for
RICHARD CURTIS
who knew what I really needed most
was a friend

*The Plainsmen Series by Terry C. Johnston
from St. Martin's Paperbacks*

BOOK I: SIOUX DAWN

BOOK II: RED CLOUD'S REVENGE
(August 1990)

BOOK III: THE STALKERS
(December 1990)

SIOUX DAWN

a novel of the Fetterman Massacre

by

TERRY C. JOHNSTON

ST. MARTIN'S PAPERBACKS

SIOUX DAWN

Copyright © 1990 by Terry C. Johnston.

ISBN: 0-312-92100-4

Printed in the United States of America

St. Martin's Paperbacks edition/May 1990

10 9 8 7 6 5 4 3 2 1

All I ask is comparative quiet this year, for by next year we can have the new cavalry enlisted, equipped, and mounted, ready to go and visit these Indians where they live.

> Gen. William Tecumseh Sherman
> from a letter written to his superior, Gen. Ulysses S. Grant, in the summer of 1866

Fort Phil Kearny was established amid hostilities. Fifty-one skirmishes have occurred. No disaster other than the usual incidents to border warfare occurred, until gross disobedience of orders sacrificed nearly eighty of the choice men of my command. . . . Life was the forfeit. In the grave I bury disobedience.

> Col. Henry B. Carrington
> Commander, Mountain District
> Department of the Platte

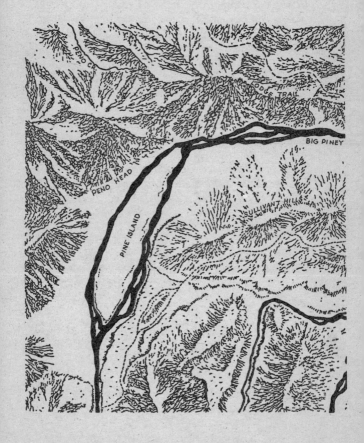

Map drawn by author, compiled from maps drawn by
Colonel Henry B. Carrington, Palacios, and the Fort Phil
Kearny/Bozeman Trail Association, Inc.

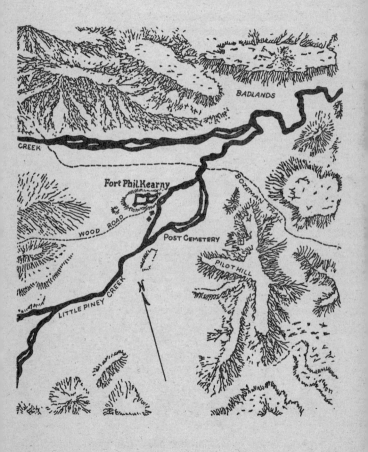

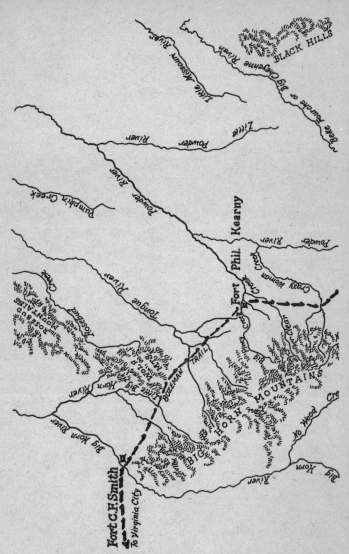

Map drawn by author, compiled from maps printed in the *Atlas of American History* (under the supervision of historian Jay Monaghan), and the Fort Phil Kearny/ Bozeman Trail Association, Inc.

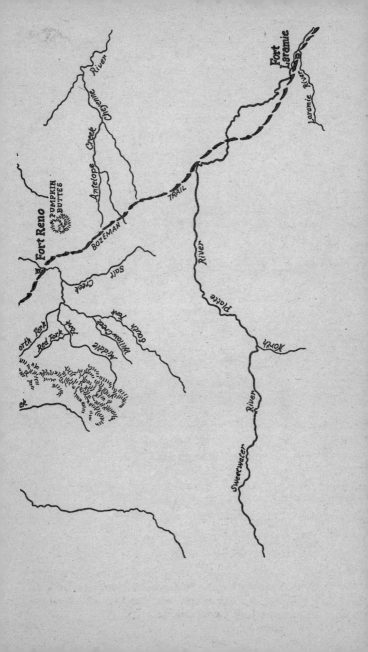

Author's Foreword

I find it important to offer a few words before this story runs its course, as a means not only of explanation, but also to set a mood and a sense of historical place for the reader.

This, above all, is the story of a time and characters largely forgotten, given the pace of our comfortable, untroubled lives. Even many of those who have a speaking acquaintance with the opening of the West know little or nothing of the tragedy of Fort Phil Kearny.

To date there have been but two other battles on the scale of the Fetterman Massacre—only two other dramas in our brief national history in which no survivors emerged. The Alamo lives on in legend and myth, as well as Custer's last fight at the Little Bighorn. For too long both battles have overshadowed the tragedy that unfolded beneath the Big Horn Mountains, a story with every bit as much pathos, every bit as much human conflict created by the passions of men colliding at destiny's call . . .

I feel the time has come for the story to be told of that bitter December day in 1866.

The writer of historical fiction assumes a perilous task: while he must remain true to history, there are the demands of fiction pressing the writer to pace, dramatize, capsulize, omit. In this case the story lay before me. All I had to do was tell it.

As a work of history, I relied on many sources, seven of which I'll make mention. The first three I called upon most heavily, drawing from them the skeleton of the story. What remained was for the novelist in me to flesh that story out.

Dee Brown's work, *Fort Phil Kearny, an American Saga,* first published in 1962, stands alone as the ideal telling of the story in a historical setting.

For flavor and mood of both time and place, I relied on two firsthand accounts, both written by women married to officers at Fort Phil Kearny during the dramatic months portrayed in the following story. Frances C. Carrington rode into Sioux country the wife of Lt. George Washington Grummond. A spare three months later she rode out of the gates of Fort Phil Kearny a widow (and years after married the man who had commanded the fort and mountain district of Dakota Territory in 1866). Her story, *My Army Life, and the Fort Phil Kearny Massacre,* first published in 1910, lends much of the bitter pall to the aftermath of the massacre. In addition, Margaret I. Carrington accompanied her husband to the foot of the Big Horns where he would build his fort and protect the Montana Road, and left us her *Absaraka: Home of the Crows,* published in 1868. Both recorded their impressions not only of the flora and animal life, but the heart-pounding sequence of events that culminated in that bloody December day on the far side of Lodge Trail Ridge.

While those three provided me with the story itself, four other sources lent muscle and sinew to its telling. In any tale of the Montana Road, one would be remiss failing to mention *The Bloody Bozeman,* the superb work of Dorothy M. Johnson, published in 1971. As much as Jim Bridger was a vital player in this drama, I found myself referring time and again to Stanley Vestal's *Jim Bridger, Mountain Man.* And because Cyrus Townsend Brady utilized many first-person accounts in the writing of his *Indian Fights and Fighters,* I turned to his pages repeatedly.

In writing Indian history (since this story is as much an Indian tale as it is a story of the frontier army), one finds himself relying on Indian information. The most monumental work on the life of Red Cloud and his Oglalla Sioux people, *Red Cloud's Folk, a History of the Oglala Sioux* (first printed in 1937), gave me insights for writing scenes from the perspective of those whose land had been invaded by the white man. And finally, I gleaned countless historical and social threads woven into the fabric of the time from *Fort Laramie and the Pageant of the West* by LeRoy Hafen and Francis Young (1938).

But beyond the mere *retelling* of history, it is left for the historical novelist himself to add something that history alone can't convey to most readers—that warm, throbbing pulse that truly allows the reader to *relive* history.

The era of the Indian Wars of the Far West is really the story of the conquest of western America. During that quarter century we witness the finish to what had begun when the Pilgrims set foot on Plymouth Rock or Sir Walter Raleigh founded his Virginia Colony. By the end of the Civil War, America was ready once more to stretch and grow. For some time the westward-moving tide had pressed beyond the Missouri and Mississippi rivers, driving before it the mighty Sioux and their allies, the Cheyenne and Arapaho. Following Appomattox, the government could now devote resources to the pacification of the West.

So what began in 1866 as Colonel Carrington's 18th Infantry found themselves the first soldiers ordered west to subdue the Indians, would not end until another bloody, cold December day in 1890 along a little-known creek called Wounded Knee.

The fever of that quarter century made the Indian Wars a time unequaled in the annals of man, when a vast

frontier was wrenched from its inhabitants, in a struggle
as rich in drama and pathos as any.

Now add the dream of untold wealth to be found by
scraping a pick along the ground or washing some gravel
from the bottom of a stream, and you'll have Sutter's
Mill in California, Cripple Creek in Colorado, and Alder
Gulch in Montana, the latest strike to land upon the ears
of war-weary soldiers, Union and Confederate alike. To
reach the northern goldfields, a man had to march west
to Fort Laramie. From there he turned north toward
Montana Territory, using John Bozeman's road, which
pierced the heart of prime Sioux hunting ground.

Any man who laid eyes on that country had to come
away understanding why the Indians guarded their land
so jealously. The whole of the Big Horn country was
laced with clear, cold streams fed of winter snows, feeding the luxuriant valleys teeming with abundant wildlife
of all description. At the edge of the eastern plains, in the
shadow of the Big Horns, roamed the mighty *pte,* the
Sioux's buffalo, a nomadic animal, followed season after
season by a nomadic people, providing the Indian with
everything he required for his survival, century after century.

Into the heart of this red man's paradise Henry Carrington was sent to build his fort, to protect the Road.
From its establishment in July of 1866 until the time of
its abandonment some two years later, Fort Phil Kearny
was under a state of seige. So constantly and vigilantly
watched by war and scouting parties, those in the fort
found little safety outside the timber stockade unless accompanied by a troop of soldiers. Even then, sheer numbers did not guarantee that the Indians would not swoop
down to harass, burn, or drive off stock. It is no exagger-
ation to state that the hostiles surrounded the fort at all
times. Not one log was cut for the stockade, nor was any
hay mowed for the stock, nor any mail moved, without a
heavy guard.

That enforced isolation and imprisonment brings about

its own kind of claustrophobia, aggravating the raw sensitivities of men too long cooped up, under seige, watching comrades whittled away by unseen, unreachable enemies.

There is no richer story than to peer like voyeurs into the lives of people under the stress of life and death. Wondering, as only a reader in the safety of his easy chair can, if he would have measured up.

Important, too, is that the reader realize he's *reliving* the story of real people. From Col. Henry B. Carrington, the commanding officer at Fort Phil Kearny whose unjust reputation for faint-hearted mismanagement of his command hung over his head until shortly before his death . . . to Capt. William Judd Fetterman, the 18th Infantry's hero in General Sherman's Civil War "march to the sea" across Georgia. So it is that good historical fiction fuses the fortunes, adventures, and destinies of numerous characters. Gold hunters and chaplains, sutlers and cowards, soldiers and those few women who followed, clinging to some man's dream. All of these individuals you will read about were actual, living souls come to play a part on that crude stage erected by the gods below Cloud Peak of the Big Horns . . . all actual people, save three. Infantryman/musician Frank Noone and his young wife Abigail.

And one other . . .

Into the midst of this tragic drama I send my fictional character Seamus Donegan, late of the Union Army of the Shenandoah, cavalry sergeant turned soldier-of-fortune, seeking a change of scenery in the West and some relief, if not escape, for his lonely, aching heart. (At this point the reader should be reminded that Seamus is pronounced like "Shamus" . . . as you would pronounce Sean as "Shawn.") Over a series of books that will encompass this era of the Indian Wars, you will follow Seamus Donegan as he marches through some of history's bloodiest hours. Not always doing the right thing, but trying nonetheless, for Donegan was no "plaster saint" nor "larger-than-life" dime-novel icon.

History has plenty of heroes—every one of them dead. Donegan represents the rest of us. Ordinary in every way, except that at some point we are each called upon by circumstances to do something extraordinary . . . what most might call heroic.

Forget the pain, the thirst and hunger. Forget the blood. Each man does what he must in the end.

That's the saga of Seamus Donegan which begins with *Sioux Dawn*. If you listen, you'll hear the wagonmasters cursing their balking mules, the warcries of Indians, along with the screams of frightened women and the prayers of untried soldiers. Test the air—you'll smell the stench of gunpowder and blood freezing on a wind that turns your cheeks to rawhide as you wait for the next rattle of gunfire or the hair-raising thunder of Indian pony hoofbeats bearing down on you.

There is, after all, a sense of something inevitable afoot here. Something of destiny's impelling course sweeping man up in its headlong rush into the future. So remember —what is written here happened. This story needs no false glamor, no shiny veneer of dash and daring. What has always been the story of man at war—of culture against culture, race against race—needs to be told without special lighting.

There's drama enough here for any man.

A very old tale indeed, my friends. One whose time has come at last. I've done my best telling the story in the pages that follow. No soul alive can say if I've succeeded or failed . . . save for that silent, simple stone monument standing alone on Massacre Hill, standing alone against the brutal wind and time itself.

Terry C. Johnston
Massacre Hill
Fort Phil Kearny Historical Site
December 21, 1989

Prologue

"*D*onegan!"

The big Irishman sprawled across the pine-frame cot in the corner of his cold, tiny cell didn't answer. A small piece of him recalled where he lay. This guardhouse in the winter shadows of the Big Horn Mountains. The twentieth . . . no, that was last night. Now the twenty-first of December. Recalling how he was trapped here by Red Cloud's Bad Face Sioux as he was on his way to the seductive gold fields of Alder Gulch, Montana Territory.

He burrowed deeper still into his straw tick mattress, swimming lazily through that thick, warm place a man finds himself when he is clawing his way up, half out of sleep, yet so far down in the dreaming soul of him.

Remembering days gone by and better times.

"Seamus Donegan!"

He heard his mother sing out, recalling the sweet sound of her voice as she would rouse him each morning to the weak tea and hard bread she set before him like a king's ransom on that cracked blue china, there in that starving land of Ireland. Land of his birth.

"You'll be late now, Seamus! Your uncles will not wait long, they'll have you know!"

His uncles. His mother's dear brothers. Each dawn young Seamus walked off between the two of them down the cobbled road, disappearing into the mist and the fog, the three of them to dig for potatoes, or hire themselves out to who might pay them a day's wages for a day's slave labors. Big, strong men, his uncles.

"And one day you'll grow every bit as big as they," his mother sang many a morn as Seamus sipped at the weak tea and tore at the hard bread that was the staple of their poor larder there in County Kilkenny.

So many died, Seamus remembered now in that warm pool of the dreaming. So many starving, wilting away. Many more simply falling ill to the sickness come to blanket the land. And always the dying shared the same look, their skin every bit as sickly gray as the molds come to rob the Irish of their potato crop. Famine descending like the locusts upon the Egypt of old, his mother would whisper in the darkness of their room at night. Whispering, as if the angel of death himself must not hear her curses on the famine that had taken her husband and one child already.

"I'm sending you to America," she had announced bravely one evening as they both held their hands over the small fire built among the moss-stones his dear, departed father had hauled to this small two-room house, one by one to build this fireplace for his new wife, expecting their first child. Their first was a boy they named Seamus O'Flynn Donegan.

"I've writ your uncles, to tell them you'll be coming to join them in that new land where they've gone."

And when young Seamus had asked why he was going, she had explained that all things would be far better for a tall, strapping lad like he in that faraway land. And in her voice he read that there was no need of further discussion.

The worst day of his life, that. Standing pressed among the hundreds of others near the rail of that rat-infested ship, waving farewell to the small woman among his brothers and sisters, all of them disappearing on the wharf in a misting rain. His mother's damp hanky soon

all he could see of her in the crowd. Great-Grandmoth-
er's linen, handed down from bride to bride, now waving
to him, clutched in that threadbare mitten missing two
fingers. Seeing her firstborn son off on his long journey to
a new start.

Once clear of the rocky point of land that each Irishman understood would be the last glimpse he would long
have of his native soil, the ship's crew began barking and
whipping and shoving and snarling. Until the Irish passengers were all below decks. "Steerage," they were
called for the first time. Like so much baggage or cargo,
kept below in the bowels of that stinking ship.

He would never forget that rocky point of land. Or
that morning's gray mist, for it was the last glimpse of
the sky young Seamus Donegan would see for the better
part of three months.

Hunkered among the living, the half dead, and the few
rotting corpses allowed to lie in their stench until taken
topside and hurled without ceremony over the rail.
"Steerage," the British sailors called them all. Among the
other crude things the British sailors called them as they
eyed the young girls and attractive women among them.

So many times at his mother's table Seamus had never
thought anything could be worse than what he and his
family had had to eat back home in County Kilkenny.
Until he looked down into a wooden bowl his first meal
on that cursed ship. One bowl a day of something thick
and slimy and mostly grease-scum. One bowl only. Far
from enough to keep the new muscle on a youngster just
beginning to fill out his tall, rawboned frame. Day after
day in the dark, rat-swarm of a latrine where the desperate Irish lay beside one another, crawling over the weak
and the dead like rats themselves. Reeking in their own
urine and feces. Once a week they were allowed buckets
of saltwater the British sailors roped down into the holds
so these Irish passengers headed for Amerikay could
wash down some of the stench. At such times they discovered a few more of the bodies that no longer moved

beneath the splashing water. No longer fighting off the hungry, gnawing rats.

Seamus remembered that while his fellow Irish grew thin and sickly, and far too many died on that God-forsaken ship, the rats grew plump and sleek. Feeding on the flesh of dead Patlanders cursed with dreaming of something better in that new country called Amerikay.

Ship-borne carnivores every bit as big and fat and sleek as the rats of Boston when that cursed ship landed, spewing forth those who had survived the trip, like human refuse upon the far shore. Shoved across the deck and laughed at, each one spat upon by the British sailors as they scurried weakly down the gangway onto the foreign soil of Massachusetts. Boston, young Seamus had been told the sign above him read. Boston—where at last his uncles would be waiting with their arms open to take him in.

Donegan found no uncles waiting. Not so much a whisper of their coming, or of their going from Boston Town, Amerikay.

And that first night of countless many he spent huddled in an alley doorway out of the cold drizzle of a March rain turning slowly to snow, young Seamus Donegan promised himself he would find the two uncles who had led a mother to send her firstborn son to the new world. Promised himself until then to fill his belly and sleep dry—no matter what he had to do. No job too dirty or immoral. He would survive. And by god—Seamus Donegan promised himself. He would never sit in the rain again. Alone. Hungry. Drenched and frozen to his marrow. And crying.

"Donegan!"

He rolled his big frame slowly onto his shoulder. It hurt where some soldier had swung a chair leg or axe-handle against the meaty part of his arm. Wincing in pain, rising slowly out of that sweet, delicious dream-state, Seamus listened as the other prisoners shouted and scuffed their way out the rough-hewn guardhouse door.

"Donegan!"

That insistent voice loomed a lot closer. In the guard-house itself. He heard the rough-hewn door of the guard-house scrape across its jamb, then slam shut. He slept on a pine-wood frame cot, the tick suspended on a woven rope netting. Room enough in the tiny cell for that six-foot bed, inches too short for his frame. That bed, and room enough for the prisoner to pace back and forth beside it. Six tiny feet by six prison feet.

Maybe they'll all leave me alone now. Let me sleep off the rest of this blessed hangover. Instead, he sensed some-one at his cell door. *By the saints! Seamus Donegan'll get no more sleep this day!*

"Talk to me, Mr. Donegan." The boy's voice pleaded.

"Don't wanna talk to nobody!" Instantly feeling sorry for the young soldier, Seamus burrowed his head deeper beneath the smelly wool blankets the army grudgingly issued its prisoners.

Too gray a day to be worrying about a bleeming thing. The army may throw Seamus Donegan in another guard-house, but they'll never have my stripes again. He peeked from one bloodshot eye. *A little sun. Fine, that is for a man with a head as big as mine. Sun, and a helluva lot of blessed cold, just four days till Christmas, i'tis. Any good Irish lad likes to dream himself about good Christmas cheer. Especially Christmas cheer.*

"Donegan, the colonel himself sent me fetch you. C'mon."

For the first time he actually listened to the clatter outside the crude log guardhouse the 18th Infantry had built here in the middle of Sioux hunting-ground upon arriving last July. The thump of feet hammered across ground frozen like an iron-hardened anvil. Men holler-ing. He'd heard that peculiar sound in throats before, when soldiers stood on the edge of battle—not one soul among them knowing if he would return.

Like a frightened bird taking flight above the clamor rose an infant's cry. Then the scream of a woman. That brought Donegan up. He swung his legs over and sat on the edge of his cot, the hair standing at the back of his neck. Perhaps it was . . . Noone's wife. The one with the new baby. He remembered her eyes. And the other. Wheatley's woman. The remembrance of the sun touching the droplets of water across the freckled skin of her firm, hardened breasts as she bathed in the Little Piney warmed him across his loins. He hoped it would not be the one he hungered for.

"Colonel and Ten Eyck want you."

"Ten Eyck?" he grumbled, his brogue thick as his swollen tongue. "What's that one-eyed Dutchman want w' me now?"

"Wasn't really the captain," the young soldier answered. "He was agin it at first." He fumbled with the ring of keys he carried nervously before him. "It's the old man himself wanted to bust you out of the guardhouse. Old man sent me to fetch you."

"The old man?" His voice was raspy, thick with the peat of his mother soil. He looked at the young soldier, really nothing more than an overgrown boy. Like he had been come to America on that stinking ship of death. And this boy before him had those same pink cheeks sprouting their first soft fuzz. Seamus felt sorry for any youth wasted in uniform.

"Yeah." The soldier swung the cell-door open and Donegan towered past him, shouldering sideways into the narrow hallway that joined six small cells.

"Ten Eyck don't want you," the soldier explained. "But the colonel said he's ordered to take you along."

"Hold on a minute, me boy." With a hand shoved against the young soldier's chest, Donegan nudged him against the log wall. Squinting against the glare, he stared out the door at the scurry of men and scrambling animals on the parade of Fort Phil Kearny, Dakota Territory. Till that moment his hungover brain had been as thick as the whiskey-dried tongue roaming his mouth. But now something sneaked in to arouse Seamus Donegan where he lived. "Ten Eyck don't want me along for *what?* Them bleeding savages swoop down on the wood train again?"

"Yeah, just about—"

"Tell Ten Eyck . . . and your colonel, too—I ain't going again. I'm tired of chasing the bleeming sons up and down the hills. The red bastirds don't stand and fight like men, they——"

"Mr. Donegan, sir." The lad was breathless. "This ain't got a feather to do with Ten Eyck or the colonel. It's got to do with Captain Fetterman."

Like a ragged piece of torn cloth Donegan's wind caught in his chest. His eyes narrowed as he turned back to study the soldier. Suddenly he read fear etched across the boy's face, etched like acid on glass. Something permanent. Unforgiving.

"Your name?"

"Meacham. Private Meacham, sir."

"Don't sir me. I ain't a sergeant no more. Colonel knows that. Knows what blaggard put me in this hole too. Brown. Fetterman's boon friend. I'm a damned civilian, I am! So, you don't 'Sergeant' me no more, Private Meacham. It's your army. Ain't mine. Hear me?"

"What about the colonel? He sent me to fetch you!"

A familiar tension sparked across the shoulders as wide as an axe handle with room to spare. In the cold, windowless darkness at the end of the guardhouse hallway, the scarred Civil War veteran felt the young boy shudder.

"Tell me what you know . . . busting me out to see the colonel—about Fetterman. He and Brown not content to put me in their hole? Eh? Fetterman hisself want my ass to stew in a fine army broth for what I done to his friend Brown?"

"N-No . . . Donegan." Meacham trembled again. He watched Donegan wipe his huge hands on the front of his bloodied wool coat. Studying the Irishman's puffy face. A black eye. The swollen lips. A cut cheek and gashed forehead, both red and angry, crusted with blood and blanket lint. Meacham remembered that just last night it had taken seven of them to pull Donegan down. Seven troopers to drag this ox of an ex-cavalry sergeant off to the guardhouse . . . to throw the man into this tiny cell. *Seven goddamned men*——

"Well, Fetterman won't get a chance to cock me like that bastird Brown did! I'll ride—straight over the hills afore the bleeming cap'n has another chance to shame Mrs. Donegan's boy——"

He stopped, listening. The rattle and creak of saddle tack reached his ears. The familiar snorts and pawing restlessness of army horses when they sensed better than any soldier what it was they were asked to ride into. With those sounds came a rush of warmth, a homey, familiar feeling of returning to what he loved to do. The tightness to his breath that once more said this was what he was as a man. A soldier. A warrior, above all.

"The colonel figures—this time it's you got to help Fetterman," Meacham stuttered.

"Help Fetterman? Brown's mate? Bloody chance of that!" he roared. By now he'd dragged the youth toward the doorway where an icy draft flung itself against his bloody cheek. A handful of new recruits yanked a half-dozen old, ill-fed horses out of the stables onto the snow-packed parade. Seamus whirled on Meacham. His gray eyes narrowed.

The young soldier gulped. "Colonel thinks Fetterman's likely got himself in trouble. He's crossed Lodge Trail Ridge."

"Fetterman's crossed the Lodge Trail?" he echoed, snagging the front of Meacham's tunic.

He nodded dumbly. "Says you're to ride with Ten Eyck. Help the captain—"

"Help that damned incompetent Dutchman?"

"Colonel says you gotta go with Ten Eyck—you're the only one can bring Fetterman back."

"The hell! Colonel thinks I should go pull Fetterman's ass out of the fire . . . when it's Fetterman himself who didn't speak-up for Seamus Donegan! Twice! When Fetterman's reeky friend Brown got a mite tight in his cups and picked a fight with the wrong man . . . me!"

"Every trooper on this post thinks there's only two soldiers here worth their salt," Meacham began, then his eyes fell to his scuffed boot-toes. "Captain Fetterman and . . . Sergeant Donegan."

"Ain't a sergeant no more. Told you——"

"You may not be a sergeant, Seamus Donegan—but you'll always be a soldier."

Meacham and the Irishman turned as one when the new voice cracked the cold darkness of the guardhouse.

"What I said is the truth, *Sergeant* Donegan." Colonel Henry B. Carrington stood at the guardhouse door, flanked by captains Powell and Ten Eyck. "Not only do the men think you and Fetterman are the only real soldiers here . . . but most of the officers feel the same. Now, if you'd be good enough to come—I've got a relief party to send out."

Carrington whirled, his face carved with worry and confusion as it gazed up at the Irishman. "Brown went with Fetterman. They've crossed Lodge Trail Ridge. The matter of Brown's charges against you can wait. For now, you ride with Ten Eyck. You're the last cavalry officer we have. Bingham died. Sergeant Garrett rode out with Fetterman." He shook his head, eyes misting in the bitter cold. "The captain might have need of your advice, Mr. Donegan."

Donegan turned to study Ten Eyck's bearded face. The Dutchman's one droopy eye, a wound he would suffer the rest of his life as reminder of that bloody war with Confederates. "Cap'n?"

Ten Eyck swallowed. "Mr. Donegan. I need your help. Sounds like Fetterman's got himself in a real . . . real——"

"Donnybrook?"

Ten Eyck nodded. "Yes."

"Cap'n." Donegan snapped himself ramrod straight

and saluted as smartly as any academy man. "Besides the bunch of green shavetails left you in this stockade, looks like I'm the last horse sojur you got. And whatever Fetterman's marched hisself into on the other side of Lodge Trail Ridge, it'll take a horse sojur to get Fetterman out. Let's ride!"

Chapter 1

"For fifteen summers," Red Cloud repeated in the stillness of the Lakota Sioux council lodge.

Come now the short-grass time of the Indian warrior, spring come to the high plains in this year the white man marked as eighteen and sixty-six. The short-grass time when ponies grew fat on the new, green shoots and young men prepared for war.

"Too long have we waited for the white man's word to grow good," Red Cloud emphasized, "to grow good like the grass that raises its head across our hunting lands and strengthens our ponies for war."

"Wait for the white man's word to grow good?" Miniconjou chief Black Shield asked. "Better to wait for tainted meat to turn sweet as buffalo tongue!"

"We have seen his every treaty used against us," Red Cloud agreed sadly. "And those treaties he cannot use against us, he breaks."

"First we watched the travelers who moved on west with the sun along the great medicine road." Red Leaf spoke this time. "This was good, for they did not stop nor take root in our hunting grounds." Red Leaf was Oglalla, of the same blood as Red Cloud. "But our eyes watched the buffalo killers and the ground scratchers follow in the shadows of those who passed on. And for three robe seasons now we have watched the others come pushing across our hunting lands: these who hurry to the land of the Crow, so they might dig at the ground for the yellow rocks. So many of these who hunger for the yellow rocks now."

"Aiyee!" Black Shield swore. "I spit on the ones who killed *pte,* our brother buffalo, only for his skin. I spit on those who scratch at the ground like gophers—more every year. My heart tells me the talking paper of the treaty-men at Laramie is only for fools to believe."

"Fifteen summers ago," Red Cloud reminded, "we gathered at the soldier's post—Laramie—with great hope that we would be left alone to hunt and live as our old ones lived for time beyond any one man's memory." He watched the older council members nod in remembering. "The white talkers told us they wanted only a road for their wagons going toward the setting sun. They said if they could have the road through our land, we could hunt as our old ones hunted long before the white man ever came." His eyes moistened. "We gave them their road."

"The white man said he came only for the road—but he has robbed us of everything else!" Black Shield shouted. "If he is not content to keep his promise . . . why should the Lakota?"

"That is for the Lakota to decide," Red Leaf replied. "The council of the seven bands must answer for themselves."

"Some are as old women," Red Cloud spat. "Those loafers who sleep each day in the shade of the soldiers' fort, telling the whiteman they speak for all the mighty Lakota nations on every treaty now—putting their marks to the white man's talking paper. Spotted Tail's Brule . . . . and——"

"They are old women! No better than toothless camp dogs, waiting to take what the white man hands them! They don't deserve to be called Lakota Sioux. Those bands who bow to the white soldiers—my mouth dares not call them fighting men!"

As one the old chiefs turned. They craned their necks, eager to see who had blurted the strong words into this lodge crammed with bodies on a breathless early-summer afternoon. A cooling breeze finally crept under the rolled-up buffalo hides of the lodge, stirring the braids and loose hair hung along the serious faces. Each of them sat upon the thick, furry robes of *pte,* their brother buffalo. Around them rose the circle of monstrous lodge-poles straining for the pale-blue sky in a gentle swirl that met at the smoke-hole above them all. The council lodge was, as always, a jumble of tobacco and sweat, cold meat and close bodies. A revered place of earth-skinned men come to decide upon mighty things.

Red Cloud's eyes found the brash young speaker.

"Curly? You speak of these as old women. Do you have council to give?" the chief of the Bad Faces inquired.

In his eighteenth summer, the tall, sinewy warrior rose quickly, beads of sweat glistening across his bare shoulders and chest. "I have, Uncle," he said, addressing his chief with a term of respect.

Curly paid no attention to the mutterings of the older warriors crowded into the steamy lodge. With the elk-horn quirt hung at his wrist, he pointed south.

"We know the soldiers will march north. Last summer we fought soldier-chief Connor and his army. He crept down on one small Arapaho village . . . destroying it . . . sending our cousins into the hills. Then he raised his dirt fort on the Powder River."

"Curly is right!" Black Shield interrupted. "We should have stopped the soldiers on the Powder."

"We were tricked . . . again," Red Cloud soothed in that voice of his, like slow water caressing a pebbled streambed. "The white man had the loafers who live in the shadow of Fort Laramie's walls sign his treaty paper."

"Connor's word guaranteed the Lakota would keep all land between the Paha Sapa—the white man's Black

Hills—and the Big Horns. . . ." Red Leaf added. "Everything from the white man's medicine road at Laramie in the south, up to the Yellowstone River in the north."

"The white man spits out his smooth promises, just to make us give him this new road into the Crow lands where white men hunt the little yellow rocks for three winters now."

"No man in this lodge put his mark to that treaty!" Curly roared. "No man here agreed to that robbery!"

Red Cloud motioned Curly to sit. "We know the loafers who camp near Laramie signed the treaty-papers for the rest of the Lakota nations."

"Spotted Tail. And the other old women like him!"

"Yes, Black Shield," Red Cloud responded. "Sadly, we have come to expect no better from them. Their council is worthless. The word they give the whiteman worth even less. My brother warriors—the real Lakota live here!" He slammed the palm of one hand against the packed ground beside him. A puff of dust rose, particles like flecks of gold spun into the late-afternoon light that slanted into the lodge. "It is here the Lakota will stay."

"You say we should not go to this great council called by the treaty makers at Laramie this summer?" Red Leaf asked.

Red Cloud shook his head. "We will go. We will listen to what the white man says. We will hear what Spotted Tail and his old lapdogs have to give away to the white treaty makers this time."

"This journey will be a wasted march!"

A new voice rose from the ranks of the young warriors in the outer circle. Beside Curly a stocky, middle-aged warrior scrambled to his feet. For many summers Man-Afraid-Of-His-Horses had raided the Crow and Shoshone for scalps and ponies. For many summers Man-Afraid had fought the white men who brazenly marched across Sioux land. Younger than most of the other chiefs, yes. But about his shoulders Man-Afraid carried the mantle of respect. A great war-chief. He was without fear.

"Man-Afraid wishes to give council?" Red Cloud inquired.

"We waste time going to Laramie, sitting with the white men and their trained fools . . . this Spotted Tail. We must ready our villages for war."

"Tell us why you make ready for war."

"The white man has repeatedly tricked old Spotted Tail . . . in a succession of treaties. I would not feed my dog the paper the whiteman had the fort-loafers sign. But now the whiteman will trick you as well!" He pointed at many of the older chiefs in the center of the great, shaded circle. "You, who think it wise to go to Laramie to listen to the white man's words! I say you have already been tricked by the white man!"

"These are strong words, Man-Afraid." Black Shield shifted uneasily.

"Man-Afraid is right!" Curly rose beside his older friend, who stood alone against the chiefs. "We must not go to Laramie. It only shows the white man we can be swayed, shows him the Lakota can be bought."

"No, my young friend," Red Cloud replied, drawing himself up with new resolve. "We will not be bought. No longer will we be fooled by empty promises. This time, the white man will be made the fool."

"How is this?" Red Leaf asked.

The chief smiled, smoothing the vanes of a spotted eagle feather across one palm. "We will go. Lakota will hear what the white man wants to tell us at Laramie. Then we will say what is in our hearts."

"And we will take his gifts?"

Red Cloud looked across the firepit at Black Shield. "Yes, we will take every gift the white man foolishly hands us."

"But he gives presents only for signing the treaty papers!" Red Leaf replied.

They all watched the smile grow across Red Cloud's

wind-chiseled face. "That is where we play the white man's cheating game better than the white man himself." He raised one arm high in the air, the single eagle feather pointed at the smoke-hole and the heavens beyond. "No longer will the white man be the only one who can lie to get what he wants. We Lakota will take his gifts. Then we return to our hunting grounds to decide what path the Lakota will walk."

"We do not have to honor the white man's treaty . . . because we know the white man will never honor his treaty with us!" Man-Afraid declared.

"It is decided?" Red Cloud peered into the dark, brooding faces. "Good. Tell your camps we will march with the rising of tomorrow's sun. To Laramie. The power of the life-giver will be warm in our faces and pride will swell our hearts. The white man will pay dearly for what he wants this time. Across fifteen summers the Lakota has learned how to deal with this creature who breaks every promise he makes us. The creature who steals back everything he ever gave us. Now, the Lakota deals with the white man and his soldier army in the only language he understands . . . and respects. The strength of our muscle. The might of our warriors."

It surprised him how cold it could get after sundown in this country. When it had been so damned hot during the day.

Private Sam Gibson pulled the wool blanket about his shoulders, shoveling his hip into the thick grass where he had made his bed.

Camped out here among the sage beside Fort Reno, Sam had overheard the talk of some of those soldiers being relieved at the post, explaining that General Patrick Conner had originally named this fort on the Powder River in honor of himself, but that the War Department had seen to it the name was changed to Fort Reno. Army posts were named only after dead officers.

Lord knows there's enough dead officers after the war, he thought.

Gibson couldn't understand why any man would make a fuss over such a miserable collection of mud hovels anyway. After his own long winter of marching out from the east on foot, watching as his regiment was plagued with desertions . . . the sleeting snow . . . men losing feet and fingers to that endless cold. Their shoes falling apart . . . wrapping burlap around what was left of them. Leaving bloody trails coming west. Marching on numb, frozen feet. Marching—to where? To do what? Some claimed the 18th Infantry was coming out to fight Indians. And not a one of them had ever seen a damned Indian in his life.

What did the army want with this country anyway? Hell. Wasn't a thing out here in all this wilderness that had convinced him it was worth taking from the Indians to begin with. But then, it would take some impressing to do that. What with him being heir to a family fortune back in Chicago—growing up among all the lace and damask and the smell of money making money . . . but none of these men camped here within earshot of the Powder River knew of his secret past. No man knew why Private Gibson had abandoned that life of wealth and ease, escaping to join the Union Army in its fight against the insurrection of the Confederate States. No man would ever know why Enos C. Bidwell had enlisted under a false name so that he might quietly disappear among the hundreds of faceless soldiers marching under the battle banners of the 18th Infantry.

Pvt. Samuel Gibson had promised himself that no man would ever know the secret that would follow him to his grave.

Second Battalion, Eighteenth U.S. Infantry under Colonel Carrington will move immediately: two companies relieving the garrison at Reno Station; four companies establishing a new post on or near the Piney Fork of

Powder River; two companies establishing a further out-
post at or near the mouth of Rotten Grass Creek. Troops
will proceed immediately so as to be able to move from
Laramie on first grass. James Bridger will be employed as
guide.

With those orders, Col. Henry B. Carrington's 2nd
Battalion of the 18th had been given just under sixty days
to prepare to march west from old Fort Kearney in Nebraska Territory. They were to occupy three faraway
posts along the Montana Road which gold seekers used
to scurry north to the goldfields. Over the next two
months Carrington had fussed and clucked, Gibson recalled, just like the administrator he was, worrying because the 2nd Battalion could muster no more than 220
men, a mere fourth of its fighting strength. But by that
shining Saturday morning, May 19, when the 18th Infantry had marched out of the old fort, past Kearney City
and Dobe Town with its watering holes and teary-eyed
whores, Carrington's "Overland Circus" marched some
seven hundred strong. Most of those foot-soldiers were
new recruits, sweating alongside the battle-hardened veterans of General William Tecumseh Sherman's bloody
Georgia campaign. For the first time since that long and
fearful war, Gibson once more felt a surge of pride in
belonging to the 18th Infantry and its decorated hero,
Capt. William J. Fetterman.

With the scurrying rush of a chilly breeze, Gibson's
spine tingled in remembrance of a stirring sight. Parading
in review beneath the eyes of no less than Sherman himself—a grand column of foot-soldiers marching beneath
the silk banners that told of their hard-fought victories
across the hard, bloody ground of the Confederacy. Iron-
ically, this same grand regiment was the first now ordered to Indian country armed with the poorest of
wartime hand-me-down weapons: muzzle-loading
Springfield muskets. Only Carrington's twenty-five-piece

regimental band had been favored with the new rapid-fire
Spencer carbines.

Gibson smiled, listening as someone nearby began to
snore musically. Carrington wouldn't think of leaving his
band behind, loving his German musicians like the
breath of life itself.

Behind the foot soldiers bound for Indian country had
rumbled fifty wagons stuffed with tents and tools, rations
and quartermaster stores. Along with Carrington's on-
ions and potatoes. Following those wagons driven by civilian teamsters rambled a thousand beeves. And behind
them all rode a mounted rear guard.

Because they had served him so bravely in Georgia,
General Sherman himself had journeyed to Fort Kearney
in Nebraska to see the soldiers of the 18th off for the Big
Horn country. Gibson remembered how the sentimental
old general's eyes had misted when he gazed over the
battered, battle-scarred veterans—the few who had chosen to stay on with the regiment for a journey into an
unknown land. Sherman had even suggested that the officers bring their wives and children along, so certain was
he in the safety of this assignment; certain, too, that the
families would lighten much of the loneliness of frontier
duty. Just a week before the regiment had pulled out,
Sherman himself had urged the officers' wives to begin
diaries wherein they could record their experiences
marching into this new land. So it was that the women
and children had come along on the army's great adventure—riding in bouncing army ambulances, wooden-
topped wagons which jolted and jarred their passengers
west then north toward the ancient hunting lands of the
Sioux and Northern Cheyenne.

"Those ink-scratchings ain't gonna help you much,
Colonel."

Gibson recalled how he watched the wrinkled scout
ease into the tent, dressed in store-bought clothes, looking more the farmer than a buckskinned frontiersman.
The former trapper and mountain man who had spent

forty-four years traversing the mountain West now stood slightly stooped with painful rheumatism. Above the old scout's collar Gibson could see the swollen mound of goiter. With a week-old growth of gray stubble across his chin, Bridger strolled up to Carrington and his officers as they scoured the new maps the War Department had shipped out as the regiment prepared to leave Nebraska Territory.

Carrington was a small, spare man who wore his hair long and his dark beard trimmed. His dark eyes bounced expressively on either side of his thin, aquiline nose. It was the look of a barrister he gave the aging scout. "True enough, Mr. Bridger."

"Call me Jim . . . won't you, Colonel?"

"Surely, Jim. The army doesn't know very much about this new Mountain District I'm to command. These maps tell me nothing. They show few rivers. See here—appears someone guessed where the mountains would be found. A few of us have even read some tattered copies of Lewis and Clark's journals to find any mention of the climate of the region. Afraid we're pretty ignorant of what we're going into."

"I got your map for you, Colonel."

"Perfect. May we look it over now?" Carrington asked.

"Not quite, Colonel. It's all up here." Bridger tapped a gnarled finger against his leathery brow. "Better'n forty-four winters out here 'mong these mountains I been roaming now. You hired me to guide you—so now it's your turn to listen."

Gibson had sat in rapt attention as the slightly-stooped, sinewy, six-foot-tall trapper had rambled through his dissertation on the country and its climate, the plant life and animals they would find in the new land.

"Ain't like nothing you've run across before," Bridger reminded, his blue eyes searching the lot of them. "Out yonder, you run across trees taller'n any house you seen back East. And if you don't watch your step, nearby you'll bump into cactus with thorns the likes of your mama's knitting needles that can cripple a horse damned fast. While you're staring off at them mountains scrubbing the underside of the sky with your mouths hung open, you'll be missing the prettiest flowers the good Lord could decorate any land with. Out there, where we're heading—that's a country with all the best . . . and all the meanest a piece of ground's got to offer. That land'll make a man outta you soldiers. Or, it can kill you just as easy."

Bridger went on in that simple way of his to warn Carrington's officers about the Sioux and Cheyenne who would guard that faraway country with a jealous, fearsome pride.

"Now, Jim—we're all aware of your experience with the Indians out here. But we're here to usher in a new era for this great land. I don't expect to encounter any opposition because I plan on reaching Laramie in time to get to know the Indian leaders gathering in treaty council there."

"Oh, you'll get a chance to meet 'em all right, Colonel. And you can skin me and nail my hide to the back of one of your wagons if what I tell you ain't so. The Sioux and Cheyenne will stand square in your way. They ain't about to give the army that road your men are sent to protect. Soon enough you'll stare some real trouble in the eye."

Carrington straightened. For the first time more than concerned with a warning from a man of Bridger's stature. The sensitive eyes beneath the colonel's high forehead narrowed. "If trouble proves to be what I find, then I'll overcome all obstacles by exercising patience, forbearance, and common sense."

"Common sense, Colonel?" Bridger scoffed. "That's one thing in short supply in the army!" His iron-hardened look bounced over the officers gathered round the table. Those cold blue eyes narrowed on the colonel. "Howsomever, I got a feeling you'll prove to be better than most, Carrington. How old you are?"

"Forty-two. And I didn't graduate from West Point. I'm a Yale man, 'forty-five. Yale law degree, 'forty-eight."

"You're forty-two, eh? I got twenty winters on you, this past spring. Why can't any of you realize that twenty year's a damned lifetime out in this country? Every season a man finds hisself still wearing his hair, he can count hisself lucky he learned enough about red niggers to stay alive one more year. Injuns out here, boys—they eager to part you from your scalp . . . 'long with everything else you own."

Gibson remembered that Bridger had waited, letting the words sink in, his hard eyes watching a handful of the young officers gulp. One even ran his hand over his bald head.

"Don't worry none 'bout *your* topknot, son," Bridger said to the officer. "What's the name?"

"Brown. Captain Frederick Brown. Regimental Quartermaster."

"You got nothing to worry about," Bridger went on, gesturing toward Brown's half-bald head. "Ain't a warrior gonna want your scalp!"

Most of them chuckled nervously, even Brown, who unconsciously ran a hand across his high forehead once more.

" 'Sides, Colonel—you got the best scouts money can buy," Bridger continued. "Jack Stead over there as your interpreter. He's had many a year with the Pawnee. Crow and Pawnee both know how fearsome the Sioux are. Fact is, I hear tell how the Sioux want Jack's scalp pretty bad."

Next he turned and pointed his quirt toward the youngest scout standing on the outer fringe of officers. "That Henry Williams there, why—he's learned about everything I can show him already. We both tried to teach General Connor a thing or two up on his Powder River expedition last year. 'Cept, Connor was all gurgle and no gumption. Figured he had knowed everything about Injuns already." Bridger let that set. He knew these young officers had heard how Connor froze nearly all his army horses, putting his entire command afoot . . . how the officer had been repeatedly whipped by the Sioux . . . how Connor had come limping back to Laramie, beaten and humiliated.

Carrington cleared his throat. "I'm sure I speak for every one of us here when I say we appreciate having men like you leading us into this Sioux country."

"Were it up to me—and it ain't—I'd be leading you soldiers through Snake country."

"I understand you took the first emigrant train from Laramie all the way to Virginia City back in 'sixty-four . . . through Shoshone land."

"Damned right, Colonel. Up the west side of the Big Horns."

"That's clearly the long way around," Captain Brown said.

"Right." Bridger glared back at the balding officer.

"And a good deal harder going, I hear," Brown added.

Bridger spit into the dirt at his feet. "Ain't going to argue with you. My road's a mite harder going than the one John Bozeman picked out."

"Bozeman laughs at your caution." Brown felt bolder now. "Thinks you're a little too cautious using that easy road of yours."

"Damned right I'm cautious—Bozeman's road runs dead to center through the prime Sioux and Cheyenne hunting ground. Maybeso that's why I still got my hair after forty-four winters in these parts. And everybody from Blackfoot and Sioux, Cheyenne down to Mormons wanting to boast of Big Throat's scalp on their lodgepole." He squinted at Brown. "But you got that right. I am a little cautious, son. I figure on lasting a few more winters."

"You'll spend this winter with us." Carrington tried out his soothing, lawyer's tone. Along with that winning smile of his. "Up near the Big Horns, Jim."

Bridger finally tore his eyes from Brown.

Gibson shuddered beneath his blankets, recalling the old scout's terse words. "That's right, Colonel. I'll stay this winter with your soldiers . . . them women and kids." He shook his head sadly. "I'll damned sure do the best I can for you. But my medicine tells me some of you paper-collar officers won't be around to see green-up come next spring. Mark my words, boys—afore hard freeze-up, there'll be scalps flying from Sioux lodge-poles . . . or I ain't Jim Bridger."

Chapter 2

*T*he breeze nudged the loose hair along his left cheek. Up here on the ridge where he always came to sit and think, Curly gazed down into the valley of the Tongue River, watching the brown-skinned lodges nippling against the gold sky of sunset, lazy puffs of smoke rising into the summer twilight.

To think. And remember.

A thousand lodges had gathered on the plains surrounding the soldiers' Fort Laramie. Oglalla. Miniconjou. And Spotted Tail's Brule.

Old *Pegaleshka*. Once a brave and daring warrior with many honors, Spotted Tail had given himself to the white man the way a new bride gives herself to her husband on their wedding night. All because his young daughter had begged him to have her baptized with water in the white man way as she lay on her deathbed. A victim of the cruel winter of starvation the Sioux had suffered. She asked of her father to be buried in the white man's cemetery at the fort. Obediently, her father had slain her four favored ponies, their tails to hang on her funeral scaffold. Sadly, Spotted Tail had told the soldiers he no longer had heart to fight the white man.

Wheat Flour was her name. The whitest thing Spotted Tail's people knew. Wheat Flour had told her father she ached to be like the white man. Eventually the weary chief grew certain his daughter's spirit had been adopted by the white man's god. No longer would he be one to make war against his daughter's adopted people.

With the remembrance of Laramie, something crawled inside Curly's stomach. Like the slow *plip-plip* of water on a rock. He straightened and sucked deep at the cooling air of twilight fallen on this high place.

Treaty-talk had been a waste of their time, after all. Better that the Lakota had followed the herds of buffalo and antelope across the prairie. Better that they had spent their time mending bows and filling their quivers with cherrywood arrows. Preparing for what surely lay ahead—now that the soldiers marched north, intent on crossing the Crazy Woman Fork. Coming to goad the Sioux into fighting for what had long been their favored hunting ground.

With a stick Curly scratched idly at the dirt before him, remembering the hairy-faced soldier chief with the slicked-back hair who had ridden up to the treaty-talk. A soldier chief accompanied by all his blue-shirted warriors. Until the moment that dark-haired soldier chief had marched into Laramie, Curly and the others had begun to think this treaty-talk might be different than treaty-talks gone before. This time the white man might talk straight.

But when the treaty-talkers had introduced the bearded soldier chief, a jolt of cold splashed down each warrior's spine. Realization as numbing as a January waterfall.

"Here stands the white chief marching north to occupy Powder River," the Sioux were told. "Going to the Big Horn and Yellowstone country."

Curly again tasted the bitter gall stinging the back of his throat. He and Man-Afraid had been right all along. The white man was indeed a treacherous devil! He would lie if he had to, making the Sioux leaders watch his right hand while his left hand plunged a knife squarely into the heart of their most sacred hunting ground. The bearded soldier chief and his columns of soldiers would be the knife the white devils would use.

But this time, the Lakota would be ready.

Even the old chiefs had admitted they had been tricked by the smooth sound of the treaty-makers' words, Curly remembered. But the bearded soldier chief had come to lead his soldiers into sacred Lakota hunting ground. And the lie to the white man's words had been laid bare. Shamed and saddened, the old ones had joined the march north from Laramie, back to their tribal lands where the Lakota would make their stand.

Curly savagely drove the stick into the loose soil at his feet, recalling the long blue columns arriving at the Laramie post. Twenty-two women and children had marched with the soldiers. This was no ordinary exploring expedition. Those women and children and wagons of household goods shouted it plain enough for any warrior to understand.

No longer was the white man content to pass through on his road to the Crow land. This time, the white man had come to stay!

"This is Colonel Carrington," the interpreter had told them that warm afternoon in the *Moon of Fat Horses*. "He comes to protect the road that crosses the Powder River. His soldiers will garrison three posts between here and the Yellowstone country of the Crows."

With that announcement Red Cloud had leaped to his feet on the platform placed immediately in front of a long table where the treaty commissioners sat. But the chief did not shout at the white men. Instead, he had turned to harangue his fellow Sioux.

"Do you see?" he shrieked. "The presence of this bearded chief and his soldiers are proof enough that the white man intends to steal our hunting grounds from us. Even without the treaty they want us to sign!"

The chiefs on the platform had stirred uneasily, hearing many of the young warriors crowded behind them grunt in agreement. *Huhn-huhn!* they had growled the courage words.

"Can you now see the white man's treachery? Is it not as plain as a hand held in front of your faces?"

Curly recalled how flushed Red Cloud's face had grown, how his old, scarred chest had heaved with short gasps of breath. Like a warrior riding into battle.

"The Great Father has sent us presents and asks us to sell him his road. But this soldier chief—he brings his soldiers to steal the road even before the Lakota can say yes or no!"

Man-Afraid had joined Red Cloud with the next heartbeat. "I have ears! I can hear the lies. I have eyes! I can see the treachery. Before this day we saw nothing, we heard nothing of the forts and the soldiers coming. Yet here we sit like fools, watching the white man's tongue wag at us with lies once more . . . while we should be making meat for the winter. It will be a long winter, this one."

"A hard winter not only for the Lakota!" Red Cloud harangued his chiefs and warriors while the treaty commissioners and army officers shifted nervously. "This will be a very long winter for the white soldiers they send to guard the road!" He had finally wheeled on the treaty-talkers, lunging at the long table to spit his words into the face of the soldier chief who would lead his troops north into Sioux land.

"For every mile you march beyond Crazy Woman Fork, a new grave will mark the dying place for one of your soldiers!"

Curly remembered how many of the young, hot-blooded warriors had growled in agreement. After fifteen winters of white treachery, each one thirsted for soldier blood.

"I swear this before you," Red Cloud had continued, his lips flecked with angry spittle as he pointed his finger like a copper lance at the soldier chief heading toward the Powder. "I will kill every man, woman, and child who crosses Crazy Woman Fork! Mark my words—for that land will be your grave!"

"*Aiyeee!*" Man-Afraid stepped in front of Red Cloud, slamming his fist down on the table. "I have been driven from one gully to the next, like a buffalo in search of grass. I have been hunted down and wounded like an animal by your soldiers. Not once has the Great Father's hand been offered in kindness to his red children. But from this day forward, we are no longer his children! I will not stand by and watch the white man take away the very ground *Wakan Tanka* gave to our ancestors in the time gone before. Lakota bones have always whitened beneath the sun above. Our land is where our warrior dead lie sleeping! No longer will your road disturb their dreams!"

Red Cloud moved to the table once more. "We have passed a winter when bellies pinched in every lodge. No man can forget the cries of the little children." He spoke softly, with words gritted between yellowed teeth. "No white men will kill our game. Nor chase the animals from our hunting lands as he travels this road into the land of our enemies, the Crow. Hear me! No more will our lodges be filled with tears and the keening of hungry women and children this winter. Your lodges will echo with the cries of widows and fatherless children!"

Man-Afraid straightened himself, still angry, his courage like a cloak about his muscled shoulders. "Red Cloud has promised you what will happen to every man, woman, and child who crosses the Crazy Woman Fork. Now this I promise you: before two moons have come and gone over your march north, not one hoof will be left your soldiers."

Smiling now, Curly recalled how the fire in those threats had shaken the white treaty-makers, especially the soldier chief, who stood riveted, his fingers pressed against his silent lips.

"Mark these words," Man-Afraid had finished, his voice no more than a whispered growl, "first we will steal your ponies and run off the spotted buffalo you bring on your march. Then we will take your scalps. One, by one, by one . . ."

Man-Afraid had leaped from the platform accompanied by the grunts and cheers of the young Oglalla warriors. Red Cloud had joined him after stomping past the soldier chief's horse and the wagon where the soldier chief's wife sat petrified in silence and fear.

Once more it stirred Curly to remember how his heart had beat with so much pride at that moment. To defy at last the treacherous white treaty-makers. To stand strong before the bearded soldier chief, warning him of the soldier deaths to come. On the horizon loomed what Curly had waited for all these years.

War.

One long, sweet breath of rose-tinged twilight he drew into his lungs. Its medicine filled Curly's spirit with this place and this time. A place of glittering, jewel-bright air. A land like no other flung beneath a stinging sun— carved by harsh winds that drove before them the endless seasons of rumbling thunderstorms and blinding winter blizzards.

A land as much a mother to him as any person could be. That ache he had carried inside for seventeen summers now. No mother to call his own. Curly had been born in the moon of *Wild Goose Honking,* during the great cholera outbreak of 1849. The white man's disease took his mother from him. This land had become his one true mother.

The sun sank like a red ache beyond the western hills, backlighting the Big Horns in one splendid moment of fiery glory. Curly rose, stiff in the sitting. His muscles tingling, ready for what lay at hand. All those years of training. Stealing horses. Learning the bow. Fighting Crow and Pawnee. Killing enemies of the mighty Lakota. Curly stood ready to protect his people against the greatest danger they had ever encountered. The white man, hungry for land.

Curly's land. Sioux land. A wild, unbridled country as savage and beautiful as the jealous and defiant folk who would hold onto it. And drive from its breast the troopers who were following behind the bearded soldier chief, marching straight into the jaws of death.

"You telling us that if we try to push on up the road on our own, you'll sick your soldiers on us?" Captain Samuel Marr demanded of the army officer seated behind the dusty table that served as a desk. From the looks of Marr, he wasn't the kind of man anyone would want to get on the down side of.

Col. Henry E. Maynadier sized Marr up quickly. "Captain Marr, you seem to know how the army works——"

"All too well." He ran a hand through the long, gray hair that spilled from his wide-brimmed hat over his collar.

Maynadier found himself almost at the end of his string with the civilians who tramped through his post like a turnstile in a railroad station, heading to the goldfields of Montana with stars in their eyes and a dream in their heart. As the commander of Fort Laramie, Dakota Territory, here in the summer of 1866, the colonel had to be the one to throw some cold water on a lot of those dreams. Most of those in whose breast burned this gold fever saw the good sense in going roundabout to Alder Gulch. Many went on west to Salt Lake's City of the Saints, found their way north from there. A few more took the northern roundabout, up the Missouri as far as steamboats could take them, on mules from there to the Three Forks and thence south to Virginia City.

First came those who had scratched the ground in California then panned in the icy streams of Colorado's high-country. But after the war the colonel began to see more come through Laramie. So damned many of them following last winter. Veterans mostly. Union and Confederate both, who had little alike to return home to. Maynadier knew any dream at all could ignite men such as these.

"Captain Marr, I'm not saying that I'll stop you from traveling north on the Bozeman Road. But the army is here to assure your safety in this part of the world."

"You yourself told us the Eighteenth Infantry left here a week ago." The big Irishman standing beside Marr squinted at the well-groomed colonel. "Told us they'd be stationed north of here to secure the road for travel."

Maynadier sighed. "Do you have a name, sir?"

"Seamus Donegan, late of the Army of the Shenandoah, Colonel."

"Mr. Donegan, surely someone of your experience and background will understand that the mere presence of our troops won't guarantee safe travel on the road."

"What the bejesus you send them soldier-boys up there for?" Marr demanded.

"Gentlemen!" Maynadier bolted out of his leather, horse-hair chair, flinging his cigar into an ashtray atop the desk. "I'll say this one last time, and then you'll excuse me. The road is yours to take. Go right ahead!" He flung an arm toward the door.

Both Marr and Donegan regarded the colonel suspiciously. A third man in their party sat unconcerned in the corner of the colonel's office, whittling at a year's crop of black soil buried beneath his fingernails.

"We'll not detain you here," Maynadier continued. "Instead, all we can do is recommend that you don't attempt any travel north of here using the Bozeman Road without military escort."

"I suppose you'll be pleased as punch to supply us that military escort, eh?" Marr asked, his old hand slamming down on the desk.

Without taking his eyes off Marr, Maynadier addressed the fifth man present in the room. "Lieutenant, read to our guests the official notification from Departmental Headquarters concerning military parties scheduled for travel on the road——"

"I don't wanna hear any more official clap-trap from your departmental——"

"Captain Marr." The colonel held up a hand. "You'll want to listen carefully to one particular item. Lieutenant, please."

As the two civilians and his superior turned their attention on him, the colonel's adjutant began to read. ". . . Detail traveling north from Fort Sedgwick, destined for final duty station in Mountain District, reporting to Colonel Henry B. Carrington, Eighteenth Infantry. Detail under command of Lieutenant George Templeton. Accompanying party are wives of two officers, two young children, and one colored servant girl. Due Fort Laramie first week of July." He looked up at the colonel. "Sir, the rest of this message goes on with——"

"I understand, Lieutenant," Maynadier replied, waving a thick hand to silence his adjutant. "There, gentlemen. You have your military escort. As I recall, there'll be four officers in the group, accompanied by fourteen enlisted men. And, you'll be happy to note, you won't be the only civilians traveling north with Templeton's detail. There're two more gentlemen who've been waiting for close to a week now for an escort north. Three days ago I gave them the happy news that as soon as Templeton arrives here, they can——"

"Bound for the goldfields like us?" Marr broke in.

"No, Captain. On the contrary—a Ridgeway Glover, photographer for Frank Leslie's *Illustrated Weekly,* out of Philadelphia. Came west for camera studies of the land and its wild inhabitants, he tells me. The other gentleman is a man of the cloth. Reverend David White. Methodist. Assigned chaplain attached to the Eighteenth Infantry . . . wherever Colonel Carrington decides to build his post."

"You know where we might be finding these two . . . civilians?" Donegan stuffed his big hands in the pockets of his gray britches, which in turn were stuffed inside the tall, hog-leg boots with mule-ears.

"Lieutenant," Maynadier asked his adjutant, "can you steer Mr. Donegan in the right direction?"

"They're camped in the cottonwood grove below Bedlam, sir."

"Bedlam?" Donegan inquired.

"Bachelor Officers Quarters. You'll go out my door, around the building, and down the slope into the trees . . ."

"Thank you, Colonel." Donegan presented his hand.

"You're quite welcome." Maynadier sighed, this ordeal over. "The army's here to protect, gentlemen."

Marr stopped at the door, July sunlight flooding into the room. "Who're you really protecting. Civilians like us? Or the Indians?"

He wheeled and pushed out into the sunshine with Donegan and Bobby Ray Simpkins on his heels. "Well, Seamus. We're on our way north to the Montana goldfields at last. So close I can smell it." He drew a deep breath, drinking deep on the dry heat of the high plains.

Donegan measured the older man again. "Still so bleeming sure those Injins won't cause us any trouble, eh?"

"Not since you and me bought those big Henry's."

"That fancy gun cost me nearly all my separation pay. But what really hurt was it took most of my drinking money to boot."

"Day'll come you'll be damned glad we got them repeaters." Marr slapped the big Irishman on the back. "C'mon, boys. I'll buy a drink over to the sutler's. Then we'll go look up these other gents waiting for an escort into the land of milk and honey."

Chapter 3

*B*rown pulled the pipe from his mouth, watching the old scout plod his way through the knee-high grass. He didn't know what it was about Bridger that made his belly go sour.

Just a harmless old man dressed like any sod-buster.

Almost laughable, with that floppy hat pulled down over Bridger's silver hair. Brown decided it might be those clear, blue eyes twinkling above the scout's ready grin. Eyes that many times seemed to mock him and his fellow officers, as if Bridger alone knew something the army did not. Whatever it was, the captain was certain Bridger didn't like him a shade either.

"Mornin', Cap'n."

Brown knocked the dollop of burnt tobacco from his pipe against a boot-heel before he answered, "Mr. Bridger."

The scout fell silent. Leaning back against the wagon Brown had been working in, his elbows propped up against the side-boards, he stared wistfully at the sunrise daubing rose light across the Big Horns. Jim cleared his throat.

"You have something to say," Brown blurted suddenly, "why don't you just say it."

"Well, I do have something what needs some dusting

off, I suppose." Bridger scratched at his gray chin-stubble.

"Be out with it. I'm damned busy these days. Counting our stores. Seeing what we've lost since departing Fort Kearney. Inventory has to be taken, what made it here unbroken . . . what the mice, rats, or weevils didn't eat. I'm damned busy, Mr. Bridger." He bent back over a sheaf of papers rustling in an insistent breeze that danced through the tall grass in rolling waves.

"The colonel ever say why he didn't want me along when he rode off to look over that country round the Tongue and Goose Crik for his new fort?"

Brown peered up from his papers. For the first time this morning he smiled. "That's right, isn't it, ol' fella? Carrington didn't take you along with him, did he?"

"It's got me some confused."

"You wanted him to choose a site farther north, didn't you? But all along the colonel's been set on building his fort right here."

"That's fair country up to the Tongue. Maybeso, even far up on Goose Crik. Better place for a fort."

"Now what would an old trapper like you know about building a fort?" Brown scoffed, his eyes raking over his papers.

"Me? Nothing, I suppose, Cap'n. 'Cept, knowing Injuns the way I does. And building that fort of mine down to the Green River country, southwest of here. Picked that spot myself. Good enough for the army, I suppose."

"What do you mean, it was good enough for the army?" Brown wet the end of his pencil on his tongue.

"Army brass figured my spot good enough for a fort that they bought mine."

"I . . . see." Brown fell back to counting.

Bridger was certain the captain knew nothing about those early days in the Rocky Mountains. *How I had to fight off both marauding Indians and Mormon raiders when Brigham Young got it in his head that this big land weren't big enough for both him and Jim Bridger to boot.*

No, this stupid captain wouldn't know nothing about how the army kept coming back for my help year after year, campaign after campaign.

He studied the balding officer a moment more, then stared off as dawn's touch of rose faded from the never-summer snows on the Big Horns hulking high above them. *This ain't that bad a spot. But why didn't the colonel take me along? Did Carrington want to be shed of my advice? Damn, if army brass ain't too oft like a cantankerous mule a'times. Never know which face they'd turn on a man with next.*

Bridger had led the 2nd Battalion of the 18th Infantry north from Fort Laramie with all hope for a peace treaty left in tatters. The old scout himself had seen the guns and kegs of powder lashed on the wild Indian ponies as the Oglalla and Miniconjou turned their own noses north, returning to their hunting ground north of the Crazy Woman Fork.

Still, from time to time, he had to remind Carrington, "Them Bad Faces under Red Cloud ain't about to welcome you with open arms, Colonel. Everything points to war."

For the first few days out of Laramie, Bridger had wheedled and worked on the colonel, the old scout trying to convince him to use the longer but safer trail north. Back in 1864 Bridger had led emigrants to the Montana goldfields up the western slope of Big Horns. Through Shoshone land. "The Snakes aren't out to lift white hair," Bridger had lectured the officers.

"But John Bozeman evidently didn't think much of your caution, Jim," the colonel had said, smiling in that administrative way of his. "He blazed his own road north that makes an easier trip of it than does yours. Saving hundreds of miles. That's why ex-soldiers from the war are scurrying along Bozeman's road, despite all the talk of danger from the Sioux."

"So where the almighty citizen wants to travel . . . that's where the goddamned government will put its road. Duty bound to keep that road open with soldiers, I suppose."

Carrington had grinned within his dark Vandyke beard. "Sounds as if you grasp the government mind, Mr. Bridger."

"I been round enough army brass in my years to know stinkum when I smell it," Jim had replied. "Come hell or war, them stiff-necked politicians back East get something in their heads, nothing's bound to change it. Even good horse sense."

Bridger had finally joined Carrington in laughing. If the army wanted to keep this Bozeman Road into Montana open, then by God, Jim Bridger would come along for the ride. Might prove damned interesting before the last dance of the ball was called.

"And you're not a man to pass up something interesting, are you, Jim?"

They laughed harder, together. He didn't know what it was, but Jim felt something appealing about the colonel. Bridger might even think he was growing to like Carrington. Still, he couldn't shake that cold, gut-grip feeling that the colonel no more belonged out here commanding soldiers against angry Sioux than a whore belonged in Sunday service.

Atop his flea-bit gray mare of a mule, the old scout had led them across the North Platte and into the desolate moonscape that swallowed the Montana Road for better than a hundred fifty miles. North by northwest they plodded across the many parched creeks, every face caked with dust, throats parched with thirst. Times beyond counting when they did run across water, they found it so laced with alkali that the mules and horses even turned their noses from a taste.

Overhead a relentless summer sun continued to bake man and beast alike. Every evening's camp brought new reports of more stock collapsed from the heat. Left for dead or the coyotes. Or the Sioux. Each dawn the new recruits marched on, prodded by the old veterans who placed a pebble in their mouths to stimulate saliva. Other old files even showed the youngsters how to carefully open a vein in their wrists. How to suck at their own hot, sticky blood. Quenching an unquenchable thirst that tormented a man almost as much as the visions swimming before their eyes.

With great relief they reached the valley of the Powder River, that flat ribbon of yellowed water crawling over beds of shifting sand and coarse gravel. It was here they stopped at the garrison of Fort Reno. A sterile, windscoured, hellish place. But Bridger cheered them all by telling the soldiers as they set about making repairs to wagons that they had passed the worst of it.

"Just look at you! The men. Your stock," Capt. Joshua L. Proctor, Carrington's new commander at Reno, had scolded the colonel in private, discussing the march beyond the Powder. "You can't possibly go on, sir. The animals and men have had nearly all they can take."

"We must push on," the colonel had replied.

"For God's sake, leave the women and children with us here. We'll get them back to Laramie where they'll be safe," Proctor had begged.

"I'm afraid it's too late to send them back now," Carrington had confessed.

Is it too late to send Margaret and the boys back with the rest? the colonel wondered. *Lord knows I've asked her time and again if she thought it best to return to Laramie, back to Fort Kearney where they'll be safe and comfortable.* Time and again she had refused his offer. She had married a soldier, she told him. So a soldier's life she would share with him. That put an end to it every time.

Yet the colonel still wondered now as he argued with Proctor. *Would the time ever come that I'll regret my decision to march on with the women and children of this regiment in tow? Would the time ever come that I'll regret not standing strong in sending them back?* At Reno his resolve quivered, like a muscle flexed and worked, beaten and abused too many times.

Carrington had simply stared at Proctor with those dark, brooding eyes of his. As if pleading for someone to understand the compulsion pulling him north. "We must go on. All of us."

For ten days he had allowed the command to tarry at Reno. Not because Carrington had wanted to—but because he had to. Making repairs to the ambulance and freight-wagon tires that split in the dry, searing heat. Repeatedly scanning the hills to the north for some sign of Lt. John Adair and his men chasing the Sioux who had roared down on Reno their very first day in camp and driven off some horses, mules and beef. Day after day they waited by the Powder, gathering strength sapped in the long march, fortifying themselves for what lay ahead. Carrington worried that Adair's men had become his first casualties until the lieutenant's detachment limped back in. Adair had located some of the stock after a long and costly chase. But no sign of feather nor bow.

Not a trace of the warriors who had welcomed Carrington's men to the ancient hunting ground of the Sioux.

"But they're out there," Bridger had chided the young soldiers, all strut and cocky for a fight with the young, naked warriors. "You best understand they're watching you boys every step of the way. When you don't see a Injun in this part of the country, then it's high time you start worrying. Like smoke in the wind. Them red niggers gone afore you see 'em. Soon enough, howsomever, you'll see more of them bastards than you'd ever care to lay eyes on."

With repairs made, Bridger had led Carrington's soldiers away from Fort Reno. Almost from the moment they climbed out of the valley of the Powder, the Montana Road took the caravan into another country altogether. With each day the breeze blew sweeter. Cooler. The men stepped livelier as the column wound its way into the shadow of the Big Horns at last. Row upon row of forested ridges fanned like velvet-draped fingers into grass-covered hills stretching all the way to the foot of the mountains. A hundred-fifty-mile spine of mountains, erupting roughly northwest to southeast into this land of the Sioux.

With cloud-draped peaks on their left, the command made the dusty crossing of the Crazy Woman Fork. With Red Cloud's warning still ringing in his ears, Carrington sent his skirmishers farther out along the high ridges. Twenty-three more miles brought his soldiers to the crossing of Clear Creek, a swift, cold, and noisy flow which would eventually find the Powder on its northward race. Rock Creek came next as the land grew lusher still. Taller timber. Richer grass. But barely a mile past the crossing, Henry Williams had come riding back to the head of the column to present Bridger and Carrington with two small boards torn from a cracker box he had found along the trail. A message scrawled on the wood told of a civilian caravan attacked here just the week before. Sioux had driven off most of the oxen and some of the horses. The message said the civilians had pressed on.

Carrington's soldiers followed. Within a handful of miles the clear, blue waters of Lake DeSmet beckoned on their right. Named after a Jesuit priest who had traversed the West some thirty years before, the lake welcomed the weary marchers by offering thousands of ducks and geese.

"An amazing country," Carrington had gushed as they skirted the lake.

"I think you're getting the idea now, Colonel. Beginning to figure out why the Sioux wanna hold onto this country." His arm swept in a wide arc. "Why they'll fight you for every mile of it. Warning what they'd do if you crossed the Crazy Woman."

Carrington nodded. "A soldier for every mile."

That afternoon they had dropped into the valley created by the two Piney forks of the Clear Fork of the Powder River. Here, halfway along the spine of the Big Horns, a headland juts toward the eastern plains, like a

mighty thumb pointing the way. The Peno Head thrusts
down amid granite cliffs and thick forests before it spends
itself along the Montana Road in what Bridger said was
known as Lodge Trail Ridge.

"Beyond that ridge, you'll find all the Sioux you'd ever
want," Bridger explained to Carrington and his staff as
they looked across the valley of the Piney forks.
"Camped down the Tongue. Up the Rosebud. Over on
the Little Big Horn. Land fat with Sioux."

Lodge Trail Ridge slanted gently south into a high valley cut ages ago by Big Piney and Little Piney creeks.
Carrington found the southern end of the valley pro-
tected by more of the great mountain range itself, while
to the east rose another spur the colonel would call Pilot
Hill. Through the narrow opening between his Pilot Hill
and Lodge Trail Ridge rushed the clear, cold waters of
the combined Piney creeks, tumbling for the Powder and
the Yellowstone, on to the Missouri and the sea far, far
from this Sioux land.

Bridger led Carrington up the Bozeman Road where it
skirted the western fringe of Pilot Hill. Here the valley
spread itself before the colonel, like a woman would open
her arms to embrace a lover, welcoming him into her
warmth, into the fire of her most private, consuming pas-
sion.

Here lay a land blessed with wild tulip and larkspur.
Hills dappled with the delicate white blossoms of wild
pea. Down in the shaded draws grew a profusion of wild
raspberry, gooseberry and red currant. Between the two
bubbling Pineys rose a low range of hills separating the
creeks. At the western end of those hills lay a large pine
island thick with great stands of timber. Carrington
breathed deep, drawing at the cool air rushing into the
valley from the glaciers hung among the clouds above.
Satisfied.

"Those will be the Sullivant Hills, Jim. Margaret's
maiden name, you see."

The old scout finally nodded without comment, watching Carrington's eyes search the approaching columns rumbling up behind them. Knowing the colonel looked for his wife. Yearning to have her approval of this place he had chosen to build his life's dream.

A mile above where the road crossed the Little Piney rose a plateau that stood near the entrance to the valley itself. Anxiously Carrington had loped to the top, where he could gaze down on the creeks and grass so tall in the bottoms that a horse might disappear in it. His eyes climbed from the ridges to the foothills, upward to the imperial peaks above it all.

With his heart racing, Carrington removed General Cooke's orders from his tunic. His dark eyes danced over the words. *'Establishing a new post on or near the Piney Fork of the Powder River.'* Carefully he re-folded the orders and replaced them against his breast.

"The Lord's seen fit to bring us to this place, Jim. It's here I'll build my fort. Down along that timbered island is more than enough lumber for construction. The creek bottoms will yield the clay to chink building timbers. Where the Little Piney flows close to the base of the plateau, I'll set the stockade's water-gates. Across the lush bottomland grows the tall grass that'll provide winter's hay for our stock. Yes, indeed, Mr. Bridger. You've brought the Eighteenth to the promised land. As in the days of Aaron, out of the bondage of the desert you've delivered us."

Bridger chewed on that a bit while he studied the colonel's face. "I think you ought to look on north a ways. Open country that is——"

"But none so fine."

"Best look it over before deciding."

Carrington watched the crow's-feet at the corners of Bridger's eyes crinkle with concern. "Yes, Jim. I promise you that. I'll look it over before I decide."

Behind them arose the clatter of hoofs. Carrington turned in the saddle, waving the two captains to his side.

"Our camping spot for the night, Colonel?" Frederick Brown inquired.

"Yes, Captain."

Tenedore Ten Eyck's left eye roamed the valley quickly. His right lid drooped, a life-long malady cursing him with a half-sleepy look. "Begging the Colonel's pardon . . . but, this looks like an ideal strategic location for your new post."

Carrington glanced at Ten Eyck approvingly. "Perhaps, Captain. Mr. Bridger has some country farther north to show me. So we'll wait to see what tomorrow brings."

Brown turned on the old scout. "Surely Mr. Bridger could never find anything so fair as this, Colonel."

Over Brown's shoulder Carrington watched the column leaders break the lip of the plateau. "True." He winked at the old scout as he answered, "I think even Mr. Bridger will agree that the Lord himself has brought us to this place. It is here destiny has called us."

Chapter 4

With his site chosen, work to erect Carrington's vision of a mountain fortress began in earnest the next morning.

Captain Ten Eyck and his pioneers first staked out the dimensions of the fort from plans drawn up the previous spring in Nebraska Territory. Atop the plateau the fort stockade itself would spread some four-hundred-feet square, its four walls enclosing company barracks, officers' quarters, a chapel and hospital, stables and laundry, warehouses and administrative buildings, a sutler's store and powder magazine, along with an impressive bandstand and parade. Next, Carrington's men staked out the dimensions of the quartermaster's yard which would enclose civilian teamsters' quarters and stables, the hay and wood yards, along with shops for wheelwrights, coopers and blacksmiths, and including the teamsters' mess. Measuring some two hundred by six hundred feet, the quartermaster's yard would reach the Little Piney, to ensure an uninterrupted supply of water in the event of siege.

Carrington sighed. The plateau was perfect. His long-dreamed-of fort fit atop it splendidly. A dream come to fruition, bringing the hand of civilization to this wild and savage land.

Now he could order horse-drawn mowers hitched so teamsters could comb down what would become company streets. Meanwhile, other soldiers pitched their white tents in row upon row across the top of the plateau.

Into the valley of the Big Piney, work details of troopers and civilians hauled the horse-powered sawmill that would begin slabbing the lumber Carrington's timber crews felled at dawn the very first morning after arrival. All along Pine Island rang the crack of axe, the whir of sawmill and the whip of men's voices at labor. Once they had finished platting the fort site itself, the mowers moved into the lush valley below, there to begin cutting the tall grass for the coming winter.

Carrington's soldiers had come to stay.

"Colonel?"

Lt. John Adair shouldered his way through the crowd of onlookers who had gathered round to welcome Carrington back as the sun was easing itself down upon the sharp spires of the Big Horns.

Adair saluted his commander. "We have a white man in custody—I've arrested him for spying."

"Spying? Good Lord!"

"Yes, sir. He approached our location furtively. I immediately suspected him of being a spy for the hostiles in the surrounding countryside."

"Jim?" Carrington turned to Bridger. "You know anything about this?"

"Can't say as I do, Colonel. First I heard about it. You, Jack?"

Stead shook his dark head.

"Let's talk with your spy, Lieutenant."

In a wall tent surrounded by four armed troopers, the colonel and his scouts were presented to a short, bearded and very frightened man. He leaped to his feet as the tent flaps were drawn back. The look in his eyes told of his fear the soldiers had come at last to execute him. Trembling, he grabbed Carrington's hand, jabbering in a mixture of Pidgin English and some French.

"See, Colonel? Just as I told you. A spy. One of those Frenchmen who hire to the English in the Canadian provinces. Inciting the Indians against Americans. Well, we have this one red-handed now—so to speak."

"Not so fast, Lieutenant." Carrington waved Adair back. "Jim, you understand French?"

"Can't make no sense of that tongue."

"And you, Jack?" Carrington turned to Stead. "What do you make of it?"

The dark-skinned scout stepped out of the shadows of twilight and spoke a few guttural words, amplifying them with his hands flying before him. A sense of guarded calm washed over the Frenchman. He wiped his dry lips nervously, his wide eyes never leaving Jack Stead's hands.

"Man ain't a spy, Colonel." The scout turned to Carrington when the Frenchman had completed his long story.

"Damn you!" Adair edged forward. "I've arrested the man for sneaking past our lines. I'll bet my life he came to look us over. Determine our strength. Before the Sioux make a go at us—just like they warned us they would at Laramie!"

"Calm yourself, Lieutenant." Carrington placed his palm against Adair's chest.

Stead shook his head. "Ain't that at all. Fella works for French Pete."

"French Pete?" Carrington inquired.

"Name's Louis Gazzous. A trader known in these parts. Beads for buffalo robes. Got him a Sioux wife, too, I hear. Been 'round for some winters, far as I can remember. Trades into the Sioux and Cheyenne villages. This man drives a wagon for him."

"One of French Pete's teamsters?" The colonel watched Stead nod. "What the devil would he be doing coming to our camp? And alone at that?"

"Seems French Pete's been trading up on the Tongue. Making the rounds since the Sioux come back from the treaty-talks at Laramie. But most of the bands ain't had time to work their hides into trading shape yet. Besides, most of the Sioux don't exactly need nothing from

French Pete yet, anyway. Came away from Laramie with some handsome plunder."

"That doesn't explain a thing to me," Carrington said.

"Pete wandered down to Black Horse's band of Northern Cheyenne, Colonel. Black Horse didn't go to Laramie, so Pete thought he'd do better with the Cheyenne. Got to the village just about the time word came in from scouts that white soldiers set up camp here in the shadow of the Big Horns. Right where the Sioux had told the Cheyenne no white men would ever come . . . nor be allowed to stay."

"The Cheyennes are siding with the Sioux?" Concern crackled in Carrington's voice.

Stead shook his head. "Not all. I got the feeling that's for you to decide."

Carrington studied the dark scout's eyes for a moment, sensing the importance of what he had just been told. "So, tell us why one of French Pete's men came here. To spy for his friends, the Cheyennes?"

"Nawww. Black Horse and French Pete wanted this one to come here . . . with a message for the soldier chief."

"A message?"

With Carrington's question, Stead motioned for the frightened Frenchman to hand over his note. From inside his greasy shirt he pulled a wrinkled piece of yellowed newsprint. Along the margin of the torn and tattered remnant of year-old newspaper, a message had been scrawled with an unsure hand. The colonel read the words formed from deliberate, painstakingly-formed letters:

We want to know does white chief want peace or war? Tell him come with the black white man.

Carrington's eyes rose from the yellowed scrap. "Black white man?"

Bridger chuckled. "They must mean you, Jack."

"I don't understand." Carrington sounded confused.

"Just look at him, Colonel," Bridger chided. "Hair and eyes dark as any Injun's. Out here in this country under the sun, his skin's tanned like smoked elk-hide. Ain't no wonder to me the Cheyenne figure Jack's a black white man."

Stead grinned. "If my mother back in England heard her youngest called a black man, she'd tear a man's eyes out, most like."

"You're . . . you're English?" Adair asked with a squeak.

"Runaway, at the tender age of fourteen years. Worked the schooners and packets until my ship went down on the rocks at the mouth of the Columbia. Made my way inland. Crossed the Rockies many a time."

"He was the first to carry word east that the goddamn Mormons were fixing to turn again' the government," Bridger added.

"Jim and me share no love for Mormons, do we, Jim?"

"Not when that bastard Brigham Young put a price out on our heads. Sonuvabitch with all his wives and a hand-picked band of cut-throats he calls his 'angels.'"

"I took a Cheyenne wife some time back," Stead answered.

"That explains a lot," Carrington admitted. "Tell me what you think about Black Horse's invitation."

"Don't know how to figure it, Colonel."

"You suspect treachery?"

"Nawww, not really. I 'spect I'm the only one they're bound to trust. Married to a Sioux and all."

"Good!" Carrington clapped his hands together, startling the scouts and the French teamster. "That settles it. You'll carry my message to Black Horse."

"If that's the way you want it, Colonel. I'll be ready to go at first light."

"No, Jack. I want you to leave immediately. I'm afraid this can't wait. Lieutenant Phisterer, fetch me some writing materials quickly."

As Carrington turned away he did not notice the look exchanged between his two scouts.

Twilight had deepened into summer's darkness, with a host of stars sprinkled overhead by the time the colonel finished the message Jack Stead would carry to the Northern Cheyenne.

To Black Horse, Greatest of Cheyenne Chiefs: Friend:

A young Frenchman has come to tell me you want to talk with me. This is good, to talk. I would be happy to have you come talk with me and tell me what is in your heart. Come when the sun is overhead in the sky after two sleeps.

The Great Father in Washington is not alone in wanting peace with his red children. All the soldiers who come with me want peace. I speak for peace above all things.

I will allow no soldier to steal from the Indians who want peace. I will allow no soldier to kill the Indians who want peace. The white men who march on the road will not steal nor kill the Indians who want peace.

Be assured when you come to talk with me, no one will harm you. And when you have spoken to me and told me what rests in your heart, you may go and be assured no harm will come to you or the chiefs you bring with you to talk with me. I will tell my chiefs and my soldiers that Black Horse and his warriors are my friends. No harm will come to you.

Come talk with me when the sun stands in the sky, two sleeps from now.

> *A soldier and your friend,*
> *Henry B. Carrington*
> *Colonel,*
> *Eighteenth U.S. Infantry*
> *Commander, Mountain District*

Shadows quickly swallowed Jack Stead and the French teamster as their army mounts carried them down the side of the plateau, riding north into the night and the land of the hostiles.

Chapter 5

"*I* see by the stripe on your gray britches and that side-arm you're packing that you were in the cavalry during the recent rebellion in the south, Mr. Donegan."

With his bony cheeks heaving like a blacksmith's bellows, the Right Reverend David White sucked the flame from a twig into his pipebowl with a succession of loud hisses, waiting for the Irishman to answer.

"Never meant to hide a thing, Reverend."

White tossed the twig into the fire. "No offense meant, sir. Just getting to know one another." Acknowledging the Irishman's friendly gesture, the reverend smiled at the two others seated round the smoky fire. A gray haze rose from the twigs and was caught in the yellow streamers of sunlight that poured through the cottonwood branches overhead. "Myself, I served with Stephen Watts Kearney down in the Mexican Provinces twenty years ago. I can well understand any man's reluctance to talk about the recent war, Mr. Donegan. I grew too old far too fast following Kearny across that brick-oven of a desert, chasing greasers and watching good men die for it."

"Never been a good war, sir." Donegan tossed down the last of the coffee in his cup. "Only men who put their good lives on the line for someone else's idea of a cause."

"Well put, Mr. Donegan." White leaned back against a saddle. "To my way of thinking, we're fortunate that we travel as civilians now. None of us here as a part of an army chasing Indians across these trackless wastes. Ex-soldiers all," he cheered, offering a toast with his coffee cup.

"You fought in the rebellion, too, Mr. Glover?" Sam Marr gazed through smoky fingers of light at the young photographer.

Glover bobbed his head of short-cropped wheat-straw hair self-consciously before answering. "Yes. Fourth Pennsylvania Volunteers." His wide, expressive eyes jumped from man to man as if ready to tell more. Then they hugged the ground, refusing to rise, like small, scared things in search of safe haven.

"Then you saw action at Gettysburg?" Marr asked.

Glover kept his eyes long on the flames at his feet before answering. "It was my first real . . . fight. Everything before that'd been just a skirmish. Gettysburg . . . changed everything for me—changed my whole life."

"Wasn't a man who walked away from that fight not changed," Seamus Donegan said quietly. "God help the generals who would lead armies into something like that hell ever again."

"You enjoyed cavalry, I take it," White asked, pointing with the stem of his pipe at the yellow stripe along Donegan's gray trousers.

"Always loved the feel of a good horse beneath me."

"You're quite a chunk of it," White said with a smile. The skin on his face shifted merrily, like a linen sheet rumpled across old bedsprings. "It'd take a good horse to stay beneath you, Irishman!"

Seamus chuckled lightly, eyes on the fire and his mind back East. "Had several good horses shot out from under me, Reverend. Each one I missed worst than the last. Most cavalry sojurs worth their salt know part of being a horse-sojur means a horse ofttimes will take a bullet meant for the rider. Lay down its life for its rider—like few friends I've known in my short time on this sweet earth. Can't say there's many men would trade places with Seamus Donegan when it came to facing the muzzles of Confederate artillery."

"You were injured in the war?" White leaned forward, the bald spot atop his head gleaming in a hazy streamer of sunlight.

"Horses, Reverend." the Irishman didn't rise to the bait. "Horses is how the cap'n here and me come to know one another. One trail after another I took when peace came and me being mustered out last winter. Found myself in Missouri. The idea of heading west struck me as the best devilment I could get myself into. Wandering as a man alone is apt to do. The cap'n was buying horses for the army in Kansas. He spotted mine and made an offer right there on the streets of Jefferson City."

"Top dollar too!" Marr added with a smile.

"This old man knows good horseflesh when he sees it."

"But Donegan wouldn't sell me his mount. Truth be, if I'd bought that horse from him, the animal never would've seen the inside of any army stable. Butchers, the army can be with their mounts. Ah, Donegan had himself a prize there." Marr scratched at his short-cropped salt-and-pepper whiskers before he swept his long, shoulder-length gray hair from his collar.

"You bought the horse after the war, Seamus?" White inquired.

"No." Donegan shook his head and glanced round at them all. "I won it—shall we say."

"A game of chance, perhaps. A race—winner take all?"

"Aye, Reverend. A game of chance. And the winner did take all," Donegan spoke barely above a hoarse whisper, kneading his big hands on the greasy knees of his gray britches. He swallowed, not wanting to tell. Knowing he would. "A Confederate cavalry officer once rode that big gray of mine."

"The spoils of war," White offered, his hand waving

expansively in the air, the long, thick-knuckled fingers working like ill-fitting sausages at the end of his hand. "Perfectly sensible. He turned over his sword and thoroughbred to the victor of the engagement."

Donegan shook his head. "Not as clean and tidy as all that, Reverend. But then, war never is, is it? No, sir. That fine Johnnie officer was a true swordsman. He drew first blood. I'll wear his saber scar across my back for the rest of me days."

White slowly pulled the pipe from his thin lips, then raked a hand back through one side of his gray hair. His bald head reminded Seamus of the walk leading up from the road to his mother's house in County Kilkenny. Worn smooth between the thick growth of stubborn grass. "And he'll mourn the loss of that horse for the rest of his?"

"I took more than the big gray from him that day," Donegan admitted in whisper. "Never have I wanted to kill a man as badly as I did him that day in the Shenandoah."

"You rode under Sheridan, then?"

"Aye."

"Does your wound trouble you still?"

Donegan studied the inquisitive minister a moment longer. He found the old man forthright in his nosiness. Besides, every man of the cloth Seamus Donegan had ever run across made a lifelong practice of getting down inside another man's britches and learning all that was hidden beneath.

"A'times, Reverend. The weather changes, I feel it in this knee. Took both a saber slash there and a ball in the meaty part of the leg above the knee here. But my back doesn't nag at me when it's coming cold. That ugly scar nags at me only when there's trouble on my backside. Like a set of eyes, i'tis. The one time I wasn't looking out for my backside in battle—a poltroon of a Confederate officer carved me up pretty good. Seems now that this scar o' mine is going to make sure no one ever sneaks up on Seamus Donegan again."

The men round the smoky fire fell silent as Donegan's eyes refused to budge from the mesmerizing flames. Long moments later Reverend White finally picked up his battered, blackened pot from the edge of the fire and poured more of the steaming brew into each man's waiting cup. Finished, he shoved more unruly gray hair back along the sides of his head, proposing a toast.

"To good friends and companions, gentlemen. They make any journey worth the wait . . . worth any effort. May our Lord God Jehovah bless us all, everyone—as we poor wayfarers travel in the good company of one another . . . each in search of his own private dream."

All four civilians drank in silence for a moment, until Marr licked at the droplets of coffee hung from his thick mustache and asked, "Reverend, what dream possesses a man like you?"

White smiled, both rows of wide teeth stained from too much coffee and tobacco smoke. "Captain Marr, my dream is to make this trip north to my new flock without serious hardship or mishap . . . and without losing what I have left of the hair on my poor head!"

White began to chuckle, running his bony fingers through the long gray strands. Though they were hands most accustomed to holding a bible or wagging a warning finger at a congregation, White's hands nonetheless showed they were no stranger to hard work. With thick-knuckled fingers he patted the baby-pink scalp taut across the full length of his head.

Captain Marr laughed even louder. He pulled his wide-brimmed hat from his own silver head, showing White that he too had a patch of valuable, pink scalp to lose. The Missourian's long, silver curls spilled well past his collar, where his sagging neck skin had begun to wrinkle.

"No Sioux warrior gonna want our two hoary old scalps, Reverend!"

White guffawed loudly, his laughter merry and genu-
ine. Pointing a skinny twig of a finger at Seamus, the
minister roared, "Let's just pray the sight of Mr. Donegan's fine head of long, curly hair will not lead the Sioux
nation into temptation!"

Chapter 6

"Colonel. Sergeant of the guard reports his sentries signaling the approach of Indians."

Carrington looked up from his detailed drawings and plans of the fort. He let only his eyes touch each officer gathered round the long table he had readied in the huge hospital tent for this very occasion. Bridger found the colonel gazing at him.

"Jim, I'll want you and Jack by my side."

"Best you bring Jack along," the old scout replied. "He talks Cheyenne better'n I do."

"But, Jim Bridger knows Indians better than any man alive," Carrington replied, straightening his shoulders, smoothing the bright red sash at his waist. He had ordered his officers into full-dress uniform at morning assembly. This would be the day—he had told them—the day the Cheyennes would come to call. "I'll want you both at my side. Have Jack ride out to escort Black Horse into camp. He must reassure the chief that he's welcome here. Among friends."

Bridger nodded, glancing at the sentry atop Pilot Hill waving his bright semaphore in the wind and riding in a circle, the signal to alert the fort of the approach of Indians. A moment later Jim recognized the bright pennons of Cheyenne warriors marching up an ages-old path crossing Lodge Trail Ridge, bright fragments of color fluttering against the brilliant blue of the midsummer sky.

This's gonna be something to see, Jim thought, knocking the dead ash from his old pipe.

Standing with the hundreds of soldiers and civilians, including officers' wives clutching bright parasols and children scampering in and out of the waiting throng, Bridger felt the warm sun high overhead beating on the leathery skin at the back of his neck.

Old Black Horse done it right. Coming here when the sun rides high.

Something down in that private place Bridger hid from other men tugged at him as he watched the grand procession work its way into the valley, heading for the white soldiers' camp on the plateau. Try as he might, Bridger still found himself a man who often felt things deeper and with more hurt than most. Right from his very first year in the mountains. A boy barely seventeen who got bamboozled into leaving Hugh Glass behind. Left behind without his rifle or so much as a knife. And old Hugh chewed up bad by that sow grizz. Abandoned by him and Fitzgerald beside a shallow grave scratched in the sand along that nameless creek.

A salty sting of moisture tapped Jim's eyes. He blinked. Thinking on all those winters since 1822.

Never did leave another man behind again . . . after ol' Hugh come looking for me that first winter. It was his right to kill me, the way I left him barely breathing beside his own empty grave.

Bridger snorted and glanced at the bright sun overhead once more. Remembering.

But ol' Glass said I was just a young pup and didn't know no better. So, for the rest of them forty-odd years . . . well, no man ever found Jim Bridger leaving a friend behind to the critters of the wilds. Or, even worse—Ol' Gabe Bridger never left a man behind for the Injuns to have a cutting spree with.

He swiped at his nose and focused on the procession

worming its way across the valley. The tail end of the caravan had made the crossing of the Big Piney.

Damn, but didn't Black Horse bring 'em all with him. Every nit, prick and stillbirth sonofabitch come along to meet Carrington and his soldiers.

"Quite an impressive sight, wouldn't you say, Jim?"

Bridger watched Carrington stride up beside him.

"That ain't no ragtag bunch of dust-tailed Injuns, Colonel." Jim almost felt sorry for the old warrior.

Black Horse almost as old as me, I'd suppose. He's seen the glory days come and go. A time few white men will ever know. Most of them ol' boys gone now too. What ones ain't gone under, they've packed up and moved on to Oregon country.

But this here's Cheyenne land much as the Sioux's. Black Horse watched his lodges rise against this very sky. He's felt the same breeze sweep down off that snow on them peaks way yonder. Down where Carrington's men cut down their first timber for the stockade, them Cheyenne found shelter against many a winter storm, I'd reckon. Sad to think—the white man's here to stay. Not like it was so many summers ago. Goddamn the settlements! Here we was the first to plant a moccasin. But where first the white man comes, next come the women and preachers.

Jim felt all the sadder for Black Horse. And the end to an ancient way of life they had shared.

"Them's Northern Cheyenne," he explained to Carrington. "Proud as peacocks. I figure Black Horse wants you to know he ain't come to beg at your feet. He's come to show the soldier chief that he's a proud warrior—that's one Injun who won't come lapping up your scraps, the way Spotted Tail does down to Laramie."

Carrington nervously straightened his tunic, freshly pressed and resplendent with brass buttons, gold braid and epaulets above the crimson sash and tinkling saber chains. "We'll welcome him as a friend."

Bridger studied the side of the colonel's face. "It's a far sight better to have that ol' warrior as your friend."

The procession reached the base of the plateau. Without a pause, Black Horse and some forty of his warriors began their slow ascent to the soldier camp. The colonel signaled Bandmaster Samuel Curry. With a wave of his baton, Curry set his forty-piece regimental band to pumping out the strains of Carrington's musical welcome.

With the blare of those first brassy notes, half the warrior ponies reared and twisted in fright. A sudden and strange medicine to these Cheyenne. Undeterred, Black Horse pressed on—his own pony prancing sideways yet under control, its nostrils wide, eyes muling in fright. Riding beside Jack Stead, he was the first to reach the top of the plateau. Lieutenant Adair greeted the Cheyenne chief with a salute and a wave of his elegant full-dress shako.

Jim turned, finding Carrington fussing like a society hostess over the details of the hospital tent, smoothing the huge American flag draped ceremonially over the surgeon's operating table. Above the excited yells of children and the soldiers' laughter, Bridger overheard snatches of an argument between Carrington and Captain Brown, their shrill voices erupting from the tent.

". . . dressing us like monkeys before these savages!"

". . . to the Indian mind, ceremony is their life breath itself."

". . . hold the bastards ransom!"

". . . I've given personal guarantee . . . we command less than four hundred men, including civilians."

". . . show them the strength of our hand—a march right through their camps!"

". . . will not be marred by your eagerness to flaunt that clenched fist of yours, Captain!"

Bridger turned when the murmuring of the crowd grew louder. The warriors halted, dismounted, allowing their ponies to be attended by young soldiers. Warily, the Cheyenne followed Stead and Adair on foot to the hospital tent.

". . . be damned if I'll give them presents, Colonel. Rifles, indeed!"

". . . bring my requisition here immediately. Dismissed."

Down through the long blue gauntlet of soldiers and civilians alike strode the anxious warriors, some aware of their vulnerability as they hid hands beneath their blankets and warshirts. Jim kept his eyes moving from one to another. *Likely got a pistol hiding there.* Yet most walked on confidently. Trusting in the faith Black Horse held in the soldier chief.

Black Horse wrapped himself in a dressed buffalo robe, the fur against his body, the hide painted with primitive pictographs of his exploits in war and pony-stealing. Just behind him walked Dull Knife, younger but proven warchief of the Northern Cheyenne. Well did he know the effect his costume would have on these troopers, for he wore a captured soldier-blue tunic, brass buttons and all. Beside him walked The-Wolf-That-Lies-Down, resplendent in brain-tanned warshirt, scalplocks dangling from shoulder seams and down both arms. Round his neck hung a ceremonial grizzly necklace, the huge claws separated by tufts of blond-tipped fur. Pretty Bear walked alone, strutting proud as any peacock, wearing nothing but moccasins and his breechclout, sporting a gay parasol at his shoulder. Undoubtedly traded from French Pete himself.

Brass armbands and beaded pipebags. Finger-rings and dentalium shells all the way from the Oregon coast hung from earlobes. Medicine pouches, quilled knife scabbards, and huge silver medals suspended on ribbon from a few necks. The-Rabbit-That-Jumps, Two Moon and Red Arm, and finally The-Man-That-Stands-Alone-On-The-Ground. Each warrior made his grand entrance through the open flaps of the tent and took his assigned seat upon the blankets spread across the ground according to his rank among the tribe. Just beyond the flaps the rest of the warriors took their places upon the grass.

Better than thirty minutes passed while the pipe made its rounds of chiefs and officers alike. A nonsmoker, Carrington attempted a brave smile as he gagged on the stem. During the long wait, most of the soldiers and spectators crowded forward, whispering at this close-up view of savage warriors. In that radiant warmth of midday, Adjutant Phisterer continued scribbling across his long sheets of foolscap, recording the proceedings. Round him the various captains and lieutenants stirred restlessly, hot in their full-dress uniforms. A few dozed. Others pinched their delicate noses, unfamiliar with the smell of the plains Indian.

Black Horse stirred, fluttered his eyes from a dreamy slumber and raised his chin from his chest. In rising, the chief allowed the buffalo robe to slip from his shoulders so that it fell round his waist, where it hung over his quilled leggings from a wide belt. White scars of many sun-dances dotted his chest. High near one shoulder he had circled the white pucker of an old bullet wound with vermilion paint.

The chief stopped halfway between his seated warriors and the table where Carrington stirred, anxious to get his conference under way.

A pink tongue darted out to lick his wrinkled lips. Only then did his hands begin to sign as he spoke, his eyes dancing between the soldier chief at the center of the table and Jack Stead, the interpreter close by Carrington's left arm.

"He speaks for 176 lodges," Jack whispered, his head turned so that he spoke into Carrington's ear while his eyes remained locked on the old chief. "In their hunt along Goose Creek, they ran into many of Red Cloud's Sioux. Man-Afraid-of-His Horses's warriors. Proud of their raids on the white soldiers."

Carrington sensed an angry stir among his officers. Black Horse, too, sensed that strained uneasiness as he went on.

"We are a brave people, but will be stronger still when

125 of our young men return from the Arkansas far to the south. They have gone with Bob-Tail to hunt and make war on our enemies in the warm country. The Cheyenne in Old Bear's band camp this summer in the shadow of the Black Hills. Our cousins in the south distrust the whites who are crawling onto the plains beside the path of the iron horse that spits smoke."

Bridger waited for a pause in Jack's interpretation. "He means the Southern Cheyenne, Colonel. South of the Republican. Along the railroad tracks they're laying."

"Red Cloud tells Black Horse that the soldier chief came to Laramie with his soldiers while the white treaty-talkers were wanting the Sioux to sell the road through Indian land. Red Cloud says the soldiers come now to take the land from us, even before our chiefs can say yes. Or no."

Carrington turned to Stead. "Ask Black Horse why the Sioux and Cheyenne claim this land when it belongs to the Crow."

The chief nodded. "It is good to answer so that you will understand why we are here . . . why the Crow live far to the west now. Many winters ago, the Cheyenne were driven here. Along the great waters to the east, the white man already grows crowded. He pushed us here. We needed this hunting ground. Mountainsides filled with the bear and elk. Valleys thick with deer and buffalo. Birds blanketed the ponds and marshes. We saw that it was good. Because the Cheyenne alone could not take it from the Crow, we asked the Sioux to help us. The Lakota share this land with the Cheyenne. Now Red Cloud asks us to help the Sioux hold this land against the white man."

"Who is the great chief of the Cheyenne people?"

"Black Horse."

"And who is the great chief of the Sioux?"

"Red Cloud," he answered, his fingertip slashing his throat in the ancient sign for the Sioux. "Man-Afraid is a powerful war chief, holding many warriors in his hand."

"Does Black Horse come to tell us he will join the Sioux in making war on the soldiers sent to protect this road?"

Black Horse shook his head. "I come to tell you these words of Red Cloud: If the soldier chief wants peace, he must go back to the mud fort he has at the Powder River. The Sioux promise not to bring trouble to the soldiers there. But Red Cloud will not allow soldiers to travel over the road he has never given to the whites. And he will not allow you to build this fort."

"Not allow us to build this fort?"

"Red Cloud wants you to understand, his Bad Faces will surround you, cut you off north and south. They plan to slowly strangle you, Colonel," Jack Stead explained the Cheyenne chief's warning. "Red Cloud promises his warriors will kill your men one at a time, or a hundred at a time. Whenever they can. Red Cloud wants Black Horse to tell you that you sit on a small piece of ground. While Red Cloud's warriors own the hills encircling us."

"Ask the chief how many warriors camp with Red Cloud now."

Black Horse held a gnarled fist before Carrington, spreading five fingers he swept across his chest.

"He says Red Cloud's got five hundred warriors," Jack whispered.

"Colonel," Bridger interrupted quickly, "you best remember that's a drop in the bucket to what he'll have come next month."

"Why more?"

"Now's the time most of Red Cloud's warriors are out hunting buffalo and antelope. By the time they lay in meat for the coming winter and head back to join the chief on the Tongue, there could be better'n twenty-five hundred warriors in Red Cloud's camp. All itching to make it a long winter for your soldiers."

Carrington nodded. "Yes, Jim. Go ahead."

"Worse yet, come next month when the tribes gather,

they meet on the Tongue for the sun-dance held each summer. A sun-dance means Red Cloud and Man-Afraid will whip their warriors into a fighting frenzy right quick."

Carrington grew thoughtful. "How far is Red Cloud?"

"Two days ride. North on the Tongue."

"Ask Black Horse if he'll join Red Cloud to make war on the new friend he has made here today, the soldier chief who sits before him."

As Jack Stead translated and signed, a few of the older warriors offered Black Horse counsel. The old chief inched closer to the council table where the soldiers waited for his answer. His voice began soft and low. Yet strong. Proud as ever.

"The Cheyenne are not many. Alone, they cannot fight the Sioux."

Carrington whirled on Stead, interrupting Black Horse. "I know that! I'm asking if he's going to join Red Cloud's war."

Jack bobbed his head several times as he signed, sensing the tension between the Cheyenne and soldier chiefs thicken like blood congealing on cold ground.

In the way of the Plains Indian, the old chief wanted to explain his answer before he gave the soldier chief his answer.

"It has been a bad year for the Cheyenne. A bad, bad winter. My people are hungry."

Carrington nodded, making no sound. His eyes never left Black Horse. The old chief's gaze never strayed from the colonel. "Ask Black Horse what we can do for him. For his people."

The chief inched closer to the table, as if shamed by having to ask. His hand rubbed his belly, and two fingers on his right hand went into his mouth. Then he wrapped his two arms around himself, sweeping them up and down his sides.

"They . . . his people are hungry. You can give them food. And the soldier chief can give them clothes."

Carrington nodded. Stead fell silent. The old chief dropped his eyes, embarrassed in what appeared as begging.

That private place inside Bridger's gut knotted for these once proud people now caught between the white man who would feed and clothe them . . . and the Sioux who would slaughter them if they went to the white man for help.

"Colonel."

Carrington started, perturbed as Lieutenant Adair bent at his elbow. "What is it?" the colonel snapped at the interruption.

"Captain Haymond, commander of the Second Battalion, just arrived from Reno, sir." He gestured out the rear of the tent. "With his compliment of troops, you have the Eighteenth about back to fighting strength, sir."

Carrington studied the clamor as four companies of soldiers, some 250 men, dismounted at Haymond's shrill order. He glanced at the Cheyennes, certain they noticed the arrival of these reinforcements.

Dull Knife angrily motioned Black Horse to the Cheyenne circle. In hurried, furtive words and glances, the chief and his advisers argued among themselves.

"Colonel!" It was Brown's whisper at his ear. Along with the smell of stale whiskey on the captain's breath. "Show the buggers our mountain howitzers. Let them see how one shell will kill many Sioux. It'll make the yellow bastards cower in fear!"

Like swatting at a troublesome mosquito, Carrington waved Brown back as he rose and left the tent to welcome his new captain. Carrington felt certain of failure.

Dear Lord, I prayed for your assistance in this meeting with the Cheyennes, asking for heavenly council. I've botched this badly. Have I asked more than these poor savages can give? Have I demanded that they make an alliance they aren't ready for? Asking that they join me against the Sioux—who would slaughter the Cheyenne as quickly as they'd slaughter my white soldiers?

Black Horse returned to the table. This time the old Cheyenne no longer held his eyes steady on Carrington. A knot of concern furrowed between his plucked eyebrows. The chief motioned Jack Stead forward. Black Horse whispered. In turn, the scout bent to whisper to Carrington. The other officers rocked forward to hear Jack's message.

"Black Horse fears that Red Cloud will find out that he stayed too long in the soldier chief's camp. Red Cloud will be angry. He'll find the village of Black Horse and sweep all the Cheyenne before him."

Palms together, one of Stead's hands flew across the other, the ancient sign of rubbing out an enemy. Carrington gulped, watching Bridger's eyes narrow. The colonel wasn't new to this sort of fear. He had seen the same fear etched on a black man's face many times before. In the fifties, the colonel had been a passionate antislaver, even before it became fashionable in the North.

"Tell Black Horse that we'll protect him. Together with my soldiers, his young men will defeat Red Cloud." Carrington straightened proudly, smoothing the front of his dark blue tunic, fingers caressing the bright crimson sash.

Black Horse shook his head only once. He whispered to Stead. Jack swallowed hard.

"The chief says you won't protect the Cheyenne. Only he can protect his people by going far away from the Sioux. All your soldiers can't help his people. When Red Cloud comes to fight . . . you . . . you'll not be able to . . . to save yourselves."

Most at the table who heard Jack stutter gasped in dismay. Carrington and his officers fell silent. For moments now the tent had drawn close, the air steamy with rancid bear grease smeared on the black braids, heavy with white soldiers sweating in wool tunics. Bridger's arthritic joints ached in sitting so long on the ladder-backed chair.

"Captain Brown." Carrington's voice cracked uncontrollably. "Bring the gifts for our guests."

The quartermaster signaled six soldiers who scurried forward, their arms heavy with gifts they laid on blankets before the Cheyenne chiefs. Into the stacks of presents the old warriors dove, the eldest and highest-ranking selecting the best for themselves: some secondhand army tunics, brass buttons polished for the occasion, every tunic seeing service in the bloody war the 18th had survived to arrive at this place in history.

When the clothing had been distributed, there remained the two shakos Carrington presented to Black Horse and Dull Knife. A few soldiers giggled as the old chiefs placed the tall, cylindrical ceremonial hats on their heads, bright plumes swaying in the air. Above the laughter, the Cheyenne murmured in appreciation. Bridger understood—to a warrior, appearance meant everything.

Next came sacks of flour, coffee and sugar. At Carrington's request Jack explained the many miles and many sleeps it had taken for these gifts of food to travel to the Big Horns. Two Moon grabbed one of the greasy, waxed bundles bound with brown twine. First he sniffed it. Then tore a strip of paper free for a better smell. Pronouncing it good, he bit off a corner of the slab bacon, a little grease dribbling from the corner of his mouth as he grinned, smacking loudly for all to see his good fortune.

Jack Stead signaled for quiet. "The soldier chief says that he does not want the Cheyenne people to go hungry. Never more. When Black Horse and his people have bellies that pinch, they should not come near the road to beg of the white people on the road. The Cheyenne must go to Laramie, where they will be fed. There the Cheyenne will receive more presents for keeping the peace with the white soldiers."

The colonel turned to his adjutant. "Phisterer. Bring the letters of good conduct I had you prepare. Jack, please explain to the chiefs what my letter says . . . what it means to them."

Before Stead began interpreting for the chiefs, he quickly read the colonel's letter of safe-conduct.

TO MILITARY OFFICERS, SOLDIERS, AND EMIGRANTS:

Black Horse, a Cheyenne chief, having come in and shaken hands and agreed to a lasting peace with the whites and all travelers on the road, it is my direction that he be treated kindly, and in no way molested in hunting while he remains at peace.

When any Indian is seen who holds up this paper, he must be treated kindly.

> *Henry B. Carrington*
> *Colonel, 18th U.S. Infantry*
> *Commanding, Mountain District*

Black Horse signaled his chiefs to gather their gifts and make ready to leave. Only then did the old Cheyenne step directly before Carrington. He laid a hand on the soldier chief's left breast. Then he tapped his own bare breast where lay the image of President Andrew Jackson on a peace medal tarnished over many winters.

"You're his friend now, Colonel." Jack Stead's voice cracked slightly.

Carrington swallowed hard against the hot lump in his throat. "Tell Black Horse that together we can see peace brought to this land."

The old Cheyenne's eyes moistened. "My people ride south with tomorrow's sun. We will stay off the road, and far from Red Cloud's camps. We . . . wish the soldier chief well." Black Horse raised an arm to the heavens, quickly brought that hand to his heart, where it rubbed his left breast before he flung the arm toward Carrington.

Jack sighed, his own eyes a little misty. "Black Horse says . . . may the Everywhere Spirit of his people protect you, Soldier Chief."

Black Horse turned, swallowed by his chiefs among their ponies. When the old Cheyenne had mounted, his new soldier tunic replacing the buffalo robe, his new soldier shako pulled down crookedly over his gray hair, Carrington strode to his side.

Squinting up into the sun, the colonel said, "God's speed, my friend. May the Lord hold you in the palm of his hand."

Black Horse signed, rubbing his chest and extending his arm toward Carrington.

"May the Everywhere Spirit watch over you, soldier chief. May he keep you safe from all harm."

A sudden cold prickled the hairs at the back of Bridger's neck. *Strange,* he thought. To have a chill under this sun. Then Jim realized why he felt such cold, clear down to his marrow. He had come to like this man Carrington. Really liked him. And the sad part of it was, Bridger realized, it would take Almighty God to protect the colonel from here on out. God, and God only. No amount of rifles nor mountain howitzers would keep Carrington out of harm's way now.

The goddamned army brass back East had sent this poor, simple . . . honest man out here to this bloody hunting ground—a man totally unprepared for what stared him in the face. The army sent Carrington here like a gauntlet thrown down to the Sioux. A slap across Red Cloud's face.

In forty-four winters of fighting to keep his scalp, Jim Bridger had never known an Indian to turn down a challenge.

Chapter 7

*A*t Bridger's urging, Carrington dispatched a rider south to Fort Reno that afternoon, rather than wait until morning. If Black Horse was right that Red Cloud was already at work sealing off the Montana Road north from Crazy Woman's Fork, then all future detachments riding up from Reno would be endangered.

While the officers at Fort Laramie were able to communicate with the outside word by using the telegraph-key, these new posts thrown up along the Bozeman Trail had to utilize the ages-old dispatch and courier system. A system that trusted a handwritten message carried by a single rider piercing the red gauntlet the hostile Sioux had thrown up around their hunting ground. More often than not, as the army would one day grudgingly admit, these couriers mounted on the swiftest horse available would not make it to their destination. Most would simply become a small notation in the record of some post— "Courier missing." All too often no trace of body, bone or even the courier's pouch itself could be found. The lonely hammering of each solitary rider's hoofbeats his only epitaph.

That brief farewell bid him as he swung into the saddle, ready to ride, his only eulogy.

Checking recent dispatches carried up from Laramie, Carrington found that a small detachment of new officers

called up from Fort Sedgwick was scheduled to depart
Fort Laramie ten days ago. If his calculations were correct, that detail would reach the Crazy Woman by
Wednesday, July 18. The colonel was relieved that the
army practiced one claim to foresight: as District Commander, he was kept informed of the makeup of parties
coming north along the trail. Always informed, that is, if
the dispatch rider himself made it up the Bozeman Road.

"Who leads the detail?" Carrington asked his assistant.

Phisterer studied his dispatches. "A Lieutenant Templeton, George. Second-in-command is Lieutenant Daniels, Napoleon H. Two replacement lieutenant's for your
staff. In addition, Alexander Wands, your new adjutant
when I'm reassigned. And a James Bradley."

Carrington chewed on the inside of his cheek, staring
off to the south, watching the Cheyenne climb across
Lodge Trail Ridge. They would be marching west tomorrow. Safe. Beyond Red Cloud's grasp.

Henry had a reputation as a thinking man, not given to
rash or impulsive acts, a trait not found among many of
his fellow officers in this postwar army. Graduating from
Yale Law School in 1848, he had begun practice in Co-
lumbus, Ohio, where he met Margaret Sullivant. A reflec-
tive man who studied the careers of great men, he read of
Hannibal, Alexander, Caesar, Napoleon—and became
expert on the military campaigns of George Washington.
Those who served with Carrington knew he made no
bones of aspiring to greatness himself.

Without turning to his adjutant, the colonel inquired,
"Any civilians in Templeton's party?"

The German cleared his throat. "Yes, Colonel. Two
women. A child. Plus an infant and a colored servant
girl. Along with a Captain Samuel Marr—retired—Missouri volunteer regiment in the war. Two others traveling
north to the goldfields with Marr. Along with a surgeon
assigned to our post, named Hines. And a chaplain."

Carrington turned, his face brightened. His eyes closed
as if in momentary prayer. *Margaret will have her clergy*

at long last, here in the heart of the wilderness. "A chaplain, you say?"

"David White," Phisterer answered, again studying his papers. "And . . . this is interesting—a photographer. Name of Glover."

"Tell me of the fighting men." Carrington turned back to watch the sun settle on the Big Horns.

"Only . . ." He looked up at Carrington, waiting for the Colonel to turn around, ". . . fourteen."

Eventually Henry dismissed his adjutant with a nod of his head. Not a word more spoken. Both sensing the dread shared between them. Carrington brooded.

My god. These civilians scurrying north to the goldfields at Alder Gulch like hungry ants. Civilians sent to the slaughter. What are those fools at Laramie thinking of? They heard Red Cloud's threat with their own ears!

The women. Children. And . . . and a baby. Every last one of them offered in sacrifice.

Louis Gazzous had spent enough winters here on the high plains to understand Indians. But the way Black Horse and his warriors had acted when they drew up to the Frenchman's camp was something altogether different. And more than a little unsettling.

After leaving the conference at the soldiers' camp and climbing north over Lodge Trail Ridge, the Cheyenne had bumped into their old friend French Pete, as Gazzous was widely known from Montana and to Dakota Territory. His years of talking straight and dealing square gave French Pete and his men a degree of safety as they made the annual rounds of villages along the Tongue, Rosebud and Little Bighorn. East to the Powder and west to the Wind River, season after season, Gazzous pulled his creaky wagons into Sioux and Cheyenne camps, trading for furs and hides. Some years he could afford more help than others. This season, French Pete fed five drivers. It would be a good year for trading, Gazzous told himself. Five wagons burdened with buffalo hides would give him the stake he needed to open a small post down along the Belle Fourche. Maybe on south to the Republican.

So many seasons of struggle and hope. Now he had five wagons and a future. So, why did the somber mood of the Cheyenne make him edgy?

Black Horse, Red Arm and Dull Knife did most of the talking around the campfire at twilight when all had finished their supper and Gazzous presented every warrior a tin cup of steaming coffee. Yes, French Pete knew, coffee always loosened tongues.

The chiefs spoke of trading and of wandering south before the season turned cold and the great honkers pointed the way. Gazzous agreed. He felt it in his bones. This would be a winter of cold like no man alive could remember. "A winter in a hundred," the Cheyenne called it.

With pride, Black Horse and the others showed French Pete their gifts from the commander of the new fort. And as the sun sank with a purple ache beyond the hills, the Cheyenne told his old friend the trader of his new friend the soldier chief. Again and again Gazzous had his Sioux woman brew pots of coffee, dumping sugar in each cup before she handed them to the Cheyenne chiefs. Coffee loosened tongues, Pete knew. And sugar sweetened the talk.

As stars came out, the Cheyenne began trading with Pete in the time-honored way. Hours had been spent in socializing, sharing both talk and coffee. They had retold old stories heard many times before. Now they could trade. But as the Cheyenne laid out a handful of dressed robes for Pete's inspection, a pony's snort crept through the trees. The *crik-crik* of many unshod hoofs trampling across the rocky bed of Peno Creek burst through the sudden silence fallen over Pete's camp.

They were surrounded by Sioux.

A party of more than eighty warriors drew their ponies to a halt, ringing the campsite. Pinning the Cheyenne in with the Frenchman and his drivers. As the flickering tongues of yellow light danced off the high branches of the pines, one warrior kicked a leg over and dropped to the ground.

Man-Afraid strode into the light at the edge of the fire and settled to his haunches, his short bow held loose before him. A slash of a smile on his wolfish face. Without a sound he nodded to French Pete. Then to Black Horse. And Dull Knife. After acknowledging Two Moons, the Sioux chief looked back at the trader.

Pete motioned his wife forward. She poured a cup of the thick coffee, dumped some sugar into the liquid, and set it before Man-Afraid. He drank noisily, slurping those last few swallows most heavily sweetened. With a finger he dug at the soggy sugar trapped at the bottom of the cup. Then wiped the back of his hand across his wet lips.

No Sioux had stirred from their ponies. No Cheyenne had taken his eyes off this feared war-chief who had appeared from the darkness.

"Trader!" Man-Afraid bellowed as he glared at French Pete. "You bring me the mirrors you promised your last visit?"

Gazzous signaled one of his men to the wagon. With his gift in hand, the trader set the heavy burlap sack at the warchief's feet. Hoping the expensive presents would mollify the fiery Sioux leader. "The mirrors you wanted, my friend."

Without a reply, Man-Afraid opened the top of the sack, pulled one mirror out and inspected it, finally smiling. "They are good, trader. You have done well to bring them to us."

Pete cleared his throat and wiped his brow, still not sure the gift would appease Man-Afraid. "T-Tell me . . . do all the Sioux admire themselves—to look at themselves in those new mirrors?"

He was startled as Man-Afraid rared back his head and laughed loudly, the sound of it harsh, like a knifeblade grating across a stone. The rest of the warriors laughed with him. Suddenly the warchief gripped the trader's shirt.

"We do not look at our beauty, trader. These mirrors are for something more important than Sioux beauty."

"W-What is that, Man-Afraid?"

He smiled, with the look of the badger come to call on a man's hen house. "We learn to use our new mirrors to talk to one another."

"Talk? You say talk?"

"Yes. From hill . . . to hill . . . to hill."

"Talk?"

"Yes, trader!" His voice showed his impatience as he glanced down at Black Horse. "Our mirrors will talk, using the sun to signal our attacks on the soldiers at the new fort."

"Signal . . . signal mirrors. Ahhh, yes," Pete replied, licking his lips nervously, relieved as the warchief let him go and turned toward the Cheyenne leader.

"Tell me, Black Horse," Man-Afraid said, beginning the conversation between Indians without the social amenities of a smoke and story telling, "tell me of your visit to the white soldier camp beyond Lodge Trail Ridge. When will the soldier chief take his men south to the old mud fort?"

Black Horse removed the hat he had received from Carrington, feeling Sioux eyes on him as never before. His skin burned under their appraisal.

"The soldier chief, he will not take his men south from our hunting grounds, Man-Afraid."

The Sioux chief spat into the fire and placed his bow across his folded arms. "He will not leave, is it? I think Black Horse failed to convince this soldier chief that his men will die—every one—if he does not leave our land."

"He was told."

"But he was not told with strong enough words. He was not told by Lakota!"

From that ring of ponies and warriors encircling the camp sprang yelps and hoots as the Sioux chided the forty Cheyenne. For the first time Man-Afraid allowed his warriors to heap insults upon the warriors of Black Horse. After several minutes Man-Afraid raised his hand. His warriors fell silent.

"Tell me, Black Horse—of the presents the soldier chief gave you."

"We had all we wanted to eat—"

"Did they give you the funny hats to eat, Black Horse?"

Like a spring flood over a beaver dam, laughter roared over the Cheyenne seated in the flickering light of the trader's fire. Gazzous wiped his sweaty palms down the front of his greasy blouse, watching in silent terror. When the Sioux warriors had their fill, Man-Afraid went on, at the same time signaling one of his men to his side. Curly moved beside his leader.

"Your bellies were filled? And your heads were covered, eh, Black Horse? Did the white men also fill your heads with silly words and your heart with fear?"

"No." Black Horse said it as calmly as his old, trembling heart would allow. "The soldier chief said he wanted all Sioux and Arapaho—all Indians in this country—to go to the fort at Laramie. There we should sign the treaty Spotted Tail has put his mark to. There, we can get our presents."

"We want nothing the white man has to give us!" Man-Afraid roared as he bolted to his feet. That sudden move caused an anxious shift in the Cheyenne round the fire. More Sioux dropped from their ponies. Tightening their noose on the fire-ring.

Deliberately, slowly, Man-Afraid marched round the fire to stand before Black Horse. He bent to spit his words into the Cheyenne chief's face.

"Tell me, Black Horse—mighty chief of the Cheyenne—why is it you take the gifts of the white soldiers when all the Sioux want is soldier scalps?"

Black Horse calmly wiped the spittle from his cheek, aware that the Sioux gathered round his Cheyenne chiefs had unstrung their bows. He sat powerless to stop what was about to happen.

More important, the ancient code of honor among Plains warriors mandated that he take this abuse without the slightest show of pain. He would instead suffer this indignity in silence, robbing his tormentors of much of their pleasure.

"For winters beyond count, the Cheyenne and the Sioux have stood together. We will—"

"You will *what,* Black Horse?" Man-Afraid shrieked, raising his bow overhead. "You will turn your back on this land and its people? You will join the white man in his war on us?"

Savagely he brought the elkhorn bow down along the cheek of the stoic Black Horse. Unflinching, the old chief suffered the brutal blows in silence. In the eyes of the Sioux drawing close, Black Horse saw that his silent, stoic bravery was admired above all else.

Blood oozed from the skin laid opened across the old Cheyenne's cheekbone. That signal released the fury of the Sioux warriors on the Cheyenne chiefs. Curly stood guard over French Pete and his five white teamsters, rifle at ready should they move to help the Cheyenne. Again and again the short, stout bows thumped shoulders, heads, and backs. With savagery the Sioux struck the helpless chiefs, two or more warriors beating each Cheyenne as they shouted their oaths and taunted with vile names.

From the mouths of the Cheyenne rose no protest. No whine. No cry. Nothing but quiet grunts of pain. Black Horse's men suffered their indignity in silence.

"Enough!"

Man-Afraid jerked round. Finding French Pete standing, his hands empty, imploring. The muzzle of Curly's rifle pressed into the trader's chest.

"They . . . they have had enough," Gazzous pleaded in Sioux.

Man-Afraid looked down at the bruised and bleeding

Black Horse. "Perhaps, trader. Perhaps they have had enough shame. For now." He motioned his warriors back. They restrung their bows and leaped atop their ponies. Curly backed off, his rifle still pointed at the knot of shaken white men.

At that moment French Pete understood why only he and his drivers had a gun pointed at them. The Cheyenne would suffer their beating in shamed silence. The Sioux knew that. And likewise the Sioux believed only the white man capable of trying something stupid. Like pulling a knife. Or a gun. Only the white man was a treacherous creature that had to be watched. Perhaps exterminated, if he could not be driven from this land.

Man-Afraid circled the fire quickly to stand before the short Frenchman. "Trader, you should be careful of who you choose as friends."

"All Indians are my friends." Gazzous tried out a weak smile, running his hand across his dry lips.

"You are wrong, Trader. Man-Afraid has no white friends!"

"We have smoked together many winters, great war-chief of the Sioux. I remember when you were a young—"

"Man-Afraid has told you, trader! I have no white friends." He wheeled on Black Horse. "You would be wise to choose your friends more carefully, old one."

Without another word, Man-Afraid and Curly were on their ponies, turning into the darkness at the creek. Gone into the night.

"You must take your woman and the others," Black Horse whispered to Pete when the Sioux hoofbeats had faded into the darkness. "Bring them with us to our village. We are going to the mountains of the wind. A bad thing—for Red Cloud and Man-Afraid will not be turned away from war."

Gazzous shook his head. "I cannot go, my friend. My family . . . these men—they depend on me to trade. To make my living."

"Then take them all now to the new fort."

"Tomorrow." Louis tried out a weak smile.

"Tonight!" Black Horse pleaded. "These Sioux will kill you. Don't you see? You are a man in-between now. Not with the soldiers. Not siding with the Sioux. Man-Afraid holds your life in his hand."

"It is late." Pete kicked at the dying coals. "We will go to this new soldier camp in the morning. Soon enough, old friend."

Black Horse hobbled to his pony, his beaten body protesting. Without another word, the Cheyenne disappeared into the night.

Shivering with a sudden chill, Gazzous reached for his blanket capote. Wondering how he could feel so cold standing near the fire. He turned to gaze into the trees along the creek where the Sioux had disappeared. Then he realized the cold came not from the night air. The cold Louis Gazzous suffered lay at the very pit of him.

"Sweet Jesus," he murmured in English, his favorite swearing language. "Sweet, sweet goddamn Jesus."

Chapter 8

*H*e'd done something idiotic.

A Civil War veteran with his experience should have known better. But he found himself in the middle of it with no way out. His only hope now was to make it back with his scalp. He was a novice at this type of fighting. Hell, all of them out here were wet behind the ears when it came to battling the Sioux.

Every man among them was used to fighting an enemy that stood up to you. Like those Johnny Rebs.

These redskins swept in on their little ponies, running off what stock they wanted, and never gave a man a target worth a damned shot. Only when those same bloody warriors found that they outnumbered a soldier detail or a civilian party along the Montana Road did they stand and give a fight of it.

Shit! This kind of fighting is new to every last soldier sent out here to this godforsaken wilderness!

Capt. Henry Haymond, commanding officer of the 2nd Battalion of the 18th Infantry, had rushed from his tent at the first shouts of soldiers and the first yelps of attacking Sioux. Pulling suspenders over his shoulders and yanking on his dusty boots, Haymond dashed to his horse in trousers and gray wool undershirt. Hollering for his adjutant to join him, and leaving orders for his mounted men to follow when they caught up their

horses, the captain galloped across the Big Piney. First
on the trail after the horse-stealing Sioux.

Following Carrington's farewell to the Cheyennes the
previous afternoon, Haymond had camped his four companies of soldiers in the valley below the fort. Then
turned the battalion stock out to graze in the lush grasses
for which they hungered after their brutal march north
from Laramie.

Was it just luck? Or, had the savages known to slip into
the herd to capture the bell-mare first? Certain the rest of
the herd would follow. Haymond urged his mount onto
the slope leading up Lodge Trail Ridge. Only once did he
dare glance behind him. His orderly was close on his tail.
A rag-tag band of half-dressed soldiers scrambled down
to the crossing atop what horses the command had left.

*The Sioux didn't waste time making good their threat to
Carrington. God damn their black souls, anyway! The
nerve! Just like the guerilla Johnnies. Hit and run! Lord,
do these savages scamper on their little ponies.*

At the top of the ridge Haymond wheeled round and
brought his heaving mount to a halt. Five minutes later
he had sixty men to follow him off the ridge toward Peno
Creek. Another five minutes found Captain Haymond's
command surrounded by more than two hundred
screaming warriors at the bottom of the ridge.

By the time he had turned his command, formed skirmish lines and fought his way back to the base of the
Lodge Trail, Haymond felt like a sucker. Drawn into the
oldest Indian trap known, like a green lieutenant fresh
out of the academy. Carrying Haymond's plea for relief,
the adjutant galloped off toward the post.

When two companies of infantry and fifty mounted
men stormed down the slope of the ridge to relieve
Haymond, the Sioux redoubled their efforts. In their
wake, the captain found two of his men dead. Three more
wounded. With the arrival of reinforcements, the soldiers
could make an orderly retreat over the Lodge Trail, back
to the safety of the fort. As they fell back to the base of

the trail leading over the ridge, with skirmishers out lest the Sioux attempt another ambush, an Indian woman and her five children burst from the willows beside Peno Creek. The captain drew his soldiers into a defensive perimeter and drove the noisy attackers off for good.

As the last Sioux warrior had disappeared beyond Peno Head, Haymond gave his attention to the woman and her half-breed children. She gestured wildly, wanting the soldiers to follow her.

Not far from the graveled crossing of the Peno, Haymond's men found French Pete's campsite. Gazzous was dead. His five teamsters slaughtered. From the looks of the camp, they had put up a fight of it while they could. A half-dozen men against twenty times their number.

"Looks to be that horse-stealing party we was chasing come on the trader while they was setting up their ambush for us," Lieutenant Nisley suggested.

"Lord only knows how the woman and her children escaped into the bushes before they were butchered too. Or why the savages didn't run off with the stock and these wagons full of trade goods."

"Us, Captain," the lieutenant offered. "Goddamned redskins didn't have the time 'cause of us."

Haymond wagged his head. This was the first he would witness of Sioux handiwork on white victims. Certain it would not be the last. "Lieutenant, have the men load what's left of the bodies into those two wagons and assign drivers to follow us to the fort. We'll give these civilians a decent burial."

He wheeled at the cries of the trader's children, the wails of the woman as they bent over Gazzous's remains. Back and forth she rocked the naked, mutilated body in her arms, keening in her Sioux tongue. Knowing she and her children had been spared because of their blood.

Knowing Man-Afraid had kept his promise to French Pete.

* * *

The baby squirmed in her arms. Too warm, Abigail figured. Too hot for any of us. She pulled the blanket from her daughter and wiped a corner of the flannel across her own brow, moist beneath the poke bonnet. This had to be the worst part of the trip so far. Frank had just said it wasn't too far to the Crazy Woman Fork now. A half a mile. Maybe a mile at the most. Not far to that promise of cool, wet water.

Her husband Frank wasn't really a soldier. His gentle, sensitive spirit would have been better suited to another occupation, something less martial. A member of Samuel Curry's regimental band, Frank Noone had been left behind with his wife back in Colorado Territory at Fort Sedgwick while Abigail delivered the couple's first child some seven weeks ago. By late June, her strength renewed, Abigail and Frank jolted north to Laramie by army ambulance, accompanied by Lt. George Templeton's detail bound for Fort Carrington.

Abigail had been relieved to find two more women on the journey. The wife of Lt. Alexander H. Wands and the Wands's colored servant, Laura. The lieutenant's young son Bobby had proven himself quite a handful already. The army families traveled in ambulances, boxed-wagon affairs often equipped with seats and high, wooden sides, a leather pucker-hole one could button closed at the rear.

Added to the party of high-walled army freighters and canvas-topped Conestogas were five civilians. Captain Samuel Marr, along with Seamus Donegan and an odd, leering man named Simpkins, all three bound for the Montana diggings. The trio had kept to themselves for the most part, occasionally bringing fresh game into camp for evening mess. Two more men had joined up at Laramie, men Abigail felt certain no more belonged out here than she. Reverend David White, a Methodist minister, announced he had been called to tend his flock among the soldiers of the new Fort Carrington. The last member of their group was Ridgeway Glover of Philadelphia, the famous photographer for *Frank Leslie's Weekly*.

The talkative reverend had plopped down beside Glover one evening by the fire. "So," he said, "why don't you share with these good folks what truly brings a man of your peculiar talents to this dangerous end of the world?"

Abigail smiled. White was the sort to squeeze a few words out of anyone. A faraway look had swept over Ridgeway Glover's face as he had contemplated the minister's question.

"I've come," he had begun, so quietly Abigail found herself leaning forward to better hear him, "eager to capture the grandeur of this magnificent western landscape. And I plan to take some cameos of the noble redman who inhabits this vanishing frontier."

Earlier in the evening at that same camp, the group's first since departing Fort Laramie, a number of Sioux had paid an uneasy visit. Abigail remembered how friendly the Indians had been, talking in a mix of Pidgin English and sign language, until she and Katie Wands figured out what they were after. The old squaws laid out a dirty blanket, heaped with beads and furs, knives and an axe—wanting to barter for her baby!

Frank and Lieutenant Wands had the soldiers scatter the old squaws out of camp, knowing the warriors were likely somewhere out in the dark. Abigail had found it hard to sleep much for many nights to come, remembering what the squaws had vowed.

If the white women will not sell their children, the Sioux promise to steal them soon enough.

Disturbing, too, was the unsettling memory of how one of the civilians watched her throughout each day's travel. Not the leer of that strange, weasel-looking Simpkins. No. The Irishman Donegan's gray eyes showed admiration for her instead. Donegan remained a cipher to Abigail for much of their journey north. While the other civilians readily sought company round the soldier bivouac each evening, the wide-shouldered Irishman kept much too much to himself.

Perhaps more disturbing still was the warning of Reno's commanding officer. Capt. Joshua L. Proctor had watched Templeton's party pull away from Fort Reno yesterday morning, after begging the lieutenant for the last time to remain at the post until a larger detachment made it down from Fort Carrington as escort for the undermanned detail. Five civilians didn't add much strength to a compliment of four lieutenants and fourteen enlisted men. Twenty-three riflemen in all, marching off into that country Red Cloud guarded so jealously.

"Better to wait for a larger convoy," Proctor had pleaded. "With those women and children—"

"We'll go on." Templeton had stood by his orders to report with all due haste. He and the four other lieutenants were badly needed at the new post, Templeton argued. "Besides, we haven't seen sign of a feather one since that first night out of Laramie. And those were only some harmless old squaws. Bartering for white children, like common beggars of the plains."

"Your orders compel you to push ahead at any cost?" Proctor had inquired.

"Orders issued by Omaha, sir."

"I see." Proctor grew grave. "Omaha has no idea yet that Sioux are marauding up and down the Road."

Templeton shook his head, his young face bright with confidence. "You must be mistaken, sir. Why, the treaty commissioners we met at Laramie told us themselves that this road is safe for all travel. I'm sure Frank Noone and Alex Wands wouldn't be caught bringing their families along if it wasn't safe, Captain. Tell me, who would know the situation better than the treaty commissioners?"

A disturbing nonchalance displayed by the young lieutenant, for not far from that adobe fort built by the Powder River, Templeton's party had run across the first of the buffalo skulls. No longer merely some glaring white, wide-eyed reminders that they had entered buffalo country. Instead, a few of the men had even murmured over the meaning of the skulls placed in neat formation in the middle of the trail itself. And each skull graphically painted in red with pagan symbols.

"I don't know what they mean, Abby," her husband had admitted, trying out an uneasy smile on her. The memory of those skulls stayed on long after the wagons left them far behind.

So Abigail had clutched more tightly at the tiny cross hung round her neck, and prayed a little longer that night before falling off to sleep. To push away the cold feeling knotting her belly like buttermilk left too long in the stone spring-house back home.

That night, their first since leaving Fort Reno, Abigail had been up and down with the baby. Every bit as thirsty as the grown-ups, constantly wanting to suckle. Perhaps it was her colic flaring once more. Poor thing, Abigail had murmured. She enjoyed the feel of the baby's mouth at her breast there in the darkness. Listening to low voices near the edge of the firelight—Lt. Napoleon Daniels keeping company with Pvt. Stanley Peters throughout the early-morning hours.

Not long after he had retired to his blankets earlier that evening, Daniels had awakened, drenched in sweat. Shivering in mortal fear of the nightmare that had jarred his safe, little world. Afraid to attempt sleep again for fear of the nightmare, Daniels wandered out to the picket line, where he located one of the guards on watch. There he had talked with the young Private Peters as if they were fast friends. Cloaked by the darkness, she overheard a lonely man's premonition of his own death confided in a young enlisted soldier.

As the baby suckled in her arms, Abigail listened to Daniels tell of . . .

". . . buffalo sprouting into wildly-painted savages who leaped at me in the nightmare. When I wheeled my horse to flee, they were right there, nipping at my heels. The faster I urged my mount, the closer the screeching savages drew until . . . their hot, hot breath—until I felt the sharp pounding of the arrows pierce my back. Next, I looked up into their hideous faces as they glee-fully ripped the scalp from my head . . ."

Perhaps the lieutenant's imagination had gotten the better of him, she reasoned. All of them were on edge, after all, following a grotesque discovery yesterday after-noon. Back along the trail they had come across a man's naked, mutilated body at the Dry Fork of the Powder. It was the first any of them had seen of Indian warfare.

"From the looks of things," Frank told her later, "it appears the young man hadn't been there more than a day at the most."

Lying facedown. Hair ripped off down to the nape of his neck. His sunburned back bristling with arrows. A leather pouch tossed nearby. Letters blowing across the dry sand of the creek bottom like cottonwood fluff.

"A courier?" Wands had wondered out loud.

"No way to tell for certain now." Templeton had tried to shrug off the horrifying discovery while watching the four men he had detailed to dig the man's grave. "Can't tell if he was coming down from Carrington. Or heading north from Reno. God rest his tortured soul."

There by the Dry Fork, Abigail recalled that Lieuten-ant Daniels said nothing as the others talked of death and the Sioux. Instead, the young lieutenant had stared trans-fixed at the butchered remains wrapped in a canvas shel-ter-half. It remained something she couldn't put her finger on, something that had changed in Daniels from that hour they discovered the disfigured body.

Minutes after the caravan had left the grave behind and resumed its march, the men had spotted a half-dozen shapes loping along the lip of a hill off to the side of the trail. Fearing those shapes might prove to be Indians, Templeton brought out his looking glass.

"Only wolves," he had announced confidently.

Templeton, Bradley and Frank had galloped to the crest of the hill, scaring off the wolves, only to confront the stench of putrefying flesh that had brought the predators to this place.

"George, that doesn't look like any Indian pony I've ever seen," Bradley admitted.

Templeton had to agree. "Army." He held a kerchief over his nose and dropped to the ground. Near the animal's carcass he found the remains of a military bridle. And an arrow shaft broken off in the animal's withers. "They took everything else. Saddle. Blanket."

"They?" Frank inquired.

"My guess is the Sioux," Templeton had answered.

"What's the horse doing out here?" Frank asked, his shoulders hunching, his eyes searching the surrounding hills.

"Perhaps," Templeton lifted himself to his saddle, "the horse belongs to that poor fella we buried back at the creek."

"He was army," Bradley said as he led down the hill. "That much we know."

"More than that," Templeton added. "No commander would send a courier along this road infested with Sioux unless it was damned important to get that message through."

Back with his detachment, Templeton told them what he had pieced together. First, he assured the women and civilians there was no need for concern. "The savages might attack a lone rider—like that poor courier riding between our posts—but they surely won't attack a detail as armed as ours."

Lieutenant Daniels hadn't been reassured. And neither had she.

A refreshing breeze brushed Abigail Noone's cheek now, nudging her awake. She had been dozing, daydreaming with the rhythmic rocking of the ambulance. Squinting into the bright sunlight, she studied the trail ahead. Ever since Dry Fork, the Montana Road had begun its climb out of the high prairie into a country knifed with ridges and deep coulees. Now, at last, Abigail saw a further change to the landscape. From this high ridge they rode along, the trail gradually descended into the drainage of the Crazy Woman Fork. To her left rose a rounded knoll south of the creek. Just beyond a fringe of trees that meandered beside the creek below arose a quiltwork of blue foothills only now touched by mid-morning light. Farther still, wrinkled peaks piled one against the other.

Abigail drank deep of the new, welcome coolness to the air, shuddering with an unaccustomed chill as she gazed down the gentle slope at the cottonwoods beckoning from less than five miles away.

Perhaps we'll find water there, she prayed. They had been promised water at Dry Fork. Instead, they had found the dead courier. *Dear Lord, let there be water by those trees.*

"Look! Just beyond the creek!" Daniels hollered like a schoolboy. "That's got to be a buffalo herd!"

Templeton brought out his glass again and gave the hillside a hard appraisal. The dark, ambling objects beyond the trees on the other side of Crazy Woman Fork did appear to be great humpbacked beasts, grazing leisurely near the creek. "By god, Napoleon! This could be our first taste of buffalo!"

"Let's ride ahead, George! Before the others scare the buffalo off. We'll cross the creek above the buffalo. Sweep down and drive them back toward the road. That way the rest of the fellows will get in some shots as the herd charges past."

"Sounds like it'll work," George said, turning to Lieutenant Wands. "Alex, you're in command in my absence." Templeton kicked his fatigued horse into a trot, straining to catch the eager Daniels, who raced down the slope toward the creek.

"Just make it a fat one for dinner!" Wands hollered after them as the pair disappeared into the trees.

Abigail slipped the damp bonnet from her head. The breezes refreshed her, enough that the sun's warmth no longer seemed all that bad. In that cool water just ahead she could soak her tired, dirty feet. Dip a kerchief in its icy chill to press against her sticky neck.

The wagons lumbered down the slope into a winding gut of gorge that led them toward the creek. Dust from the wheels twisted upward in gold ropes toward the clear, cloudless blue overhead. Tall cottonwoods momentarily hid the buffalo hunters from view. Still, those left behind could hear the enthusiastic yelps as the two lieutenants galloped into the herd.

"We're twenty-six miles from Reno, dear." Frank glanced at his wife, beside him on the ambulance seat.

Abigail glanced back at the rest of the wagons. Thick, glittering dust rose in sheets from the spinning wheels as they plunged into the gorge that would usher them to the cool, waiting water. Down to the shade of trees and thickets of chokecherry, plum, and rock grape. Fragrant, verdant growth mixed with the smell of axle grease and the sweet sweat of the mules. Rays of morning sunlight slanting off the nearby ridges turned the dust screen to a shower of gold.

"Heave! You brutes!" Frank slapped the reins against the team's rumps. Like huge paws grabbing at the wheels, the deep sand of a dry wash made their wagon lurch and list. Slowing almost to a halt. "Hup! Hup!"

In one arm Abigail held fast to the baby, her other hand clutching the bouncing seat-board. Suddenly they careened onto firmer ground, rolling more easily.

"Must be a dry course of the creek back there—come spring runoff," Frank volunteered, sweat beading his forehead. "But these mules smell the water now. Look at 'em!" He smiled at Abigail. "They're pulling better. Won't be long now, dear."

Wands loped past on his horse, headed back along the column. "Keep 'em moving! Don't let 'em slow down in that sand. We'll never get those wagons out if you bog 'em down now! Hump it, fellas!"

"Goddamn!" Sgt. Patrick Terrel hollered as his team

slowed then lurched to a complete halt in the dry sand. He looked at the shaken passenger beside him. "Sorry, Reverend. At times we Irish have a way of sprinkling our speech."

"Q-Quite all right, Sergeant. You and Seamus Donegan both," he replied as he wiped his brow. "I sympathize with your sentiments for these brutish animals we find ourselves hitched to!"

Wands reined up beside them, signaling his enlisted men. "Reverend, if you'll be good enough to step down. We can use you in back of the wagon."

"Certainly, Lieutenant."

"Sergeant, when we start pushing, I want you to shake these sonsabitches like they've never been shook. You understand?"

"Completely, sir."

"Put your shoulders to it, men!" Alex reined away. "Heave on it! Slap those mules, Sergeant. Slap——"

The wagon broke free of the sand at the exact moment something else snagged Abigail's attention, drawing her eyes back to the creek. An unearthly cry. As if wrailing out of the land of the damned itself. She gazed up at the steep walls of the gorge ahead, where the hellish wail of death seemed to echo. Surely it must be her imagination. This tight, closed-in place, like the belly of a tomb.

Pounding, pounding, pounding hoofs. The buffalo were coming! At once she grew frightened, hoping the wagons would not be turned over. Her baby trampled. Then, that unearthly cry again. Something inhuman. Almost like a beast . . . in great pain.

A clatter of gunfire echoed along the gorge. Arrows like swift, iron-beaked birds whispered into the sidewall beside her. Frank swore as his left arm swung abruptly back without warning, knocking her and the baby into the wagon. Her last glimpse of the bare ridges hemming the gorge froze Abigail's heart in her breast.

Never before had she seen naked, painted warriors. Shrieking like demons from hell. Shaking their rifles and bows. Cavorting along the ridgetop as they fired down on the wagons again and again and again . . .

Naked, brown demons freed from her worst nightmares. Lieutenant Daniels's nightmare come true. Glistening brown bodies sweeping down on the helpless wagons. To butcher them all.

"Not my baby!"

That voice screeched in her ear so loudly Abigail could not recognize it. A voice hollering those three words over and over again as she mantled herself like a sage hen over the infant.

"Not the baby!"

Not sure who kept screaming in her ears, until her own throat began to burn.

Chapter 9

The foul taste of his own stomach flung itself against his tonsils, burning his nostrils. All too well Ridgeway Glover remembered that taste of fear so intense it caused him to vomit. Again and again during the war he had crawled off and hidden himself after dark, certain no man would find him—afraid he would have to fight the next day. Each time certain even God Himself couldn't see how he cowered from the gunfire.

Glover swallowed and kept his stomach down. His limbs wouldn't move at first. Petrified. Forcing him to stand riveted by the wagon tire as the soldiers raced for their rifles and cover. Captain Marr and the Reverend shouted for him to dive beneath a wagon. Then a bullet smacked into a mule beside him. The beast dropped in its traces, kicking in its death throes, brassy lungs shrieking out a death song. Deafening in his ears.

Glover was yanked off his feet.

Like a doll, Donegan flung Glover along the wagon, shoving him beneath the box. Reverend White pulled the photographer into the shadows.

"Welcome, brethren!"

"Addle-minded sonuvabitch was fixing to get himself punctured out there, Reverend." Donegan cursed with a smile as he rolled his rifle into position.

"What in God's name is that?" White asked.

Donegan sighted along the weapon, fired, then looked at the minister. "This? Called a Henry." He pulled the trigger again.

"Blessed God!" White marveled. "A repeater."

"A blessing indeed, Reverend!" Seamus aimed and fired. "Sixteen shots worth of repeater, i'tis."

"We'll ask our Heavenly Father to see to it those sixteen shots mean sixteen heathen souls sent scurrying straight to hell!"

By the creek the first wagon shook and shuddered. A mule went down, braying in its pain. The other three answered with their own brass-lunged cries, exploding in three directions at once. Unable to handle the reins and keep his seat at the same time, the young driver leaped from the wagon. He caught an arrow high in his throat with the next jolt of the mules. With a whimper, the soldier tumbled over the sidewall to the sand, gurgling as he drowned in his own blood.

She had never watched a man die before. At least Abigail supposed he was dead. The soldier didn't stir. Mesmerized, she watched the body to see if it would move— breathe or quiver. Death . . .

A painted face leaped into view at the front of the wagon, scrambling onto the ambulance seat. She shrieked, not sure if she had made a sound at all. Twisting to the side as the warrior raised his tomahawk, deciding to shelter her daughter to the end. His grinning, painted, savage smile—

The ambulance jolted, throwing the warrior off-balance for an instant. He clambered back to his feet just as a blue blur hurtled itself against the glistening brown body. Abigail slapped a hand across her mouth.

"Frank!" she screamed.

Like a true soldier, Noone grappled with the muscular brave, not the trumpeter he was nor the concert musician he had always hoped to be. Again and again he wrenched on the arm that held the hatchet, until the warrior lost his footing and fell back against the cushioned seat.

Frank fell with him, choking the brown neck with all the strength left in his hands. Frantically the warrior fought back, pinned beneath the blue fury. For a moment they both held the tomahawk. Then Frank found it in his hand alone, watching in fascination as it streaked high over his head and plunged squarely into the middle of the warrior's face.

Abigail felt the hot sting as flecks of blood and brain slapped her face and neck. Tasted the Indian's blood on her lips. She watched Frank slowly release the tomahawk, gulping. The first man he had ever killed. Right in front of his wife. She knew he would need her. Needing him. To feel his arms around her. To take the horror away—

"In God's name, Abby—stay down!"

Obediently she fell back to the floor of the ambulance, among the baggage and clutter of what an enlisted man's family was allowed to bring west to a new household. Crawling like some maimed animal on knees and one hand, clutching the wailing infant against her breast. Sobbing harder still as she watched Frank leap from the seat, disappear. He was gone. Alone again with the baby.

"Cut that one loose!" she heard some man cry out. "He's done!"

Abigail hoped he meant a mule in harness. Not another soldier. None of them would last long if the Indians cut soldiers down so quickly.

"Pull the harness loose!"

"Pull it, hell! Cut the goddamned straps! Slash 'em!"

Another mule cried out. Abigail shuddered as bullets slammed into flesh with a sickening smack.

"Dear, merciful God—watch and protect Frank—"

"Jesus, that was close!"

"Cut it loose," another, deeper voice hollered, banging into the ambulance. From the thickness of his brogue, it sounded like that standoffish one, Donegan. "Too late! Too late! Here they come for another go a'tus!"

As if ordered by that stern voice without, Abigail fell

to the floor among the canvas bags, blankets and a straw tick. Coming from a foggy daze, she suddenly heard her infant daughter wailing. Hungry and frightened by all the noise thundering against the canvas and wood of their little sanctuary. Whimpering, feeling so alone—Abigail unbuttoned her blouse and freed one engorged breast, guiding the rigid nipple into her baby's mouth. The infant grabbed the nipple, suckling lustily. Abigail cried in silence, her hot tears splattering her bare breast. It was all she knew to do, remembering the horror of the squaws' promise to take her baby.

"Behind you, Noone!"

Abigail jerked as she heard Wands's voice cry out. A man yelped in pain. Not knowing if it was Frank or not, she clenched her eyes shut with all her might, hoping the horrid sounds would be shut out as well.

"Watch it!"

She heard Frank shout.

Beside her an arrow ripped through the thick canvas, burrowing its iron head into the board siding behind her. *They're above us . . . on the ridge!* She cowered. *Firing down on us—we're like helpless animals. Lord, the baby's not safe——*

"Abby!" Frank's voice shrieked.

"W-We're . . . we're all right, Frank!"

Blessed God, savior of man, she began to pray. And wondered if that Methodist minister was praying as well, clutching his worn bible between his wrinkled, veiny hands.

"Reverend! Get down! Great ghost, but White's a fool!"

It was that man's voice again. Donegan.

In the next breath the wagon lurched as a body flung itself against the rear gate. Abigail's heart surged into her throat, fearful another warrior had made it to the wagon. Desiring her. Wanting her baby even more.

Through the buttoned leather pucker-hole at the rear a wild spray of gray hair appeared. In the middle of its disarray hung a bright red circle of wrinkled flesh, White's veiny nose suspended beneath two wild, marble-like eyes.

"Dear woman!" the reverend shouted in at her. "Pull me in, for the grace of God. Pull me in!"

She dragged a dirty hand beneath her runny nose and flung it his way. Clutching the hand, White dragged himself into the rear of the wagon.

"Dear Lord!" she gasped, looking him over at close range at last. "You're . . . you're bleeding."

"Nothing to worry the Lord over, dear lady." White smiled, trying out his wounded arm by combing at the wild gray hair that stood out in thick sprigs along both sides of his head. At the top, where the reverend was very much bald, a second wound. Long, ugly, and bleeding. He dabbed fingers at it. "Nothing at all." Then used his sleeve. "Afraid I didn't keep my head low enough as I took cover beneath a wagon. There, now. Better still. My bag, Mrs. Noone. I need my bag."

With that imperative ring to the minister's words, Abigail scanned the ambulance for his bag. He pulled his legs into the wagon at last, took one final glance out the rear then searched for the bag himself.

"Ah, blessings upon us all!" he cried, leaping for a canvas satchel topped with thick leather handles. He crabbed over Abigail to get at it.

Nimbly his old fingers fought with straps and buckles until a wrinkled hand dove into the satchel. Extracting a stubby object of dull pewter. Ugly as a pond-toad, she thought, staring at those seven round holes backing the squat barrel. White cracked the pepperbox in half, quickly checking each chamber before he slammed the barrel back in place.

"The Lord helps those who help themselves." He held the pistol before his chest like a chalice at communion.

"P-Pray for me . . . us," she pleaded, her eyes imploring him to remember the babe suckling at her breast.

White glanced at the firm, milky flesh and gulped, his

eyes leaping back to her face. His cheeks crimson. "Our Heavenly Father, may we all live to see this child grow to your glory! Amen."

He brushed by her, again at the rear of the ambulance. Turning, he seemed to decide on a better plan of action. Crawling past Abigail again, White slid over the back of the driver's seat and tumbled to the ground.

"By the saints, Reverend!" Donegan cried out. "I thought you'd hidden yourself off somewhere to pray for us all!"

"Pray? HELL! Comes a time for praying . . . and a time to slay the heathen Levites!"

"You'll get plenty of that today," Donegan added grimly. He pressed his Henry into his shoulder. "You any good with that stub of a pistol?"

"This?" White held the pepperbox high in his hand as he slid in beside the Irishman. "Don't have to be. Got seven chances to dispatch them straight to Lucifer himself!"

As the wave of warriors rushed past, smoke puffed beneath one pony's neck. A young soldier on the other side of Donegan lurched backward, clumsily. The trooper moaned, eyes rolling back in his head.

Donegan stared down at the youngster for a moment. "He's gone now. Better off, he is too—a man stops one in the belly like that, Reverend."

Wands bolted up, helping Marr and a soldier drag the quivering body behind a wagon. "We can't stay here," the lieutenant explained, rising from the body soon to turn cold. For an instant the lieutenant surveyed the creek bottom, then the hills and gorge surrounding them. *We're like clay targets here.* Wands swallowed, his nostrils already fetid with the stench from the young soldier's punctured bowels. *Our only chance . . .*

"None of us will last pinned down here!" Donegan grabbed Wands by the shoulders. Swung him round. "Best get your wagons moving afore we're just a greasy spot on this crossing!"

Wands glared back at the big Irishman a moment, ready to lash back. Instead, something pushed him back to the saddle. He spurred away, riding low at the horse's neck, shouting, "Back to the hill! We've got to make a run for it. Follow me! All of you!"

Back again by Donegan and White, Wands slid to a halt, kicking up sand. "You! Irishman. Grab the reins to that wagon! Chaplain—you'll drive that ambulance. Noone—the other. We'll run two wagons up front . . . then the two ambulances. As a rear guard we'll bring up the last four wagons. I want the Irishman to lead the way. Now, ride like your necks depend on it!"

Savagely the lieutenant sawed his reins to the left, his mount tearing back toward the creek and the waiting ambulances, his hat flying into the air. "Bradley! You spotted Templeton or Daniels?"

He shook his head. "Not a sign, Alex. I'm afraid both were cut off up ahead. Never make it back—"

"It's up to you now. Take the point. To the high ground—yonder!"

"I'm on my way!" the young lieutenant answered. "Sergeant Terrel. You five—no! All the rest of you, FOLLOW ME!"

"Hep-haw!" Donegan urged his wagon full about through the sand, back into the throat of the gorge behind the soldiers charging ahead on foot.

"Blessed are the beasts of the earth!" Reverend White screamed to his mules, urging them into the hairpin turn on two wheels. "Pray they deliver!"

By the time Wands had his wagons backtracked into the gorge and headed toward the knoll south of the Crazy Woman, Bradley's dozen foot-soldiers were scampering up the sandy hillside, leading the way for some snorting, protesting mules. To the troopers' surprise, three dozen yelping horsemen burst over the far lip of the high ground, every one of them brandishing a bow. Reinforcements arriving to seal the ambush as tight as a puckered buffalo totem.

"Arrrggghhh!" Bradley plunged straight up the side of the slope without stopping, hoping to confuse some of the warriors, frighten the rest. Like a man possessed, his thick legs churned like pistons in a steam engine, intent on blurring things just long enough for everyone to reach the high ground. The rest of those in army blue followed blindly in his wake, their lungs bellering their best cry, certain to put fear in a Confederate heart or a Sioux breast.

That noise, the headlong assault and confusion—Indian ponies reared, pitching their riders backward or thumping into others galloping up from the rear. Shrieks of rage and challenge fell down upon the soldiers, but nothing more deadly. Surprised at the fierceness of the soldiers' gallant charge, nearly forty warriors turned tail, scampering back down the slope to the west, where the Crazy Woman came tumbling down to the crossing.

"Ho, you bastards! Pull with all you've got!" Donegan urged his team.

"Close up! Close up!" It was Wands, riding in their midst, exhorting the drivers.

"If these old gray whores'd do what I want—"

"Bring it up!" Wands hollered, then brought his horse around, reining back toward the top-heavy, swaying ambulances having a tough time keeping up. They had lagged far behind the other high-walled freighters and Conestoga wagons. From the corner of his eye the lieutenant caught a sudden glimpse of wild movement. To his right appeared a dozen or more mounted warriors, screaming down on his rear guard. He slowed his horse, watching the gap widen between the wagons and the lumbering ambulances.

"Bring it up, Frank!" His horse pranced around in a circle. "Dammit, Reverend. Drive that wagon like you were chasing an offering plate!"

Far behind the other wagons, both ambulances surged forward in a final, valiant effort to reach the knoll. Up out of the gorge, their drivers slapped reins over the wild-eyed teams like mad charioteers. Wands felt the bullet scorch past his cheek before he ever heard the crack of a rifle. The six freight wagons raced on by him before he dug his heels into the lathered flanks of his animal.

Too late, he cursed. A dozen warriors had cut the ambulances off as the rest of the wagons reached the top of the slope.

Abigail watched naked horsemen flit like streaks of multicolored light past the front of the ambulance where Frank stood behind the seat, leaning into the reins, slapping and hollering at his team. Never before had she heard him sound quite like this. A shiver of January water spilled down her spine as she realized a banshee must sound much tamer. But the maniacal screech of her husband's voice as he dove into the midst of those warriors would cause more than the hair on the back of her neck to stand on end. She closed her eyes. Dreading to witness his death.

Our Father, which art in heaven . . .

Chapter 10

$\mathcal{F}$rank Noone simply refused to let the horsemen sweep to one side or another as they bore down on him. He saw no other way out—either he was going to force his way through the trap or the rest would watch one hell of a collision. When the Sioux veered to the left, Frank yanked in the same direction. The warriors dodged to the right. Noone pointed his lethal wagon straight for them. Swaying back and forth until . . . the brown-skinned phalanx parted like water round a rock in a stream at the last moment.

Abigail heard the shrieking monster drain from her husband's throat. As the screams of the warriors faded down the slope behind them, she dared open her eyes. Frank glanced round at his wife, smiling that brave, sensitive smile of his. The unashamed tears cut a wide swath down his dirty face.

With no specific orders, the drivers brought their wagons into corral at the crest of the knoll as if they had performed the maneuver in a thousand Indian surrounds. Donegan wheeled the first wagon close to the sharp lip of a ravine at the south end, leaning back into the reins, his brake-lock snarling against the iron tire. The second and forth wagons spun up on the left. The third and fifth skidded to the right. To begin shutting the corral, the reverend rolled up in his ambulance. Frank Noone rode as file-closer, lumbering to the crest with his three-mule team, accomplishing what the other drivers had with a full harness.

Frank leaped inside to embrace Abigail. With no words spoken, their tears mingled a moment before he disappeared through the leather hole at the rear. Only then did she feel the baby wriggling against the iron-like lock of the arms she had clamped around her.

Without warning mother and child pitched backward. The wagon shuddered and pitched convulsively. Back and forth, side to side. Abigail clung to the sidewall. The baby had long ago lost its hold at her breast. The infant shrieked, wanting that nipple ripped away from her back in her little mouth.

A mule sang out. Two men cursed as they grappled with the wounded animal, wild with the pain of two iron-tipped arrows sunk shaft deep in its flanks. The mule strained against the rest of the team.

"Cut it loose, for God's sake!" someone hollered.

"No. No time for that," Donegan objected.

Before she could catch her breath, Abigail heard a rifle shot, followed by a loud, sodden clump striking the ground.

"Now," she heard the big Irishman say, calmer this time, "you can cut the son of a bitch from its harness."

"They're gathering up again, brethren!" White hollered above the rising shriek of the onrushing warriors.

Donegan listened as the pounding, thundering earth-beat crescendoed, watching in fixed admiration as the Sioux sat lightly atop their galloping ponies until, by some secret signal, they dropped from sight. Years he had spent fighting some of the world's finest horse soldiers: J.E.B. Stuart's "Invincibles," who consistently ripped apart Union cavalry formations. But these naked warriors were a pure marvel, surpassing all. Never before had he seen any riding to equal what he witnessed this bright morning near the Crazy Woman Crossing.

By instinct, he brought the heavy Henry to his shoulder, sighting along the gleaming blued barrel.

Mark this day, Seamus—the first you've found a man in the sights on this rifle.

He held, led a striding Indian mount, then squeezed.

The rifle slapped his shoulder. More of it came back to him now. The firing of a carbine pointed at the butternut uniforms. The cries of the wounded in the dark, shadowy woods. Always the smell of death thick in his nostrils. Suddenly he gazed down at his hands. *There'll always be enough dead soldiers.*

"Can't see the red bastirds no more!"

Glover jerked up at the sound of Donegan's voice. Every man behind the wagons watched the mounted warriors disappear from view down a long, gradual slope to the west. Toward a hidden bend in the creek. Among the shelter of a belt of cottonwoods.

"Just keep your heads down, soldiers!"

Someone else hollered on the other side of the corral. Glover swallowed hard, gripping the rifle like life itself. *Where did the weapon come from?* Someone must have put it in his hands. *That big man, the Irishman. Maybe the gun belonging to the soldier with the gut wound.* He remembered now. The young soldier wouldn't be needing the rifle anymore. Black thoughts flooded through him. Ridgeway Glover had never had a problem keeping his head down.

"Everyone ready?" Wands dashed up behind a knot of men, his hand on Glover's shoulder. "When they come, make every bullet count. Don't aim high, for God's sake. Make sure you hit something."

Glover felt the fraternal slap on his shoulder before Wands scampered off to the north side of the corral. *Perhaps this officer isn't like the ones I've known,* he thought. *Maybe we'll all pull through this.*

"Stay ready! Here come those sons again!"

Glover gulped, hearing Captain Marr's warning, and swiping at his misting eyes. By damned, he wouldn't let the gut-wrenching sickness wash over him again as it had month after month and year after year. All those battles where he tried to lose himself in the brush and the smoke and the bodies. A coward. Afraid of fighting. Afraid of running even more. He knew what they did to the ones who ran. *No more,* he promised himself. His eyes clenched shut, tears streaming as he brought the rifle to his shoulder. It shook uncontrollably.

"Easy, lad. Easy."

He opened his eyes, finding Donegan at his side.

"You fired a weapon like this before?"

Glover nodded.

"Just slow down. One target's all you need. Take your time."

He winked at Glover with those piercing gray eyes of his, then slid away along the side of the wagon. The words helped. Glover sucked deep at the hot air. Held it. His stinging eyes cleared, focusing along the barrel. A warrior dared stay atop his pony longer than his companions. Glover found him, squeezed. And felt better.

"By damned!" Donegan cheered. "You got the bastird! Nailed him in the lights, lad!"

As if by rote, Glover rolled onto his back, hunkered down behind the wagon wheel and yanked the ramrod free. Powder. Ball. Start the ball down the barrel. Behind him the ponies thundered past the wagons, sweeping away down the long slope. Through the spokes he watched the warriors roll back atop their ponies, galloping out of range. Shaking their rifles and bows in triumph.

Like a rush of hot air that won't let a man breathe, another band of fifty or more pressed toward the corral. Most of the soldiers hadn't finished reloading. Donegan grumbled, finding only one other man ready for the new wave. Marr with his Henry. The two of them would have to brave the rush until the soldiers had reloaded their clumsy Springfield muskets.

Glover twisted round at the thundering hoofs. The

ramrod stuck in the barrel. Without another thought the Philadelphia photographer slapped the rifle to his cheek and found a target. A glistening chest bearing down upon the wagons. Weaving back and forth behind his pony's wide-eyed head. *Wait. Wait. Wait . . . squeeze!*

Back over the horse's rump spilled the warrior, toppled by both ball and ramrod.

"By the saints! You can use a weapon!" Donegan cheered.

Glover slid behind the wheel once more, intent upon finding another rifle, listening to the cries of the wounded and dying. The tally of wounded grew each time the Sioux tore by, sending their whistling death among wagons and mules.

"Dammit, Sarge! Another rush or two like that, won't be enough of us to keep them off the wagons!"

Glover recognized the panic in that voice. That was the voice of fear he had never been able to utter. Too afraid even to speak.

"Shuddup, Meeker!" Sgt. Patrick Terrel growled back. A wiry infantry sergeant who had served under the 18th's banner throughout the war. "Ain't never been in battle before, 'ave you?"

"We gotta do something!"

"Go tell the lieutenant!" Terrel hollered. "I ain't in charge 'round here. Tell Bradley!"

"I c-can't, Sarge. He's out . . . cold."

"Dear Mither of Saints!" Terrel muttered, crossing himself and swiping the sweat off his brow. He gazed down the slope. "Well, I'll be . . . sweet, sweet, Mither of——"

Glover watched the sergeant rise off his knees with some of the other soldiers. Staring dumbfounded down the slope, the troopers gathered next to the wagons they had just used to race to this knoll. Struck by the eerie silence. No shrieking warriors. No thundering hoofs. Quiet enough to hear the soldiers muttering their curses. Mumbling their prayers.

Out of the brush and up the slope lumbered a riderless horse. *Army.* Glover knew that much from its size and color. As the animal raced closer to the corral, he could make out the arrows dancing from its neck, more along the ribs and flanks. Bristling like dried cornstalks before a winter wind. Glover slowly stood with others. Every man in awe as the wounded animal sought companions in its pain and fright. Perhaps it recognized the wagons as something familiar.

Topping the knoll, the horse staggered toward the corral. It was then Glover noticed the saddle swinging beneath the heaving belly. An empty saddle. Swaying back and forth until the animal collapsed, rolled on its side, struggled to rise on its rear legs and fell a second time. Then lay still.

Terrel crossed himself again. A woman shrieked. To Glover it sounded like the colored maid riding with Lieutenant Wands's family. Then another woman cried out. Glover rose, his shoulders hunched in a flush of fear that he'd make too good a target when the next wild rush came.

Only another lone horse lumbering up from the creek. Yet this second army mount carried a rider slumped over its withers like a wet sack of oats. Hatless. Weaponless.

As the horse brought its load closer, Glover could make out the arrows deep in the withers where the soldier clung. His eyes instantly drawn to the one long shaft quaking in the middle of the rider's back. As the soldier neared the corral, he raised his head slightly. His white face a mask of horror. More pain than a man should be asked to bear. It was——

"Templeton!"

Glover started at the sound of Wands's voice. Rushing toward the north side of the corral, Alex was the first to rescue his fellow officer. With a few final, faltering steps, George Templeton was among them, falling from his horse while muttering something incoherent. Donegan led the wounded horse to the edge of the corral, pulled

the cavalry revolver from his belt and fired one bullet into
the animal's brain. The mount twisted then dropped at
the Irishman's feet.

"Templeton! For God's sake, talk to me, man."

Wands cradled his friend across his lap, supporting
Templeton's arms so he wouldn't jar the arrow stuck between the shoulder blades.

"Daniels? Daniels!" the wounded man cried out.
"Great ghost, they're not buffalo! Ride, man, ride!"

Templeton's voice cracked as he moaned, twisting this
way and that, trying to relieve the pain of the arrow, the
pain of his dash to freedom.

"Help me, will you?" Wands implored, staring at the
soldiers circling him. "Into the ambulance."

Three of them carried Templeton to the wagon. But
they struggled getting Templeton's feet over the back
wall. His legs gone limp. His arms like rags.

Donegan leaped into the ambulance and hefted the legs
over the back-wall so he could drag the unconscious lieutenant over Abigail Noone. Placed on his side, Templeton
appeared to breathe a mite easier.

"For the love of God, you've got to pull that out of
him."

Donegan looked up. Wands's eyes implored him from
the hold at the back. For Seamus it suddenly grew un-
bearably hot inside the ambulance. Close. Suffocating.

"This arrow?" he gulped, his mouth gone dry.

"However you do it," Wands nodded, his eyes pleading, "take it out of him."

Donegan blinked to clear the sweat in his eyes. Maybe
they were tears of anger. Or frustration. When he looked
up, the face was gone. He glanced at Abigail. She shook
her head violently to answer his unspoken question. He
knew she wouldn't do it. Couldn't do it. His gray eyes
drawn to her flesh. The creamy breast stood naked, rigid
from her blouse. The nipple still wet from nursing.

"All right, faith," Donegan murmured, slowly tearing
his eyes from her flesh. "Up to me to do, is it?"

Gently he rolled Templeton onto his belly among the baggage and blankets. Stuffing an end of the straw tick beneath the lieutenant's head, Donegan watched the eyes flutter, trying to focus on who was ministering to him. The tip of his tongue raked along his dry lips below the dark, shaggy handlebar.

"Water . . ."

"Soon enough," Donegan replied, then gazed at the woman. "I'll need bandages." He searched, straining to keep his eyes off the bare breast. "There, faith. Your petticoat. Please."

Abigail nodded, looking down at the rumpled dress a'swirl like seafoam around her legs. Unselfconsciously she tucked her breast back inside the blouse before tearing three strips from her dirty white petticoat. From the floor the lieutenant's breathing grew ragged, grinding like a coarse file drawn over cast iron.

Never before had Donegan been handed a problem like this. He drew in a long breath and pulled at the arrow. Templeton shrieked. Seamus released the shaft as if it were a bright red branding iron. That plan was not about to work.

"The blighter! It's . . . it's hung on something." Talking to her as if he had to explain it.

His eyes frantically sought something. What it was, Donegan didn't know. Then he saw it. Stuck in the side of the wagon wall hung an arrow. Seamus yanked it free, then measured the distance from the tip of the iron point to the end of the sinew binding point to shaft. His finger and eye felt along Templeton's arrow. That was a relief.

"Begod, and thank the Holy Mither." He made it sound like a prayer for what was to come. "T'isn't buried deep enough to cut the lung, praise be."

"Do it!"

Donegan gazed up at Abigail, finding her wide-eyed with fright. She shook her head. He gazed down at Templeton.

"Now, dammit!"

Obediently the civilian grasped the shaft, low, his
hands soppy with the lieutenant's warm blood. Pulling,
Seamus measured the resistance. Templeton's whole body
rose as Donegan pulled. The lieutenant's nails raked
again and again across the floorboard. Donegan rose,
placed one knee just below the shaft and drew upward.
Steadily. Grunting in his own effort against the unearthly
shriek pouring from the man pinned below him. With all
his weight he pressed Templeton down as the arrow
inched free.

Abigail bit a knuckle anxiously, until she was sure she
had drawn her own blood. She clenched her eyes, shutting out the bloody scene as she heard the shaft scraping
bone, tearing muscle and sinew like a moist, sucking
wheeze.

Templeton's body sagged when the shaft broke free.
The arrow hung dripping from his hand before Seamus
tossed it aside. Then he ripped the lieutenant's shirt open
down to his belt. "The bandages, faith."

Abigail opened her eyes. Handed him the strips.
Watched the stranger fold the cloth into a thick bandage
he stuffed over the ugly, red-purple hole. "Find something to wrap 'round his chest," he ordered. "He comes
to . . . no, wait."

She watched him push and shove against the bags in
the ambulance, searching until he yanked the one he
wanted into his lap. Brown, scuffed cowhide, with his
initials emblazoned below the silver clasp. From it
Seamus pulled a tin flask. About to hand it to Abigail, he
thought better. Worrying the cork from the neck, the
Irishman drank long and deep. She watched in fascination at the bobbing of his Adam's apple between the muscular neck muscles while he pulled hungrily at the liquid.

Finished, Seamus inserted the cork again and handed
her the flask. "He comes to, give him some of me potion.
Better still, bathe the wound with a little of it after I'm
gone. Wait till I'm gone, faith—for I can't stand to see
good devil's brew wasted on a wound. Damn the luck of

it all! Sounds like the h'athens are back on the rampage out there." He studied her, his eyes settling on the cleavage between the two swollen breasts where her blouse remained unbuttoned. "You'll minister to the lieutenant, aye, colleen?"

She nodded.

"Some on the wound. Bind it all with a strip from your dress. And give him some of me potheen to drink when he comes 'round. He'll . . . he'll bless you for that whiskey. A time like this—any man would."

Donegan smiled at the woman, quickly licking the last drops of the potent whiskey from his lips. Then he disappeared from the front of the ambulance.

Alone once more, Abigail Noone gazed down at her infant, asleep through it all. Her tummy warm and full of milk. Her little lips moist from mother's body. The flask grew heavy in her hand. She didn't think she could possibly move to tear another strip of cloth from her petticoat. Much less pull the bandages off that ugly, oozing wound just to pour some foul whiskey on it.

Whiskey.

She always forbade Frank from drinking. Even in the company of his friends. Evil brew. Just thinking what it did to man. What it made a man want most of all . . . she had recognized that glint in the Irishman's gray eyes. The flask grew heavier still in her hand. No strength remained to help the lieutenant.

Outside, the shrieks of warriors and the pounding of pony hoofs pierced her private world. Soldiers cursed. Mules brayed and jostled against the ambulance. Rifles roared and bullets slapped against the wood side-walls closing in around her. Abigail tried lifting the flask. So heavy.

The cork will be lighter, she decided. *No man's ever looked at me the way that Irishman did. Not even . . . my husband Frank.* The cork popped free with no effort at all. Her head seemed to swim once more with the sudden smell of the whiskey, as it had reeked on the

Irishman's breath. *Funny, with the cork out of it, the flask isn't all that heavy anymore.* She brought it to her lips, fighting the revulsion she felt from the smell and tilted her head back just as she had watched the civilian do. Past her tongue and down her throat washed the potent liquid, sending a shockwave of heat through her being.

Abigail knew she would lose her stomach and prepared to vomit. Lightheaded, she pulled at the flask again and again, fighting down the waves of nausea by choking down more whiskey. *No sense wasting it all on that oozy hole in the lieutenant's back.*

At last she tore the flask away from her dripping lips. Now that the immediate revulsion had passed, Abigail felt better with every breath. Warmth spread through her like a gentle wave, replacing the cold knot she had suffered from the very first view of those writhing, naked brown bodies. *Whiskey. So. Not so bad after all.*

But it'd be her little secret. She took one more long gulp and shook the flask. *Best leave some for the lieutenant.* Abigail retamped the cork and set it aside. Feeling like she could wait a while before she had to do anything else. Feeling much like a soggy bag of oats as she sank against the side of the wagon. And licked her lips, listening to the shrieks of warriors and the moans of dying soldiers nearby.

Irish whiskey, she thought to herself. Not so bad after all.

Chapter 11

$\mathscr{F}$ollowing every mad rush, the soldiers scraped at the hard, flaky earth with anything a man could use to make himself smaller. Skillets from their mess-kits, bayonets, or rifle-butts. Even bare hands. Every able-bodied man digging at the dry crust cracked like an overripe melon long ago, gone bone-dry beneath a relentless summer sun.

On the north and west wings of the corral the defenders eventually scratched rifle pits out of the unforgiving soil, each trench dug just beyond the ring of wagons. Those men still able to move scraped and sweat, surrendering what precious little moisture their bodies might still possess to that one-eyed monster in the sky above. Far from Fort Reno, Templeton's men found themselves with little water left among the barrels lashed to each wagon. It had been their hope to refill the water-barrels at Crazy Woman Creek after finding Dry Fork a tongue of parched sand yesterday.

The only good thing, they muttered to one another as they grubbed at the soil like frantic gophers, was that the warriors hung back—waiting.

"The bastards skittish now," Captain Marr explained. "Reckoning on the range of your big guns."

Donegan licked his lips, taking secret pleasure in the potion of salty sweat mingled with strong whiskey.

A potent libation.

Through the spokes of a wheel he burrowed up the dirt so that he had more to hide behind. Relieved for the moment that he had only to gaze across the slope at those mounted warriors milling about, waiting for their next charge.

"They look so . . . very wild and savage while galloping around us, Mr. Donegan," Glover muttered with a weak smile. *Perhaps,* he thought, *I've conquered this immobilizing fear after all.* It had proved itself a more powerful enemy than Confederates or Sioux warriors ever would. "Yes. How I'd love to set up the camera and make some views of their riding feats. Mounted horsemen swooping down on us . . . like frantic swallows darting out of this dusty, yellow gloom."

For a moment Seamus stared at Glover, disbelieving, though Donegan had seen many a man cope with the stress of battle in odd ways. Behind the photographer an old soldier growled.

"By damned, forget that nonsense of your camera! You best shoot them with that rifle of Rooney's."

"Rooney?"

"Plopped back there." He gestured with his head. "Gut-shot. And dead for it, thanks be. Awful way to go."

"Lookee there!" Terrel pealed. Heads rose, following his arm as he pointed to a high piece of ground to the west, above the clearing where the warriors gathered to wait. "See that buck? I'll bet he's commanding officer o' the whole shebang. They all gathering like rebel cavalry waiting to grind us down now, boys. Charge after charge —and that bastard calling the tune. You watch . . . see? Keep your eye on that buck up there with the blanket."

Donegan's eyes climbed from the fluttering feathers worn by the milling warriors to that single Sioux, stoic atop the hill. A red blanket hung from his arm, dangling off the side of his pony. As he watched, both were deftly flung into the air, the blanket swinging round and round over his head. Answering his command with a wild demonic cry, more than a hundred warriors pounded heels against ribby flanks, tearing up the slope toward the soldiers waiting in their trenches.

"Told you." Terrel scratched at his bony chin before he eased it along the stock of his Long Tom Springfield. "That boy's running the whole shooting match, or I ain't Mither Terrel's smartest boy."

Riderless ponies thundered up the rise. At times Donegan caught only a glimpse of a foot strapped atop a pony's flank or the bobbing shadow of a dark head pressed behind an animal's neck. But to most of those hunkered behind their pitiful mounds of dirt, it looked like just another stampede of riderless mustangs. Riderless, that is, until those ponies spewed arrows or spat random rifle-fire. Once again those still able to hold a gun answered back, the clatter of their weapons hollow in the dry air above the west and north rims of the corral.

This time the shrieking horde thundered closer still to the wagons. Closer than they had yet dared. Arrows hissed by or smacked into the dry wood. Keening bullets kicked up dirt in front of the dugouts or whistled overhead. Too often one of the soldiers would hear that unforgettable sound of a bullet slamming into flesh like a thick smack of a hand against wet rawhide. The red tide washed past as the young warriors reined away from the rifle pits, swinging onto their ponies, flaunting their inviting umber backs at the soldiers.

"Damn, but he's a heavy one. Gimme a hand here, Sarge."

Donegan turned to see a dusty soldier yanking at the body of a young trooper. As they rolled him off the edge of the wagon and pulled him back into the corral, Donegan saw the thickening wet stain over the heart.

"Hope my bunkie didn't felt a thing when it hit, Sarge," the soldier muttered morosely. "Only way to pass on 'round."

"Shit." Terrel helped heave the body behind that of

Templeton's dead horse. "Never do feel a thing when you get hit with the bullet that snuffs out your candle!"

"No pain a'tall?"

"None."

"Thanks be to God!" The soldier laughed, until he turned away, crying.

Donegan looked away when the young trooper gently tugged his dead comrade's eyelids closed, caressing the peach-fuzzed cheek.

On the hill above them the crimson blanket fluttered into the still air. A hundred voices clamored like cawing blackbirds rising to the clear, translucent sky overhead.

"Another go at us, boys!" Wands hollered.

On the warriors thundered, their ponies wide-eyed in the race, nostrils funked in the exertion of their chase, each animal laying flat-out toward the wagons. Straining up the slope, tearing from west to north.

"I'm tired of having nothing to shoot at but the bastards' arses!" Terrel laughed grimly.

"Well, dammit—shoot the jackanapes' ponies instead!" Donegan hollered.

"Hurroo! Anither Irishman!" Terrel answered back, his voice rising in joy. He rose a moment to glance down the line at Donegan, tipping his hat in recognition.

"Who else would you see out here 'neath this merciless sun, letting redskin h'athens have a flog at us, eh? None but the stupid Irish!" Donegan roared.

"A right fine notion—shooting their horses, Mr. Donegan!" Reverend White raised his assent.

"Dandy idea, if I don't say!" another soldier agreed. "The ponies it'll be!"

"What we do after we shot a Injun's horse?" a soldier whined.

Terrel leaped up, hand on his hip. "Who's the dumb mither's son asked that question? I dare you own up to it! Ah, none of you children'll fess up, eh? For those what don't know what to do after you got one of them red buggers knocked off his horse—you shoot the bastards!"

"That's the idea, Sergeant!" Donegan agreed. "Put 'em afoot!"

"We topple Mr. Donegan's red heathens from their ponies to slow 'em down," White hollered in that high, grating preacher's pitch, "we'll have a better chance of hitting them afoot."

"Kick 'em outta the saddle!" Bradley yelled weakly back in the corral, a bandage smeared with a brown stain wrapped round his skull.

"'At's it, Lieutenant!" Terrel cheered. "Glad to have your rifle to bark back at these red mongrels."

With the next charge three warriors found their ponies pitching headlong as they approached the wagons. One did not rise from under his struggling animal. A second crawled to his feet, was shot by a soldier, then lumbered to the edge of that ravine to the south where he pitched out of sight. The last warrior tumbled across the sage and dust, springing to his feet. Flinging his broken bow aside he dashed toward the corral, axe in hand.

"That'un's yours, Terrel," Donegan offered.

"No, sir. I think the bastard belongs to you. After all, t'was your fine idea knocking 'em outta the saddle. Besides, appears he's coming to call on a fine civilian gent like yourself."

"Naw," Donegan replied, wiping the sweat from his eyes. "He's looking for a sergeant . . . Sergeant."

"But you'll shoot 'im for me, won't you, Donegan?"

"I don't want——"

"Damnation on your black Hibernian souls," the reverend shrieked. "Will one of you bastards shoot that godless heathen before we'll be on a first-name basis with the red bugger?"

"For a man of the cloth," Donegan stood, pressing his Henry to his cheek, "I'd do anything, Reverend."

A puff of smoke burst from Donegan's muzzle. A blossom of red exploded in the middle of the Indian's chest, shoving him back three steps before he plopped into the dust. Donegan lowered himself into his pit.

"Too damned close, you ask me," muttered one of the soldiers.

"Didn't hear a goddamned soul asking you, Harris," Terrel barked, jumping to the defense of his fellow Irishman. Then he laughed, causing more soldiers and Donegan to laugh with him.

Seamus had to admit, it felt good to laugh. When a man had nothing else to do but wait. Watching that lone warrior and his blanket on the hillside. The rest of the devils gathering and milling. Waiting. He'd always hated the damned waiting.

"Simpkins is down," Marr groaned as he knelt over the old friend bound for the Montana goldfields with him. "Relax, boy. You'll be no good to anybody now—'cept when they make a last rush on us."

Marr gazed up at Wands. The lieutenant motioned him away from the wounded men.

"Casualties mounting up, Captain Marr." Wands chewed at his lower lip.

"No call to address me as Captain. Seems like a long time ago, son—that war back yonder. You see action, Lieutenant?"

"Yes, sir. Enough to realize we aren't going to last a whole helluva lot longer at this rate. They get one of us most every run-by."

Marr nodded. Looking up at the bone-yellow globe hung at mid-sky. "If the Injuns don't get us, then that goddamned sun will. But they keep coming at us like they have, it's all over before mid-afternoon."

"You got an idea, tell me," Wands pleaded. "I'll go along with you."

Marr looked round the little corral. The wounded moaned in pain and thirst. The rest tried to hide from the sun. Inside one of the ambulances a baby cried pitifully. From the other came a child's whining as little Bobby Wands begged to go outside to play.

"Lieutenant, I ain't got an idea one. You and me both are used to fighting Johnnies. Even guerillas like Quantrill. But . . . these Injuns are something else altogether. Face up to it—none of us know how to fight like this."

Donegan pushed himself up to the pair. "One thing you got the power to decide," he whispered, glancing down at the toes of his dusty hog-leg boots, "is that when those red bastirds make a final push to run over our position, who among us will take care of killing our wounded . . . and which of us will take care of . . . of the women and children."

His gray eyes sought the lieutenant's. Wands swallowed hard. Wishing suddenly for some whiskey in his belly. Better yet, some brandy right now. He liked brandy laying warm in his gut. Something to make what they were talking about a little easier to swallow. Finally he nodded.

"All right, Donegan. I think we understand each other. It comes down to it, I . . . I'd like to have you two take care of the women . . . and the children." His eyes flooded and he turned away.

"I think it best, Lieutenant." Marr briefly clamped a hand on the young lieutenant's shoulder.

"You and Terrel see to the wounded, Lieutenant. We don't want a one of those bloodied lads falling into the h'athens darty paws," Donegan said, and was gone back to the trenches.

Down the slope the Sioux slipped from their ponies, settling on their haunches like they were going to make council. Talk matters over. Make some adjustments in their approach to the soldiers forted up atop the knoll. Up the far hillside loped three warriors. They dismounted to talk with their leader who carried the red blanket.

Things fell quiet as cotton down in the corral as the defenders began to broil between earth and sky.

"Hottest part of the day," Donegan grumbled as he looked back, seeing Marr had resumed his place in the rifle-pit. Seamus glanced round their miserable refuge, finding Wands standing at the back of an ambulance.

Whispering with his wife. Her head appeared momentarily. The lieutenant tenderly kissed her. Then the little boy's upper body popped out from the back. Wands hugged his son, kissed the boy's cheek, and wheeled away suddenly, swiping savagely at his nose.

Donegan sensed a hot sting in his own throat as he turned away, feeling dirty like a thief for stealing a glance at the lieutenant's little family—three people who might not have all that much time left together now.

He cursed himself. Like a darty thief, stealing a peek at happiness coming to an end.

Those few veterans of the war, sweat-stained and grimy down in their trenches, seemed the most calm. They had been under fire before. Donegan recalled his own nightmares. Hardest part was this waiting. Once the fighting began, a man didn't have time to think. Gazing now at those grim, dirty, powder-burned faces full of wrinkles and a life's share of miles, Donegan realized he was one of them. He couldn't escape it. Though he'd tried, he had never really left the army. Realizing that he, like the rest of those old files who'd fought that dirty war between the states, all sat alone, assessing some narrow odds.

Seamus Donegan knew no one worth his salt ever spoke out loud about the odds.

Chapter 12

O ver the corral, a steamy silence fell like a mantle of torture round them all.

From the Wands's ambulance came the sobbing of women. Little Bobby cried out, confused and frightened. In the second ambulance the baby fussed, crying from time to time. At one point things even grew so quiet Donegan thought he heard the woman praying for her baby daughter, for her husband. Praying too for the lieutenant who lay bleeding at her feet.

Seamus closed his eyes, recalling the creamy fullness of her breast. Then the wounded mules rose in chorus all over again, drowning out the woman's praying with their brassy *scree-haws*. In the tomblike lull between their tortured screams, a nearby horse tore at the weedy ground and dry bunch-grass, chewing noisily. And when all fell silent, Donegan listened to the rustle of a breeze nudging the canvas tarps lashed over the freight-wagons. He gazed down the blue octagon barrel and the dull-brass hardware gleaming in the bright sun, watching the warriors squatting on the ground over his sights. And wondering why the red heathens had quit. Wondering, why it had to be so damned quiet——

Out of a pale sky arrows fell like sparks of iron-tipped fire spewed from the sun. In that moment of terror a man yelped in pain, digging at the arrow that had fallen out of the sky and pierced the back of his neck. Clawing at the shaft, he bolted from the trench like a wounded animal. Two others burst from their pit, one tackling the wounded soldier, holding him down in the yellow dust. The other braced a knee against his comrade's shoulders, yanking at the arrow until it wrenched free.

"God damn you all!" Terrel leaped to his feet, his rifle in hand, the muzzle sweeping the horizon, a man hungering for a target. Any target. "C'mout here and fight me like men! Show yourselves, you bloody bastards!"

A second shower of arrows rained from the heavens.

Wands sprinted toward the southern side of the corral. "There!" he screamed, pointing, shaking in anger and frustration. "Dammit! They're coming from the ravine!"

Other voices rang out—some in pain as arrows struck them or friends. Most in shock. No man immune from fear now—finding himself vulnerable to an unseen enemy.

"They're in the ravine!" Wands whirled, screaming to the men as they dashed up. A few kept craning their necks to the sky as they hobbled toward the lieutenant. He stood there, shaking his head in frustration, pounding a fist against his forehead. Not near so certain of their safety now as he'd been when he ordered the wagons toward the lip of this ravine.

Sure that this southern side of the corral would be safe from attack. Like having our backs to water. So damned sure the warriors couldn't sweep 'round our southern flank. Almost on the verge of tears that he hadn't so much as considered——

"Watch out!" someone shrieked.

Like a covey of flushed quail, the soldiers scrambled for cover. Arrows hissed out of the ravine, a hundred pieces of mirrored light, glinting, winged into the dry air. Each one rising into the sun, stalking predators curving in flight to plummet down into the unprotected corral. A mule struck—braying in pain, kicking wildly. A soldier cowering under the mule rolled free of the thrashing legs.

Like cruel retribution for his stupidity, the mule's wild dance found the wounded soldier again and again and again . . .

"By all that's holy, Lieutenant," Terrel grabbed Wands with his free hand, "let me have a dozen men. I'll clear out the ravine before the——"

Wands laughed crazily. "A dozen men, Sergeant? We don't have a dozen! I can't spare a goddamned one!"

"Bejesus, sir! We can't fight like this. None of us has ever fit a enemy what won't stand up to you—a enemy what's gone like a breath of smoke. Shooting us from behind. We ain't used to this, sir!"

Wands gulped, his eyes narrowing. "Looks like us soldiers got a lot to get used to out here, Sergeant."

"Here, Lieutenant." Reverend White shoved his rifle into Wands's hand. "I won't be needing that."

"What? Good God—don't need your rifle?"

"Not down in Daniel's den of lions!" White's mouth set in a tight line of determination.

Wands studied the minister, wild-eyed and powder-burned. "Lion's den——"

"The ravine, Lieutenant. I'm going to flush the buggers out for you."

"You'll do no such——"

White pressed a veiny palm against Wands's chest, shutting him up. "I'm called for the job, you see. The power of the Lord rests in my hand." He raised the old pepperbox aloft.

"At least take your damned rifle with you!" Wands pleaded.

White shook his head. "The face of the Sioux is red, Lieutenant, but his heart is black. Jehovah saw fit to arm little David with nothing more than a sling when he stepped forth to battle the mighty Goliath."

"I can't allow a civilian——"

White shoved the lieutenant aside.

"My god, Reverend!" Wands lunged for White, "You're wounded."

White stopped and turned, tapping the pepperbox against his left arm where the broken shaft of an arrow poked out of his bloody shirt-sleeve. "A mere flesh-wound, my son! I'll take one other . . ." His eyes scanned the soldiers nearby before Wands could protest further. "You, son. Gird thy loins! Verily I say, we shall slay the Philistines with the jawbone of an ass! Come, race on the heels of the Lord!"

"Halt—Fuller!" Terrel roared, dashing to the young soldier's side. Quietly, he asked, "You wanna do this?"

Fuller nodded eagerly. "Way I figure it, Sarge, they get me now . . . just save 'em the trouble of rubbing me out later."

Terrel watched the boy-faced recruit tear from his grip and follow White, leaping over a wagon-tongue. He watched, mesmerized, as the pair stopped at the lip of the ravine, glanced over, then plunged from sight as if a huge maw had opened to swallow them both. Terrel turned to Wands.

"Better that boy than another, Lieutenant."

Wands nodded, watching the sky for more arrows. "Can't really spare any man now, Sergeant."

"You three!" Terrel shoved the soldiers away from the wagons. "Watch them red bastards out there. They mount up—you sing pretty for me! Off with you!"

From the ravine echoed two quick shots. Immediately a volley of shots rumbled over the lip of crumbling earth. Then a final, lone crack of a rifle. And a wild, demonic war-cry screeched to the skies.

The hair at the back of Donegan's neck rose. He had never heard anything so hideous. Like the scream of a banshee itself. Knowing, like the others, that the minister and the young recruit were done. *Each man alone to wonder whether t'is better to put things off . . . or stare death in the face——*

"Bejesus!" Donegan growled. "Lord Mither of Gawd! Lookit!"

From the upper end of the ravine, where it swept toward the western hills, raced a haggard band of warriors. Not one dared glance behind him as they sprinted toward the slope where the other warriors watched in astonishment.

"No-o-o!" one of the old soldiers wailed.

"They killed 'em both!" Frank Noone groaned, swallowing hard. Thinking of the two he had back in the ambulance. Thinking of what could have been for his little family. "We gotta be ready now. Watchit . . . those bastards'll come right outta——"

The ravine belched up a dark head. A madly grinning head. Fuller, the boy-faced infantryman. Over the crumbling, sage-covered lip poked the gray-headed eagle. Wild-eyed still, his face almost unrecognizable for the dark smudges of burnt powder. Arm in arm the two scampered to the wagons amid cheers and hearty back-slapping until White winced in pain when the celebration jostled his wounded arm.

The reverend shook the pepperbox before him. "Went off all at once." His high-pitched voice quaked with conquered fear. "Can't understand it."

Fuller nodded eagerly, his youthful smile bigger than ever. "Like to cut that big'un right in half—that pepperbox going off all to once."

White shook his head in disbelief that he stood before them still whole. "Always worked proper before, Lieutenant. Yet," he grinned weakly, "who am I to question the ways of the Lord Jehovah!"

"That one buck got tore up to pieces," Fuller explained. "The rest bolted off like skeered cottontail. Flat skeedaddled!"

"Listening to their wild shrieking," White smiled, "seems music fitter for the bounds of hell!"

"Sarge!"

Terrel wheeled.

"They're coming at us again!"

"Lieutenant." White patted Wands on the shoulder. "Appears we've only angered them. I'm heartily sorry."

Wands laughed. "Reverend, with the way that bunch was flinging arrows into us, we'd not lasted much longer. I'm proud to have you along, sir. What you did took courage. Foolish—but no question of guts."

"My loins were gird with the power of the Lord!"

"C'mon, Reverend." Wands took off at a trot. "Let's send a few more of these savages straight to hell!"

The warriors no longer raced wholesale toward the corral. Ridgeway Glover figured they must have decided the soldiers had been knocking too many down each charge to keep flinging themselves against the wagons time after time. And losing two of their number down in the ravine to the reverend's mighty gun that shot many times in the hand of the gray-headed one surely proved a bit disconcerting to the Sioux.

What had started off as easy pickings had grown into hot, dirty blood-letting. Work. And that was one four-letter word a warrior wanted no part of. Still, occasionally throughout the afternoon, a brave handful would rush the white men, swinging from their ponies to fire a bow or rifle. Whittling away at those white men still capable of holding a gun. By the time the sun sank midway toward the west, over half of the corral defenders lay wounded or dead.

Glover realized most of the wounded wouldn't see another sunrise without proper attention.

Funny thing about pain, though. As the shock of a wound fades, the pain grows. Like a strangling fist gripping 'round a man's throat. Through the lengthening shadows Glover studied the wounded who had been pulled together at the center of the corral. He himself had talked Katie Wands and Abigail Noone into helping him nurse those who lay helpless and terrified—waiting for the next thunder-roll of pony hoofs or clatter of rifle-fire, or simply a whispered curse as another man fell quietly to the yellow dust. Each time the Sioux galloped out of range, Glover laid his rifle down and returned to help the women.

Abigail knelt beside Glover as he wrapped some clean muslin over a shoulder wound. "Don't you think you should get some rest like the others?"

He looked at the rifle-pits as the first fingers of sundown stretched out of the west. What men still held weapons lay exhausted, drained, the juices sucked out of them in dusty, blood-soaked holes burrowed into the ground. "I . . ." he tried to explain, "I'm afraid if I stop . . . I'll never get started again." He watched her smile before moving away without a word.

"Besides, ma'am," he whispered so that no one would hear, "I'm finally doing what I should've done back in the war. Too long I hid from the fighting, and those wounded in it. Not hiding any more. No man'll take that from me now."

A raspy whisper interrupted his reverie. Glover crawled close to the old veteran. The soldier tugged him down to his cracked, bleeding lips, coughing sounds into the ear Glover held close.

"Wah—uhghh—wah . . ."

The soldier collapsed, his hand freeing Glover's shirt. Faint with the effort. Glover gazed down into the wrinkled face, for the first time noticing the long, thick scar worming from temple to jawbone. Saber, he figured. Nothing else would cut so clean nor lay a man open quite like that. *To survive a wound the way this old soldier has . . . only to march west all the way on foot . . . and die in the dust on this hill.*

"Yes, my friend," he answered the soldier's pleading eyes. "We'll have some water soon. Real soon."

Glover found Wands looking in on Templeton. He waited until the lieutenant had stepped down from the back of the ambulance. "We need water," Ridgeway explained. "Some of your men are in a bad way and won't last without it. I'll go alone if you can't spare a soldier," he rushed on, not waiting for Wands to object. "Just get me some buckets and I'll climb down the ravine to the creek."

Wands stared at Glover for a long moment, numb and dumbfounded. White and Marr came up before the lieutenant found the will to speak. "You're right about getting the water for the wounded. Except . . . I'll lead the detail."

"But if something happens to——".

"Captain Marr, I'll lead the water detail myself. Is that understood?" He waited. No word was raised in objection. "Good. While Peters and Wallace fetch some buckets from the wagons, I want Terrel and the captain here to pull Templeton from the ambulance. Lay him in the shade over there with the others. That way we can keep an eye on him. You'll see he's cared for properly, Mr. Glover?"

"I will," he answered. "But——"

Wands turned. "Get those buckets ready for me, men. Now, Reverend, I want you and Fuller on the point leading the way. Secure the ravine for us. We'll follow you down to the water. That set by you?"

"We're on our way," White answered. "Private? Shall we march once more into the land of mine enemies?"

"After you, Reverend!"

"Don't exactly know how far down the ravine it is to water, Lieutenant," White said. "But we'll help you fill buckets, and boots if necessary. Singing the Lord's praises as we do!"

Buckets appeared moments after White and Fuller had disappeared over the lip of the ravine. Wands waited with Peters and Wallace at the south side of the corral for a few minutes, intent on every sound below them. Only when he was certain his two scouts had not run into an ambush did the lieutenant lead his water detail down the slope.

From sloshing buckets all three poured the cold, clear liquid into kettles and mess kits. Then turned around for a second trip to the creek. Every step of the way Wands held certain he was watched by at least a hundred enemy eyes. Sensing half that many arrows and rifles pointed at his back. *Perhaps they don't jump us because they think we're positively crazy.* Reaching the corral with White and Fuller after the last trip, Wands had finally convinced himself it had been a crazy, suicidal stunt. But for some reason, one he had pulled off.

A few minutes later the lieutenant understood he wouldn't get away with his trip to the creek scot-free.

"Lieutenant!" a soldier yelled.

"It's Daniels, sir!" screamed another.

He ran to the northern edge of the corral overlooking Crazy Woman Crossing. Down by the cottonwoods, backdropped by the glittering gold-dappled stream itself, stood a distant figure in an army-blue tunic and gray britches. The figure stumbled and weaved out of the water, shoulders gyrating until he ripped his hat off, revealing two long, black braids. With a howl the lone warrior began his savage dance. Round and round he stomped the dust while the soldiers watched in fascination. Two more Sioux dragged a limp, naked body across the stream, up the bank to join their friend dancing in soldier clothing.

Wands choked. "Yes. *That's* Daniels, Private."

As Glover watched, Donegan shoved two young soldiers aside, swapping his Henry for a trooper's Springfield. Seamus dropped to his belly smoothly, pulling the Long Tom into his shoulder. Quickly he gauged the distance, windage, then squeezed the trigger. His lead ball landed far short.

"That's enough, mister," Wands ordered. "It's a waste of precious ammunition. You'll never hit anything that far off."

"Man's gotta try—"

"Daniels is beyond caring now," Wands said.

"He's *your* bloody friend!" Seamus growled. "You won't even try?"

"I can't allow you to waste our ammunition," Wands ordered as he reached down to stop the Irishman. Marr and White yanked the lieutenant off Donegan just as

Seamus figured the meaning of the warriors' creekside performance.

"Sonsabitches!" Donegan muttered, fumbling with the sights and watching the scene unfold below.

No man was prepared for what came next.

While his two companions held Daniels' body propped between them, the dancer ripped off the lieutenant's scalp.

Donegan cursed under his breath, clicking up the first of the long-range leafs on the rear sight. He squeezed off another round. The ball kicked up some dust a few yards from the dancer. The warrior turned, exposing his genitals to the enemy.

Some on the hilltop groaned in helpless frustration. Yet the Sioux had only begun their sport. The warrior laid open first one thigh. Then Daniels' other thigh spread apart, muscle pink and mottled before blood gushed free.

A second leaf clicked into place. Seamus squeezed again. The ball dropped into the dust, closer still. Yet not close enough to threaten the dancer's bloody game.

With one savage swipe from the knife, the lieutenant's belly fell open, gut tumbling free like purple snakes writhing to the ground. Beneath the coils the dancer performed his bloodiest work, finally shaking his trophy aloft at the end of his arm.

The Sioux spun around, pushed Daniels' head back and stuffed the genitals into the lieutenant's mouth as a final desecration of the body.

"What'd he just do?" one private inquired.

"You don't wanna know, lad," Donegan growled over his rifle, snapping the third and final sight-leaf into position. "Believe me, you don't wanna know."

He held on the warrior's head, about high as he trusted himself to hold. Sucked a deep breath, let half of it out and squeezed again. This time he knew before the muzzle-smoke even cleared. The others cheered before he watched the damage for himself.

Down below, the warrior wheeled slowly on his heel,

his chest a bright red, staring at the gushing hole in astonishment. Instantly, the other two dropped the lieutenant's body and dove into the trees. Leaving the dancer to die in the dust beside the soldier he had mutilated.

"An eye for an eye," White growled bitterly. "An appalling spectacle of savagery."

"Tarradiddle, Reverend." Donegan rose to his feet. "No eye for eye . . . just take twenty of these bastirds for every one of us now!"

The Irishman whirled and cut a swath through the soldiers, stomping back to his trench.

As Seamus left, Glover watched a young private crumple to his knees, gagging, his belly throwing up what bacon and hardtack was left from breakfast.

"It's . . . just like he said it'd be." The soldier choked, then wiped his hand across his mouth.

White helped the young man struggle to his feet. "Just like who said it'd be?"

The boy pointed to the creek. "Him, Reverend. The lieutenant. Daniels talked with me last night, most of my watch. Couldn't sleep. Had a nightmare . . . 'bout his own death. That dream he told me . . . 'bout the Indian attack—it's all come to pass here today!"

"What's your name, son?"

"P-Peters."

"Private Peters, I want you to remember something," White soothed as he helped the boy stumble toward the west wall of the corral. "If thy right hand offend thee, cut it off. If thy eye offend thee, pluck it out. We have been offended. Oh, merciful Lord, have we been offended! And mark my words, Private. We'll do much cutting and plucking before this day is out!"

The cool water had done much to bring three of Glover's wounded around so they could return to the trenches in time for a renewed attack on the corral.

In their first charge up the slope the Sioux didn't rein up out of range for the soldier guns. Instead, they circled, continuing down the slope, then raced right back toward the corral in a frontal attack.

"They mean to ride over us, Donegan!" Marr shouted in warning. "You got that Henry of yours ready?"

"These h'athens've learned about sojur guns." Donegan tried to spit, but found his mouth full of cotton. "You and me have a wee bit of a surprise to hand 'em, won't we, Cap'n?"

"Do what damage you can, Seamus," Marr encouraged. "Boys, you best hurry for they don't figure to give you time to reload!"

"Get your powder down quick, brethren!" White exhorted. "Let not the ball tarry behind."

"You are a one, Reverend!" Terrel roared loudly. "We get our arses pulled outta this fire, I'll give thought to changing me faith from Catholic!"

"Why, Sergeant . . . I'll take that as a compliment! And a promise as well." White brought the rifle to his cheek.

Instead of gliding away along the west wall of the corral as they had done all afternoon, the warriors thundered on in a red wave. Here and there a pony stumbled in a prairie-dog hole, a rider sprawling. Yet for every one who fell, it seemed three more appeared in his place. The tidal wave rose, drumming closer and closer.

When close enough, the two repeaters barked and chattered. Marr and Donegan pumped their Henrys as fast as they found new targets. White fired, then dropped the heavy, one-shot Springfield and pulled the pepperbox from his belt, preparing for a hot time of it at close quarters.

The more he fired the weapon, the more Donegan liked the way the Henry bucked in his hands, the smooth action of the lever, the way he could lay the front blade on a brown chest and squeeze, assured that warrior would tumble off the back of his pony.

"Holy Mither of Mary," he marveled out loud, "this is some sweet rifle!"

"Your partner there'd loan me his gun, my Irish friend," Terrel called out lustily, "we two'd show these red bastards what real shooting's all ab—"

Marr turned in time to watch the sergeant pitch backward out of the trench, his long rifle slowly tumbling from his grasp as he stumbled among the mules lashed between two freight wagons. Glover had watched the arrow hit the wiry sergeant. He found himself at Terrel's side before the soldier had settled in the dust.

"The . . . g-gun, me boy," Terrel whispered roughly. "Use . . . use it."

Without hesitating, Glover raked the big rifle into his shoulder, kneeling right beside the sergeant's body. Squeeze and fire. He helped turn the tide. One final wave of warriors swept over the battlefield, leaning from their nimble ponies to drag away their wounded and dead.

Glover rose to his feet, shaking. Squeezing on the musket trigger still. Yanking and pulling and . . . until Marr grabbed his hand.

"It's over, son. Over for now."

The photographer nodded, letting the captain take the gun before he fell to his knees beside the sergeant.

"It's only me stomach, boy." Terrel tried to laugh weakly.

Glover looked down at the growing patch of moisture spreading across the blue tunic. In the center of it Terrel's dirty paw clutched a feathered shaft. He swallowed hard.

"Not to worry, I tell you . . ." Terrel's eyes misted as he tried to focus on the faces gathering close above him.

"That's right," Donegan soothed, on his knees, leaning over the soldier. He blinked his own stinging eyes. The shaft trembled, heaving in with a tremor, out with a whimper. "Not to worry, Sergeant."

"Shit." Terrel fell deadpan a moment. "You know better than that, Paddy. Man takes a hit in the belly, it don't hurt all that much. Just . . . just his ol' heart floods his belly till there ain't no more Irish red left to pump." He turned his head to the side, spitting up some bright fluid.

Donegan wiped the sergeant's chin as one of the men moved up with some muslin bandages.

"Sergeant," the photographer from Philadelphia whispered, "you got nothing to worry about now."

"Shit. This bleeding Irishman here with me knows better than that, boy." Terrel coughed more dark blood up. "That's right. *You*, Irishman." He gazed steadily at Donegan. "What with all you know 'bout war . . . and men dying."

"Save your strength——"

"Maybe you can fool these others, hiding outta uniform the way y'ar. But you're more a damned soldier than any these others, Paddy. More a warrior than them red bastards what killed me for sure," Terrel replied.

"Hush," Donegan prodded. "Say it after me: 'O, my God . . .' "

Terrel seemed to smile within that face of his gone gray. "Last rites, eh, Paddy?"

" 'I am heartily sorry . . .' "

". . . 'for having offended thee—' " Terrel choked on his own fluid. "Your kind won't fool me, Irishman. Just a shame we both come through that big, dirty war to die here . . . in this dirty, little war."

". . . 'I detest my sins most grievously . . .' "

"Difference is, Paddy—" Terrel broke off in a spasm, coughing up dark blood. "Difference is that out in this frigging war, nobody'll remember a one of us."

With the sergeant's next breath, Seamus recognized the gurgle at the back of Terrel's throat. A heartbeat later the sergeant lay quiet. Seamus eventually slid his hand over the edge of the dark, moist stain. Hoping to feel the slightest movement.

Seamus Donegan lowered the body to the ground, turned and loped away before any of the rest would see his tears.

Chapter 13

*A*bigail prayed the Irishman wouldn't find out she had watched him cry. She knew that would shame a man like Donegan. Though he had every cause to cry. Twice this day she had watched him do what must be done. First for Lieutenant Templeton and that bloody arrow. Then for the sergeant who only needed someone to know he had lived, to know he had died.

Lieutenant Wands had Peters build a fire near the wounded men. Having pulled the last of their firewood from the sowbelly under the wagons, he used the greasy sage to keep the tiny fires burning. Then Wands put Pvt. William Wallace to work butchering a dead mule.

"Can't be one dropped back this morning," Captain Marr advised. "If these men going to eat mule meat, Private, best you make that meat fresh."

He sliced each strip from the mule's muscular haunch, sniffing at the stringy meat to tell what was palatable. At least he figured the meat could be made edible, what with a little cooking over that smoky fire Peters was nursing. Soon enough both privates had the bloody strips of mule hung over the tiny flames, suspended on bayonets they jammed in the soil, circling the fire-ring.

Through most of the afternoon Abigail, Katie Wands and her colored servant Laura had bandaged and fed the severely wounded. Three more had been added to their number after the last rush which claimed Terrel. Three more to bleed in the center of their desperate, little compound. Every one of them waiting to die as the shadows lengthened and the sun fell headlong toward the Big Horns.

Abigail Noone crawled from soldier to soldier. Scraping what dirt she could from their faces. Brushing away the insects that gathered wherever the sticky blood collected. Earlier in the day ants and grub beetles had discovered the dead horse and mules. Searching out the stench of decaying flesh growing putrid beneath an unforgiving sun. By late afternoon the insects were busy on the wounded.

"Frank?"

Noone turned, finding her standing behind him at the edge of the shallow trench, wringing her hands in her once-starched dimity dress. Now it hung in lumpy folds, smeared with the blood and vomit of the wounded.

"Abby." He got up, nudging her back where they could talk in private. "The baby?"

"She's sleeping now. Katie's watching her. I . . . I need to feel you."

She hurled herself into his arms, still not sure how she was going to ask this of him. How any woman could ask it of the father of her child. She brought her face away from his chest, lifting it, inviting. Frank kissed her fiercely, ignoring the taste of stale whiskey on Abby's tongue.

She tore away, sobbing. Able to control her tears no longer. A cheek finally pressed against his chest, Abigail began. "Don't let them kill the baby . . . our baby, Frank! Please."

"What're you talking about?" He held her away from him for a moment, until she wriggled back into his embrace.

"Don't you see, Frank? The Indians wanted the baby. They've wanted her all along. It's as plain as I'm standing here. They told us they'd steal her if they had to—"

"You're talking utter nonsense, Abby," he soothed, his own mind fogged in fatigue and fear.

"No," she argued. "They wanted her at that first camp north of Laramie. Remember? For God's sake—let them have her before . . . before the end."

Frank slowly held her away from him again, studying Abigail's stained face, eyes swollen from crying. "The end, Abby?"

She nodded, sobbing uncontrollably. "We're not going to make it. But she can! They want her. She'll live! All I want is my baby to live. Don't let her die with us!"

Abby's knees went out from under her. Frank caught her as she fell, lowering his wife to the ground, where he clutched her against him, leaning back against a wagon wheel as he cradled her in his arms. She felt so very small whimpering against him now. Gently he stroked her hair, whispering his assurance.

"I'll see that she lives, Abby. With God as my witness. What happens to us won't happen to her. You must believe me."

He rocked her back and forth in the lengthening shadows, cradling her as the sun sank lower and the breezes chilled, sliding off the foothills. Frank pulled the shawl round Abby's shoulders, whispering into her auburn hair.

"I'll see that she lives—on my oath. I'm her father, for God's sake."

Back in the shadows behind that wagon, Reverend White sighed, his old heart shaken. Moments ago he had stepped outside the corral to relieve himself in privacy, slipping back to the circle when Frank had pulled Abigail away from prying ears. White found himself caught with nowhere to turn, embarrassed to overhear Noone's secret promise to his wife. As he listened, White kneaded the sore muscles of his left arm where Abigail herself had pulled free the broken arrow shaft.

Praying that no one else must know their secret.

Careful now of where he laid each boot, the minister

crept along the backside of the wagon, sliding into the corral several yards from the couple.

"Lieutenant Wands."

"Reverend. Care for a slice of mule?"

He waved his wrinkled, waxy hand. "No, thank you. I've come to appeal to you. For the mercy of our little band."

"What're you talking about?" Intrigued, Wands rose along with his voice.

"One of us must make a ride for help."

"I know," Wands admitted sadly. "But I can't spare a single one. Any of my men capable of sitting a horse would surely be capable of holding a rifle. I can't allow the loss——"

"I'm not requesting permission of you as my superior officer, Lieutenant. Best you understand that." His words yanked Wands up short. "I'm a civilian." Wands nodded in answer. "You've got no authority over me, Lieutenant."

"That's where you're wrong." He wanted to say this as gently as possible. "You're a civilian destined for a military post in the Mountain District. Traveling along a military road, guarded by the army. You are under my authority, Reverend. Like it or not."

"Then," White grew thoughtful, drawing himself up, "you'll either agree to my appeal on the grounds of humanity, or you'll have to shoot me as a deserter."

"A deserter?" Wands squeaked, watching Donegan and Marr inch closer to the fire and the argument.

"That's what I'd be if I rode out of here—on that strong horse of yours over there. Right, Lieutenant?"

"Well . . . I don't——"

"The way I've got it figured, son, I can make it back to Reno in four hours."

"Hard riding. Perhaps." Wands agreed reluctantly.

"How long Captain Proctor and his boys take to get ready to march?"

Wands stared at the sun impaled on the sharp peaks.

"Best you should figure two hours from the time you ride in till the time they march out."

"So if it takes me four hours to ride horseback there . . . it means they'll be at least twice that long marching back here."

"Even double-time," Wands added.

"If they're able, Lieutenant," Donegan argued. "They'll be marching that road in the dark."

Wands shook his head, then stared into the dirty, wrinkled face before him. He had to smile at the gray-headed old man. "You are something, Reverend. After all you've done today—now you're volunteering to go on this fool's errand."

"Not just me," White answered. "I want one of your young ones to ride with me. In the event one of us . . . one doesn't make it."

"No! Absolutely not, Reverend. I've heard enough of your nonsense. Now understand this, all of you. This cockamamy idea of White's doesn't hold water. Fifteen hours it'll take. Hell, fifteen hours from now . . . that sun'll be high in the sky once again. And by then . . ." He paused, sucking in a long breath like dry rawhide dragged over sand. "By then I figure there won't be a one of us left here to rescue anyway." Wands let that sour a moment before he plunged ahead. "No, Reverend. I need you here. With the rest of us. With *me,* for the love of God."

White paused, studying the faces of the troopers gathered round him. He gazed down at those faces etched with pain. "Sorry, son. I don't figure a one of your soldiers will shoot me in the back if I walk over there and climb on your horse."

"Perhaps they won't," Wands growled, feeling like he'd been backed into a corner. "But you're forgetting that *I* will."

"No." White shook his head. "Especially you, Lieutenant. You won't shoot me."

"L-Let him go, Alex."

That voice shook Wands to his heels. He looked down, seeing Lieutenant Templeton struggling up on one elbow.

"George——"

"Let White go. If I gotta make it an order——"

Wands shook his head. "But you're . . . the wound—perhaps your thinking is fogged."

"The reverend cleared the ravine!" Lieutenant Bradley urged.

"That's right!" Peters cheered. "He cleared the ravine. If any one of us can make it to Reno and bring back some . . . some help—the reverend here can."

"Damn right!" young Fuller agreed.

"If I can't change your mind . . ." Wands whispered when things grew quiet. "Take my horse."

"And a volunteer can ride mine." Captain Marr pulled his thoroughbred stallion into the group. "Finest animal this side of Independence, Missouri. He's got the bottom to make the ride."

"Wallace?" Wands asked, waiting for the young private to step forward. "Will you go . . . William?"

He saluted smartly and nodded. Never had he had an officer address him by his first name. He glanced at White eagerly. "The two of us make a dandy ride of it—won't we, Reverend?"

"Best of luck, Reverend." Wands saluted the preacher, then presented his hand.

White shook it. "Won't be luck I'll need, Lieutenant. I'll count on your prayers."

With a rustle of cloth Abigail and Katie pressed forward, brushing their tearstained cheeks against White's before he was helped atop Wands's mount. Boyish William Wallace stood petrified and red-faced as both women kissed his cheeks. Marr and Donegan boosted the young soldier onto the thoroughbred's back.

"He starts to fight the bit, son," the captain explained, "you give him his head. He'll get you to hell and back if he has to. Bring him back to me if you can, soldier. God's speed, gentlemen!"

With that, Marr slapped his stallion on the rump and sent him off. Marr wheeled away, swiping at his nose, knowing the odds of ever again seeing that beloved animal.

White whirled the army horse in a tight circle, saluting the compound's brave defenders. "May you wear God's protection like a shield about your shoulders! Mrs. Noone—I'll expect to kiss your daughter's tender cheek when I return!"

Startled, Abigail watched the old man yank his reins to the side, bringing the army horse round beside young Wallace. Both riders whipped their mounts over the tongues of two wagons, galloping straight toward the sharp slope dropping from the east side of the knoll. Almost instantly a wild cry arose from the warriors milling down the western slope. Half a hundred leaped atop their ponies, beginning a race down the south ravine to cut off the escape of the white riders.

"Just look at their faces, Alex," Templeton urged from the ground. "Look at our men, every one! The hope they share right now is worth a hundred times more than White's gun would ever mean to us. That hope——" He broke off coughing, clutching his chest in pain.

Without so much as slowing their breakneck speed, White and Wallace spurred their animals over the sharp lip of the knoll, forcing the horses to skid and slide through the sage and loose sand like two maddened, four-legged beasts. Careening straight down the east slope to the Montana Road that would lead them south toward Fort Reno, away from this crossing at Crazy Woman Fork.

For an anxious moment it appeared to those left behind that the warriors might cut the couriers off by reaching the road first. But the reverend had seen and heard the devils coming, putting heels to his animal. Wallace was instantly at White's knee, low along the thoroughbred's neck, his cap long ago swept off in the wind. From the corral there rose a brief cheer amid the tears and back-slapping as the pair reached the road a few hundred yards ahead of the Sioux.

In seconds the riders disappeared from view. Only the fading hoofbeats and bitter screeches of the pursuers told those left behind that the chase continued. Leaving behind the crossing at the Crazy Woman. That wild race, of many miles yet to go.

And too few hours left to pray.

Chapter 14

A cooling breeze whisked down the creek drainage, born of icy snows forever frozen on the peaks above their little corral. Twilight sank like gloom around them. Most of the defenders realized they were alone once more. In the middle of this wilderness. Surrounded by hundreds of Sioux. Waiting for sunup. And now counting two less riflemen among their desperate number.

"Guard will be mounted every hour," Wands explained moments after White and Wallace galloped away. "I won't take the chance of a man falling asleep because he's pulling a two- or four-hour watch. We'll need four able-bodied men on a watch. One picket on each side of the compound. Peters, Higgins, Lewis and I'll take the first watch."

Then he stopped. And counted. Wagging his head.

"Lieutenant." Peters inched into the firelight. "There ain't enough of us left to pull watch, sir."

"He's right." Frank Noone moved up. "Let's just figure on keeping each other awake tonight. We can . . . we'll get through till sunup, sir."

Wands swallowed, that knot of sentiment thick in his throat. "Till sunup, men."

For the first time in all those evenings on the trail west, Ridgeway Glover really marveled at the texture of colors wrought by thin, high air of this country at twilight. As silence slipped down upon them with the darkness, he studied how each succeeding range of hills and high peaks contrasted with those stacked before it—from a deepening black of those most close at hand, to the purples and violets found farther away surmounting the rugged necks of the mountains. A tint of rose brushed the fringe of those hills dippling the northern skyline, making this foreign land seem less sinister for the moment. Somehow less cruel and punishing here as day hung in the balance before sliding headlong into the black unknown of night.

In that distant fringe of rose along the hills beyond the Crazy Woman hung a thin cloud of dust. Glover finally noticed Wands intent upon the same cloud. Photographer stood silent by West Point lieutenant for minutes until he whispered, "You think that's more of the savages?"

Wands nodded. "Yes, Mr. Glover. Out of the north—only thing it could be. No one else up north knows we're here. Only the Sioux. Likely sent for reinforcements to join in the sport they're planning here come morning."

Frank Noone joined them at the north wall. "Probably won't be so bad after all, Lieutenant. Whole thing'll be over before the sun's full up."

"Yes, Frank. One good rush would do it now. Not that many of us left can hold a gun."

Glover watched Noone glance back at Abigail cradling their daughter near the firelight. Rocking and murmuring a lullaby to the infant.

Maybe I'll be able to do it at sunrise, Frank thought. Just before dawn he could hide her little body among the baggage and blankets and the old straw tick in the wagon. The Indians would be sure to look . . .

He blinked his eyes, smarting at the tears he didn't want the others to know he couldn't contain.

They'll find her. The Sioux will. They'll raise her like one of their own. Just a baby now . . . she'll never know

*what happened here in this dirty little corner of no-
where . . .*

A change in pitch in the nightsounds brought a sudden
chill to every man in the compound. North, along the
creek itself, arose a new hum to the darkness. The kind of
change in sound a man might miss during the day when
his mind crowded itself with shrieking savages and the
cries of the wounded or the braying mules. Nightsounds
now as plain as the hand in front of his face at twilight,
now that things grew quiet and a man could no longer
ignore the fear that lay in his belly like a cold stone.

Glover flinched as the magpie called, *creee-awww-
hawww-awww.* Then burst into flight from the trees by the
creek.

"We're all a little jumpy," Wands admitted. Nothing
more to be said. Every man among them silent, nursing
his own thoughts of home, of what might have been if
dealt a better hand.

The land sank into quiet once more, a quiet so intense
a man could hear the greasy sagebrush popping back in
the firepit or the wounded moaning deep down in their
fitful dreams. A coyote yipped, at home among the western hills, up where the warrior and his red blanket had
called the tune throughout their long summer's-day
dance. To the north another coyote took up the call.
Then a third—much closer—down in the creek-bottom
cottonwoods.

"You see that . . . down there, Lieutenant?" Glover
pointed north.

"Yes . . . I think I can."

More a feeling than anything a man could see, they
each sensed the movement of men and ponies beyond the
creek. Faint yet unmistakable sound crept to their ears,
carried on the breezes sweeping off the west slope of the
knoll. The Sioux were on the move.

"Back East, when I was planning on making this trip
west—I was told the plains Indian didn't attack at
night," Glover admitted with a sad chuckle.

"Seems we don't know as much as we think we did—about this land. And its Indians," Wands replied.

"Already?" Frank asked, his voice unable to conceal his panic, eyes flicking at Abigail and the baby. "You mean they'll rush us at night?"

"Looks that way," Wands gritted. "Gathering down by the creek. In this darkness they can creep up lot closer before making a full-scale assault on our position . . . on what's left of us." He turned full round, facing those still standing, to talk all the quieter. "Don't any of you forget—save that last bullet for yourself."

Frank sniffled, then drew himself up and wiped his hands down his dirty tunic. *That's what it means, this being a soldier . . . keeping a last bullet in your gun for your own head. Always wanted to be a musician. Never did mean to be a soldier.* He steeled himself. *Today's as good a day as any to start being one, I suppose.*

"Perhaps it's better after all," Noone looked back at Wands and Glover. "Better than waiting till morning."

"Yes," Glover agreed, responding to the young soldier's courage. "I doubt I'd make it through a long night of waiting again myself."

Donegan had stayed in his trench. As far out of the firelight as he could, allowing his eyes to swell with the inky immensity of nightfall swallowing the high plains. While he listened to the murmur of voices behind him along the north wagons, Seamus made of his ears another set of eyes piercing the gloom.

So many nights like this before, he recalled. Yet, those nerve-twisting hours during the war were filled with the sounds and smells of horses. Listening to the quiet murmuring of your fellow soldiers passing among themselves a canteen of warm water or strong whiskey or sharing a plug of chew. This . . . this was something altogether different, Seamus decided. Easy it was for him to wait out the Confederates. Come dawn, a man knew what to expect. They were, after all, white men.

This Indian fighting was something new to them all.

And the not knowing sent a cold spray of ice water down Donegan's spine as he lay in his trench, trying to make sense out of the night sounds and the shadows, spat where his eyes strained most to see.

Confederate Johnnies he could figure out. These naked, screeching warriors were something else.

"Seamus!" Marr held up a hand. "Look," he whispered hoarsely, waiting for the soldiers and Glover to grow quiet. "Out there. Along the crest of that hill." He pointed north.

If a man concentrated hard enough, he could make out movement of men and ponies along the ridge. But instead of Sioux riding down into the valley of the Crazy Woman, the warriors trailed northwest. Out of the valley. Away from the Montana Road. Leaving behind the knoll and its little band of defenders.

"They're going?" Frank asked, desperation in his voice.

"Don't count on it," Marr answered.

"You think it's a ruse, Captain?" Wands inquired.

"Have no idea. I'd be ready for those devils to pull any kind of trick on us now. No telling what——"

"Lieutenant!"

Wands jerked with Donegan's call.

"Over here—double-time!"

Every man who could run bolted for the western trench where the big Irishman stood his watch. One by one they dropped into the dust and the dried blood, pulling their weapons into readiness.

Then fell silent. Waiting.

"What'd you see?" Wands whispered at Donegan's ear.

"Nothin'. *Heard* it. Out there." Seamus pointed down the slope. "Hoofs. On some rocks. Maybe down by the creek."

Every set of eyes strained into the murky gloom. A thumbnail moon limned overhead amidst a sprinkling of stars dusting the darkening horizon to the east.

"There!" Donegan shouted, spotting the rider.

"I see 'im!" Marr levered the action on his Henry.

"Hold on!" Wands whispered harshly. "There's only one."

"One means they come to ask for our surrender," Marr argued. "Rather'n wait till sunup."

"No surrender," Noone protested, his mind on Abigail and the baby. *Should I go now . . . to be with them before it's too late?*

"No, Frank. There'll be no surrender." Wands inched himself out of the trench to stand on the prairie.

By now the lone rider was plainly visible, sidling up that slope the warriors had hammered all day long. A horseman briefly backlit by the far-fallen sun peeled behind the Big Horns. The faint, plodding hoofbeats carried to them on the night-breeze.

"The blaggard ain't in no hurry," Donegan whispered.

"Red bastard don't have to be," Marr answered as he dug his left elbow into the dirt, making a firm rest for his rifle.

Wands wasn't all that sure—but from the dancing shadows, it appeared the rider wore a low-crowned, floppy hat. It was just a hunch he felt before he bellowed, "Halt where you are!"

Instantly the horse stopped, and set about nuzzling among the sage and dried grass, grazing for a tasteless morsel. Its rider as still as a statue.

Wands waited. Then waited longer. When the rider didn't move nor speak, his gut churned with worry anew. Scratching his chin, he stepped forward three steps, slipping his pistol from its holster.

"Who goes there, dammit?" he demanded, stronger this time.

A thin, reedy voice sang out of the gloom. "Friend."

Wands grew concerned—yet relieved at the same time. Whoever was out there sure as hell knew some English. "What's your name?" he yelled.

"Jim . . . Jim Bridger."

Wands turned as the others whispered behind him.

"A white man, by God!" peeled one soldier.

"Lordee! A white man!" sang out another.

"You believe that!"

"Ride on in, Mr. Bridger." Wands didn't know whether to holster his pistol yet or not. "Slow—mind you. Real slow."

"Like you say, son. I'll come in slow." Bridger nudged his old gray mule into her lazy walk again. When he saw the riflemen backlit by the tiny fire, he snorted, laughing quietly, realizing every muzzle pointed his way. "A powerful lot of guns you boys got there. 'Specially when it takes but one to put this ol' man under. I ain't much a coup—no more'n parfleche and bones, boys!"

"How you come to be out here . . . this time of night?" Wands had a thousand questions he burned to ask.

Without a word, Bridger slid from his mule and led her straight past the soldiers into the compound. There he stopped, stunned by the wounded he saw gathered in the dust round the fire. The three grimy, bloodied women. A little boy hugging his mother's knee, staring in wide-eyed wonder at the old gray-beard. And last, his eyes fell upon a little newborn suckling at its mother's breast in the pale glow of the tiny fire. New life amid the stench and pain and blood.

"Lord a-mighty," he murmured, tearing the old felt hat from his head. "Ladies," he apologized. "Man out in this country long as I been tends to forget his manners a'times." His eyes landed on Wands. "Officer, I'm scouting for a stupid captain, name of Burrowes. Out of Fort Carrington, up north a ways."

"W-We're bound for there!" Noone gushed.

Bridger nodded. Looking over the wounded. "How many you dead, son?"

Wands swallowed hard. "Two. Lieutenant Daniels down by the creek . . ."

"That's the body I found," Bridger admitted. "Any more?"

"Sergeant Terrel." Wands pointed. "That's all."

"Just two?"

"Yes," he answered lamely, looking over the wounded himself, his eyes resting on Templeton. "The lieutenant there, he's commanding the detail——"

"Only two, you say." Bridger sighed. "Be real proud what you done. I just watched a whole passel of Sioux warriors hotfooting it over the hills yonder. Tell me, just how long they have you forted up here?"

"Just after sunup, Mr. Bridger." Templeton raised himself painfully. He didn't feel as feverish, what with a cool breeze blowing through camp now.

"In all my forty-four years in these mountains, this the first time the Injuns done this sort of thing."

"What sort of thing?" The big Irishman edged forward.

"A surround," Bridger answered. "Stop you, circle you till you run outta water or ammunition. Whatever come first. My, my," the old scout clucked. "This little rag-tag outfit of your'n held off all them warriors?"

"We had two more with us . . . earlier."

"Where they?"

"Gone for help. Down to Reno." Wands pointed south. "Took our best horses."

"And a mess of them Sioux on their tails," Fuller added.

Bridger sank to his haunches by the fire, warming his hands. "They'll make it. Them horses stay under 'em . . . your friends'll make it to Reno just fine."

Donegan knelt beside the scout. He worried the cork from the neck of his tin flask and presented it to the old scout. "Mr. Bridger, a betting man'd wager you could use this."

Jim sniffed at the neck. "I thankee, son. You figure it's the proper thing to do, offering me some of your barley-corn. But scouting's my business. To stay alive in this country, a man's gotta smell and see and listen like a sharp-eared wolf. Awake or asleep. Hard drink like that gonna bumfuzzle my senses. Not that this child's ain't had many a hurraw in his day—selling my beaver to rendezvous. Love to taste that on my tongue—just don't dare now."

"Man never gets too old to have a drink, Mr. Bridger." Donegan gulped the fiery liquid.

"Ain't a matter of age, son. Only a matter of knowing when. Maybeso someday, we'll have us a drink and palaver. Now's just not the time . . . and here's not the place." Bridger's eyes squinted as he studied the wounded and blackened faces illuminated by the cooper light.

Wands dropped beside Bridger. "I'm still confused. You say Burrowes's troops scared the hostiles off when they saw him coming . . . how did *you* know we were here."

"Didn't. Just knowed someone was bound to have a fight of it down this way. Black Horse—he's a Cheyenne chief in these parts—he warned the soldiers up to Fort Carrington. From what he said, I figured there'd be trouble with the Sioux along the Road. And hell to pay at the Crazy Woman. But cheer up boys! That paper-collared captain Burrowes got two hundred men with him, and they're not long behind on my trail."

Templeton tried a smile, the first since racing across the Crazy Woman after the buffalo at Daniels's side. "How'd you know there'd be trouble here at the crossing?"

Bridger sniffed at the dark meat hung on the bayonets. "That mule? Smells to be. You folks mind I have me a chaw on some?"

Wands handed him a piece, but before Bridger ate, he continued. "Captain Burrowes—now, he is a stubborn one. Were it up to him, he'd be in camp right now up to the Clear Fork."

Wands gasped. "What do you mean? That's north of us . . . miles away."

"You're right about being way back yonder, son."

Bridger tore off a chew of the stringy meat. "Ahhh . . . nothing like a mule haunch when a man goes hungry. In all my winters out here, I've tasted the best. Some claim it's buffler hump. Others stand by beaver tail or painter meat. My, but I've always favored a fat mule haunch."

Bridger chewed thoughtfully a moment, then went on. "Had to pester that captain something fierce all day after running onto sign telling 'bout the big fight. Hell, if'n I didn't make myself a burr under that captain's ass, he'd be plopped down at Clear Fork right now . . . and you folks'd be waiting for sunup to be rubbed out, I'd reckon."

Wands gazed down at Templeton. George nodded weakly.

Wands turned back to Bridger. "You still haven't told us how you knew there'd be trouble here at this crossing. Those Cheyenne of yours?"

"Injuns, yes. Cheyenne, no." With the browned stubs of old teeth, Bridger chewed on more of the unseasoned meat. "Plain as I ever seen it writ in forty-four winters. To any man what wants to read." Bridger studied the eyes round the fire. "I reckon you figure me for a man don't write or read. Well, you're right. Not English, least-ways. But this child learned Injun long ago—in a Sho-shone lodge, it were—I first come to these'r mountains."

"These Injins wrote down that they were going to jump us here?" Donegan sounded dubious.

Bridger nodded and swallowed. "Told you. The Sioux painted it on every buffler skull from here clear north to Carrington's fort. All saying the same thing: 'Big fight at the Crazy Woman. All come fight the soldiers.' "

"Painted on buffalo skulls?" Fuller inquired.

"Yep. The creek here. With pictures of rifles and arrows, son. Rifles broke in half . . . says the Sioux would whip you soldiers. Sure as sun I knowed there'd be hell to pay here on the Crazy Woman. Almost had to shame that captain into following me here."

"We're damned lucky you nagged Burrowes into

marching down." Wands sighed, leaning back, some of the tension draining from him at last. "I suppose the captain'll bivouac down by the creek. I, for one, vote that we stay right here for the night . . . since we're safe now."

"I agree. It won't do to move some of your wounded yet, Lieutenant," Glover said.

"Thank God it's over." Frank Noone pulled Abigail close.

"Yes." Wands swept young Bobby into his arms. "I think we can thank God for our deliverance from a certain and horrible death."

Bridger snorted loudly and pulled a stringy piece of mule haunch from his lips. "Damnation! To hear you all jabbering 'bout thanking your Lord for delivering you from them savages. Wagh!" he snorted again. "Better you thank Jim Bridger, this child thinks. Fact be, better you all thank that hunched-up ol' Shoshone woman who forty-odd winter ago taught this pilgrim to read Injun!"

Chapter 15

"**M**r. Donegan!"

Seamus turned at the sound of his name, finding Lieutenant Wands waving him across the parade toward the wall-tents serving as Carrington's headquarters.

"If you'd be good enough——"

"Can't be stopped. On my way to see Cap'n Brown. Said he had something for me to help him with this evening."

"Perfect!" Wands replied. "That's just where I'm asking you to take these three men. To Captain Brown. They'll apply for quartermaster employment."

"Aye," Seamus answered with a quick wave of his arm, appraising the three men and the big rifles they carried. "Come along. To Cap'n Brown i'tis." He led off.

Something about the young lieutenant had come to trouble Donegan. Where there should have been a camaraderie, borne of what the two of them had survived at the Crazy Woman Crossing, there was instead something itching in the Irishman's gut that told him Alex Wands was not the same man now that he had arrived at Fort Phil Kearny. Now that the lieutenant had become one of Capt. Frederick Brown's inner circle.

Donegan wheeled suddenly, watching the three newcomers halt in their tracks.

"You got horses, gear you'll want to fetch?" he asked of them.

"Back yonder." One man, the oldest, threw a thumb. "Six horses and some pack animals. There's a woman— my wife—and my two boys. We'll go back for 'em later."

"Aye," Donegan replied, his eyes studying the rifle the older man held close, like it was part of his arm itself. "My name's Donegan. Seamus Donegan. Currently in the employ of the army once't again. Cutting . . . hauling wood. Figured what with the Injuns sealing this post off, making such a scare of the Road and all, it'd be best to lay over the winter here among the army blue. Push on to the Montana diggings come green-up."

The older man stepped forward, smiling like he'd made a friend, presenting his hand. "Name's James Wheatley. My friends and I—we was bound for the Bozeman country ourselves. Down at Laramie the soldiers warned against coming north. Told us there was a passel of trouble clean to Montana. None of us believed it."

"Not a soul out there has idea one what's really going on up here in Red Cloud's country." Donegan laughed. "Bleeming idiots back east, every one. Thinking the lion has laid down with the lamb in the shadow of the Big Horns. Horseshit!"

Wheatley gestured at the other two men. "Just figured that kind of talk was army jitters. Back to Nebraska where we come from, word is the Sioux signed the treaty and took their presents—meaning they won't trouble the Road no more."

"Discovered the truth out a hard way, didn't you?" Seamus inquired. "Just like the rest of us had to find out how the army lies to civilians."

"Our first brush weren't so bad," Wheatley went on. "They didn't get nothing off us. All we done was we pee'd our britches. First time any of us seen a honest-to-goodness war Injun before. Don't know who it scared more, the missus and my boys . . . or me! So, we decided right there that if we was going to travel along the

Road, it'd have to be after dark. Ride till sunup. Hide out during the day. Only way we made it up to Fort Reno."

"Why didn't you stay there?" Donegan asked, eyeing the octagonal barrel on Wheatley's rifle again.

"They tried to talk us into doing just that. What with my woman and boys along. Captain Proctor said another group come through Reno just the week before us, only to get jumped on the Crazy Woman. Had women and kids in their party too. Like us."

"I was there." Donegan said it flat. Like a hand slapping wet wood. "Lucky as not, if Cap'n Marr and me hadn't carried big Henrys like hangs at the end your arm there, the Sioux would've pounded sand up my arse. I'm here to tell you how bleeming lucky you three are—packing your woman and a pair of wee ones along as you did."

Wheatley glanced at his partners. They studied the ground sheepishly. "I suppose we pushed on past Reno 'cause we figured we could make it all the way to Montana just the way we'd been doing things—traveling at night. Pulled in here this afternoon. Colonel himself made a believer outta me—that it ain't smart to push on. We're staying the winter."

Donegan smiled with wide rows of teeth, sticking out his big paw to the second man. "Glad to have some civil company for the winter, my friends! These sojurs not the proper association for a man who's had his fill of brass, braid and orders."

"We all fought," the second man said. "Missouri Volunteers. Issac Fisher's the name. Pleased to make your acquaintance, Mr. Donegan."

"Seamus to me friends!" He presented his hand to the last newcomer.

"John Phillips," he offered quietly. His eyes still dug anxiously at the ground, sensing the big Irishman's appraising gaze. Not much of a social animal. In fact, he seemed almost scared of folks. John Phillips appeared a man yet to be tested. "But I'm known to some as Portugee."

"Portegee, is it? How'd you come by that?" Donegan asked.

"My mother." He glanced up into the Irishman's face quickly. "Have more of her blood, so I'm told."

Seamus rocked back on his heels. "Gentlemen. 'Tis a pleasure to have some more old sojurs like you here at the new Fort Phil Kearny. We'll while away our winter regaling each other on our favorite stories. I've grown weary already of all the prattle the others can tell. You'll be welcome in my camp anytime!"

"Thank you kindly," Wheatley answered with a big grin. "And likewise you, Seamus Donegan. Any man what carries a Henry rifle can't be all bad—now, can he?"

"Aye, James Wheatley," Seamus agreed. "Nor can he be called a stupid man."

On the third of August, Carrington bid farewell to Bridger. He wanted the old scout to accompany captains Nathaniel C. Kinney and the impetuous Thomas B. Burrowes in their march north, under orders to establish a third post along the Montana Road, on the Bighorn River some ninety miles north of Fort Phil Kearny.

"You'll be pleased to learn that General Cooke's office has selected a name for the new post to be commanded by Captain Kinney," Carrington announced to the entire regiment, his voice booming across the parade. In formation on horseback, ready to march, sat the two companies to garrison the new post. "Fort C. F. Smith, in honor of one of our own. A hero of the Eighteenth Infantry during the Mexican War. May his bravery and selflessness in service to this grand Republic prove a constant inspiration to us all."

Stepping up to Kinney's horse, Carrington presented his hand. "Captain, I've given you and Burrowes what extra mounts I could spare. I'm sorry there weren't more.

We simply lost too many when the Sioux rushed Haymond's camp last month. You both know what we've been through here already. Not a day has gone by that there's not some alarm. The beef herd attacked, our stock run off. A civilian woodcutter or one of the mowing crews killed."

"Red Cloud's made a damned nuisance of himself, Colonel," Kinney replied.

"I pray his warriors won't harass your men farther north. I've tried to make up for the lack of ammunition and stock by sending one of the mountain howitzers along with you."

"We won't have a problem, sir." Kinney saluted.

At Kinney's side Captain Burrowes saluted a bit less enthusiastically, still smarting that he was forced to take Bridger along once more. Nothing had ever eaten at him quite as much as how savvy the old scout had been concerning the Sioux attack at the Crazy Woman Crossing.

Carrington brooded as he stepped up to the captain, realizing that Burrowes supported Brown's approach to the hostiles. Burrowes appeared to him no different than so many of his junior officers—believing they knew why he was held back from his unit while they fought the war. They'd never accepted the fact that he was cloistered in the north as the war ground on. Then the War Department had sent him to Indiana to build prisoner of war camps. That done, he was needed to help quash the Copperheads. Secretary Stanton kept him busy in Ohio—yet Lincoln himself sent Carrington to Indiana to capture the traitors in the Northwest Conspiracy, which culminated in hanging.

"Captain Burrowes." Carrington presented his delicate hand. "This time it's your turn to take care of Mr. Bridger. See that you pay heed to his counsel, and that he has all the provisions he requests before he departs the site of your new post for the Crow villages."

"Sir." He answered with barely a whisper, his eyes focused straight ahead, never looking at the colonel.

Carrington turned toward his chief of scouts. "Jim, you have my complete confidence."

"Proud of that, Colonel."

"I'll tell you something now that I wasn't certain how I was going to handle. About a week back, in departmental dispatches, General Cooke sent his personal order releasing you from service."

"You say?" Bridger eyed the colonel, squinting. "This mean I'm fired now, or after I get back from the Big Horn country?"

Carrington chuckled. "Nothing of the kind. I rely on you like no other." Carrington felt the eyes of the rest of his officers hot between his shoulder blades as he admitted it. "So, I wrote on Cooke's order the words, 'Impossible of execution,' and sent it back. As long as I'm in command of the Mountain District, Jim Bridger will serve as my chief of scouts. So for now you must learn what you can about the mood of the Crow and the other tribes in the area, what with Red Cloud pressing his war on us. Then hurry back here to give me your intelligence."

"You bet on that, Colonel," he answered, stroking the neck of his old mule. "And by the way, I thankee for your trust. Not heeding Cooke's order. That fog-headed fool. Seems most of them army brass back East don't know what the hell's going on out here. Why, just look at all them traders and miners gathered down in the valley, ready to pull out behind us."

Bridger pointed. "While we're up to our asses in redskins madder'n wet hornets, folks back East being told everything's plumb friendly out here. Likely as not, folks being told Red Cloud's waiting for white folks on the road with open arms."

Carrington nodded into the rising sun. "One more irritation among many I must endure. Indian Superintendent Taylor spreading his twisted version of conditions out here, claiming relations with the Sioux exhibit a 'most cordial feeling.' All that wishful thinking of his has done is lull travelers into a false sense of security. They limp in here by the skin of their teeth. That Merriam train down in the valley lost two men between Laramie and here."

"They was damned lucky, Colonel."

"The Kelson train down there lost fifteen men, with five more badly wounded already. Why the army continues to tell civilians it's a Sunday picnic out here, I fail to understand."

"I'll say it again, Colonel—you ain't like a lot of these other paper-collar soldiers." Jim threw a thumb back at a knot of men seeing the Kinney command off. Brown, Wands, Powell, and Surgeon Hines sprawled in the shade of a tent. "There's a few around you who'd poke a stick in a hornets' nest—if you'd let 'em. Best watch 'em while I'm gone, Colonel. I'll go see what Red Cloud's up to. Just don't you do nothing to invite him and his brown-skins down on your little post here."

"I'm afraid nothing more dangerous than construction of a new fort will go on here." Carrington stepped back, waved his captains into motion.

Cooke has no idea what's going on out here. With these troops marching north, I'm left with 220 fighting men. Counting band and clerks, no more than 260. Many of those left here have less than a year of their enlistment to put in! But that's the way of things with the bloody 18th. At Stone's River half of the regiment's officers and enlisted men lay dead or wounded. That pompous ass Cooke has no idea what he's asked me to do.

A hand shading his eyes, Carrington watched both companies parade off the plateau, cross the Big Piney and climb the road onto Lodge Trail Ridge. In the dust kicked up by those two hundred horses rumbled a long cordon of wagons. For the past week two civilian trains had camped near the new post, refusing to attempt the road north without a military escort. Now at last they could leave Fort Phil Kearny and the danger of Sioux territory behind.

* * *

Overhead a hot August sun tortured those men scattered across the timbered slope of the Pinery, the name given the hillsides above Big Piney Creek here, more than five miles west of Carrington's plateau. Civilian and soldier alike labored in small crews, whipsawing through the thick trunks of old growth to fell the pines. As a cutting crew moved farther along the slope to a new site, a trimming crew would take its place. Working over each of the fallen trees left behind, the trimmers whaled away with their singing double-bit axes as they topped off the huge trunks and trimmed away all troublesome branches.

And as if the work itself wasn't enough for a man to worry himself about, they each kept their eyes roving the higher slopes, watching the Peno Head as well. Those wood-trains hauling timber to the fort site weren't the only ones needing to keep a sharp eye on the skyline for hostiles. The warriors themselves were becoming as pesky as the troublesome mosquitoes right here in the Pinery itself.

"Carrington says he can't send any more men down here," Capt. Frederick Brown had explained to an angry crowd of woodcutters after the Sioux had made their first successful attack on Pine Island, fleeing with a half-dozen mules. Leaving behind one dead civilian and two wounded soldiers. "We had more troops, the colonel would not be stretched so thin. We're stretched thin enough as it is, fellas."

"Difference is, your soldiers came out here figuring to fight Indians," James Wheatley said as he stood to draw Brown's attention. "We're here only to work, Captain."

Brown had nodded as the crowd murmured their agreement. "Yet you each stayed on, knowing the odds, didn't you, Mr. Wheatley?"

Seamus remembered how Wheatley's neck turned crimson.

"Damn you, Brown! No man gonna call James Wheatley a coward, you strutting cock!"

"Wasn't calling you a——"

"We'll damn well do the job we contracted to do for you," Wheatley went on. "For your end, you damn well better provide the protection you told us we'd have when we signed on."

Donegan had risen from the rear of the crowd. "Wheatley's right. Besides, Cap'n Brown, best you remember we'll get a lot more timber brought to your fort if we got the protection we need."

As he stopped now for a breather, Seamus remembered how Fred Brown had huffed and grown red himself, fuming to a parboil before he responded. "Donegan, isn't it? Well, Mr. Donegan, we'll just have to see what protection the fort operations can spare a fella like you, won't we?"

"Sounds like a threat, Cap'n Brown."

"Oh, it's no threat at all, Mr. Donegan. Just want you to understand that I figure for the time being, you'll have to just take care of yourself and keep your mind on your work. Keeping your nose out of army business. That is, if you care to stay on as my employee. Do we understand one another?"

He recalled smiling at the quartermaster. "Keep my nose out of army business, Cap'n? We most certainly do understand one another."

He remembered how Brown had glowered at him in those days since, like a man making a mental mark in a ledger kept always at the forefront of his mind.

"What you staring at, Cap'n?" Seamus hollered now as his axe came to rest, finding Marr studying him some distance up the slope.

"Never seen a half-nekked, red-breasted Irish jaybird before!" he answered, chuckling. "Not one for much bird watching."

"G'won with your sawyers, old man!" Donegan yelled upslope, flinging his hand in impatience. "Man gets hot swinging this axe, fighting branches aside that all but swallow me up—by the saints, you bet I'm gonna take my shirt off."

Marr swiped his brow. "Hot enough to sweat the tallow off a horsefly, you Irish whelp."

"Ain't only that, Cap'n," he replied, dragging a piece of coarse sacking across the back of his neck. "I go and tear a shirt on these'r branches, it leaves me only one shirt to me name. Not about to buy anither at the sutler's prices!"

"You belly up for his whiskey quick enough, Seamus Donegan."

"Damn right I do, horse-trader!" He laughed, taking up the hickory axe-handle once more. It gave a solid, comforting feeling to his callused palms, much like the feel of his Henry repeater. "Fact be, yourself owes me a drink as well. I'll be expecting payment in full this evening."

"This evening it is," Marr replied, staring back over his shoulder. "My, but you're all muscle," he marveled more to himself. "No wonder they've got a lad like you swinging that big axe."

Stuffing the damp sacking in a pocket of his cavalry britches, Donegan put his blades back to work, steadily working his way up a trunk, trimming the branches from sides and top. That very first day working on civilian contract for Capt. Frederick Brown some weeks ago, Seamus realized the other men went at this trim-work all wrong. They started at the top of the tree, working backward down the trunk, stumbling over the thick branches they had yet to cut.

Wasn't too many trees and a lot of blood drawn from his punctured hide by broken limbs before the Irishman figured another angle at it. While the others fought their way down the trunk, Seamus worked his way *up*. Starting at the bottom, he trimmed the lowermost branches. Then stepped up for the next series of limbs, never stumbling or faltering in his task.

Took no time at all before the subcontractor to the army, watching in awe, saw that the Irishman was completing better than two trees to every other man's one. And seeming to do it with half the effort as well.

"Tell you what, Irishman," Aubrey Pitman declared one afternoon after his wood crews had been at work on the slopes of the Pinery for about a week. "Make you a handsome proposition."

Seamus eyed him warily. "What's that, Mr. Pitman?"

"Son, if you continue to chop more wood than the others, I figure one of two things gonna happen."

"Here I was, fixing to ask you for a raise."

Pitman snorted with a chuckle. "Cain't do that. Captain Brown fixes the quartermaster employee wages. As a civilian you already make more than them thirteen-dollar-a-month enlisted boys."

"So, since you'd give me no raise, you figure I'll just go back to cutting no more than the slowest men . . . since he's getting paid the same as me."

Pitman nodded. "Aye."

"No sense in busting a sweat then, is there?"

"There's still the deal I wanna offer you."

His gray eyes narrowed on the contractor. "So, tell me."

"Every sundown you finish with a tally of logs twice that of the *best* man in the trimming crews for that day, I'll give you a bonus."

"Dollar a tree, you say?" Seamus asked, chuckling.

He wagged his head. "Cain't do that, but I will see you get what you're worth. You cut twice as much as the best man—I'll see you get a extra day's wages."

Seamus licked his lips, drawing long on the damp, blanket-wrapped canteen, wishing the warm water something more heady. "A man can always use more drinking money, can't he, Mr. Pitman?"

Aubrey's head bobbed. "Is it a deal, son? You cut twice as much as the best man, you get twice the pay?"

He flicked his tongue across his chapped lips again, tasting success already. "Lad like me can hardly go wrong—now, can he?"

"Donegan!"

They both turned to see a pair of civilians fighting a team of mules up the slope in their direction. One of the pair hollered out again.

"You gonna sit there rubbing on the bossman all day? Or you gonna help us get these'r logs o' yours hitched up?"

Donegan clambered to his feet, flinging the canteen down on the grass beside his shirt as he watched the two men back their mules into position where they could hitch the animals to three long logs the mule-team would haul downhill. Once across the Big Piney, the team would be unhitched and return for another load of three logs, while the workers below at the trail-head of the wood-road hefted those logs brought to them onto the running gears of wagons, from which the men had removed the freight boxes so the thirty- to forty-foot logs could be carted past the Sullivant Hills to the site of the army's newest post in this heart of Red Cloud's hunting grounds.

"Yeah, Mr. Pitman." Seamus held out his sore hand, waiting for the contractor to scramble to his feet. They smiled at one another as they shook on their private bargain. "Twice the money, for twice the work. We got us a deal!"

Chapter 16

Your bleeming mind's playing tricks on you, Seamus.

The big Irishman ground to a halt, cocking an ear downstream. And listened to the soft, almost inaudible sound of a woman's song. She was humming to herself.

If any man could recognize the faint sound of the female voice, that man stood beside the Little Piney at this moment, a smile slowly beginning to crease his beard.

All around Donegan the robber jays dove and squawked and protested. From time to time the breeze nustled the summer-dry bullberry leaves among the nearby willow at the stream's edge. But there it was again. That same soft whisper of a woman's voice. As enchanting, as alluring, as seductive as any siren song young Seamus had succumbed to in his life.

He had ridden back to the civilians' camp downstream from the water-powered sawmill engineer Gregory had planted in the middle of the Little Piney. Come here alone to fetch some jerked meat and two canteens of water for Sam Marr's midday meal. The felling of trees and the loading of the timber was hot and sweaty work these late-summer days down in the Pinery miles away. Like any man among those laborers, Seamus welcomed this chance to ride back to camp. Far better than swinging that double-bladed axe or yanking on one end of a two-man whipsaw.

Seamus had convinced himself the ride back was
enough pay in itself. Until he heard her voice.

After hanging the canteens over the horn and stuffing
Marr's jerky into a saddlebag, Seamus lashed the big
gray's rein to a tent-peg, where the animal could nuzzle
among the sunburnt grasses. Then he set off on foot.
Downstream. Following the sound of that liquid voice.
His mind grew busy, imagining who he would find having herself a midday picnic, far from the bustle and noise
and dust and wood-shavings blown about with the fort
construction.

A picnic. Alone by the creek. And downstream was
not the safest place for a woman to be. Whoever she was,
he decided, she needed reminding to move upstream,
closer to the stockade.

As he pushed through the willow and creeper hemming Little Piney creek, Seamus mulled on the female he
might find. Maybe Carrington's wife. Or some officer's
woman. Perhaps . . . even the young mother who had
nursed her infant at the Crazy Woman. Remembering her
swollen breasts engorged with milk, pale, opaque droplets
clinging to the rosy nipples, made Donegan's heart race a
bit faster.

She's a married one, he chided himself as he tromped
on through the willow, with each loud step drawing
closer to the sound of that sweet voice singing a soft,
lilting tune. *That woman's got call on her.*

Rounding a soft bend in the creek some distance downstream from the sawmill itself, Seamus was in no way
prepared for what, or who, he found. And how he found
her.

Through the thick copse of willow and gray-backed
bullberry, he now saw no picnic blanket spread upon the
grassy bank. Instead, the first thing the young Irishman
spied was the long folds of a woman's dress flung carelessly across a willow branch. A few feet beyond, his eyes
found the worn ruffles of bloomers swaying on a
bullberry bush. Beside them hung the lacy, unbuttoned

bodice dancing lightly on the August breeze. Farther down the bank, the heavy boots of a working woman.

He stood, petrified, confused for the moment. This ain't no soldier's woman, he decided from the look of the clothing.

Beside those scuffed, dusty boots lay the thigh-length woolen stockings. Atop them a faded, yellow kerchief Seamus imagined the woman tied round her hair.

He held his breath. Eyes narrowing through the willow. Donegan could not see the woman yet, but he could hear her splashing in the cool water just on the far side of a clump of willow that overhung the stream. A few yards away . . . and Donegan found himself swallowing, suddenly nervous. Palms sweating.

Should he go on, to warn her of the very real danger? Was it proper out here . . . proper for such concern, such manners?

For a moment he remembered what Sam Marr mentioned time and again to him: that Sam found it odd how the hard, ofttimes cold and resolute Donegan, a man who could be stingy with his feelings, became suddenly of manners in the presence of women.

Seamus laughed to himself. Women deserved to be treated different, he figured. No matter how pretty or ugly they might be. No matter the circumstances or where a man might find them. Manners was manners, his dear mother had taught him early among the green hills of his homeland.

Then he decided, convinced that no man he knew would find a thing wrong with warning the woman. So Seamus stepped round the clump of willow that overhung the gurgling creek, shielding her from view.

Stopping in his tracks, Donegan's breath caught in his throat. With a mouth gone suddenly dry.

No two ways about it, that woman standing in the quiet pool where the Little Piney eddied against the bank had to be the most beautiful thing his gray Irish eyes had ever laid upon. Even more beautiful than the sweet colleen who had taken him out of the Boston alleyways and into her room above those stinking streets. The sweet colleen who made her living entertaining fine-dressed gentlemen callers but gave herself willingly to the skinny, dark-haired adolescent Seamus Donegan through the rest of that cold, damp winter and into a rainy spring when first he came to Amerikay.

It shook the Irishman to his heels to realize this water sprite had no rival in his memory. More beautiful was she than his wildest imagination.

Her back was to him as he clung in the willow. She had her head turned sideways, scrubbing a slip of old burlap over the back of her shoulders.

He swallowed hard, finally realizing he needed to breathe. Greedily, Seamus sucked at the hot, steamy air of the high plains. And found himself sinking to his knees. Not yet ready to interrupt the water sprite's bath. Nowhere near ready to end this incredibly beautiful, provocative scene.

Sunshine and the breezes played with her hair the way a kitten would play with a ball of yarn. Tossing it about. Splaying color and hues and hints of crimson and rust in that long, curly, auburn mane of hers. Most of the tresses hung wet along her shoulders or spilled down her graceful, curved back as she rose from the surface slightly. Then turned full sideways to him, unaware that her breasts hugged the gently rippled plane of the creek. Their pointed firmness broke the surface like twin muskrats nosing their way in tandem across a prairie pond.

Seamus had never seen such breasts.

For a long, languid moment, the young woman flung her head back, eyes closed to the bright light pouring down upon her. As if glorying in its warming caress upon her body. Then she ran her hands slowly over those breasts, wringing the water from her freckled flesh.

He felt himself growing hard, watching the young woman stroke her own flesh. Sun rays played like a thousand bits of rainbow light in each water droplet that trickled down the fine nape of her ivory neck, across the soft curve of her shoulder. Onto the rounded melons the likes of which Seamus Donegan was certain he would not see again, would he live a century of searching.

By the saints! She's . . . she's so young . . .

Quickly he raked the back of a hand across his dry lips, puzzled on what to do. Let her finish her bath so as not to scare her? Yes . . . yes!

His eyes poured over her pale skin freckled by rose and umber, caressed by both sunlight and the cool waters of the Little Piney. Seamus swallowed, with each passing second becoming more unconscious of himself, so absorbed in the young woman in the water.

"By the saints . . . preserve me!" he blurted out in a whisper.

Surprising himself as it slipped from his lips.

Frightened as the woman whirled about. She sank to her chin in the stream. Head bobbing side to side, darting from bank to bank.

"Who . . . who's there?" she called out anxiously.

He wiped sweaty palms down his damp shirt and rose from the willows.

"S-Sorry, m'am," Seamus stuttered. "Didn't mean to startle——"

"How dare you scare me like that!" She flung her sudden anger at him, cheeks flushed and green eyes flashing every bit as liquid as the creek itself. Eyes every bit as fiery as the sunlight refracted off the water that danced around her shoulders as she covered those magnificent breasts beneath her folded arms.

"Didn't mean to scare you . . . truly didn't," he said, finding himself a bit tongue-tied. Seamus pointed upstream, foot shuffling. "Heard you singing . . . come down here . . . figured to tell you——"

"Figured to take a peek at me, didn't you?"

By the love of the saints, she is a feisty one, is she not?

"Come to warn you."

"Warn me of what?"

His head bobbed downstream. "Injins, m'am. They're all 'round us. No one's told you?"

For a moment that made Seamus even more anxious, she only stared back at him. Then she slowly rose from the stream. Now he could see most of her freckled arms. And the beginning of deep cleavage, a hint of fullness hidden beneath her hands. He was certain the woman was unaware she was showing so much of her flesh to him as she rose from the water.

At the same moment, Donegan felt strangely uneasy— not quite certain she was not toying with him, taunting him with her flesh.

Without warning she flung back her head, exactly as she had to feel the sun upon her face and neck moments before. That same graceful curve to the ivory neck. Strong muscles. The press of windpipe against the surface of her flesh. The strong chin that said this one had fire in her. And this time, she laughed loud. The trickle of that laughter rang about him like the waters of icy, Big Horn snow-melt tumbling over a pebbled stream-bottom. Merry and cheerful. Without a care.

"Indians?" She laughed some more. Louder still. "Looks instead like what I've got to fear most is some peeping Irishman creeping up to spy on a lady's bath." She stared him in the eye, as if suddenly uncertain of it. "You sound Irish."

"I am—was, I mean I am—yes. Come to America before the war."

She measured him a moment before replying. Then nodded. "My husband fought in the war as well. Union."

As she spoke of her husband, the woman sank back into the creek until the water rippled at her chin. Hidden once more.

Seamus nodded. "Union. Second Cavalry I was, m'am." Then, of a sudden, he remembered more of his mother's teachings and swept the soft-brimmed hat from the shock of curly, dark hair that rubbed his shoulders.

"Seamus Donegan, m'am. Sorry. Should introduce myself."

She giggled, lightheartedly this time. "Thank you for your manners, but, I'm not really in the position to shake your hand right now, am I, Mr. Donegan?"

Feeling like a sham dodger, Donegan's eyes raked the grassy bank as his sweaty hands rolled the hat-brim. "My manners don't always show at the proper times of it, I suppose."

"You'd be most good-mannered if you'd simply leave, Mr. Donegan."

"The Indians, m'am. They've been at their killing every day now."

"You needn't explain that to me, Mr. Donegan!" she snapped, those eyes flashing their sudden anger.

Now he nodded. "You're right . . . yes'm. Best that I just leave." Seamus slapped the hat back atop his head, then surprised himself by a quick bow from the waist. "And best you get dressed quick and scoot back close to the camp and the stockade. Much safer it'd be for a beautiful woman like you than out here alone."

Her eyes followed the Irishman as he rounded the big clump of willow, until he was a good twenty yards upstream, his back growing smaller with each long stride.

"Mr. Donegan!"

He stopped and whirled about before she had it all said. "Yes'm?"

"Do your manners also say you should allow a lady to introduce herself?"

He bobbed his head, grinning. "Sorry, m——"

"Jennifer," she interrupted his clumsy explanation. "Jennifer Wheatley."

Seamus swallowed. *Damn!* This angel of a creature belonged to that saint of a Nebraska sodbuster, James Wheatley.

"M-Met your husband, Mrs. Wheatley. Fine . . . fine man. I work with him up in the Pine——"

"Yes. Jim is a . . . fine man, Mr. Donegan."

"I best be going," he admitted, tapping the brim of his hat.

"Mr. Donegan, let's just tell Jim you . . . we bumped into each other. Won't do for him to worry about me out here with the Indian scares. Best if he didn't know I came down here to bathe . . . where you bumped into me."

"I figure that's best, to let him know we . . . we just bumped into one another, Mrs. Wheatley. Just so's there's no talk."

"And you?" Jennifer began, then paused as she pushed a handful of auburn hair from her cheek. "You'll forget you ever saw my . . . caught me bathing, Mr. Donegan?"

For the first time now he chuckled lightly, and wagged his head. "Sorry, m'am. Won't promise you something I know I can't possibly do. Truth is, I'll never forget such devastating beauty as yours."

Seamus had turned and was gone among the willow as those final words dropped round her. Not at all sure if he really heard her whisper to his back as he plodded upstream.

"I was hoping you'd say that Mr. Donegan. Praying . . . you'd not forget me."

Chapter 17

"**R**ed Cloud's five hundred lodges on the Tongue ain't all there is, Gabe," mulatto Jim Beckwourth said as he leaned over, whispering to his old friend, "Big Throat" Jim Bridger.

Together the two had trapped from the Marias and Milk rivers clear down to South Park in the Colorado country. When beaver was prime. Then years ago Beckwourth had parleyed his dark skin into a place of honor among the Crow tribe as one of their respected warriors. Jim's father, it was rumored among the trappers of the old west, had been a wealthy Virginia landowner who sired his son by one of his plantation slaves. Rather than owning up to his paternity, Beckwourth's father had instead granted that son his freedom. After years of homeless wandering, Jim found himself happy among the mountain trappers to whom a man's color simply didn't matter.

Ultimately the Crow, who had captured Beckwourth in a horse raid many years back, believed the man with the remarkable mole on one eyelid a long-lost son returned home to his people at last. The tribe had treated him so regally that Jim couldn't bring himself to leave. Instead, he had chosen to stay, marrying and helping the Crow in their wars on Blackfeet and Sioux, earning himself a place of respect among the elder counselors of the river Crow.

"You're telling me there's bound to be more than just Red Cloud's boys hankering to kill soldiers, eh?" Bridger whispered, feeling Seamus Donegan's cold, gray eyes on him across the fire.

"From what Rotten Tail says here," Beckwourth gestured toward the old Crow chief seated across the lodge-fire, "those soldiers got something to worry about."

To Bridger those words had the flat sound of a beaver tail smacking water to warn its neighbors of trouble. Yet, he had to admit, it was just as he had feared, and figured.

"Others joining up with Red Cloud?"

"Yep. Rotten Tail says I should tell you that he rode through the camps as the Sioux was gathering on the Tongue himself. A half-day's ride, he says it took him. Near as I can figure what he claims, says there's fifteen hundred lodges coming together."

"Must means the Miniconjou have joined the Oglalla, eh? Hunkpapa, too?"

"From the sounds of it." Beckwourth nodded. "I hear Sitting Bull's the nigger to watch in that band. He's a seer —has his powerful dreams and visions."

"Big medicine to them Sioux," Bridger admitted. "Where the rest of them Lakota stand for war?"

Beckwourth waited politely as Rotten Tail smoked his pipe and passed it on to the other old ones, respected counselors of this band of Plains Crow who followed the buffalo across the seasons, up and down the valley of the Yellowstone. Bridger knew as well as any man that it would not do for him to have Beckwourth rush the old chiefs. Injun etiquette dictated he politely, and silently, wait while the formal smoke went its four rounds of The Tail's lodge. Jim winked at the young Irishman seated on the far side of Beckwourth. As if to say Seamus was to settle back and relax.

Looks as if we're going to make a night of it here,

Bridger mused to himself in the smoky lodge. No sense in hurrying things now.

The better part of a week ago, Jim had invited the Irishman to ride along on this errand for Colonel Carrington. The army commander had dispatched his chief-of-scouts to visit the Crow, see if he could glean anything on the mood and disposition of Red Cloud's Sioux.

Seamus Donegan had jumped at the chance to ride along with this new friend, Jim Bridger. Anything to escape sawing trees or building Carrington's new fort. Besides, the Irishman told Bridger, he could learn a damned sight more from the old trapper than he could any number of lug-headed soldiers who always figured they knew everything already.

Despite the fact they were totally ignorant of this new country. Every bit as ignorant about fighting Sioux and Cheyenne.

Across five days Bridger and Donegan had followed a pair of Crow guides, nosing their ponies north by northwest. Up to the country of the Tongue, down to the Big Horn itself. Then straight across country to the wide Yellowstone that would take them west into the heart of Absaroka—land of the Sparrowhawk people.

For those hours spent in the saddle or during cool nights beneath the biggest, starriest sky the Irishman had ever seen, Bridger talked and talked. Normally a quiet and reticent man, more prone to keeping his mouth shut than running off at the tongue, Jim thought it strange a time or two that he palavered with this Irishman so damned much as they traveled along or sat around the evening fires. Yet long ago Jim Bridger, known as Gabe to his friends, had learned to accept things as they are. As well, he accepted the bond growing between them. This old trapper in the seventh decade of his life. And the young, scarred ex-soldier who hungered for knowledge and information, drinking in everything Ol' Gabe had to say like parched desert soil sucks down a spring rain.

The young fella was smart, about as smart as they

came, to Bridger's way of thinking. Jim had met the best across forty-four years in the West. Of a recent time the old trapper had thought there was none who could shine with the likes of Jack Stead and Mitch Bouyer for plain gut-savvy. But there was now a third. This Irishman had him the makings of plainsman. Pure and simple, Jim Bridger figured, this boy Seamus Donegan would do to ride the river with.

From first-light to moonrise Jim found a pair of eager ears to listen raptly to all his stories and frontier lore. An apt pupil who asked questions that many a time made Bridger smile and puff out his chest like a prairie cock. The sort of questions few men would think to ask. Questions that showed young Donegan truly realized he was in the company of the finest of mentors.

Jim liked that feeling Seamus gave him. The sense that he believed there was none better for teaching him what he needed to know about this high country, its animal and plant life and all a man could learn about the Indians who lived the seasons upon the face of this tumbling, kneading, rugged land.

So by the coming of that fifth morning, Jim had quietly hobbled over to the young Irishman, his rheumatism giving fit to an old hip injury. Bridger had grasped Donegan's arm and gazed up that tall frame of his, into those gray eyes, and told the lad something meant for their ears alone.

"I crossed these'r mountings more'n most men I know, Irishman." He stopped there, not sure where this was going, then plunged ahead. "Seen my share of niggers come and go. Some I'd lay store in. Most I'd as soon spit at."

Jim ground to a halt once more, digging a toe into the pine needles beneath his moccasins.

"I figure what you're telling me is . . . is you like me. Right, Gabe?"

Bridger nodded. "Only knowed a handful of fellas in my years out here who I'd figure I could go into a fight

with. Be it Blackfoot or a watering-hole brawl. But . . .
I sense you're the kind to trust at my back, Irishman."

Jim turned away with it said. Dragging that bum hip
over to the old mule, where he fussed with the cinch and
smoothed the blanket. Never aware of the mist that he
had brought to the young Irishman's eyes. So intent was
he in fighting the salty sting of moisture in his own.

Late that fifth day out, the Crow guides had led them
to Rotten Tail's village. Down from the umber and pine-
green rocky ridges they rode, accompanied by camp-
guards and a crier who announced their coming. Dogs
barked, nipping at the ponies' hoofs. Children darted
among the horsemen, laughing and holding hands up to
the whitemen. Shy young women and haughty old
squaws peered at them all from both sides of a long
gauntlet that gathered to escort them to the council
lodge.

The smells of that sundown entrance to camp seemed
like old friends welcoming Jim Bridger back among
them. Frying antelope tenderloin and boiling puppy. Siz-
zling boudins and broiling humprib. The fragrant perfume of strong coffee a'steam, mingling with the savory
fire-snap of greasewood and quaky. Warm, beckoning
flames were lit before each lodge as twilight sank upon
the Yellowstone but a rock's throw beyond. The familiar
smells of bear grease and smoked hides rose from the
gathering squaws.

Smells that reminded the old trapper of a younger Jim
Bridger, and what Crow squaws could arouse in a man.
Seductive fragrances that made him think on what these
dusky-skinned ones could do to make a man's juices boil
within him. Old Gabe had glanced over at the young
Irishman. Donegan's eyes filled with the new sights and
excitement of it all, as Jim remembered his first visit to an
Indian camp forty-four winters gone now.

And something turned warm inside the old trapper as
he gazed on Seamus Donegan. Realizing that things were
as they were meant to be. That squawing was for the

young ones. Truly a time, as he remembered the Bible-spouting Jedediah Smith oft repeating, a time for all seasons to a man's life.

Old Gabe figured that this twilight was perhaps his cue. Mayhaps this coming winter should be his last robe season in the mountains. Mayhaps come the time for him to retire to a warm lodge somewhere and quit pushing back against fate and gambling with chance. Time to let the younger ones seize their moment on this fading frontier.

Mayhaps it weren't so bad after all—what with youngsters like this Seamus Donegan to carry on.

Beckwourth watched Rotten Tail set his pipe down before he resumed his questioning. He quickly glanced at his friend Bridger before he spoke. "Uncle, Big Throat asks who joins Red Cloud on the Tongue."

The old chief fished in the warm kettle for a soft morsel of puppy he could chew using the brown stubs of his old teeth without too much pain. Bridger waited patiently as the Crow chief ate, understanding exactly how another old man with teeth problems felt.

For as old a man as he was, Rotten Tail's skin hadn't yet sagged. Instead, it was hung on his dark face as if it could have better been the bark of a black walnut tree, heavily seamed with the lines of many winters. And like Bridger's hair, the Crow chief's was flecked with the iron of many seasons hunting the nomadic, shaggy beasts of the plains.

Beneath his huge nose, Rotten Tail's fleshy lips rolled, and finally spoke. "Tell Big Throat the Miniconjou warriors of Black Shield wish to rub the soldiers out."

"Yes, we understand, Uncle. Are there more?"

"I have seen many Hunkpapa warriors under Sitting Bull."

Beckwourth nodded and winked at Bridger, though this was not a happy revelation.

"The Northern Cheyenne are split," Rotten Tail said as his hands flew apart. "Black Horse goes one way, to

the south away from trouble. The warriors under Two
Moons join Red Cloud as we speak."

· He chewed thoughtfully while Beckwourth and
Bridger fidgeted across the smoky fire. Old Gabe prayed
for a draft to drive away the oppressive, late-summer air
of early evening stagnating along Clark's Fork of the Yellowstone.

"Tell Big Throat we hear of more joining all the time.
Not only Arapaho, but the Gros Ventres are said to journey from the north, come to fight the soldiers."

"Big Bellies, Gabe," Beckwourth moaned.

"Not only Gros Ventres," Rotten Tail continued, "but
the rest of the Blackfoot confederation: Piegan and Blood
are ready to fight."

"Every Injun in the entire territory ready to ride down
the warpath," Bridger growled. "Can't say I didn't figure
on it. This is something the tribes been waiting for—a
chance to drive the white man from their hunting lands."

"Red Cloud's showed 'em a way to do it," Beckwourth
moaned. "When will they attack, Rotten Tail?"

The old chief paused a moment, whispering with chief
White Mouth to his right. "They gather close to the fort
now. Will go closer still when the leaves change. Word is
told, the attack will come before the snow flies."

"Gotta hump it on back soon, Jim," the old scout said
to Beckwourth as he shook his head sadly. "Get word to
Carrington. If trouble ain't started there a'ready."

"Damned good chance of that, Gabe. What with Sioux
coming off the Powder, the Rosebud and Big Horn for
the big fight Red Cloud promises to make of it."

"Jim, best ask Rotten Tail where his stick floats on
this," Bridger remarked. "See what the Crow will do,
push come to shove and the whole country's afire with
war."

At first the old chief shook his head, studying the faces
of his chiefs while he considered how he would answer
Beckwourth's question. When he had taken the council
pipe into his hands once more, Rotten Tail spoke, sadly.

"Our villages are small against the great Sioux gatherings," he began. "The Crow have always fought hard to hold onto what we call our home, Absaroka. Not many winters ago the Cheyenne and Sioux joined to drive us from our old hunting grounds along the Rosebud and Big Horn. Now, with this talk of war and sweeping the white man from those ancient hunting lands for good, our young men grow hot to join the fight. They want their hunting grounds back."

The mulatto shook his head emphatically. "If our young men hunger for a fight, they must join the soldiers against Sioux and Cheyenne," Beckwourth urged, "to drive them away so we may regain Absaroka land—for the Crow."

Rotten Tail wagged his head. "I wish they heard my words as well as you hear. The young men talk loud about joining the Sioux to get our lands back."

"Why would they join with their enemies to win back the land?"

The old chief gazed into the fire. When his tired, rheumy eyes finally raised to stare at Beckwourth, "The young men wish to join those who will win the war that is coming as sure as winter snows will soon cover the land. When the Sioux have killed many soldiers and driven all the rest from Indian hunting grounds, our young Crow warriors want to be on the side of the victors. No Absaroka wishes to be shamed siding with the soldiers who have lost the fight and run away."

Rotten Tail stared at the fire. "You must understand— our warriors do not want to see Crow scalps hanging bloody from Sioux lodge-poles when Red Cloud's warriors dance in victory over the soldiers."

Chapter 18

$\mathcal{T}$he Sioux hit Aubrey Pitman's wood train on its first run of the day as the wagons lumbered up the wood-road from Pine Island some four miles south and west of the fort. While the Indians' signal mirrors flashed across the timbered hillsides, the warriors down in the valley managed to kill a single civilian driver who threw his fate to the winds in trying to outrun them.

Even before the stockade sentries along the banquette heard the first shots, a picket stationed on Pilot Hill began wagging his semaphore flag. Most of the compound was out in force following the bugle call sounding the alarm, every man, woman and child watching the approach of the wood train and its escort when the wagons nosed free of the Sullivant Hills.

Henry Carrington glanced over at Ten Eyck. "Appears the men beat off the attack, Captain."

"Wait, Colonel—I'll be damned, there's a body in the back of one of those wagons," Capt. Tenedor Ten Eyck announced, taking the field glass from his good eye.

"Let me have a look."

Carrington peered into the valley, blinking, wishing his eye could pierce the morning haze. He stood on the ban-quette, a catwalk constructed atop his new headquarters building for just this purpose. It was here he had run with

Ten Eyck and adjutant Wands when the first alarm rang out.

"Perhaps you see things more clearly than I, Tenedor," he said, handing the glass to Wands. "I can't tell much of anything so far away."

"The captain's right," Wands announced as he peered into the valley. "I see a body . . . yes, it's been stripped."

Without warning, Carrington slammed a fist down into his open palm. "Damn them! I've resisted all efforts of those who want to attack the Sioux. I've restrained my officers and men from striking back—not only to finish our construction, but to show Red Cloud that we can garrison our post in peace with them. I vowed not to practice any offense against them! Yet they play me the fool!"

"Second thoughts, sir?" Wands inquired, interested.

"Anger at this point, Lieutenant," Carrington answered guardedly. A week ago Ten Eyck had informed the colonel that Carrington's young adjutant was often seen in the company of Fred Brown. And Brown clearly stood as the center of all opposition to Carrington's policies, if not Carrington himself.

"May I suggest, Colonel . . ." Wands began.

"Suggest what, Lieutenant?" Carrington snapped. "A change in policy? Vacillate? Attack the Sioux and stir up trouble for us from here clear down to Laramie?"

"Perhaps, the time's come——"

"Colonel!" Ten Eyck shouted, silencing the others. "Pilot Hill!" He pointed. "Look!"

Atop the flat ridge to the southwest christened Pilot Hill, a solitary trooper waved his semaphore again. Three times the man raised his flag high then lowered it to his right.

Ten Eyck checked his codes and announced, "That's the signal for 'small party on the Reno Road.' "

"Thank God. Not another attack." Carrington sighed,

glancing down along the wood road to check the progress of his timber train returning with its lone victim.

By now the first riders in that small party pressing toward the fort could be seen along the Montana Road. Three wagons, escorted by mounted troopers who dogged both flanks.

"Tenedor, see that the gates are opened. It appears we have some supplies arriving from Laramie."

"Colonel, Pilot Hill's signaling again. Another small party coming up from the south on the Reno Road."

"Surely there can't be another group."

"There is, Colonel," Wands said, handing the glass back to his commander.

Carrington peered into the valley. Several thousand yards behind the first three wagons, a second group rounded the base of Pilot Hill and began their descent to the crossing of the Little Piney.

"The mail escort, gentlemen. And it appears they've brought us a guest. See that wagon loaded with personal baggage and furnishings. I'd bet the ambulance in the rear holds a new replacement."

"Officer, sir?" Wands asked.

"Yes. My command's been whittled away by Omaha. Too many of my officers siphoned off. So I requested replacements."

"Fetterman?" Wands's voice rose in anticipation.

"You've heard of Fetterman?"

"Oh yes, sir. Much. Fred . . . excuse me, Captain Brown's told me much of Fetterman."

Carrington's eyes left the lieutenant's crimson face as he peered into the valley. He was watching the three groups approach when a mounted detail of soldiers clattered off the Sullivant Hills, ambling leisurely toward the fort.

Must be Bisbee's scout, Ten Eyck mulled. He loves playing the soldier, Bisbee does.

"I'm sorry to disappoint you, Lieutenant," Carrington said quietly as he turned back to Wands. "And disappoint

Fred Brown." He gave the name a certain cordial empha-
sis. "But I doubt that ambulance contains Fetterman. I
have yet to decide on calling the captain up."

Wands turned, hiding his disappointment. Carrington
noticed that Ten Eyck had watched it all—nodding at the
young lieutenant and smiling back at Carrington. Know-
ingly.

"A second casualty?" Carrington moaned, stepping off
the rough-hewn porch of his headquarters office. He had
expected only one corpse when Wands announced a civilian had been killed by the Sioux that morning along the
wood road. He combed a hand through his dark beard as
he stopped beside the riderless horse.

"Pull it back, Lieutenant," he whispered to William
Bisbee.

His order obeyed, the canvas-shelter half was drawn
back slightly.

"Who is it, Colonel?" Jack Stead asked from the shade
of the porch.

"Glover," he answered quietly. "Ridgeway Glover.
The photographer."

"We warned him," Bisbee argued. "So'd the timber
crews down at the blockhouse. Said he'd been down at
the island for two weeks. Just up and took off back here
yesterday. Alone. Paid 'em no heed when they warned
him to wait for an escort."

Donegan inched closer to the corpse. "You mind, Colonel?"

Carrington looked the Irishman over a moment. "No.
Not at all."

Seamus drew more of the canvas tarp from the body.
"They had some time to practice their devil work on poor
Glover, they did." He sighed, wagging his head.

"Found him in the middle of the road, sir," Bisbee
explained to Carrington. "Halfway out to the island."

"Locate any of his equipment?" the colonel inquired.

"Just him, " Bisbee answered with a shake of his head.

"The way you see him. Stripped and cut. Facedown in the middle of the road."

"Facedown, he was?" Seamus asked, still studying the body.

Bisbee regarded the Irishman a moment. "I said facedown."

"A shame," Donegan replied, covering the corpse. "Never saw Ridgeway Glover for a coward—the way he fought at Crazy Woman Crossing."

Jack Stead stepped down to the Irishman's side. "How you know so much about Indians?"

"Why ask me that?" His gray eyes narrowed.

"Find it strange that you'd know something like that," Jack began. "Indians will lay an enemy facedown . . . to show he was a coward. Care to tell me how you'd know that?"

"Didn't." He answered it short and flat. "Simple as that. Learning about Injins from an old trapper. But more than that, I figure the savage mind isn't that different the world over. In the land of my birth, ancient Celts would've done the same, I suppose. Important thing is," Seamus strode around the horse, gazing at Carrington, "Ridgeway Glover wasn't a coward. Not the way he fought in the trenches at Crazy Woman Crossing. Every bit a man as any of us there that day."

"I'll vouch for that, sir," Wands replied.

"Lieutenant Bisbee, see that Glover is prepared for burial," Carrington instructed, "then bring me his personal effects. I'll ship them East. Next of kin."

"A sad thing," a new voice said, "this civilian getting himself killed this way."

Carrington wheeled to find himself gazing into the eyes of a stranger dressed in a second lieutenant's uniform, complete with insignia identifying him as an officer of the 2nd Battalion, 18th Infantry. "Who have I the pleasure——"

"Grummond, sir." He saluted snappily. With a smile

flashing beneath his dark, bushy and very droopy mustache. "George Washington Grummond."

Carrington returned the salute. Then presented his hand. "Good to meet you at last, Mr. Grummond. Heard much about you." He waved Bisbee's detail to stables before motioning the new lieutenant up the headquarters steps. "Please. Let's go in and get acquainted."

Seamus turned to watch Bisbee's detail plod away as the pair disappeared through Carrington's pine-plank door. Every horse but the one led across the parade toward the hospital with its grisly burden.

"Mr. Donegan?"

Seamus turned at Jack Stead's familiar English seaman's accent. The young, buckskinned scout came down the steps from the headquarters' porch.

"You must be the one Bridger said he'd take to the Crow camp. He mentioned your fight of it at the Crazy Woman as well."

"An interesting journey, both were. Like the old man, I do. Sorry he's staying up at Fort C.F. Smith after visiting the Crow. He wouldn't say, but I suspect his rheumatiz was acting up. Me, I come on down straight-off."

"Seems he took a shine to you, Mr. Donegan. Even told me you were trying to make some sense of the Indian's code."

"Their signal mirrors? I've been trying, with no luck as yet."

Jack Stead fell silent a moment as he watched the Irishman gazing after the riderless horse plodding toward the infirmary. "You knew him?"

"Glover?" Donegan turned. "No. Not really. We rode up from Laramie together. A quiet man." Seamus fell silent. Either the wind whipping its way across the dusty parade, or perhaps something altogether different turned the Irishman's eyes moist.

"Name's Jack Stead." The scout presented his hand.

"Yes, I know," Donegan's voice boomed thick and low. "Pleased, Mr. Stead."

"Besides being a man who knows something of the Indian's ways, Seamus Donegan appears to be a man of some sentiment."

Donegan appraised the scout for a moment. "I might be, that. Who might be asking such a question of me?"

"A man who respects Jim Bridger more than any other. And when Jim Bridger tells me he's taken a liking to an Irishman name of Donegan—that's says a lot in my book. But when I see you troubled by another man's death, out in this land where so many are bound to die—and soon—well, Mr. Donegan, that tells me even more of the man you are."

Donegan smiled. "You're for certain a cully Englishman, aren't you?"

"Born outside Liverpool. But I left British ways behind long ago."

"Never met an Englishman I liked, Jack Stead."

"Not asking you to like me, Seamus Donegan. Besides, I'm no more English now than you are. We're free men. On the boot in this wild and savage land."

"Free men, eh?" Donegan smiled, his rows of teeth gleaming in the sun. "We're Americans, I take it?"

"Nawww," and Jack shook his head. "Men like us belong to no country. These soldiers—now, they're the Americans. And the Sioux—they have their homeland too. But you and me are a breed apart. We've no home but what we make for ourselves. Cast about as the loners in the world, Seamus Donegan."

The Irishman clapped a big paw across Stead's back. "C'mon, me cully friend." Smiling, he yanked Jack along at his side. "I've got me a turrible thirst and I hear the sutler's opened his barrel for the day. There's nothing that cuts the lonely of this dangerous place like drinking with a new friend."

"My Margaret will be fluttering around your Frances soon as she learns you're expecting a child, Lieutenant." Carrington showed Grummond a chair.

"She dreaded the loneliness of frontier duty, yet followed. I believe Frances understands that it's here that my career will be made," George Grummond replied.

"Yes. Many careers will be forged here in the West," Carrington agreed, his eyes scanning the papers Grummond handed him. "Forged in sweat and toil, blood and bone."

"We watched your timber train pull in just before we drove through the gates. Unfortunately, Frances saw the naked body of that poor worker. Hacked to——"

"I apologize your wife had to view such a scene, especially in light of her condition."

"She's strong, sir. Good family stock. I'm just afraid it won't be her last shock as an army wife."

Carrington looked up. "That's something I'm sure we could all put a bet on, Lieutenant. Well, in reading over your record, I'm most impressed! I asked for experienced, proven officers—and Omaha actually sent me one. You served with a Michigan volunteer infantry regiment. Was Frances a childhood sweetheart?"

"No, sir. We met during the war. A daughter of the South. Tennessee, born and bred. A genteel slip of a girl, Colonel."

"The breeding I've heard so much about, no doubt."

"We exchanged vows after the war. Her family wouldn't hear of marriage while they waged their cause against the Union. The North won its war. And I my bride."

"You sound like a romantic, Lieutenant."

"We both are, sir. Incurably romantic."

"Good. I see that following the war you applied for a regular commission, which you were awarded because of your brilliant war record. You were breveted Lieutenant Colonel of your regiment for heroism in face of the enemy."

The lieutenant's eyes found the floor. While proud of his war record, George Washington Grummond still found himself embarrassed.

"Come now. No need for modesty, young man. This is a record to be admired. You're just what your colonel ordered! This has become a splendid day . . . despite the deaths." Carrington turned back to his desk and swept up some other papers. He looked at Grummond. "You arrive to join my staff. And a contract commissary train from Laramie pulls in just before you with sixty-thousand rounds of rifle ammunition. Why, I had each soldier down to his last three rounds! We've been virtually cut off by the hostiles for weeks now, Lieutenant."

"They've laid siege to you, sir?"

Carrington nodded, blinking. "We're surrounded . . . in the midst of this great wilderness. Now, after all this time, I finally receive the ammunition I've requested!"

"Glad to hear of its arrival, sir."

"So, let's see what this letter from General Sherman has to say, shall we?" He spread the foolscap open and began to read.

"He writes from Laramie. Where he visited the end of last month. August. On his tour of western posts. He goes on to say:

"I shall instruct General Cooke to reinforce his force at this post so that expeditions in sufficient strength can go out to punish the Indians. We want to avoid a general Indian war . . .

"I'm glad as hell to have Sherman say that!" Carrington gushed.

". . . as long as possible, until we get the new army further advanced in recruiting."

Grummond cleared his throat. "Seems they're having a hell of a time getting the regiments rebuilt after the war, sir. What with the volunteers being mustered out and so many troops ordered South on reconstruction duty. It

amazes me that the army has any soldiers to send west to
fight Red Cloud at all, Colonel."

"Let's just hope we don't have an all-out fight with
Red Cloud, Lieutenant. It appears the army's not ready
to give me what I'd need to fight that war I'm afraid is
coming. Never enough soldiers. A dire shortage of good
officers like yourself. And they're stingy with the ammunition. I'll never . . . but Sherman goes on:

> "The Indians seem to oppose the opening of the new
> road, but that must stimulate us to its protection, and
> you may rest assured that you will be supported all that
> is possible . . .

"Perhaps Sherman can nudge General Cooke to support me a bit more ably, Lieutenant. All Omaha can do is
chastise me for not getting my mail to them on time. I
beg for men and weapons. While Cooke demands his
mail!

> ". . . We must try and distinguish friendly from hos-
> tile and kill the latter, but if you or any other command-
> ing officer strike a blow, I will approve, for it seems
> impossible to tell the true from the false."

Carrington fell silent, contemplative as he wordlessly
reread the last line. "Isn't that the truth?" he asked
aloud, his eyes glued to the page. "Here we are, in the
middle of this wild country—completely surrounded, and
virtually cut off from the outside world by Red Cloud's
warriors—and Sherman tells me I'll find it hard to tell
the true Indian from the false. Little does he know I've
found my real problem telling my true friend and officer
from the false."

Chapter 19

$\mathcal{H}$enry Carrington hunched over his desk far into the night. Among the letters the dispatch rider carried up from Laramie he found one from Cooke, once again chastising Carrington for his mail getting to Omaha late. Nothing said about reinforcements. No mention of ammunition forthcoming. Instead, Cooke scolded him about the many newspaper accounts reporting civilian murders along the Montana Road.

Repeatedly reminding Carrington that as commander of the Mountain District, he was answerable for the administration of his duties. Reports. Dispatches. Rosters.

When Henry shuffled to the sheet-iron stove to warm his mug of coffee from the battered pot Wands had left bubbling, he sensed the draft sneaking in around the plank door. As he peered out the smoky window, autumn's first snowfall whipped and skipped across the dark parade. *It will be a long, long winter, I'm afraid.*

Sipping at the scalding coffee, Carrington scanned his report to Cooke, recognizing for the first time that pent-up intensity evident in his cramped scrawl as it raced across the pages.

Mail has arrived. I send directly back. Lt. Gen. Sherman wrote me from Laramie to endeavor to keep you more frequently advised. I am doing all I can with my broken-

down and famished horses, not having received a pound of corn yet . . .

. . . No women or children have been captured or injured by Indians in this district since I entered it . . .

. . . While more troops are needed, I can say (and I am in the very heart of the hostile district) that most of the newspaper reports are gross exaggerations. I gather and furnish you, as requested, all the bad news, neither coloring nor disguising facts . . .

. . . contract commissary arrived this date from Laramie. 60,000 rounds of badly needed ammunition. From same civilian contractor I was able to purchase a few tons of some badly-needed corn for our weakening stock. Have not received the promised shipment of grain . . .

. . . not near enough ammunition. I ought to have, if possible, a hundred thousand more, and from Laramie more ammunition for my 12-pound field howitzers . . .

. . . Red Cloud is known to command the parties now immediately engaged . . . they are determined to burn the country, cut off supplies, and hamper every movement . . .

. . . those hostile parties now effectively sealing off the fort and placing us under a state of siege have made effective use of small mirrors for communication in their constant harassment . . .

. . . chief of scouts Bridger has sent word through dispatch rider from Fort C.F. Smith. In talks with Crows, Bridger informed of more than five hundred lodges of Sioux camped on Tongue River. All very hostile, and some even armed with latest rifles. He heard reports of a renegade white man among the Arapahos. Additionally, hears many reports of other "squawmen" and Confederate soldiers who have joined forces with hostiles to drive other miners and all white men from the Montana gold country . . .

. . . in the midst of my sad report, this bit of happy news. Near sundown a brigade of miners arrived, down from the north. Had left the Montana fields to search new

finds in the Big Horns. They were repeatedly attacked en
route. Two men killed yesterday on the Tongue. Their
elected leader, one Wm. Bailey, a former scout & prospec-
tor in this region for 17 years. I immediately hired more
than forty men of Bailey's group—all crack shots and
frontiersmen, cool under fire. Capt. Brown will have no
trouble finding work for these men, who will receive cav-
alry pay as you suggested in your 11 August telegram.
Miners put the matter to a vote and have elected to stay the
winter. I now have secured the equivalent of an armed and
mounted cavalry regiment!

   . . . with Ten Eyck's arms inspection this date, I am
informed of their sad condition and want of proper arms to
prosecute our aims in the Mountain District. Many
Springfields unserviceable. Some men not armed at all,
because of thefts by deserters and others. Badly need pis-
tols and carbines, as rifles no good for mounted men . . .

"Thank you, Tenedor," Carrington said. "That . . .
that'll be all."

Carrington watched Ten Eyck lick a tongue across his
chapped lips. He's hungover again, Henry thought to
himself as the captain turned to go. *He drinks more and*
more every day. And sleeps when he's not drinking. Yet
Brown drinks two bottles to Tenedor's one. And works on
—early each morning to late at night. Damn Kinney's
alcohol anyway! Were it that none of them drank . . .

Three days had passed since Grummond's arrival. *Al-*
ready, George sides with the Brown clique. Damn them
all!

Without purpose his eyes swept over the lazy scrawl of
Ten Eyck's report on the skirmish at the Big Piney Crossing yesterday morning.

Can you really blame the man, Henry? he asked himself.

Forced to surrender his unit twice during that bloody
war down south, Ten Eyck had been thrown in Libby

Prison by the rebels after Chickamauga—where the men who survived limped out with one affliction or another.

Ten Eyck's chronic diarrhea and hemorrhoids . . . the blasted man drinks to forget more than memories. Each of us has his own private pain. . . .

Carrington glanced at the calendar. The twentieth of September already. The first snow come and gone. *Levi Carter's mowing crews forced to cease cuttings. Not only melting snow and rain hampering their labors, but the Sioux harass like a tormenting plague. Worse still, winter stares us in the face . . . yet I can't speed the men to hurry against the advancing season. Their officers oppose me . . . more openly every day.*

Is there sufficient reason to oppose me? Lord knows the Indians aren't helping bring peace to the road.

"Bring Fetterman up," Carrington muttered, peering out his smoky window. "That's all I hear. On the parade. At mess. During retreat each night. Bring . . . Fetterman up."

If only to rally them 'round me once more, I would—— Carrington shook his head. Refusing the inevitable still. *If need be, I'll stand alone.*

Knowing he stood alone already.

His right hand, Ten Eyck, had sunk to a drunken mediocrity. His closest adviser, Bridger, gone for weeks and not expected back until October. Generals Sherman, Cooke, and Hazen recommending stern measures: *Chastise them! they say. Strike back at the red hand that hampers your own!*

Carrington swilled at the last of the coffee grown cold in his cup while he peered through the frosty pane. Welcoming the warmth beside the sheet-iron stove. With a fresh cup, he brooded over the troubling report of another ambush on Carter's hay operations just hours ago. Across Peno Creek in the Goose Creek Flats, a large warparty of Sioux and Arapaho had discovered the mowers and their guard under command of Lt. Winfield Scott Matson. The lieutenant and his civilian workers had themselves pinned down for the better part of three days, until Carrington had learned of their predicament and ordered out a relief column from the fort. Carter's men returned with their mowers and what empty hay wagons the Indians hadn't burned. Four wounded. Three more bodies stacked in one of the bouncing carts.

He recalled what Quartermaster Brown had argued when word spread of this recent attack on a hay party. "We won't find a single civilian who'll work out of sight of the fort now! For the love of God, Colonel—you've got to strike back now, and strike fast. Wring one, just one victory from all this defeat and despair! Be something more than a . . . damned garrison officer!"

Still, Henry steadfastly refused to mount an expedition against the Sioux. Forced to watch his civilian workers whittled down by the hostiles.

Yet, that ambush troubles me less than Matson's report that he encountered a white man during the battle. A white man, dressed in warrior's clothing!

If what Bridger reports is true—that white men are joining Red Cloud's hostiles—it would confirm Matson's startling confrontation during the skirmish. He told me the white man was missing the fingers of one hand!

Pain needled through Henry's head. Dreading the walk over to the hospital, begging a powder from Surgeon Horton. *Even he's calling to have Fetterman reassigned to my post. Where are those——*

Carrington located the notes Phisterer had transcribed almost two months earlier, during Henry's questioning of Jack Stead concerning the mood of the Cheyenne in the area. *I was right. Stead did mention a renegade. Missing four fingers on one hand. The one called Captain North.*

Closing his eyes for several moments, Henry fought the pain pricking his skull. *We still remain vulnerable on two fronts—down in the timber cuttings, where the men work in scattered groups . . . and atop Pilot Hill itself. Where the pickets can only warn us of their own imminent danger.*

His head nestled atop his forearm, Henry waited for the pain to pass. Brooding on the man he had ordered to remain behind at Fort Sedgwick when the regiment marched north to Indian country.

Damn him! He's everything I'd ever hoped to be. Born in Garrison—son of an old army officer. Inbred with that singular instinct and ambition of a born soldier. A graduate of West Point . . . while I was too sickly for acceptance. The handsome devil even has a reputation for gentlemanly manners. Everything . . . I ever wanted——

The cold began to creep along his legs, and his fingers grew chilled.

The fire's died out.

Then opened his eyes. Removed a sheet of paper from a drawer. For a moment he stared at its ivory purity. Then dipped his pen and wrote:

20 September, 1866.

Henry suddenly froze the pen over the page, his mind brooding on dark thoughts. Remembering the stories he heard repeated so many times on their march west. Those tales of his very own beloved 18th Infantry in battle . . . the siege of Fredericksburg . . . later their siege of Atlanta. He shuddered again. Recalling how it was said Fetterman and Brown maintained control over the 2nd Battalion during those fateful days with Sherman, marching to the sea. Though time and again Henry had heard of such rumors on other units during the war, it had proved something altogether different when he overheard reports of his own officers maintaining their control of the battalion by . . .

Not only shooting deserters, but shooting cowards! Men who simply——

Carrington shook his head. *To shoot a man simply because he's nowhere near as rash nor foolhardy as Brown. Simply because Brown believes any man not ready to dash into the jaws of death is a patent coward.*

Carrington shuddered, finally scratching feverishly at

the paper. Sweating as he thought on men who would
murder their fellow soldiers.

His breathing hard. His heart pounding. Muscles
tensed, knotted. Afraid of admitting his private fears to
anyone.

When he had finished, Carrington folded the page and
stuffed it into an envelope upon which he printed:

Colonel Henry E. Maynadier
Fort Laramie
Territory of Dakota.

He returned to the window, watching the snow melt on
the frosty windowsill where his breath collected and froze
in patterns of glazed sugar.

Carrington wondered if he had done the right thing,
ordering up Capt. William J. Fetterman.

Chapter 20

*D*amn you, Carrington! Fred Brown seethed to himself. Struggling to control his rage. "Don't you see them for what they are?" he demanded.

"Explain yourself," Carrington replied.

Brown studied the faces of the others crowded in Carrington's small office. His heart pounded, fired by anger. By his humiliation before the Sioux warriors his detachment had chased off Pilot Hill less than an hour ago. And exasperation that no one saw Carrington for what he was. *An incompetent, bumbling coward unfit for command.*

"We came upon that band of Cheyenne while they were parleying with the escaping Sioux I was following, Colonel."

"Weren't parleying at all, Brown," Jack Stead advised, his arms crossed, balanced on the balls of his feet. "Two Moons tells me they came from Black Horse's camp in the mountains. Just nine old warriors, Colonel. And a squaw. They don't own enough belongings to sag that travois being pulled by a skinny pony. They've come to ask Black Horse's friend, the soldier chief, if he'll allow them to hunt in the valley of the Tongue this autumn. They're poor."

"Bastards're in league with the Sioux who've run off my cattle! They get a few more almost every day!" Brown hollered.

"Two Moons's Cheyenne bumped into the Sioux, who were running from the captain here." Stead addressed Carrington, but he kept his eyes on Brown. "Some of them Sioux were the same warriors who beat the Cheyenne chiefs in French Pete's camp, the night before the Sioux killed the trader and his teamsters."

"So what's this got to do with that soldier shot down at the Pinery today?" Carrington asked.

"He was shot by Sioux, Colonel. Not Cheyenne. When the fleeing Sioux rode up on Two Moons's bunch in the middle of the trail this afternoon, they asked the Cheyenne where they were headed. Two Moons told the young warriors that they were coming to the fort. That got the Cheyenne another beating. Those Sioux had to be pretty worked up—scalping that soldier down with the timber crews. Then rushing your pickets on Pilot Hill. All that effort for one poor scalp."

"One poor scalp!" Brown shrieked. "Private Smith was scalped and left for dead. By the grace of God and that brave soldier's guts—he crawled for help." He pointed out the door to the busy parade. "Colonel, you have no idea what's going on out there right now. Those soldiers are pretty worked up themselves . . . seeing one of their own brought in here butchered like that. Blood and all. Smith's scalp in tatters 'round his face. Those broken arrow shafts in his back——"

"We're all aware of the seriousness of our predicament here, Captain Brown." Carrington tried saying it calmly. "Every man feels the same sense of desperation . . . that sense of utter isolation, under siege here——"

"Colonel," Brown interrupted, lunging forward, "the men don't just feel utter isolation—every one of them feels utter desolation that you won't strike back while we are picked off . . . one by one . . . day by day. Until you get the balls to send two companies out there to destroy those red bastards!"

"Captain!" Carrington shouted more loudly than he had wanted. "Unlike you and the rest of those who want me to delay the building of this post to send a punitive force against the Sioux. Unlike all of you, I have two enemies. While we both are cursed with the Sioux as enemies, I have another—perhaps even more formidable —enemy."

Brown fumed, chewing on his lower lip, waiting. "Just who the hell is that more formidable enemy? Me?"

The colonel shook his head. "As much as you might like to flatter yourself, Captain, you are not my most formidable enemy. Instead, the enemy I fear most at this time is winter itself."

"W-Winter?" Brown squeaked in disbelief.

"Winter, Captain. Unless I use every available man and every hour of daylight left us, this post will not be secured before winter comes to this land."

"B-But . . . your problems getting this post built has nothing to do with those Cheyenne out there . . . going free after they've scalped and maimed——"

"Jack? Today's attack doesn't have anything to do with the Cheyenne, does it?" Carrington had turned to his scout, his voice growing desperate.

"It sure as hell does have everything to do with those Cheyenne!" Brown roared, lunging toe to toe with Carrington. "I saw the Sioux talking with your beloved Cheyenne, Colonel."

Stead stuck his thumbs in his belt. "Like I said, Captain Brown, Two Moons's people were getting a beating when you rode up. You're the only reason the Sioux skedaddled and left the Cheyenne be."

"Spies!" Brown roared. "Those Cheyenne you've just given bacon and coffee to—they're spies! You've even let them camp down on the Big Piney, like they were guests of ours. And tomorrow you gave them permission to ride on to the Tongue River to hunt for the season. They're spies, Carrington! Headed to Red Cloud's camp on the Tongue!"

"Jack?" Carrington appealed to his scout.

"They're Black Horse's chiefs. Most of 'em old men,

Colonel. A handful of 'em even have your letter of good conduct you passed out when they were here last. When they showed your pass to Captain Brown here, he threw it in the dirt on the road, spat on it, and then had the gall to have his soldiers search 'em for weapons."

"Damn right I did!" Brown whirled on the scout. "I wasn't about to let them sneak a weapon into this stockade."

"Most of 'em are poor, ill-fed, old men. Looking for a place to hunt," Stead protested.

"Spies, I tell you. You'll see. Damn their red hearts, anyway! If Indians aren't sneaking around behind your back, the red bastards are running away from a fight. Won't stand up to you like a man! And that bunch of Cheyennes—they're worse than the rest. Sniveling cowards, afraid to look me in the eye when I surrounded them. Sorry now I didn't order my men to finish them off."

"That would've been more than folly, Captain. Some poor judgment," Carrington said quietly.

He's a fine one to be talking about poor judgment, Brown fumed. "Been better for the red bastards in the long run," he growled, then flung an arm toward the parade outside the colonel's office. "None of you have the slightest idea what's going on out there among those soldiers. They've seen what Stead's Cheyennes done to Private Smith. Almost every day it's another poor soldier butchered——"

"Wasn't those Cheyenne, you pigheaded fool!" Stead roared.

"Maybe it wasn't," Brown answered quietly. Intense. "But, out there, it doesn't really make a difference right now. Lotta soldiers got blood in their eye. So, Mr. Stead, it really doesn't matter now who scalped Private Smith!"

"They hacked his damned scalp off and he didn't even whimper!" one of the civilian woodcutters grumbled at the pinewood bar. He banged his empty cup down loudly.

Judge Jefferson T. Kinney poured him a stout pull, then placed another mark beside the man's name in his ledger. A short, thick man with a large head that gave him a top-heavy appearance, Kinney's flat nose topped a sensual, feminine mouth. A good evening for business—two dozen soldiers and civilian workers jostling each other at his bar or squatting on stools and chairs, eating the judge's crackers and grumbling over the afternoon's Indian attack.

"Smith ain't giving up. Not Patrick," an old soldier said, taking up the chorus. "Just come back from the hospital where that surgeon don't figure he'll last to morning."

"Gawd-awful way for a man to die," a third whined. "Your scalped ripped off afore your eyes. Laying there—not making a damned peep of it!"

Donegan sat alone in the corner nursing a cup of rye. Moments ago Captain Brown had strolled in, muttering and growling "Carrington this" and "Jack Stead that." With a pale, puffy hand, Kinney poured the captain a tall one. On the judge. Seamus sensed the sutler wanted to warm things up for the evening—Kinney's marble eyes twinkling mischievously above the fleshy pouches. Donegan figured the judge for a man who loved to stir things up then watch them come to a boil—all from a safe distance.

Across the room sat Reverend White, alone at a tiny table, scratching at his notes or thumbing through his grease-stained Bible. Thursday night. And already preparing his spiritual message for Sunday service. He sipped his coffee, acknowledging Donegan over the lip of his cup before his gray head bent over God's word once more.

"But Private Smith's only one," Kinney said, his tone dripping with sarcasm within his gray-flecked goat's whiskers.

"What?" a teamster shrieked, not realizing he'd been baited. "Damn you any——"

Kinney threw up a hand. "That's right . . . just one!" He flung a plump, oratorical finger at the ceiling. "How many will it be tomorrow?"

"He's right!"

"Judge got a proper head on his shoulders!"

"How many?" Kinney repeated. "Two? Three the day after? What next week?"

"By damned!" roared the woodcutter, slamming his big hand down on the bar. "Enough is enough!"

"We have nothing to say about it," Brown grumbled into his whiskey. Though he whispered, the entire room fell quiet as he spoke.

"By Gawd, it's high time we had something to say about——"

"You don't. I don't." Brown turned slowly, his elbows sliding back, resting on the bar, the cup sloshing at his belly. "The red bastards are working themselves up into a killing frenzy."

The others nodded, pressed forward. This was going to be good. If it wasn't Kinney stoking them up, then Brown could put on his fire-breathing speech. Some muttered between them, then studied the captain, eager for the show.

"What we've seen—them hitting my cattle herd, running off horses, burning the hay wagons—all of it . . . one thing's for certain: they're working themselves up for something big!"

"It's just like he says!" someone rumbled.

"Who's gonna be next?"

"Each attack gets worse." Brown pointed his cup out at the crowd. "More of them bastards hit us every day. More of us get scalped."

"Damn right!"

"So!" Brown roared, tossing whiskey down his throat. "When do we strike back?"

"High time we fight!" the teamster shouted. A friend pounded him on the back.

"You've seen the blankets waving every time they attack," Brown kept kneading his audience. "Can't miss all those mirrors they flash from every hill!"

"Passing the word!"

"Working up to something big, like the captain says!"

"Now they sent some among our number, right, Captain?" Kinney inquired, watching Brown turn slowly. The judge refilled the captain's cup and smiled, nodding his big head with satisfaction atop a wattled turkey-neck.

"That's right," Brown answered. "Stead and the colonel think those Cheyenne just harmless old men. Wanting to hunt buffalo up on the Tongue. But Red Cloud's camped on the Tongue. Sitting pretty. Waiting for his spies to come riding back from our fort!"

"Red bastards!" the woodcutter cried. "Killed Smith!"

"We don't know that, Frank!" another argued as loudly.

"What you mean?" Frank roared back. "A Injun's a Injun. No difference."

"He's right!" a soldier shouted at the bar. "I rode with Captain Brown this afternoon. We saw them Cheyenne with our own eyes . . . watched 'em talking with the Sioux. Ain't that right, Captain?"

Brown nodded. "Completely right."

"They was in on it. I told you!" the wood chopper shouted. "Told you they was the one's got Smith!"

"Where'r they?" a teamster growled.

"Colonel said they could camp down on the Lil' Piney. 'Cross from the sawmill."

"I say we settle the score," Frank hollered, his face mottled with fire. "Ten of them bastards for what they done to Smith!"

"I don't figure it," Frank's friend moaned. "How they scalped Smith . . . coming from the south where the captain's group seen 'em?"

"Red's red, far as I'm concerned," Kinney replied, his oath filling the cabin.

"Judge's right," Brown agreed. "Not a Injun I know of doesn't want to fry any white man's gut . . . he had the chance."

"He's right!"

"Both of 'em right!"

"They're sitting down there by the mill crossing—right now." Brown swiped a hand across his lips, taking the thick beads of whiskey with it. "Probably laughing at Colonel Carrington himself right now. Laughing at us!"

"By Gawd! I'd give those red devils something to laugh at!" the woodcutter shrieked, waving a thick fist.

"They're Cheyenne, though," the quiet civilian among them whined in vain. "It's Sioux causing all the trouble, killing——"

"Red's red, like I said before, son," Kinney said, jumping into the fray again. "An Injun's like a leopard. Won't ever change his spots."

"They're same as that murderin' Red Cloud and his bunch!"

"Colonel give 'em a place to stay the night!"

"Coffee and bacon as well."

"Bacon? When we get moldy sowbelly for breakfast. And there ain't enough coffee to fill a working man's gut each morning?"

"Made them Cheyenne beggars feel right to home!"

"Them as drove off the cattle?"

"Sacked the hay mowers!"

"Set fire to the sawmill too!"

". . . scalp of a honest white man!"

". . . red is red!"

". . . we're prisoners here!"

"That's right," Brown replied. "Held prisoner here if we do nothing about it." His dark eyes glowered at the Irishman in the corner for the first time. He must have wondered why the big, bearded stranger had not joined in the mob's call.

"And I know just what to do!" Frank the woodcutter pulled the big Walker Colt revolver from his waistband. The blued steel glimmered like dark water in the yellow light of a half-dozen lamps. The room fell quiet.

Donegan glanced over at White. The reverend clenched his Bible, eyes studying the growing ugliness. Seamus figured White understood as well as he what was coming to a boil.

Another teamster drew his pistol, held it aloft. "No time better'n now to burn me an Injun. I'd like to watch 'em cook slow for all they done." He guzzled the last drops in his cup.

"No!" Kinney cried out. He watched all of them turn his way. Disbelief colored their faces. Now that he had their silence, he almost whispered, "You can't go now. Not even dark yet, boys. Wait till the cover of night." It was a dangerous gamble, betting the mob would hold its grim resolve.

"He's right!"

"When?"

"After tattoo!" another suggested.

"Yeah! We'll go down then."

"Who's gonna do it?"

"Any of us!"

"Tell the others!" a soldier cried out. "Pass the word. Go down together."

"Colonel could hang a handful of us," an old corporal hollered. "He can't hang the whole bloody regiment!"

"Wait till tattoo—after bed check."

"Meet at the water-gate . . . above the sawmill."

"Who's gonna get a key to the damned gate, let us out?"

"Fellas." Judge Kinney held up a pink hand for silence, then pointed out the officer standing at the bar, slowly sipping his whiskey and glaring at the silent Irishman in the corner. "Any damn fool knows Captain Brown's got a key to his own gate!"

Chapter 21

Reverend White shivered as the last notes of tattoo echoed from the stockade walls. He was cold. And too old for a stunt like this. Yet something drove him to these shadows across from the log barracks. Watching lamps twinkle out, one by one. *Those soldier boys never go to sleep this quick. Something's afoot for certain.*

The reverend waited. Listening. His eyes long ago grown accustomed to the darkness. Shivering, wondering if he should've grabbed the Irishman to come along. Wishing he had as the first shadow flitted along a barrack wall. Then a second. Scurrying low, crouched over. Then more.

Like damned rats. A whole nest of 'em.

More than two hours had passed since he closed the Bible around his crumpled sermon. Angry with himself now for waiting to be sure.

Should've gone to the colonel earlier. Have to be quick about it now. And careful.

"Private Sample." Carrington turned to his orderly spare moments later. "Hurry to Captain Ten Eyck. Have him meet me here, with the Officer of the Day and the Sergeant of the Guard. The sergeant needs a half-dozen men."

Reverend White watched Sample slip out the door.

The minister had awakened the orderly by rapping on Carrington's door. Getting here by staying to the shadows, hugging the dark places. "Just got too quiet, Colonel," the reverend explained.

"I believe you," Carrington muttered, like a man disbelieving. "But, I must . . . get dressed now."

"Quickly, Colonel."

"Yes. There's no time to waste."

By the time Carrington emerged from his private rooms, buckling a pistol at his waist, Ten Eyck and Lieutenant Bradley swept into the office.

"Who the devil's attacking the Cheyennes down at the mill?" Ten Eyck demanded, his tongue thick with whiskey and his eyes gummy with sleep.

"I'll need you to post a guard around the Cheyenne camp, Lieutenant." Carrington ignored Tenedor for the moment. "You have six men?"

"Yes, sir," he answered. "Four waiting outside. The other two I sent off to——"

"Lieutenant!" A young private burst into the room. "F company . . . the barracks . . . they're gone!"

"Captain." Carrington turned on Ten Eyck, "Let's pray we're not too late."

"By all means, Colonel." Ten Eyck whirled, flinging his arms and shooing soldiers out the door.

"You coming along, Reverend?" Carrington asked as the troopers scurried into the night like starlings.

"Wouldn't miss a prayer meeting like this for the life of me, Colonel."

"What're we waiting for?" the big teamster growled, his pistol weaving, muzzle pointing here then there at the nine old Cheyenne close around their small fire.

"Not a gawddamned thing!" Frank the woodcutter snarled, leveling his own pistol at Two Moons.

From the moment these white men had crossed the creek to surround their little camp, the Cheyenne hadn't budged. Only the old eyes swept round, from white face to white face illuminated in the copper firelight. Better than ten-times-ten, whitemen stacked like cordwood, pressing in on the fire-ring to watch. To witness another man's bravery. To hang back in the anonymous darkness and watch.

Every now and then flames jumped restlessly along a limb. A soft, yellow glow shimmering off the unmoving copper faces. Even the old squaw sat silent, motionless. No longer did she stir the coffee she'd been boiling in the old kettle. A gift from the soldier chief—a treat for his friends, the Cheyenne. Until these white men had poured out of the darkness.

"Well, we gonna take care of business?" someone shouted.

"Let's do what we come for!" another yelled from the ring.

The ringleaders fidgeted. Frank spun the cylinder on his Walker. Once round, hammer clicking back on each chamber. Somehow, he sensed the fire in the mob had flickered and gone out. Not as warm as up at the sutler's.

"Hey, Judge!" he hollered. "We got the bastards now."

"That's right," Kinney sang, a bit hollow. No grand oration. His lower lip hung out like a slice of raw calf's liver—pouting. "Look at 'em. You ever see a more guilty bunch than this?"

"Never!" Frank tried to whip them up again the way they had snarled and foamed for blood back at Kinney's place. "I'll take the first one. Who want's another?"

"I'll take that fat one there!" a teamster barked. "Like to see him squirm when I shoot his balls off first. Watch him beg for his life."

"Smith didn't get no chance to beg for his life!"

"This'uns for Smith!" someone across the fire hollered.

"For all the rest they murdered!"

Frank spat into the fire. "It's time," he muttered, striding right over the low flames until he stood before Two Moons, jerked the Walker down, and pressed the muzzle to the old Indian's head.

"That'll be far enough, mister!"

Frank spun with the others at the voice clawing out of the darkness.

"What you're about to do is murder."

The big woodcutter's eyes blinked as he watched Jack Stead stroll into the firelight. He saw the scout carried a pistol. Stuffed in his belt.

"You're a brave man, aincha?" Frank challenged.

"Sorry, can't say the same for you." Jack strode full into the firelight, stopping before the woodcutter. "Shoot an old, unarmed Indian."

"Murderer—what he is!"

"This old man didn't scalp that soldier today." Stead pointed at Two Moons.

"Others say differ'nt."

Stead gazed round the circle. "I can see. Lots of 'em. Ninety to nine doesn't sound like fair odds to me."

"What kind of odds did they give the soldier today?" Kinney puffed into the circle beside Frank.

"These Cheyenne weren't anywhere near Pine Island today." Stead measured the crowd, listening to the muttering voices all around him. The slow, sliding of bootsoles on sand. He was surrounded too.

"Odds, you ask?" he flung his voice over the group, ready to see what the mob was made of. "Funny that cowardly dogs always travel in packs . . . like you, Frank."

The woodcutter slashed with the Walker, catching Jack across the cheek. Stead stumbled backward, falling against two of the mob. They heaved him out of their arms. Dazed, Jack sank to his knees in the sand.

"He's no better'n these red bastards!" someone hollered.

"I damn well know that!" Frank replied. "Squaw-man. That's what he is. Same mongrel filth as these redskins!"

"Kill Stead!"

"Yeah, do him first! Injun-lover!"

Frank spat a stream of tobacco into the small fire.

"Stead's got him a Injun wife, Judge. Bet this bastard's been feeding the red niggers all kinds of information on the fort."

"Could very well be," Kinney chimed in.

"I said, let's kill 'im!" someone hollered.

"Why not?" Frank growled in agreement, looking over at Kinney. "Judge?"

"Be my guest, sir," Kinney answered. "Stead had no business here to begin with. I figure a man always gets the judgment he deserves."

"My sentiments exactly." Frank lowered the Walker muzzle, pressing it against the scout's temple. "Why, he ain't even American."

"Kill 'im!"

"Shoot the son——"

A shot rang out from the hillside above them. Frank yelped, spinning, the Walker flung into the sand. He gripped his bleeding arm. A loud voice hurled down on the mob like a boulder from above.

"I'll shoot the next bleeming fool who so much as pulls his weapon!"

"And I'll put the rest in the guardhouse!" a second voice answered, this one even closer. On the sandbar.

The mob ring parted in four places. A half-dozen armed troopers stomped out of the night, holding their carbines on their fellow soldiers and civilians. Through the final crevice strode Carrington and Ten Eyck, following the sergeant who had threatened arrest.

"I believe I've got more here'n I can handle, Captain. Guardhouse won't hold 'em all." He waited a moment, watching the men shuffle their feet as one of his pickets pulled Stead to his feet. "What say I just arrest ringleaders? Charge 'em on attempted murder. Send 'em down to Laramie to hang——"

"We ain't gonna hang!" someone shrieked.

"Nobody got hurt!" another voice defended.

"It were Brown's and the judge's doin'! Not ours."

The crowd surged against itself. A few began backing away, inching across the pebbled creek-bottom.

"Halt, soldier!" the sergeant ordered. "Identify yourselves!"

That was all it took. The rest bolted like a flushed covey of blue hens. Crashing across the creek, stampeding past Gregory's sawmill.

"Halt!" the sergeant roared after them, almost chuckling. "I'm pressing charges for desertion!"

"That's quite enough, Sergeant." Carrington stepped into the firelight.

"Think they got the idea, Colonel? Scampered back to their bunks fast enough, didn't they?"

Carrington turned from the sergeant, stepping before Two Moons. "Jack?" He waited for Stead to come up. "You tell the chiefs to see me before they leave in the morning. Tell them how important it is."

When the chiefs had grunted their approval, the colonel turned back to Ten Eyck, the pickets, and the night-watch sergeant. Carrington didn't know whether to congratulate the man or chastise him. "That was a damned foolhardy thing to do, Sergeant—firing into crowd the way you did. Might've gotten yourself killed very easily——"

"Wasn't me, Colonel!" he answered, shaking his head.

"Who? If——"

"Wasn't your sergeant," Jack piped up. He flung a thumb back at the shadow ambling down the slope toward the fire. "My new friend."

The shadow strode into the firelight. He stopped just behind the ring of Cheyenne chiefs. "Gentlemen."

"Who the devil——" the sergeant began.

"You care to explain this, Jack?" Carrington turned on the scout.

"Certainly, Colonel. My friend stayed back in the dark . . . case things got nasty."

"From the looks of your face, things turned nasty."

Carrington gazed at the newcomer. "And what were you doing hiding in the dark?"

"Wasn't hiding," he answered softly. "Hanging back if my friend needed me." He tapped his Henry. "I'd taken sixteen with me had there been trouble."

"Trouble?" Carrington growled. "Seems you two came here this evening looking for trouble."

"On the contrary, Colonel," the stranger replied. "Jack and I came here to stop *your* trouble. Never counted on your guards getting here in time."

"The nerve," Carrington fumed. "From the smell of it, you've both been at the bottle."

"What'd you think holds my gun hand so steady?"

Stead laughed. "Colonel, don't believe you've had the pleasure of meeting Mr. Seamus Donegan, formerly Master Sergeant, the Army of the Potomac and Shenandoah, Union cavalry."

Chapter 22

*T*o his tongue, his mouth was like the bottom of muddy boot-sole, and tasted worse. Bad part about it, Seamus Donegan's head felt as if it were a painful saddle boil, ready to burst atop his shoulders every time he tried to move it.

Brushing some crawling insects from his cheek, the Irishman became aware of the sun grown hot on his skin. Gathering the strength, Seamus blinked, opening his eyes into the new light.

"Top o' the morning, Irishman!"

Donegan sat up slowly, staring full into the face of Jack Stead as he held his swollen head between both hands. "Thought you drank much's me last evening, cabin-boy."

Stead chuckled. "I did. Least before we came down here to help out the Cheyenne."

Blinking, Seamus recognized some of the old men gathered around the smoky fire nearby. "I recall you brought with you a bottle of your own."

"Aye, Seamus." Stead slapped him mercilessly on the back before rising to go kneel by the fire. "So I'll be a long time in forgiving you for drinking that bottle damned near all yourself!" He set the pot down and shuffled back to the Irishman.

"What's this?" Donegan growled, opening his eyes again as the steam wafted into his nostrils.

"Coffee? Your nose so stove-up you can't smell coffee?" Stead laughed easily, which caused the old chiefs to laugh along as well. "Must be in some bad way, not to smell the coffee that's going to make a new man out of you."

"Coffee, eh?"

"Well . . ." Jack sighed, suddenly serious, plopping onto the grass beside the Irishman. "I tried the only other way I know to make a new man out of you last night."

Donegan eyed the Englishman suspiciously over the lip of his dented tin cup. "How?"

"Her."

Seamus followed Jack's arm, the finger at the end of which pointed to the old, squat Cheyenne woman who smiled back at Seamus. Toothlessly among her wrinkles.

Donegan sputtered on his coffee, turning to Stead with a look of helplessness. "I . . . *no!* I couldn't have. Could I? Did I, Jack?" He stared into his coffee and whispered so the Cheyenne chiefs and the squaw could not overhear. "Was I drunk enough to . . . to do . . . to . . . her."

Suddenly Stead was roaring, laughing so hard he fell over backward, rolling on his side and thrashing his legs in merriment. When he gathered himself again, swiping the tears from his eyes and crawling to Donegan's side, more of Jack's teeth showed than Donegan could recall seeing.

"You were worried, weren't you, Irishman?"

He swallowed, looked down at his cup of coffee and considered flinging it into the grinning face. "Damned worried—still am!"

At that moment she was there between them, presenting Seamus with a long, wide, nondescript strip of dried meat. Thing about it as she held her offering up before the Irishman, the jerky seemed alive with green-backed bottle flies. Swarming, in mass, like the meat itself throbbed. Donegan fought the empty heave of his belly. Bile threw itself against his tonsils.

He shook his head and pushed the rotten meat and the squaw's hand away.

"Careful, Seamus," Jack whispered. "Them old men had that woman come over and offer you some of the little they have to eat."

He swallowed down his revolting stomach once more. "I . . . I'm sorry, Jack. Their offer . . ." Seamus nodded and tried to smile on the woman.

"You had no supper so they figured you could do with some breakfast."

He belched, unable to rid himself of the sour but familiar taste pasty in his mouth. "Looks's if I slept right here."

"When you got through drinking and dancing."

"Dancing, was it?" he squeaked feebly, headache worsening.

"First you had those old boys up and shaking their legs with you in a Yankee jig," Stead declared, then laughed. "So for good measure, they had you dance Cheyenne with them as well."

He wagged his head, holding it with one hand while the other sloshed steaming coffee on his boots. "But I didn't . . . didn't touch," he begged, wagging a finger at the woman now.

Stead grew serious. "Not while you were awake, at least. You passed out sometime after the moon sank out of the sky. But she stayed right beside you. Did you ever make a show of it—moaning in the throes of pleasure, Irishman."

"P-Pleasure, Jack?"

"Sure, you had that old woman rubbing what you claimed was your 'poor, bleeming back'!"

"Rubbed me back, you say?"

"Until you passed out on her, and she had to waddle back here to the fire while you snored."

"So," he gazed up from his coffee, "I didn't . . . you say you didn't see me . . ."

"No, you didn't touch her," Jack confided. "Besides, I don't think she'd crawl in the robes with you now, anyways."

"H-How's that?" Seamus inquired, his pride suddenly pricked.

"She come back to the fire last night, telling all them chiefs how the big whiteman must not really have the donicker of a buffalo bull after all."

He swallowed, brow knitting. "She . . . she did, did she?"

"Yeah. She said the big whiteman must have him a tiny donicker of the weasel . . . seeing how the whiteman didn't have enough of a donicker to share with her!"

Seamus sipped his coffee in silence while Jack, the chiefs, and the wrinkled old squaw laughed at him round their smoky fire. And he flushed in embarrassment when he caught himself staring down the loose neckline of the woman's skin dress, gazing at those saggy, discolored dugs of hers.

As bad as the coffee tasted this morning, Donegan was sure it in no way tasted near as bad as would those flabby, dried-up teats.

Not long after the 2nd Battalion's veteran bugler, German Adolph Metzger, had blown reveille, the nine Cheyenne chiefs presented themselves at the south gate. For close to an hour they waited patiently while Carrington dressed, sending adjutant Wands to scare up Jack Stead.

His office filled with aromatic pipesmoke, the colonel had his interpreter begin by asking the whereabouts of the troublesome Sioux.

"Red Cloud and Man-Afraid," Jack began, "both are on the Tongue. They're your biggest threat."

"But by no means my only problem, Jack."

"A chief goes by the name of Buffalo Tongue—he's causing trouble for Reno and the Powder River country."

"What of the other tribes, Jack?" Carrington rocked forward in his chair. "I want to know if they can confirm any of what Bridger learned from the Crows."

Back and forth the interpreter talked in Cheyenne and sign. When at last Jack straightened in his chair, he looked squarely at the colonel.

"The Hunkpapa and Brule have come in to join the fight. Along with a big band of Arapaho, making war under a white renegade they call 'One Thumb.'"

"Do the chiefs have any notion what the Sioux and Arapaho plan against us?"

The Cheyenne whispered among themselves for several minutes before Two Moons turned to give Stead their gripping report.

"The Sioux are going all out for a winter campaign against you. When the first snow flies."

"That first snow has come and gone, Jack."

"*Winter,* Colonel. You haven't seen anything like cold yet. When old-winter-man blows the snow right out of the north itself . . . that's when the Sioux are planning to cut your post off. That's when the chiefs say the Sioux plan on one big fight with the soldiers. They'll raid your herds no more."

"One fight?" Carrington sounded doubtful.

"The Sioux brag that what soldiers they don't kill in that big fight . . . will all be driven away. Like snowflakes before a summer wind."

Carrington grew thoughtful, face gray with concern. "Do the chiefs know where the Sioux plan this big fight . . . where they'll kill so many soldiers?"

Jack bit his lower lip. "Over Lodge Trail Ridge, Colonel."

Carrington relaxed. He slapped his palms down on his thighs, grinning. Causing Jack to wonder if the man had lost his mind momentarily.

"That's good news, Jack!" he explained himself. "All I do now is finish my post as I've planned all along . . .

and simply forbid my officers from pursuing any warriors beyond Lodge Trail Ridge!"

"That might be easier said than done," Jack said. "Hardest thing to do is stop a man from crossing the Lodge Trail when he's got his fighting blood up."

"Not when its an official order," Carrington smiled to ease the harsh sound to it. "Official policy."

"Won't stop the Sioux from trying. They get your men riled enough—like they were last night down at the Little Piney—someone will bolt on over the ridge."

"I pray you're wrong about that, Jack. As wrong as you and Bridger were right in your intelligence. What news Bridger himself sent us tallies squarely with what these chiefs are saying. I think I can believe them. And," he looked up at Lieutenant Wands, "allow them to leave on their hunt for buffalo along the Tongue River."

Stead watched the fire smolder in the lieutenant's eyes, though Wands refused to let his face show his hatred for the Cheyenne—how he despised the colonel for letting the Indians pass on to the Tongue River country where Red Cloud reigned.

"I must register my protest, Colonel."

He gazed at Wands. "You want it for the record you don't approve of my giving the Cheyenne free passage?"

"That's correct, sir," Wands replied, stiffly.

"Protest registered, Lieutenant."

"Time was," Stead said, "the Sioux and Cheyenne were great enemies. For many generations there was nothing but bad blood between them."

"They've allied against us as we speak! Allied to kill us!"

Stead gazed at the adjutant no older than himself. He replied quietly. "The army has no one else to blame but itself for that mistake. No one else to blame."

October swept down on the Big Horns with the stealth of a mountain cougar. None of the bluster of a silver-tip grizzly. Instead, it crept up on a man so he didn't realize autumn had come to the valley of the Pineys until he finally noticed his water buckets were crusted with ice every morning. Noticed the lacy cordons of ice-scum along the creekbanks that melted when the sun rose high in the crystalline-blue skies. Across the higher slopes of the mountains the aspen had begun its autumn dance of gold, quaking on breezes that bit and chilled to the marrow.

The sun rode lower in the southern skies. A man's breath greeted his every word at reveille. Violet and rose streaked the sky with morning's chilly arrival. The seasons had turned. And with it, the tide and time of man.

By now Capt. Fred Brown had lost better than six hundred head of beef to the Indians, meaning Fort Phil Kearny had fewer than a hundred left—a cheerless situation for any soldier worried about fresh meat in his belly with the coming of winter. That wasn't all the stolen beef meant. While once a common sight on the tables of officers' families, milk had now become a rare commodity.

In time the talk among the enlisted men turned to desertion, most amazed that but one man had gone over the wall, taking his "grand bounce."

Seamus Donegan chuckled at the idea of soldiers deserting as he leaned against Kinney's pine-slab bar. Time and again he asked if any man among them would care to pit himself against the wilderness of the Big Horn country. That, and run the gauntlet of the Sioux who flashed mirrors from every hill, or waited in every coulee.

"Nawww," Seamus laughed, "safest place for a man to winter is right here. In this post. With a lot of friendly fellows gathered 'round him. Besides, that one fellow deserted had to be daft. That, or the bleeming fool was a Protestant!"

On the last day of September, Supply Train Number 33 had rumbled through the quartermaster's gates, ending its tortuous sixty-six day run from Lone Tree, Nebraska. Civilian contractors James Hill and James Henning had hauled up tons of sorely-needed corn and oats for the ribby mounts of the 2nd Battalion. Anxious at first to leave the post on their return trip before winter set hard upon the land, Hill and Henning reluctantly pulled wagons and teamsters south. Damned scared too. Little had they known when they contracted to haul supplies north that in two months the Sioux had killed four soldiers and twenty-six civilians.

Fred Brown looked over the new grain shipment just arrived.

Perhaps that sniveling Carrington won't be able to refuse us our strike at the hostiles now. Every day more and more officers join forces with me against the craven coward! While every day we get closer to striking back. Yes! With our horses well-fed, we'll be ready to strike a blow soon, when we can catch the Sioux nestled in their lodges for the winter. Now that their ponies grow gaunt for want of grass. And ours grow strong on oats and corn once more.

"By damned, ain't they a pretty sight!" Marr shouted, slapping Donegan on the back this bright, chilly November second.

In silence Seamus suffered a hot knot of sentiment stuck back in his throat.

"Always did have a soft spot in my heart for cavalry myself, Seamus," Marr said, more quietly this time. "Think I know what you feel, son."

Donegan tried a smile. At least he showed rows of wide teeth and tried to make his misting eyes twinkle. *Ol' Cap'n Marr just might understand Seamus Donegan.* Among a crowd of cheering soldiers and civilians, they watched from the stockade gates as two columns of dusty-blue cavalry approached the fort.

He counted but sixteen men in the first group, yet every one of them sat proud as could be. Backs saber straight. *Horse soldiers. Damn, but don't Mither Donegan's firstborn son know what it means to be a horse soldier!*

Still, something about the way one of those riders sat

his horse tugged at a wee part down inside the pit of him,
unsettling Donegan. Causing him to remember things
painful and less than sunny. Those bright yellow
chevrons the rider wore.

*Maybe, 'tis only that. You sat a sergeant's saddle once,
Seamus Donegan. Was a time you gave shine to no man.*

On the sergeant and his fifteen rode, down to the crossing of the Little Piney. Beside the sergeant pranced the
color-bearer, his standard held high in the new breezes
rustling off the Big Horns. Over his shoulder the stan-
dard-bearer wore his bugle on a braided cord. Horse
soldiers. New to this land, but here to stay.

Something caught his attention. From the corner of his
eye. The flashing of small mirrors from first one hillside
thick with a carpet of timber. Then a second. A third and
fourth. And soon it seemed to him that every slope spat a
bright flash into the valley.

Below him on the parade three small boys stood suddenly still in their play, pointing first to one hill then
another slope. Yelling out for others to notice the signal
mirrors as well. He recognized one of Carrington's boys.
The oldest.

"Who're they?" he asked Marr.

Marr seemed perturbed that his attention had been
drawn away from the cavalry unit riding into the valley.
"Oh, just boys."

"Whose boys?"

Marr glowered at him a moment, then gazed down on
the parade where the youngsters went back to chasing
one another in a wild game of blind man's bluff. "Carrington's eldest, Seamus. The other two belong to Jim
Wheatley."

Wheatley, he repeated to himself. *She has two boys,*
Donegan found himself marveling.

"By the by, Seamus." Sam Marr of a sudden wanted to
talk again. "You ever make sense of them Injun signals
like you was figuring you could?"

He wagged his head as he turned back to study the

boys below. "Not making much headway at all on it, Cap'n. Doesn't see to be much rhyme nor reason to the signals."

"Trouble is, Seamus, you're trying to figure things out like a white man."

Donegan laughed. "Perhaps you're right, old man. To make some sense of those mirror signals . . . I've got to learn first how to think like a bleeming Injin!"

"Seamus!" Marr gripped Donegan's arm suddenly, wheeling him around on the catwalk. "Take a look, boy! You ain't seeing what I see—are you!"

Donegan nodded, staring down into the valley at the Reno Road now. Choking on a hot knot in his throat. He had seen. Blinking his eyes free of stinging tears.

"By god! That's your old outfit, Sergeant Seamus Donegan," Marr shouted for all to hear. "That's the Second Cavalry!"

By glory if it t'aint, Seamus thought, looking at the proud battle streamers the boy was carrying high in the breeze. *Not a man wouldn't be proud to ride under those banners!*

Colorful streamers like fragments of life itself held aloft for all men to admire. Pieces of history. Moments in time when the clock stood still and man pitted himself against man in a war that no cause won. Gettysburg. The Wilderness. Cold Harbor. Antietam. Spotsylvania. Petersburg. Manassas. The Shenandoah.

"Faith, and begora!" he whispered at last, reading the red and white flag at last.

Marr gazed down at the fluttering guidon that announced what company climbed up from the crossing. He turned to stare at the big, keg-chested Irishman and smiled too. Hugging Donegan's arm and nodding. Knowing how young Seamus must feel.

"C Company?" the old soldier inquired in a whisper only Donegan could hear.

"Aye, Cap'n." He nodded. "C company, i'tis."

Silver, bronze and blue bands on the battle streamers

told the story. Meritorious service in the face of the enemy. Courage under fire. Time and again—death before retreat. The ring of places now foreign, once as familiar as old friends: Bloody Angle, Five Forks, Shiloh, Harrison's Landing, Missionary Ridge, Saylor's Creek, Ashby's Gap, Beverly Ford, Catlett Station, Dinwiddie Courthouse, Hartwood Church, White Oak Swamp, Tom's Run . . .

On the green parade bandmaster Cully marched with his baton. Brass horns pumped out the familiar, energetic strains of the popular, "Ain't I Glad to Get Out of the Wilderness." Carrington's personal welcome to Fort Phil Kearny.

"The colonel's Germans playing sojur music again." Seamus choked, smiling behind the mist in his eyes. *What the call of bugles do to a warrior's heart . . .*

"Germans, you say?" Marr asked, smiling as he clapped in time with the music. "Why, I'll bet there's two tons of Irishmen in that company."

"Aye," Seamus whispered. "Were it not for we Irish and the Krauts . . . why, there'd be no bleeming American army!"

He found his own thoughts drowned beneath the cheers and shouts of glee and welcome rising to a sustained crescendo. Crossing the Little Piney came the second and larger group of 2nd Cavalry. Forty-five enlisted men, led by a young Minnesota veteran, Lt. Horatio S. Bingham. A Civil War veteran himself, leading sixty-one men of C Company to Fort Phil Kearny.

Bingham and twenty-seven of his number had reached their final duty station.

A moment more and Donegan understood why the men of the 18th cheered so raucously. Not for the 2nd Cavalry. Not for Company C nor Lieutenant Bingham. Instead, they cheered for a lone officer who had spurred his mount out of formation. Prancing ahead of Bingham and the cavalry. Waving. Standing tall in his stirrups as if he were returning home. To friends.

Donegan turned to an old soldier nearby. "Is he what all the hurroo's about?"

The old soldier eyed Donegan up then down before he answered. "I'll say." And he smiled broadly. "You don't know who he is, eh? Well, you will one day soon, boy!"

"You care to explain it, we'll both know," Marr said.

The soldier eyed them a moment more, and smiled again around missing teeth.

"These places mean anything to you fellas? Peach Tree Creek? Jonesboro? Resaca? Corinth? Eh? Didn't think so. Well, let me tell you they mean something to the Eighteenth and its fighting Second Battalion. While that damned Carrington hisself squatted behin't a desk back in Ohio, that young officer down yonder led us into and outta every dad-blamed battle. Lord, did the Johnnies try to turn us back time and again! But did we retreat?"

The old soldier shook his head so hard Seamus feared it might fly off.

"Not one goddamned retreat! Not with that man leading us—there would dare be no turning back. We dug our earthworks by night and bled by day. But retreat! Not at Stone's River! Not at Atlanta! By god, not at Kennesaw Mountain! Sweet Jesus, but I'd follow *that* man into the jaws of hell again, I would."

Seamus watched the old veteran swallow hard, shifting his tobacco-cud with his tongue and not caring about the single tear that slipped down his sunburned cheek.

The soldier glared at Donegan with the look of a man daring another, challenging. "So, let me tell you boys something—that officer down yonder, that's *Cap'n Fetterman!*"

Chapter 23

"*B*arkeep!"
    Every man drinking in Kinney's cabin turned at the brassy call from the tall man who stooped through the door. It was the way of him. To charge into a room the way he seized Confederates on the battlefield. Without mercy. Taking no prisoners. There was a swagger about him even as he stood with blue-gray eyes slewing over the smoky room.

"A tankard of your finest corn whiskey," the tall man ordered. "And pray that it's better than Bullock-and-Ward offer down at Laramie."

Kinney nodded his gray head, eyeing the newcomer suspiciously. "Much better, friend. You'll not be disappointed."

He ripped open his wool coat and bellied the pine-plank bar. "Best that I not be disappointed, my 'friend,' " he mimicked the trader. "I've no liking for you popinjays who trade off professional soldiers."

Kinney set the mug before the man. Studying him. Perhaps his mid- to late-twenties. A massive head of curly hair the color of strawberry wheat. Hard, muscular jowls. Clean-shaven but for the bushy mustache that drooped round heavy lips then curled upward once again at his square chin. A big paw wrapped itself around the mug.

Swallowing, he swiped the back of a hand across his lips and smiled. "Aye, barkeep. You're a man of your word. I'm not disappointed." He sighed, turned round to tear the wool coat off his thick arms, slinging it across the bar. Shrugging his shoulders, he leaned back, scanning the room. His glowing, feral eyes came to rest on the dark-haired man seated alone in the corner by a sheet-iron stove.

"Glory be of glories!" the newcomer boomed in that cannon of a voice. "I've heard of God-given miracles before, barkeep. But this is a moment for wonderment. Four days ago I ride into this slip-trench latrine of a post —assigned to the end of the goddamned world itself. Where everything's new and every man's a stranger. But this night of nights, I find myself sharing a drink with an old, *old* friend."

"I see you still wear my chevrons, 'old' friend," the dark man replied across the grave-still trading post.

Tapping a finger at one of his yellow patches, the sergeant grinned. "When you gave 'em up—the army had to find a man who still had some fight left in him. You'd carried the stripes around long enough, far as most was concerned."

"Only way you'd get my stripes," the dark man answered, "I got busted down . . . or they signed peace at Appomattox."

"Gents!" the blond sergeant announced, raising his mug. "To the Grand Army of the Potomac. And Phil Sheridan's Army of the Shenandoah!"

The spectators raised their cups and drank with him before the sergeant turned back to the man seated in the corner. "How you been, Seamus Donegan?"

"I've been better," the Irishman replied. "Quietly enjoying my whiskey amongst me friends. Till the first sergeant of C Company, Second Cavalry strolls in—and Kinney's whiskey don't taste good any longer."

"What about me, Donegan? We was friends once. How 'bout you drinking with me?" He dragged his wool coat from the bar and was three steps across the floor when Donegan stood.

"On a time, Eli Garrett was my friend." Donegan nodded to Jack Stead and Sam Marr. They rose from their table, edging for the door. "That friendship died in the Shenandoah . . . along with too many good men."

Garrett pursed his lips, drawing his mouth into a thin line of unconcealed hatred. "Funny that you should mention the Shenandoah, Seamus. Where so many of us finally found you didn't have the stomach for war."

Donegan turned his back, slowly. He pulled his thick mackinaw coat over his shoulders. Only then did he turn around. And wasn't surprised to find Garrett at arm's length.

The Irishman casually shoved buttons through their holes. "You always was one to sneak up on a man, Eli Garrett."

"Ain't sneaking up on you now, Seamus." Flinging his coat onto a chair, he spread his arms wide. "Just wanted to get a wee bit closer when your back was turned . . . see if it's really true what they said about you in the Shenandoah. Front Royal. Had to see for myself that broad stripe of yellow down your back——"

Before any man in the room realized it, Donegan had slammed his fist into Garrett's jaw. The sergeant stumbled backward three steps, crashing into the pine-plank bar. Shaking his head, he dabbed the trickle of blood at the corner of his mouth.

"Good punch, Seamus." He grinned and jiggled his jaw. "But nowhere near as good as you had during the war. But then, you always was just a big, stupid youngster. Only one thing I hated about you more than you being my sergeant—you was a mick!"

Every bit as fast as Seamus had connected, Garrett pushed off the bar, diving into the Irishman, swinging both fists like pistons and jabbing a shoulder into Donegan's belly. Back into a small table and a handful of chairs they tumbled. Seamus clawed at the back of Garrett's blue tunic, trying to pull free so he could swing again. In the next heartbeat the soldier had wrenched Donegan to his feet and flung him against a second table. Garrett swept a clay mug off a table and held it in the air, ready to swing it into a dazed and very foggy Irishman's head——

The shotgun roar filled the little cabin with its startling racket.

Garrett wheeled, scowling. Watching trader Kinney lower the double-barreled fowler and point it at his belly.

"Right barrel I keep loaded with buckshot," the judge announced as the cabin fell to silence. "The buckshot went into the ceiling."

Kinney watched Garrett glance up at the roof. "This other barrel, you're asking? Loaded with buckshot and salt. Makes for a painful, oozy wound, you see. Now." He pointed with the muzzle of the shotgun. "I want you both out of here. One at a time. And should I find need of replacing tables or chairs, I know where I'll come to find the funds, gentlemen. Sergeant Eli Garrett, right?"

The soldier glared at the judge, finally nodding once as he raked some of the strawberry curls from his eyes.

"Good," Kinney replied to the unspoken answer. "I'll talk with your Lieutenant Bingham should I need replacements, Sergeant. Grab your coat and be gone."

No one moved as Eli Garrett yanked his coat about his shoulders, then stomped to the bar and swallowed the mug of whiskey without wincing.

"Good whiskey, trader," he growled. "I drink lots of good whiskey. I'll be back."

"You'll be welcome," Kinney pointed the muzzle to the door, "when you learn manners. Got all the whiskey you can drink, and then some. But when you come to Kinney's, you're on my ground and you play by my rules. Good night, Sergeant."

Thumping his empty clay mug against the plank bar, Garrett turned on his heels, crossed the room, and yanked open the door. Jack Stead stepped over and grabbed the latch, slowly closing the crude pine door once the tall sergeant had swept into the night.

"Now you." Kinney brought the butt of the fowler to rest on his right hip. "Pick up the tables and chairs for me."

"And if I don't?" Donegan replied with a bloody-lipped smile.

"I suppose I'll have to impose upon my friend Captain Brown to see that he no longer requires your services for the winter."

Seamus nodded. "Lose me job cutting timber, eh? I see the picture you're painting, trader. You get me fired—I can no longer stay at the fort. Right?"

"Unlike Sergeant Garrett, I won't dare accuse you of being stupid, Mr. Donegan."

Seamus straightened his mackinaw then bent to set tables and chairs upright. "You've three busted chairs. What's your verdict, Judge?"

"You'll pay me for one," Kinney answered, laying his fowler on the bar. "The other two will be Sergeant Garrett's to pay. Seems to me he began the fracas."

"A fair judgment, Seamus," Captain Marr replied with a nod.

"Sound's fair," Donegan said as he swiped at the blood oozing from a cut above an eye. "Considering."

"I'll take payment in gold." Kinney squirmed behind the bar. "Two dollars."

"Don't have gold," Seamus replied, feeling the hackles spur up on his back. "You'll settle for the army script what Cap'n Brown pays us that works for him."

"No gold?"

Donegan eyed the trader. "Army script's good enough when I drink the saddle varnish you call whiskey . . . it ought'n be good enough to pay for your bleeming chair."

"Two dollars in script it is," Kinney said firmly, slapping a palm on the bar.

After he paid and left, Donegan stood on the parade

with Marr and Stead. His tongue licked at a sore row of teeth while he glanced at the cloudy glitter of stars above.

"Be a cold one tonight," Marr muttered, afraid to raise what lay on each man's mind.

"Faired off quick, it did," Stead responded.

Donegan watched his friends toe the snow and wriggle as nervously as a couple of boys carrying bullfrogs into church. "Whyn't the two of you get the gumption to ask me?" Seamus whispered to them. "Unless you do, it'll eat a hole in your belly afore morning."

"All right, dammit!" Marr replied. "Tell us what Garrett's talking about. Claiming you had a yellow stripe down your back."

"Not that we believe it, understand," Stead chimed.

"No," Marr agreed. "I know you too long, Seamus. Watched you tackle bushwackers in Missouri to Injuns at the Crazy Woman. No man knows you can say Seamus Donegan's . . ."

"Yellow, Cap'n? Was a time that Seamus Donegan wondered for himself if he was a coward. I'll tell you while we walk. Not a night for a man to be standing— freezing his bullocks off."

Halfway across the parade he began. "Like Garrett tells it, trouble began in the Shenandoah. 'Sixty-four, i'twas. But Eli and me go back to the beginning. Army made us horse soldiers together . . . to fight the Johnnies. Together. Until the Shenandoah, that is. Was best of friends—drinking and carousing, we were. Watching each other's backsides in every battle across three long years of blood and bone. I carried him or he carried me. And everytime I had me stripes ripped off me arm, they give 'em to me friend Garrett. He'd grin and say, 'Seamus, my boy—I'll wear these stripes for you till you want 'em back. Can't have no other man getting 'em away from you for good. A friend'd do no less.' Time was, Eli Garrett was just that sort of friend."

Marr cleared his throat. "Sometimes, the best of friends . . . make the worst of enemies."

"Truly said, Cap'n." He walked in silence for a few moments. "Sheridan had us burning and looting our way down the Shenandoah. Hell, we'd come all the way to Harper's Ferry in but a month. And then General Devin and Custer both were given the word. Orders from Grant and Sheridan. We were to find Colonel John Mosby's raiders at all cost . . . and hang every one."

"I heard tell Mosby dogged Sheridan like fleas on a hound," Marr said.

"Worse. There was no end to Mosby's treachery and evil. Grant wanted Mosby bad. So he turned the problem over to Sheridan. And Little Phil turned us loose on those raiders."

"How'd they come to call you yellow?"

He glanced at Marr. "Came about when we caught a batch of them raiders in the first drag. They fought us like hellions. Brave they were—let no man mistake that. Captured six. But when Custer dropped a rope from a tree limb at Front Royal, fixing to hang their leader . . . that's where I drew the line."

"Found yourself alone on the wrong side of that line?" Stead asked.

He nodded. "Custer had his hanging—a sick, sad affair. Had the rest tied to a tree and shot. Pinned notes on the bodies . . . telling Mosby he'd be caught soon enough. That very day Custer saw to it Brigadier General Thomas C. Devin busted me back to the ranks for refusing to hang or shoot a one of those bushwackers."

"Insubordination?"

"Aye, Cap'n. And waiting for court-martial, if Custer'd had his way. That blue-eyed sonuvabitch's a man you don't want to rile . . . or find yourself on the bad side of."

Stead sighed. "Seamus, care to tell your friends why you didn't want to see those men hung . . . even shot. It was war, was it not?"

"Aye, Jack. I't'was. But to Seamus Donegan, war never gave no man the right to excuse what's a crime

committed on any other field." He wagged his head.
"Mosby's men was sojurs. Plain and simple. Doing what
any sojur would do to harass our march down the Shenandoah."

"And you wanted no part in killing them."

"No Cap'n—I wanted no part in murder," Donegan
replied.

"So Garrett got the chevrons ripped from your arms,"
Marr continued.

"Custer saw to that."

"Why Eli Garrett?"

Donegan sighed. " 'Twas my old friend who threw that
rope over the tree at Front Royal for Custer himself.
Then handpicked the firing squad to shoot the rest while
the leader swung."

"What became of friend Garrett wearing your stripes
to keep 'em safe from others?" Stead asked.

"This was different, Jack. From that very moment, in
that grove of oak and shadow at Front Royal, Eli Garrett
wanted my stripes for himself. We was no longer the
friends we'd been. I was no longer a sergeant in Company
C, Second Cavalry."

"Had wondered why a union sergeant wouldn't stay on
in the regular army after the war," Marr commented.
"You wasn't a sergeant come Appomattox, eh?"

"From the summer of 'sixty-four till it was over—just
a sojur. Fighting Johnnies, and watching over my shoulder. Wondering when Sergeant Garrett was next to come
rubbing on me. Giving me all the dirtiest details. Sending
me off on the wild missions he figured I'd not return
from."

"But you came back," Marr said as he slapped Donegan on the back.

"No," the Irishman whispered. "You see a different
Seamus Donegan than rode into the Shenandoah Valley
in 'sixty-four. Ever since Front Royal, I ain't been the
same. Neither has Eli Garrett."

They walked for several minutes in silence, nearing the fires of the civilian camp by the Little Piney.

Donegan stopped by a large ring of coals. "Time'll come, Cap'n. Time that Eli Garrett will want to finish what he started two long years ago in the Shenandoah."

Two days later, on the eighth of November, Carrington relented.

Fetterman had made himself a thorn in the colonel's side from the moment he had arrived at Fort Phil Kearny. Back in the arms of his Civil War comrades, Captain Brown and Lieutenant Bisbee, Fetterman devised a plan that he practically affixed to Carrington's desk. For five days he doggedly argued the merits of that plan before the district commander he loathed as nothing more than a desk-pounder.

Through the window Adolph Metzger watched the stars fleshing out a crooked strip of sky. Silently nursing his ration of whiskey in a tin cup, the German-born Metzger gazed over the sutler's cabin. Civilian and soldier alike huddled around tables and sheet-iron stoves, gabbing and waiting for Fetterman's trap to spring and catch the unwary Sioux. Metzger shivered in the corner, wondering how fared his old friends out there in the dark. Down in the cottonwood and willow along the Big Piney. Waiting for the Sioux to show.

Surely, the Indians will come, he thought in his painstaking English. The bugler sipped at his whiskey, enjoying the warmth each gulp spread through him. *The Sioux cannot pass up the mules.*

Three days ago Metzger had ridden with Fetterman, Bisbee and Brown into the surrounding hills. Sweeping across Pine Island, the Sullivant Hills and up atop Lodge Trail Ridge, Bisbee and Brown had thirsted to show the country to their wartime comrade—Brevet Lt. Col. William Judd Fetterman.

Once beyond the tattling ears of the stockade, Fetterman had turned to his friends and confided, "I want you to be the first to know that Carrington's not long for this command."

Bisbee laughed and slapped his thigh, gushing. "I knew it! Tell me more!"

"Just before I left the East for this assignment, a friend at the War Department informed me of some changes in the wind."

"I want to hear all of it!" Brown begged.

Fetterman grinned. "There's a reorganization under way . . . a postwar thing. And, so I'm told, that reorganization will place me as the new commander of Fort Phil Kearny."

"What of old yellow britches himself?" Brown growled.

"Carrington?" Fetterman asked with a smile. "I suppose the army will find something suitable for a man of his talents. A desk job. Recruiting for the new army. While the fighting men of the old army are given new fields to conquer!"

"Gad, Judd!" Bisbee cheered. "Tell us when."

"Soon, is all I know. Back in Washington City they're burning to have Congress enlarge the frontier army. Plans are to use our Second Battalion of the Eighteenth as the core for building the new Twenty-seventh Infantry!"

"With Captain Fetterman in command!" Bisbee roared.

"No, Bill," he corrected. *"Colonel* William Judd Fetterman." He clenched his gloved fist. "Colonel Fetterman, in charge of crushing the Sioux."

Brown reined up. For a moment the three officers sat, staring down into the valley of Peno Creek as Metzger had dismounted, letting his horse chew at the winter-dried grass blown free of snow.

"Such wild, pretty country," Fetterman admitted at last. "Let's ride down and take a look."

"Can't," Brown grumped. "Orders."

"Whose?"

"Carrington's," Bisbee answered. "Who else?"

"Why?"

"We aren't to cross this ridge," Brown answered.

Fetterman pointed down the north slope. "What lies there?"

"Sioux!" Brown shouted, flinging his fist into the frosty air. "Twenty-five hundred of them, Judd! Waiting for us."

Fetterman grinned with that look of a timber wolf catching its first whiff of prey on the breeze. "Boys, those red bastards won't have long to wait!"

After dark on the eighth, as Metzger sat drinking his gill of whiskey, Fetterman, Brown, and their eager recruit, Lt. George Grummond, had led a detail of enthusiastic soldiers down to the Big Piney, where they staked out some mules to graze, certain their bait would draw warriors into their trap. In the cold and snow along the creek, Fetterman's heavily armed troopers waited. And shivered. Wishing they lay warm in their bunks or stood at Kinney's bar with the rest.

Those left behind passed the long winter evening rereading worn newspapers from the last mail brought north from Laramie. Others played with soiled, greasy decks of cards. Some gambled next payday's wages on a race or two of lice across a warm tin plate. Most drank and talked, and waited too. Listening for rifles to crack from the Big Piney.

When the guns bark, Adolph thought, Fetterman's caught his Indians.

Beside a stack of calico and flannel on the bar, Jim Bridger sat, rocking back and forth in his chair, half dozing at times while he listened to others boast of what Fetterman would do to the Sioux once he got his hands on some of the slippery devils.

"Won't stand and fight like men!" one old soldier barked.

"Exactly what the colonel told Fetterman," Metzger said. "Told the captain he could not figure to fight Indians the way he fought the rebels."

"What would Carrington know about fighting John-nies?" the old veteran growled at the bugler. "Colonel knows even less 'bout fighting Injuns!"

By midnight most had abandoned the trading post for their bunks and blankets. A pale moon shed milky light along the Big Piney, revealing Fetterman's inviting bait. Down in the tangle of brush and snow, the eager detail struggled to keep their chattering teeth quiet. A lucky few dozed. But most shuddered in the cold, nursing their first doubts in Fetterman's scheme to whip the Sioux.

As the gray of dawn slithered out of the east, Fetterman led his shivering detail back to the fort. The captain crawled beneath his warm blankets just as bugler Metzger blew reveille.

Chapter 24

November was eleven days old. The weather continued bright as a polished brass button, the air
cold and crisp. Overhead hung a sky as incredibly blue as
the water of high-country beaver pond.

Ever since his arrival nine days ago, Captain Fetterman stole every spare moment to drill infantry and
cavalry alike. Carrington, on the other hand, had a fort
to build. He ordered every waking hour of these shrinking autumn days to be used for construction. To assure
that the men would remain soldiers, Fetterman ordered
his troops out before reveille and kept them drilling long
after the last notes of retreat had echoed across the
parade.

For over a week the men had struggled to maintain the
pace, serving two taskmasters. One ordered them to raise
a post before snow blanketed the land. The other ordered
them to be soldiers, first of all.

"The snow be damned!" Fetterman had growled more
than once. "Let the colonel worry about the weather. I
want Red Cloud to worry about losing his scalp!"

They were cheering words to men who too long had
suffered one embarrassing defeat after another. Fetterman's words bristled with bravado. Easy enough for
Donegan to realize why old veterans and new recruits
alike harkened to the captain's siren call.

There's a boon of courage among most warriors, he thought to himself, until the hell of battle begins.

Leaning back against a raw-boarded wall outside officers' quarters, Seamus dreamily watched soldiers drill back and forth across the parade. He sighed, enjoying the high-morning sunlight. A Sunday off. On the autumn breeze floated the tinny piano pounding out an old hymn, "There Is a Light in the Window."

Reverend White at it already, he mused. Calling his flock to worship.

From time to time even the strident notes of the out-of-tune piano disappeared, drowned beneath the profane curses of the tall, blond-bearded sergeant of Company C. Donegan closed his eyes, vowing neither Methodists nor cavalry sergeants would intrude upon the peace of his Sunday morning.

Eventually he found himself in that warm pool where a man swims halfway down into sleep. Half dreaming, yet still able to make some sense of what his ears overhear. The noise on the parade grew to a chanting roar. The sort of rumble Seamus Donegan recognized. The sound of men making sport of a fight. Goading one combatant or the other. Cheering for the winner. Catcalls for the bloodier man.

Doubting he should, Seamus cracked his eyes open into the bright light caressing his face. Sorry just as quickly that he took measure of the brawl. For what he saw was not at all to his liking.

Eli Garrett, Sergeant, Company C, danced easily as a cat back and forth within the ring of soldiers who had broken off their close-order march to watch their drillmaster lay into a hapless green recruit. What began with a severe tongue-lashing now found Garrett shoving the private back, back, back into the swelling mob. Time and again the private ducked away from Garrett, who pursued the recruit like a cat toying with a mouse.

Seamus eased down off the porch, slow to shake the

kinks from his shoulders. Shame it had to be the likes of
Eli Garrett to ruin a fine Sunday morn, he brooded.

"You stupid son of a bitch!" Garrett spat into the private's face. "Never be a soldier! Knew it I first laid eyes
on you at Jefferson Barracks!"

This time Eli swung a big fist and connected. Squarely
on the breastbone. Knocking the private down, making
him gag for wind. With an arm like an oak fence post,
Garrett swept down and locked hold of the youngster's
tunic. Yanking him to his feet like a wet rag-doll, still
gasping for air.

"No-no-no!" he sputtered, bubbles spurting from his
lips as he threw his hands up.

"I'll show you, Burke!" Garrett shouted. "You'll not
frig up again in my unit!" His eyes swept the growing
crowd, his words meant for all in his company. "You
each see what awaits the soldier what frigs up in Eli Garrett's troop!"

He whirled, shaking the private at the end of one arm.
"Gonna make an example outta you, boy! Watched you
frig up one thing after another . . . for the last time,
Burke!"

When Garrett's fist connected against the youngster's
jaw, it reminded Donegan of the crack of a wood chopper's axe against a hardwood tree. Solid. Destructive.
Still, Seamus hung back at the edge of the crowd.

Army business, he tried convincing himself. Best to
stay far from it.

"You been trying to make a fool of me ever since you
joined, ain't you, Burke?" He scraped the semiconscious
private off the brittle autumn grass of the parade.

Burke tried mumbling something, his eyes fluttering,
spitting some blood from his lip as he stared up into the
new-day sun, watching the shadow of Garrett's arm
swing his way again. Eli connected under the jaw. Burke
sank to the ground like a sodden rag.

"We're not done yet, Burke!" Garrett screeched. "Been

waiting just as long as you to settle this. 'Cause you're no soldier!"

Standing over Burke, Garrett looked to his left, seeing Fetterman among others atop the porch in front of headquarters. Bisbee, Wands, Powell, Brown, and others watched too. Yet Fetterman made no move to stop the beating. Nor did any other officer. Garrett nodded to Fetterman. Instead of nodding in reply, the captain merely crossed his arms and leaned against a porch timber. That simple gesture told the cavalry sergeant all he wanted to know. With the approval of Capt. William Judd Fetterman, wasn't a soldier on this post going to stop Eli Garrett from giving Pvt. Thomas Burke the beating he so richly deserved.

He savagely drove a dusty boot-toe into Burke's ribs. Donegan listened to the familiar crunch of bone as Garrett struck a second time. Grunting in agony, the private rolled over, struggling to crawl onto his knees, with one arm protecting his ribcage. With his fist driven like an oak mallet, Garrett smashed the back of Burke's neck. Driving the private's face into the dust and dried grass.

Donegan parted the men before him like sheaves of wheat, paying no attention to the faces or the uniforms they wore.

"Fact be, you frigging bastard!" Garrett screamed as he snatched the back of Burke's collar, yanking him off the ground, swinging his limp body around. "I think I'll finish the job 'stead of waiting for Red Cloud to do it for me. I'll finish you first my——"

The cheering stopped. Fell silent. As Eli Garrett slowly turned round, his huge right fist held aloft, ready to swing at Burke—but imprisoned for the moment in the grip of the dark-haired Irishman.

A look of surprise, then shock. Finally something like raw pleasure crossed Eli Garrett's face as he came face to face with Seamus Donegan. The Irishman recognized the crazed, feral eyes. Seeing something in their raw, red depths that told him not only had Garrett been punishing the whiskey early this morning, but something even more frightening and foreign lay behind them. Something Seamus had only rarely seen. That look of a timber wolf as he closes in on a hamstrung buffalo calf.

"Seamus!" he bellowed, happy to see Donegan. "Surprised you're out of your blankets this early to a Sunday morning. Going to church, are you?"

Donegan gripped Garrett's fist all the tighter as the sergeant struggled to wrench his arm free. "Ought to let the boy go, Eli," he said calmly, squeezing. "Youngster like him don't go a hundred fifty pounds, what with a sackful of old horseshoes in each hand. I figure you can find something better for your darty hands to be doing."

"If I ain't whoring, I'm drinking," Eli replied, struggling to free his fist. "And if I ain't drinking, I'm fighting."

"Smells of you holding Sunday service atop Judge Kinney's whiskey barrel this morning. You been burning your goozle with his saddle varnish already, eh?"

"Was a time we drank and fought side by side, Seamus Donegan," Garrett replied. "Afore you lost your taste for fun and soldiering. Afore you growed a yellow band down your spine."

Donegan flung Garrett's arm backward, spinning the sergeant off balance. Eli recovered on the balls of his feet instantly, rubbing the fist Seamus had crimped.

"Taken me better than two years now," Donegan said as his left hand popped the horn buttons from their holes on the front of his mackinaw overcoat. "Think now I figured out about you and me . . . and that grove of hangman's oak at Front Royal in the Shenandoah back to 'sixty-four."

"You're yellow! Plain and simple!" he roared, listening as many of the soldiers laughed with him. "Didn't hang that rebel leader. Didn't raise your gun to shoot the rest of Mosby's raiders neither. Admit it, Seamus Donegan— you gone coward!"

Donegan sighed, his gray eyes flitting over the crowd

for an instant. Even at his young age, a man found Donegan's face etched with the fine seams of experience a long and bloody war had given him. A lifetime for any fighting man.

"No, Eli Garrett," he replied quietly. "You're the coward." He waited while the sergeant quit laughing. "You're afraid to stand before a man on equal terms, aren't you? Like Mosby's men who you hung and shot for Custer at Front Royal. You're a mighty big man when the enemy can't fight back, eh, Eli?"

"Goddamn you! I'm no cow——"

"That's it, ain't it? You screamed long and loud about me being a yellow-back," he said as he flung his coat down. "But, Eli Garrett can only work up the nerve to kill when the enemy's already beaten. Like those bushwackers you and Custer had strung up and shot. And," he glanced at Burke slumped in the grass, "like that poor sojur there. Ain't got no more a chance against you than a boy."

"By the gods, I'll cleave you, Donegan!" he shouted, trembling.

Seamus brought up his fists, glancing at the officers watching from the shade of their porch. Across the parade stood a group of four women and their children. Carrington among them.

"Got your chance, Eli Garrett." He backed up a step and shuffled to the side as the sergeant dropped his gunbelt and saber. "You and me now. Like you wanted three nights ago in Kinney's place."

"Yeah," he growled hungrily, swaying his long arms from side to side. "Something I wanted to do for a lot longer than that, Seamus. A long, long time."

"C'mon, *Sergeant* Garrett," he goaded, bringing his big paws up before his face, hunching his powerful shoulders. "Show me you're not a coward. Show me you can fight a man on even terms."

"More than that, Seamus Donegan," he spat his

words. "I'll show these soldiers how Eli Garrett kills a man with his bare hands!"

Garrett swung. His blow as quickly blocked by Donegan's left, their arms cracking together like hickory axe handles colliding. Seamus spun in with a quick right snaking under the soldier's jaw. Driving Garrett backward two steps. Eli tapped his lip with a finger, tasting blood. He smiled at Donegan. Without warning he dove headlong into the Irishman's belly, planting his big head squarely below the ribs. Seamus felt the wind explode from him, his legs going to soap as Eli pumped against him. The Irishman sank against the ring of soldiers. They gave way. Donegan collapsed beneath Garrett.

Garrett swung once, twice, a third time. Connecting with his longer reach and oak-mallet fists. Before Seamus realized, the soldier towered above him, a foot cocked back and headed for his face. He snagged the dusty boot inches from his nose, gripping it as he'd cling to life itself. Twisting slowly against the strength in the tall man's leg. Eli hobbled closer, straining to yank free. One hop too many.

Donegan flung the soldier's leg up and back. Garrett crashed with a snort. Shook his head and rolled onto his knees. He turned just as Donegan stomped up, and drove a fist into the Irishman's groin. Seamus doubled, stumbling back, and wheeled, sinking to his knees. Shards of sharp pain flickered through his body like the burning fumaric acid they had poured in the saber cut across the great muscles of his back. His stomach lurched as stars fluttered across his eyelids and dripped to black. Sucking for air, Seamus tried to blink his eyes clear of the blinding meteors——

Like a raging badger Garrett fell on the Irishman before Seamus had settled to his knees. Yanking Donegan's head back with a fistful of hair, the soldier whipped his right fist back and forth from jaw to jaw. Holding Seamus upright as he struck again and again. Watching the Irishman's eyes puff from blood. Grinning madly as cuts opened on the brows, along the cheekbones, trickling free bright, glistening crimson. Laughing now as Donegan's lips puffed and cracked, blood dribbling into the dark whiskers. Fiercely, he brought his knee up beneath the Irishman's chin.

Donegan catapulted back blindly as the knee cracked under his jaw. Beneath his wet cheek he welcomed the dried, freeze-cured grass. Listening to the cheers and taunts of the soldiers ringing him. *Gawd there's something about a fight. Makes a man feel more purely alive being this close to death, it does.*

Between sagging shoulders he raised himself slowly, blinking his eyes clear. Hearing more clearly Eli's taunts. He rolled onto a hip and brought a leg under him as a shadow flickered at the corner of his eye. On instinct Seamus swept the ground before him with a thick, hewn-timber of a leg. He connected, sensing more than seeing the soldier topple beside him.

Still blinking his eyes clear of sweat and blood, Donegan rolled toward Garrett's grunt. Pouncing. He dug his fingers into the curly blond hair. Whipped the head back and drove his maul-sized fist down into those blue-gray eyes.

Donegan struggled to his feet, yanking the blond head up with him. Then flung his rail-splitter's fist at Garrett's bloody face again. Eli sagged at the knees. The Irishman snapped him up for a third pummeling. He flung a fourth blow into the washboard belly. Again and again, enjoying the animal grunt that burst from Garrett's lungs each time Donegan drummed the face with his hardwood fist.

"That's enough!"

Seamus blinked his bloodied eyes, a flicker of blue and gold braid passing before him. Hands reached out, clawing at his arms. Like swatting flies, he flung the soldiers away. Then realized Fetterman's inner circle had dashed up behind Garrett.

"Arrest that man!"

Stunned, still drunk with adrenaline, Donegan watched Fetterman bellow his orders.

"By god, we've got this mick bastard to rights now!"

A different voice this time. *Brown.* As he thought it, the weight of several bodies collapsed atop his back at once. Seamus flung Garrett free, then shrugged his powerful back free of the soldiers clawing over him like a dog shook water. The Irishman started his turn, fist poised in the air—when the click of the revolver pierced the loud clamor. And everything got quiet.

Swiping a hand across his bloody, sweat-stained eyes, Donegan recognized the gaping muzzle of a regulation army .44. Aimed at his puffy nose. At the business end of the pistol hung an officer's trembling hand. Captain Brown.

"Just make a move, *Mister* Donegan," Brown growled. "Please. Any provocation whatsoever . . . and I'll oblige you by blowing some army lead through what you've got for brains."

Seamus swiped his eyes again. Watching Fetterman and Bisbee, Grummond and Wands gather on either side of Brown, their mule-eared holsters unsnapped. Two more hands filled with revolvers while Fetterman and Bisbee struggled to haul Garrett to his feet.

A big load, that one, Seamus thought. Donegan brought his arms up, slowly—hands empty.

"Want no trouble from an armed man," he sputtered, his lips swollen.

"That's all you've got now, mister!" Fetterman bawled. "Interfering with my sergeant's drill."

"Drill?" Seamus replied with a quick chuckle, eyes on the muzzle of Brown's pistol.

"You're fired from my payroll." Brown said. "Don't want you cutting timber on army wages no longer. Knew something stunk about you first day you rode in here."

"Arrest him, Fred," Fetterman goaded. "He deserves some time to cool his heels in the guardhouse."

"Yes! Perhaps you're right," Brown replied. "Not only

fire him off the rolls, but lock the bastard up as well. *Interfering with military discipline!* Well, Mr. Donegan— how does that charge do your uncivilized Hibernian heart now?"

Seamus smiled. Too often he had watched things just like this run their course. *If it wasn't such a bleeming shame, I'd laugh in their faces!*

"Every man here saw Garrett beat that young sojur over there," Donegan said. "All of you watched. But done nothing——"

"Burke's been a problem for some time now!" Fetterman said with a smile. "I knew there'd come a time when he'd have some 'soldier' knocked into him."

Donegan squared his shoulders, sensing the mass of troopers at his rear. "You career officers all alike, ain't you now, Fetterman? To you bastards, sojurs are nothing more than cattle. Fit to be prodded and manhandled, with the whip or pistol butt."

"Dare you question military——"

"No," Seamus interrupted. "I don't question military authority, Cap'n Fetterman. But what I watched Garrett do today had nothing to do with your military authority."

"What the goddamn hell do you know about the military, you stupid sonofabitch!" Fetterman seethed.

"Served under plenty of arrogant martinets like you, from the first battle of Bull Run," he answered, licking his bloody lip, "all the way to the time we swallowed up Uncle Bob Lee in Appomattox Wood."

Fetterman eyed the Irishman severely. "Just who the frigging hell did a jackanape like you march behind?"

"Never marched behind nobody, Cap'n. I rode."

"Cavalry?"

"Aye," he answered, glaring at Garrett for a moment. "Of a time I wore those stripes Eli Garrett's got sewed on his tunic."

"Company C?" Fred Brown squealed.

"Aye, Cap'n. Second, by god—Cavalry."

"Sergeant of the guard!" Brown hollered. "Bring two of your men. I want this man locked in the guardhouse. Now!"

The sergeant and his two guards grabbed Donegan as Brown stepped back.

"Every one of you halt! Right where you stand."

Seamus put the voice with a face, and came up with Carrington.

"Care to explain yourself, Captain?" he snapped.

"I'm locking this civilian in the guardhouse, Colonel."

Donegan wasn't sure, but it seemed Brown was the sort of man who could strut just standing still.

"I know damned well what you're about to do," he sputtered. "I want to know *why!*"

Carrington's sudden, fuming anger caught Brown by surprise. "He . . . Donegan, I'm saying—interfered in army business. I'll have charges written up later. For the time, he'll sit in there and rot till——"

"You saw the whole thing happen, did you?" Carrington inquired.

"I did, Colonel. Sergeant Garrett here drilling his men. Correcting a problem when this civilian——"

"Captain, best you understand I watched as well," he interrupted Brown. "Right over there." Every man's head craned as Carrington pointed across the parade to the tiny knot of women and children clustered at the front of the chapel.

"And, I might add," the colonel went on, "every woman on the post—all eleven of them—heard every word of the altercation as well. My boys subjected to the . . . earthy vocabulary Sergeant Garrett used. As well as the . . . shameful words used by members of my own staff. Captain Brown and . . . you—Captain Fetterman."

"Sir." The captain nodded his head. "I'm sorry if any of my language——"

"My own two sons, captains!"

"Our apologies, sir," Brown replied, contrite. "An unusual circumstance. Now, if you don't mind, we'll see that the flap's put to rest and the sergeant's free to drill his men once more."

"I don't think you understood me when I said I watched it all, Captain Brown. In full sight of the garrison, its women and—God forbid!—its children. This sergeant," and he flung a finger at Garrett, "reviled another soldier in language which has no place among Christian peoples."

"Colonel, I damn well don't believe it fitting that you should interfere with your officers in the performance——"

"Captain Fetterman!" Carrington wheeled, shouting. "You have the gall to . . . to swear at me?"

"By damn if it takes that to make my point!"

Carrington fumed a moment, then whirled on the guard detail. "You'll see Sergeant Garrett is locked up."

"You're letting Donegan go free?" Brown howled.

The colonel turned back to his scowling officers. "No. They'll both spend some time in the guardhouse. While we sort this out."

"The duty of a commanding officer should be to enforce what his officers——"

"Don't lecture me on the duties of a commanding officer, Captain Fetterman!"

"Someone ought to! Appears you don't have a frigging idea one what it means to *command!*" The compound fell to a hush. "While the rest of us placed our lives on the line in battle, you were pushing pens——"

"Before I say or do something I'll regret, Captain Fetterman—you're dismissed!" Carrington snapped, near the end of his string.

"Colonel, if I may?" Adjutant Wands stepped between his superior and the captains. His face glowed with anger. "Not backing your company commanders in their exercise——"

"Mister!" he shouted at Wands. "I have a post to run. And I'll run Fort Phil Kearny as I see fit."

"As long as it's yours to run," Brown growled.

"What was that, Captain?" Carrington seethed.

"This is your post . . . for *now*, Colonel," Brown replied, turning on his heel and stomping off.

"Sergeant?" Carrington demanded.

The guard got the message, taking both brawlers into custody, shoving them across the parade toward the lockup. As the milling crowd of soldiers dispersed, the colonel turned. On the headquarter's porch he recognized Bridger and Stead. Farther down the company street he watched the women disappear into Reverend White's chapel. Only Margaret Carrington remained frozen to her spot. Young Harry and Jimmy clutched the folds of their mother's long overcoat.

Donegan looked over his shoulder to see the colonel flick his hand, sending his wife and sons into Sunday service. Two soldiers yanked on his big arms, hurrying their prisoner.

Seamus strained to overhear what Carrington said to Fetterman when the two officers finally stood alone. From what he saw, Donegan realized no man would ever know what was exchanged in private between those two determined men at this crucial moment.

Chapter 25

$\mathcal{P}$ulling the flannel housecoat more tightly about her shoulders, she tiptoed into his office adjoining their private quarters. A few moments ago she had awakened sensing some dread and flew to the boys' room. Four of her six babies had been snatched from her at birth or infancy. A cruel curse for any woman to suffer. Both slept soundly. Her babies safe.

But she didn't find Henry asleep in his tiny cloister off the parlor. From the day of their arrival here at the foot of Cloud Peak, she and Henry had slept in separate rooms. For her, it made things easier. To his way of thinking, it made sense. He worked long into the night, writing reports and dispatches, mulling over construction details. And her? Why, she knew separate quarters made sense too—when the fire had gone out of their marriage and she hadn't the slightest desire to rekindle even the smallest of flames.

"Margaret!"

She watched him turn wearily at his desk, his papers spilled beneath yellow lamplight. His long hair messed. The blue tunic tossed carelessly over the back of another chair. Margaret moved to his side, sweeping his head against her bosom as a mother would a child. More frantically than even little Jimmy would cling, her husband hung to her in that desperate moment.

"Henry," she whispered. "Please. You must come to bed."

"I . . . I'll be there soon."

She sensed his need. Not for her body. There had been nights for that in their past. Afraid this time, she sensed Henry needed more from her than he had ever needed before.

"Tell me what it is," she asked, still cradling his head.

There came a strained, empty moment of silence before he answered in a weary voice. "My command, Margaret. I am . . . so alone."

"No, Henry," she whispered. "I'm right here with you. I always will be." Then felt him shudder.

"We're all so alone here. I don't know how long any of us can last under these conditions. Virtually cut off from our other posts. Not knowing if any mail gets through. Every day, Margaret . . . every day it's another skirmish. A running battle with some Sioux horsemen. Civilian woodcutters killed. Couriers missing. Private trains attacked on the road both north and south."

"We all sense the same isolation, Henry. Believe me."

He took his head from her bosom, gazing at the desk littered with maps and plans, orders and correspondence. He held a letter aloft. "It's from Cooke. Another of his scathing rebukes, Margaret. I'm certain one of my staff is sending Cooke reports on me. Giving the general the wrong impression of conditions——"

"You have an idea who it is?"

"Anybody." He shook his head. "Everybody! They're all more versed in warfare than I—there's the rub. War! They want to attack. And I need to finish the construction."

"Those were your orders."

"*Were* my orders, Margaret." He fluttered the letter again. "The bloody discontent among these postwar officers. Too damned many of them and too few positions that will allow for advancement. The war did that to us. The bloody war! It created far too many chiefs." He snorted. "I'll wager Red Cloud doesn't have the problems I do!"

"Henry——"

"Every damn one of my staff—lieutenants and captains —held high brevet rank during the war, Margaret. They chafe—Lord, do they chafe—now that they're bucked to lower rank and pay . . . with little prospect of promotion. Even dimmer prospect of command."

"But you command, Henry."

"By my teeth, dear. I hold on by my teeth!" He banged the desk with his fist.

"What's happening with your officers?" she asked, pushing a stray lock of Henry's hair from his eyes.

"Some . . . some have evidently accused me of being inept," he answered, his head slung between his weary shoulders. "As the chasm widens between me and my battle-hardened staff, I hear myself accused of tolerating insubordination . . . even from those I am tolerant of."

"Brown?"

"Yes."

"Bisbee? Hines? Wands and Powell?"

"Yes," and he nodded.

"Fetterman."

Henry looked up at her. No sense in hiding it. She knew. "Yes."

"They encircle him, don't they, Henry? He's their . . . their Mars. Their god of war, isn't he? Riding into *your* post, to become *their* savior. It's what Fetterman says that stings you most, isn't it?"

He nodded once. Finally looked back at her when she settled on the edge of the desk. "Brown's been saying I'm lenient toward offenders against military discipline."

"That awful incident with the fight two weeks ago . . . Sunday morning——"

"Yes," he answered quickly. "Brown is probably just Fetterman's mouthpiece. They both cross me. In front of the men. Right in front of my command!"

"What else are they saying about you, Henry?"

He raked a hand across one eye in exasperation. "Margaret, word has it I go to pieces under any pressure."

"I've never seen you fall apart, dear."

"I haven't—that's just it. Just one more imagined flaw reported to Cooke."

"You really believe some member of your staff is undermining all your noble efforts here?"

"Yes. This arrived in the mail today. I didn't want you to know——"

"Read it to me," she commanded.

He swallowed. "It's from Cooke."

"I know."

"Colonel: You are hereby instructed that so soon as the troops and stores are covered from the weather, to turn your earnest attention to the possibility of striking the hostile band of Indians in their winter camps.

An extraordinary effort in winter, when the Indian horses are unserviceable, it is believed, should be followed by more success than can be accomplished by very large expeditions in the summer. With two hundred or three hundred infantry, with much suffering, perhaps you might accomplish more than two thousand troops in summer.

You have a large arrear of murderous and insulting attacks by the savages upon emigrant trains and troops to settle, and you are ordered, if there prove to be any promise of success, to conduct or to send under another officer, such an expedition."

"Henry, you must give up ever making General Cooke understand the realities of what you face here. So far from Omaha. Surrounded by Sioux——"

"Again tonight I've written, telling him how unreasonable it is to propose an attack on the camps of Red Cloud's warriors. I lack more than a hundred Springfields. And the cavalry he so graciously sent me? Why, they're busy performing escort duty for the wood trains. I again begged for the carbines promised for the cavalry. Until they arrive, those horse soldiers must content themselves with outdated and wornout Starr carbines."

She waited when he fell quiet. "Henry, what are you going to do about Cooke's order to attack the Indians?"

He gazed into her moist eyes. Perhaps sensing something there in the way she looked at him that had too long been absent from her eyes. "It was an order, Margaret. A direct order. And I am, above all else——"

"A *soldier,* Henry Carrington."

"Yes," he whispered. "So I replied," and he read to his wife: " 'I will, in person, command expeditions, when severe weather confines the Indians to their villages, and make the winter one of active operations, as best affords chance of punishment.' "

"You . . . you have a plan?"

"Yes," he answered, seeming to really smile for the first time since she had entered the room. "I believe I can capture one of their raiding parties, Margaret. Like a hammer on an anvil, I can capture the warriors between a relief party I'll send out under one of the men. The hostiles know we always send out a small relief party."

"How will you capture the warriors with a small relief?"

"By pinching them between that relief party and a main attacking force I will lead."

Margaret felt the air freeze in her lungs. "You . . . you'll go yourself . . . lead the attack?" her voice sounded small.

"I must. For the sake of my command. My career, Margaret. For the future of this post and all our dreams."

"What the devil do you think you're doing, Mr. Donegan?" Carrington demanded.

"Breathing my first as a free man this fine morning, Colonel," Seamus explained as his horse joined Carrington's. Together they loped down the trail toward the crossing of the Big Piney that would take the colonel's detail of twenty-four soldiers climbing Lodge Trail Ridge.

"I know," he snapped. "I signed your release order myself."

"That doesn't explain what he's doing riding with us, Colonel!" Lt. George Grummond flared. He and Carrington led one half of the pincer movement the colonel hoped would catch some of the warriors who had attacked a wood train south of the Sullivant Hills early that afternoon.

Donegan smiled at the dark-headed lieutenant with the bushy mustache that hid his lips, then touched the brim of his floppy hat. "A good day to you too, Lieutenant. By the by, for a man who's spent time enjoying your hospitality, Colonel—I've lost track. What day would it be?"

"The sixth," Carrington answered.

"December?" Seamus shrieked. "Locked up since the eleventh of November!"

"Damn right," Grummond answered. "Funny, ain't it, Colonel. Been real quiet without this trouble maker stirring things up."

Donegan shook his head. "Nigh a month of me life stole in that cold pine house of yours, and neither of you the least bit grateful to see Seamus Donegan and his Henry rifle ride with you on this little set-to."

Carrington's eyes settled on the rifle the Irishman cradled across his thighs. "Mr. Donegan, we'll undoubtedly use every able man to settle a score with Red Cloud's warriors this day."

Nodding at Carrington, Seamus glanced at the undisguised loathing he read in Grummond's eyes. Damn, if army officers ain't all the same, he thought, easing back into the column of twos struggling up the slope behind Carrington. *North, south . . . or west. Most of 'em a bag of wind—and what officers ain't, they're a bag of bad-smellin' mule-droppings.*

The sun had dawned bright in a sky as clear as rinsed crystal that Thursday morning. Donegan had squinted some as he stepped from the guardhouse door, rubbed his eyes, then gazed for a long moment at the snowy mountains shouldering the sky. Freed at last, he had scampered down the hill to the civilian camp along the Little Piney. Fires smoldered, dying. The camp deserted. Every man at work—hay-cutting, wood-chopping, laboring in the quartermaster's stockade.

In the tent he shared with Captain Marr, Seamus found his rifle well-oiled and wrapped in a piece of old canvas. "Like as not," he had said aloud to himself, "the cap'n didn't have the foggiest when I'd come free, neither."

After tugging on a clean pair of long-handles, Seamus stuffed a clean shirt into his gray cavalry britches. The cleanest pair of stockings were pulled onto his feet before he stuffed them once more into the dusty, hog-leg cavalry boots. When he had filled himself on some jerked elk Marr had left behind and drunk his fill of creek water, Donegan strolled over to the civilian corral next to stockade. There he found his big gray well-fed and curried.

"Thankee, Cap'n Marr," he had whispered while stroking the gray's muzzle. "You're a gentleman among uncivilized, selfish poltroons." He nudged the bridle gently. "I best take you down to camp, boy. Seeing how we're no longer in the employ of this fine army establishment—best you stay near me. No telling when we've got to make a run for it, eh? Red Cloud's warriors love to get their paws on the likes of you, wouldn't they?"

A little past noon Donegan had been awakened from his nap by distant gunshots. Using a mariner's brass looking-glass, Seamus spotted several mounted warriors descending Lodge Trail Ridge toward Big Piney crossing. All along the Peno Head and Lodge Trail, signal mirrors flashed, spitting back light like fractured pieces of sunbeams dappling the valley. Rifle shots cracked in the distance. Miles off, along the south slope of the Sullivant Hills.

"A wood train, no doubt," he had grumbled, eyes

searching the tent for his pistol and extra ammunition. Every pocket in his trousers, vest, and mackinaw he stuffed with shells for the Henry. Quickly slapping the saddle blanket and his old McClellan atop the gray, Donegan nudged the bridle back in the horse's mouth and swung aboard.

As he wheeled the animal, wondering what direction to take, the Irishman had the decision made for him. Out of the fort's sawmill gates clattered the cavalry, a squad of mounted infantry struggling to bring up the rear. Seamus figured he'd be less than welcome joining that group. Eli Garrett hurried his troopers down the slope. And riding just in front of him, leading the relief itself, rode three officers to make four of a kind. Lt. Horatio S. Bingham, commanding cavalry, assigned to Capt. William Judd Fetterman. Between the two rode the man who loathed Seamus Donegan no less than did Eli Garrett—Capt. Frederick Brown.

"Won't do to join that pack o' snarling wolves, boy," he had whispered, kicking heels. "Let's see what we can scare up elsewheres. While Fetterman's crew scampers after the wood train, we'll look into all those mirrors. Hep-hah!"

He had swung north around the brow of the low plateau to bump into the troopers galloping out of the main gate behind Carrington and Grummond. To a veteran horse soldier, it made sense.

"C'mon, boy!" he urged the gray. "Fetterman's bunch'll drive the Injins into retreat . . . and Carrington'll cut that retreat off sweet as kidney pie. Let's ride!"

When the colonel's detail reached the Big Piney north of the fort, they found the crossing sheeted from bank to bank. Beneath the translucent mica an icy cascade tumbled across the gravel bottom, creating great, boiling bubbles of trapped air that foamed and flutted downstream. The roving bands sighted across the creek barely moments ago had disappeared like woodsmoke in the wind.

Only three warriors sat atop the ridge now, watching the soldier advance.

Carrington signaled a halt, turned his stallion into the creek to break the ice for those to follow. Several yards from the bank the ice still held, until the colonel's horse balked, terrified, fighting the bit. Its iron shoes skidded. Wide-eyed, it twisted, clambering back to the bank, crashing through the ice. Floundering in the bubbling flow, Carrington sputtered, drenched to his chest. He yanked the stallion across on foot, kicking the ice free with his sopping boots, wading in freezing water that lapped at his gunbelt.

"Go back to the fort, Colonel! I'll take it from here," Grummond shouted as he reined up beside his drenched commander.

"N-No," Carrington stammered, lips numbing. "Can't allow my men to think me a c-coward!"

"You're a damn fool," Grummond snorted contemptuously, speeding on.

"I . . . thought they'd see . . ." Carrington crawled aboard his horse. Clumsy. Shivering. Teeth chattering.

Donegan halted beside him. "Some men too busy to recognize another man's courage . . . because they're so busy worrying about their own. Seen it. Many a'time."

"I've g-got to lead——"

"Ride on, Colonel!" Donegan slapped the rump of Carrington's horse. He stayed with the colonel as they raced past some of the slower horses straining up the side of Lodge Trail Ridge. Out of the trees and into the stiff wind that rawhided down from the Big Horns.

As the soldiers climbed to the top of the first spur, they spotted four warriors waiting on the Bozeman Road beyond.

"A wee bit late setting up their decoy for you, Colonel," Donegan shouted, pointing.

Into the bushes on either side of the road disappeared more Sioux.

"I counted thirty-two, sir!" Grummond hollered.

"Where there's thirty," Carrington signaled his men to follow, "a safe bet is there's sixty!"

"Even more come to join the party," Donegan announced, pointing his Henry into the valley of the Big Piney.

Fetterman's soldiers had dashed to the relief of the wood train, sweeping more than a hundred Indians before him exactly as Carrington's plan dictated.

"Time for us to break their party up, Mr. Donegan," Carrington said. He turned to Grummond. "Lieutenant, we'll attack those hostiles waiting for us in the valley!"

"Damn right we will, sir! About time!" He twisted in the saddle to holler back at his men, "Pistols ready! Guide center—at a gallop . . . ho!"

Seamus Donegan felt the surge of adrenaline through his veins. The cords along his neck pumped heady juices to his brain as he slapped heels to the eager gray beneath him. Along the columns rose eager shouts and cheers. He turned and glanced at the flushed young faces as the drumming of hoofs and the clatter-clang of saddle gear drowned out all else. *Recruits . . . getting their first raw taste of horse soldiering this day.*

Near the western end of Lodge Trail, Grummond brought his mount galloping alongside Carrington. "Unless we kick straight down the slope at a full gallop, we won't make the valley in time to cut off the warriors Fetterman's herding before him!"

"At a gallop, Mr. Grummond. Just be sure that none of the men get scattered heading down," Carrington ordered.

"Right!" Grummond pulled back to pass the word.

A moment later the lieutenant tore past Carrington, careening down the slope toward the flats near Peno Creek and a hundred screaming Sioux.

"What the devil!" the colonel screamed.

Grummond did not respond, racing low, his face along the horse's neck.

Carrington looked for help. "He's headed for certain suicide—the damned fool!"

"Suicide?" Donegan demanded, pulling his collar up against the wind.

"Jack Stead told me . . . the Cheyennes' warning."

"Warning?"

"When the snows come," Carrington explained, "Two Moons and the Sioux would give us a big fight."

Seamus gazed into the heavy, gray sky. "Snow any time now, Colonel."

His lips threaded into a line of determination as he fought to keep his teeth from clattering. "Warned us— the Sioux would bait us . . . drawing us to our own destruction."

"Where?" Seamus asked.

"Beyond Lodge Trail Ridge."

Donegan twisted to his left, gazed down into the valley of the Big Piney. "I'll be damned, Colonel—but it looks like we've come to the end of the Lodge Trail now."

"Down there—that fool Grummond is about to throw his life away!" Carrington shouted into the rising wind.

"I'll pull him, Colonel!" Donegan shouted into the clatter of hoofs and saddle gear as he sped off, pounding heels against the gray's flanks.

As his horse pitched headlong down the slope, Seamus whispered into its ear, "Let's pray there's nothing but wind to a Sioux promise."

Chapter 26

*I*t wasn't as if this were his first battle at all. German-
born bugler Adolph Metzger had six years of service
under his belt before the rebels fired on Sumter. Stayed
regular army after Appomattox, finding the promise of
three squares and a warm bunk some security for a man
who didn't know but twenty words of English when he
first donned army blue. Now, eleven years later and
sporting a tinge of gray at his temples, Metzger wasn't
one to let a bunch of screaming Sioux rile him. Was a
time he'd thought about a pair of sergeant's chevrons,
like they gave that wild young Irishman during the Rebellion. But Adolph had quickly figured it much safer to
remain a common soldier.

What with the way sergeants went at it. Two he had
known during the war tossed in the guardhouse. Eli Garrett set free two days later. And Donegan, Adolph
thought, left to rot in the dark for the better part of a
month.

Minutes ago he had followed Fetterman, Brown, and
Bingham around the brow of a hill to discover the wood
train corraled near the middle of the road. Some of the
soldiers rasped their glittering sabers into the sunlight.
Others began firing even though the Sioux were still more
than a half mile off. For all the shouting and bravado,
they watched the warriors turn to flee then immediately

split into two bands. Fetterman ordered Bingham to follow the group sweeping right, heading toward the western end of Lodge Trail Ridge, while the captain's own platoon followed the band galloping into the valley of the Peno. Metzger stayed with his company commander. But it hadn't taken long for Bingham to lose his head.

None of us knew what we was in for, fighting Indians, Metzger thought as he watched Bingham race ahead with a handful of men, following a few warriors baiting their trap. *Not a man among us knew these Indians would not stand like Confederates stood and fought . . . like white men! None of us had an idea what we was facing.*

A moment later Metzger realized how alone he and the other fourteen men left behind really were. He threw up his hand and looked round at the young faces tight with fear. Dry-mouthed, Metzger realized he was the oldest man there. Not an officer in sight.

Metzger swallowed. Calmed himself and hollered, "We'll take cover, men!" Sweeping an arm toward the Peno Creek cottonwoods better than fifty yards off, "Stay together at all costs!"

Before his squad even began their ride, the cottonwoods belched half a hundred screaming warriors. The soldiers rolled over one another in a jumbled mass, dashing for the base of the ridge where some huge boulders stood that might give cover until rescued. Then, as suddenly as the warriors had materialized, they disappeared. Back down to the creek, across and gone. Metzger reined up, signaling his green fourteen.

"They'll bunch for attack!" he shouted, remembering how Confederate cavalry bushwackers would whittle away at small detachments of Union horse. "Dismount, boys! Fight them where we stand!"

"They've run off, you dumb Kraut!" one young red-haired soldier cheered.

Metzger wheeled, watching the warriors disappear over the knobs and knuckles of raw landscape. Turning, Adolph understood as he watched the horsemen ripping down the bare slant of ridge in their direction. Carrington reined up near the fifteen dismounted soldiers, his detail a noisy clang and squeak of cold saddle-leather.

"What the devil you doing here? Who're you with?" the colonel demanded.

"Lieutenant Bingham, sir," Metzger answered. "C Company, Second—"

"Where's Bingham?" Carrington snapped.

"Gone that way," he answered, pointing west across the Peno. Into the snow swept hills where the fifty warriors had suddenly appeared, then flitted off like spring butterflies. "Gone down the trail——"

"He rode ahead of you?"

"Outrun the rest of us, sir."

"A bloody lot of that happening today," Carrington muttered bitterly.

Metzger watched the colonel seethe a moment, his lips pursed into a grim line of consternation.

"By god," Carrington growled, "Fetterman's off in one direction, his unit torn apart . . . Bingham dashing off God knows—I go to one of them, soldier, the other is sacrificed."

Metzger nodded. "Bring 'em to you, Colonel."

"Bring them to me?"

Adolph pointed to what he carried on a thick, braided cord over his shoulder. Carrington nodded with half a smile.

"Bugler?"

"Sir?" Metzger replied enthusiastically, bringing the brass horn to his lips.

"Sound Recall."

Metzger licked the cold mouthpiece, blew the call once, then twice more before his breath moisture froze in the bugle.

"Colonel—" he started to explain.

"Good enough, soldier." Carrington flung an arm forward. "You men mount up. We've got to——"

The trees and tumble of brush erupted with rifle fire

and a flight of arrows. An iron-tipped shaft hit Carrington's stallion high on the flank. He fought for control as the soldiers about him hollered with struggles of their own.

"Fall back! Fall back! Skirmish formation!"

"Say, bugler!" An old infantryman dashed alongside Metzger. "Like old times, eh, friend? Appears the ball's opened for sure now!"

"With one hell of grand march!"

"Old soldiers like us—always love to fight to music, don't we?"

"Gottamn!" Metzger replied, tugging at his lunging horse. "If we had Curry's whole band here, we could play these savages a fine number!"

Pvt. James McGuire pitched from his horse in the melee and lay senseless for a moment in the dust and old snow along the road. Carrington himself rushed forward when he spotted a warrior dashing out, ready to swing his warclub at McGuire. His action scared the warrior off, but it drew a phalanx of arrows from other Sioux.

"By the gods! Under fire at last!" the colonel roared lustily.

"More've come to join the dance, bugler," the old infantryman yelled grittily as he pulled his ramrod into action.

"More a hundred now," Metzger replied sourly, reloading his old Starr carbine.

"Tell you what, bugler," the old soldier replied. "You shoot only your share. You hear? Leave half for O'Malley!"

"Half I'll leaf you, O'Malley!" Adolph cheered.

For more than fifteen minutes, each moment as heavy as an hour, the warriors circled and stabbed at the defensive perimeter the soldiers had thrown up at the base of the ridge. With constant reminders from Metzger and a handful of others, most of the green recruits fired slowly. Firing only with a target in their sights.

Close enough I could spit on 'em, Adolph brooded, struggling with his heated Starr carbine.

On the warriors swept across the creek and along the brow of the hill. Smoke hung heavy in the cold air. *Thicker than those Virginia hickory ham-sheds.*

Arrows whispered through the thicket like nervous, probing, iron-tipped fingers. Across the slopes of Peno Head, above the fight, signal mirrors flashed in the pale, frosty light. Moments later the warriors withdrew, as if swept over the hills by a broad hand. Only then did the soldiers understand what the mirrors had been signaling.

Fetterman's command dashing to Carrington's rescue.

Lieutenant Wands had watched Fetterman turn in his saddle, both of them startled to hear the pounding hoofs clattering up behind them. Their detail had scattered the warriors swarming over the wood train. Already Bingham had dashed off to pursue a splinter band with half the troops. Wands recognized the familiar bearded figure spurring the little calico pony beneath him, straining to catch up.

"Fred!" Fetterman shouted into the cold wind.

"Judd!" Brown answered breathlessly. "Alex!"

"What took you so long to join the fight? You suffering from Carrington's cowardice, eh?" Fetterman yelled.

"You dare mention my name beside that spineless bastard's!" Brown growled. "Had to wait till the old fool set off with Grummond. You damn well know he wouldn't let me join the attack—much less ride with you!"

"Let's all raise some scalps!" Fetterman flung an arm forward, wolf-grinning at Brown and Wands.

Across the base of the Peno Head the trio led their troops in the wake of the fleeing warriors. No man paying any attention to glittering mirrors signaling above them.

Down off Peno Head they clambered, their quarry flitting through brush and thicket. Wands swept the horizon, making mental note of the narrow spur of broken land jutting north, spreading the two branches of Peno Creek the way a woman opens her legs for a lover.

Ah, Katie, Wands moaned silently.

Fearlessly they raced after the warriors into the yawning maw of the Peno. Down slopes carved by centuries of erosion, over raw scars of narrow ravines. Through brush and bramble thick enough to conceal an ambush.

"Fred!" Wands shouted into the wind. His voice whipped along his cheeks like the cold tears streaming from his eyes.

"FRED!"

Brown turned.

"We go down there." Wands pointed into the thickets ahead, "none of us come out!"

Fetterman and Brown laughed metallically.

"You lost your nerve of a sudden, Alex?" Brown demanded.

"Been trapped before," he explained limply. Shamed before them. "Crazy Woman——"

"Leave the goddamned command to us!" Brown hollered into Wands's face, spittle on his lips.

He only wants to be certain his order's understood, Wands brooded, trying to lessen the sting of Brown's words.

A moment later it didn't matter who was right or wrong. They were all in the thick of it. Surrounded. Horses turning, skidding, bumping. Soldiers dropping to the ground to fight. Every man screaming.

"By god they'll stand and fight now, Judd!" Brown raised his shrill voice above the clamor, struggling with the skittish calico.

"Damn right, Fred! Here's our chance to get our licks in!" Fetterman cried.

Behind them along a thin rib of bare ridge, more than thirty feathered warriors blotted a span of skyline. Pouring down toward the bottom of the draw. Wands pointed, begging Fetterman to realize what he had ridden into.

"More keep coming!" Wands yelled. "Till we run out of ammunition and they overrun us!"

As swiftly as the thirty warriors raced off the rib, they were followed into the ravine by Bingham's squad. Down the face of the slope his cavalry charged toward the cheering troopers penned down with Fetterman and Brown. Straight through the center of the ravine the warriors scrambled. Bingham driving the Sioux before him in a wild charge through Fetterman's position.

"Lieutenant!" Fetterman hollered at Bingham as he raced up, then swept on by without slowing.

"BINGHAM!" Brown leaped from cover to holler after the lieutenant.

Fetterman and Brown stood their ground at the bottom of the ravine, holding their rifles in the air, shouting, ordering Bingham's troops to stop.

"It's an ambush!" Brown shouted.

"You'll be killed, you follow him in there!" Wands joined the captains. Surrounding the trio, lathered horses snorted, their riders fighting for control.

"C'mon!" Bingham hollered to his men as he disappeared around the brow of the ravine, a handful of troopers hot on his tail. The rest fidgeted, confused, halted by Brown and Wands. Staring at the officers' carbines.

"First man moves to retreat . . ." Brown screamed maniacally, "just one of you rides anywhere—I'll shoot!"

The quiet grew eerie as the pounding of iron-shod hoofs disappeared with Bingham's handful of faithful cavalry. The whoops and screeches of warriors faded over the bare, windswept knobs. Beside Wands a young horse-soldier's teeth rattled like dice in a horn cup. Off in the distance he thought he heard a bugle. He couldn't be sure—this high, thin air might play tricks on a man. Might only be the wind . . .

Alex thought it almost quiet enough to hear the cold breeze nudging the brittle grasses in the thicket. Like the rattle of arrows seeking him out. The nightmare of the Crazy Woman returned to haunt him still.

"Mount!" Fetterman bawled.

"Mount up, men!" Brown echoed. "We're going after those warriors."

"Let's raise some scalps!" Fetterman hollered, leading off. "Show the red devils what real soldiers are!"

As Alex climbed into the saddle, he finally realized his own teeth were chattering like a box of dominoes.

Chapter 27

"Carrington can rot in hell!" Grummond flung his words back at Donegan. "I won't go back. Won't retreat . . . he's a craven coward!"

The lieutenant spat his words into the cold wind as they scrambled down the scarred slope of Lodge Trail Ridge together.

"You'll be killed!" Donegan repeated. "What can one man do——"

"I'm not alone!" Grummond pointed.

Directly ahead appeared Lieutenant Bingham and a handful of troopers, chasing more than thirty feathered warriors over a raw finger of bare ridge. Into the badlands north of the Lodge Trail.

"Bingham's a fighter, by jove!" Grummond wore a wild smile across his mouth normally hidden beneath a bushy mustache. "Carrington can rot in his goddamned post—and leave the fighting to real soldiers!"

Donegan turned in his saddle, fretting what to do. The long, brittle slope of Lodge Trail had disappeared behind another knuckle of scarred landscape. Carrington and the rest were back there. Somewhere. A damn poor choice . . . but at least he knew where he could find other men. Straight ahead. Ride with Grummond. Join Bingham. Chase the Sioux. Shoot some warriors while hoping the blood lust cooled in these mad officers.

Get back to the post before the Sioux backtrailed and surrounded them.

By the time he and Grummond overtook Bingham, only one Indian remained in sight. On foot. Tantalizingly dashing from thicket to bramble. Luring the hot-blooded soldiers. Seductively.

"Can't you see it's a trap?" Seamus hollered into the wind.

Both Bingham and Grummond smiled mechanically at him. *As if they don't bloody care that they're leading these men to their deaths!*

"It's a bleeming decoy!" Donegan shrieked.

Angry beyond words, the Irishman turned in his saddle, reining up for a heartbeat, haunch-sliding the big gray to a stop. And felt the hair along the back of his neck rise. Dozens of warriors sprang from the bushes on either side of the backtrail.

They're closing the bleeming trap on us!

"LIEUTENANT BINGHAM!" he bellowed like a wounded bull.

It didn't matter. Bingham and Grummond already had their hands full at the moment. As soon as the warriors behind Donegan sprang from hiding, even more Sioux leaped from the brush up ahead. Eight soldiers and one angry civilian trapped.

Donegan raked his heels along the gray's flanks. He'd stand a better chance joining the soldiers than fighting off the screaming savages hot on his tail.

Too late for . . . Bingham flung his arms in the air, the side of his head a red blossom sprayed in the frosty air. He tumbled from his horse into the trampled snow.

"Sergeant!" Grummond hollered at the soldier with bright chevrons. "Form up the men!"

"Form up?" Bowers asked. He was infantry. "Damn well know how to fight on foot," he yelled back, struggling with his unruly mount as the warriors closed in. "Gimme a chance to——"

Three warriors using a rawhide lariat yanked Bowers

from his saddle. More loops whistled through the air as the Sioux worked at pulling the soldiers from their horses. Not risking a gun battle that might kill the valuable soldier mounts.

Donegan flung aside a lariat sailing toward him. Watched another loop tighten about a soldier ten feet ahead. In a spray of snow and icy slush, the trooper slapped the ground, rolling over, hollering for help as a warrior leaped over him, pinning him down, a gleaming tomahawk held high. The pitiful screech——

As the soldier's face disappeared beneath the Indian's bloody weapon, Seamus recognized those sensitive eyes of a musician. The terror-filled eyes of Frank Noone.

"By damn—follow me!" Grummond yelled.

"Where, sir?" Pvt. John Guthrie shouted.

"Out, goddammit! *OUT!*"

Donegan saw the lieutenant rip his saber from its scabbard. Flinging his empty pistol away, Grummond swung the saber from side to side like a scythe lopping wheat.

Seamus yanked the Henry to his shoulder. Swung the front blade about. And peered down the frosty, blued barrel at a white man dressed in buckskins and capote. Hollering orders at the warriors. Directing them. *Commanding the h'athens!*

He blinked his eyes to be certain of what he saw, then watched the white leader turn his way, arrogantly staring for a long moment as Donegan eased back on the trigger. Looking down the barrel at that white man watching in disbelief as the mounted Irishman shot him in the belly.

Gawddamned renegade!

"Arggggghhh!"

He wheeled, seeing Grummond slashing on all sides as he urged his rigid horse back, back up the hill.

Seamus and the four soldiers still left in the saddle swung their rifles like clubs. Muzzle-loading Springfields emptied and useless now. Warriors breathing too close for Donegan to use his Henry.

Bleeming hand to hand——

A rigid shock thundered through his shoulders as the Henry's stock cracked against a copper head or smashed a ribcage. At his side rang the familiar *crick* each time Grummond's saber cleaved skull or bone.

Their retreat splattered with sinew, brain, and blood. A savage, slashing dash back through the gaping maw of hell.

"If you'd supported Bingham—"

"Captain Fetterman!" Carrington roared. "I'll not be badgered nor lectured——"

"A cowardly act of a post commander," he shouted, his voice crackling like a quirt on still air. "Abandoning your officers——"

"I didn't——"

"Withholding your support!"

From the moment Fetterman and Brown had led their troopers after the fleeing warriors and bumped instead into Carrington's squad, the young captain had been jabbing an accusing finger at the colonel. Brown sat silent, his lips a thin line of undisguised hatred. He could tell from the look on Carrington's face that the colonel well understood his post quartermaster had disobeyed orders to join Fetterman. Fred Brown seethed to join the argument. He dared not. Not, just yet.

"By god, you're a spineless bastard!" Fetterman exploded. "I vowed as an officer that within sixty days of my arrival that I'd regain the honor of this regiment . . . an honor you've done your bloody best to destroy!"

"That's quite enough!" Carrington snapped.

A distant clatter of iron-shod hoofs coupled with the frantic yells of men interrupted their heated debate. Over a bare knob raced a soldier jabbing his horse in the flank with a saber. On his trail charged another soldier whipping his mount into a lather. At the rear galloped a big gray horse, its rider wearing a plaid mackinaw coat.

"Lieutenant Grummond!" Carrington hollered as the trio skidded to a stop on trampled snow.

"George!" Brown cheered. "Your horse—bleeding——"

"Spurs weren't enough!" Grummond growled. "I stuck him to make the bastard move!"

"More than once from the looks of it, mister," the colonel accused.

"If you'd supported your men, Colonel Carrington!" Grummond wheeled on his commanding officer, his eyes aflame. "You left it to me to support Lieutenant Bingham —while the rest of your command gets chopped to pieces."

"Exactly what I told him!" Fetterman agreed, nodding at Grummond. "You've acted like either a prissy fool, Colonel, or the damned coward every man says you are."

"You'll not bully-rag me, Captain!" Carrington barked.

"I'll grant you this Indian war's quickly become a hand-to-hand fight—requiring the utmost caution," Fetterman allowed.

Carrington appraised the captain suspiciously. "Thank you, Captain Fetter——"

"But that caution's no excuse for abandoning your troops."

"Gentleman," Carrington soothed, trying to calm his own anger, "have you forgotten about Bingham?"

"Wasn't he with you, Grummond?" Brown inquired stridently.

"He was," George stuttered. "Or, I was with him——"

"Lieutenant's dead."

Their heads turned to look at the red-cheeked Irishman.

"Last I saw of him—the side of his head blowed off." Donegan pointed.

Brown watched the Irishman's eyes settle on him.

"We slashed our way out," Grummond explained.

"Mr. Donegan." Carrington threw a hand up to silence any more conversation. "Take us."

"Aye, Colonel." He sawed the big gray around, pounding heels.

"Troops at a gallop!" Fetterman hollered. "Center—
HO!"

Minutes later they found Bingham's body flung over an old stump. More than fifty Sioux arrows bristled from his naked corpse. The scalp ripped from his skull. His scrotum obscenely jammed into his mouth.

In a nearby clump of bullberry Donegan found Frank Noone, split wide open from crotch to chin. Most of his organs lay on either side of the body. It reminded him of a Christmas goose his mother would stuff. The neck and giblets and heart . . .

Not far away they located Sgt. G. R. Bowers lying in the trampled dust of a game-trail. His coat, shirt and trousers stripped from his body, along with his boots. Brown vaulted from the calico at a run. Kneeling beside the sergeant, he gently took Bowers's bloody head in his lap. The sergeant's eyelids fluttered against a glittering dance of frost crystals afloat in the bright December sun.

"Don't try to talk, Greg," Brown said, wiping dirt from lips trembling to speak.

The side of the sergeant's head was missing where a warrior had split it with a tomahawk. Bowers's blood and tissue soaked into the captain's blue britches like a splatter of dark molasses as Brown cradled his Civil War comrade.

"I'll walk the last few steps beside you, Greg," Brown whispered. "You've not far to go now. I'm at your shoulder—here till you no longer need a friend."

"Bowers said he got three of the devils before . . . before they got him, Frances," George Grummond whispered to his wife huddled at his side.

Even his remark could not take her eyes from the young widow dressed in black, her face hidden from time to time by the veil that the wind refused to honor. Her baby clutched to her breast, wrapped in a dark scrap of bunting. Perhaps no older than Frances herself.

The poor . . . poor Abigail . . .

A cold scut of wind knifed along the bare ground without remorse, rustling her black crinoline dress and petticoats. Frances wondered if she'd ever be warm again. What a lonely, forsaken place the colonel chose, she brooded to herself, and leaned against George.

For the post cemetery Carrington had selected this high rib of ground jutting off Pilot Hill, overlooking the valley where the Pineys began their march across the plains. Overhead the low-running clouds made Frances Grummond's little world look like the bottom of a slate-colored pool.

Nearby waited the hundreds come to watch three more boxes lowered into the frozen earth. Other red-eyed women and fellow soldiers.

Too many funerals, she thought, eyes wet behind her black veil. Then Frances recalled how three days ago she and Margaret Carrington had stood frozen in terror when the picket rushed up shouting that the wood train had been attacked and all killed. Remembering now that look on Eleanor Bisbee's face. Her husband rode escort that Thursday.

Ironic that Bingham, not Bisbee, had been ripped from this earthly veil, Frances brooded.

Now Bisbee and poor Eleanor leave for Omaha. Soon as we commit these poor soldiers to the ground. God bless her —he's been reassigned, and Eleanor's getting him out of this . . . this hell that will swallow us all.

A pale December sun had spread milky light while it fell atop the Big Horns that Thursday the sixth. As quickly the temperature had fallen. While women waited, watching from the sentry platform headquarters. Waiting until weary horses brought the soldiers home.

Sergeant Bowers had died before Fred Brown allowed his friend moved. Besides Bingham, Bowers and Noone, a sergeant and four privates had been wounded. For all their trouble, the Indians had gotten their hands on but two horses. The soldiers had abandoned eight wounded animals in the bushes as they escaped the ambush. Carrington ordered five of them destroyed before he turned his angry, wound-licking command back to the post.

A civilian and Pvt. John Donovan were the only men who rode into the ambush with Bingham and rode back out unscathed. Again and again George had tried to soothe his wife's fears, laughing lightheartedly for Frances these past three days.

"Dear girl," he had said smiling at his brown-eyed daughter of the old South, "were it not that the Sioux wanted horseflesh more than scalps, your George would not be standing here in your arms!"

In hushed whispers she had overheard how close her George had come to joining Bowers and Bingham on this horrid hilltop. She had listened to bitter talk of blunders and mistakes, disobedience, cowardice and recklessness that marked the skirmish with the Sioux on December 6. Almost every man held Carrington accountable. Yet somehow even Frances realized no one man had to shoulder the guilt alone. Wands had joined Fetterman's squad though ordered to ride with Carrington. Bingham dashed ahead of his frightened, confused squad of raw recruits—racing to his death. Even her beloved George had ignored Carrington's order, galloping off alone—for some reason escaping the ambush that took the lives of three soldiers they buried today.

Every day it seemed to her that the men grew more desperate here to end their isolated struggles against the land, against the winter, the calendar, and the Indians themselves. And that unrelenting strain, Francis realized, was showing in those cracks ever widening between Carrington and his officers. At times some of the women even whispered in private that the staff command at Fort Phil Kearny fought among themselves with more tenacity and zest than they fought the Sioux.

When George had returned that cold afternoon, snow

lancing out of a ground-hugging, gray sky, Frances found it impossible to speak at first. Instead, they sat arm in arm for the longest time as darkness swallowed their little cabin. Sharing tears at his deliverance.

From that first brutal moment of uncertainty, Frances had been unable to shake the presence of dread that made sleep a fitful, nightmarish torture. Haunted by a recurring dream where she helplessly watched her George galloping frantically away from her, a score of Indians hot on his tail. Awaking each night as she heard him scream out for help. For his life.

There had been other deaths. Soldiers. Noncommissioned officers. But never a widow left behind. Never before . . . an orphan like Abigail Noone's baby girl.

"Ten-shun!"

The shout of the old line sergeant brought Frances back to the hill. And the cold seeping through her coat. To her marrow.

She watched the seven troopers slap their carbines against their legs as the procession of wagons and mourners topped the rise, drawing to a halt near the three mounds of frozen spoil wrenched from this hard ground. Twelve troopers slid the tin-lined pine coffins from their wagons, lowering the boxes beside the dark holes as the wind swept skiffs of icy flakes along the ground. Nudging dresses and coats, mufflers and hats they struggled to hold.

It's as if the sky itself . . . this very land, were in mourning for Abigail . . . alone now. Frances bit down on her lower lip till it hurt.

Afraid to pay too much attention to Reverend White's religious service, she watched her husband instead. That hard line clenched along his jaw. The press of his thin lips beneath the bushy mustache. Realizing she really didn't know the man all that well. But sensing George fought back his own tears of anger. Fought down the knot of fear at his own deliverance.

Thank you, God, she prayed. *Thank you for sparing him.* Frances felt the baby move. For the first time. She placed a hand on her belly. A hard kick beneath her ribs, then it slept.

". . . as were our fathers, and their fathers, lo—we are wayfarers and strangers before Thee. Our days are but shadows on this bitter earth. None will abide but Thee."

She listened to Reverend White drone on. Nothing wrong him being a Methodist, she thought.

". . . yea, the prairie sea of this earth grips the moldering dust of our fallen heroes. So oft unsung. So oft unhonored. But where a rare stone is placed to honor the name and deed in their passing . . ."

Better funerals conducted by Baptist preachers.

When White completed his simple service, he nodded to George Grummond. Solemnly the lieutenant stepped to the precipice of the middle hole, pulling a white handkerchief from his pocket which he hung from his coat belt for want of a Masonic apron. As six fellow Masons joined him at the graves, Grummond opened his ritual book, choking through the last rites to be read over fallen comrades.

"Captain Brown?" he asked, finished at last. Turning, he stuffed the book and handkerchief into the pockets of his overcoat.

Fred Brown stepped to the middle coffin, raised its lid. On Sergeant Bowers's breast the captain laid his own medal for bravery awarded during the Civil War. From Stone's River to Fredericksburg and on to the siege at Atlanta, Brown and Bowers had forged a fast friendship. Now Brown's "Army of the Cumberland" badge would rest for all time on the breast of his old friend.

Frances watched Brown swipe angrily at his drippy nose, touch Bowers's gray hand a last time before he lowered the coffin lid and stood.

"Port arms!"

The 18th's old funeral sergeant droned into his commands.

"Ready!"

Frances steeled herself for the coming roar, cradling the muffler over her belly to shield her unborn child.

"Aim!"

She watched the seven step back on their right feet, the dirty-gray barrels pointed forty-five degrees into the heavy sky.

"FIRE!"

She shuddered. Through all those years of war round her home in Tennessee . . .

"FIRE!"

. . . she had never grown accustomed to the cruel and obscene . . .

"FIRE!"

. . . thumping clatter of gunfire.

"Present arms!"

On the brow of the hill some thirty yards away, Metzger brought the bugle to his frozen lips. *Taps.* Slow and measured—a much-practiced death march.

It's over. She finally took a breath, afraid now to look at the woman in black.

As the gunsmoke scudded along the frozen ground, a sad chorus sang over the graves. Six of Curry's German bandsmen, Catholics all—their quiet, Teutonic dirge reverberating around the mourners who filed past the coffins, dropping hard clods of spoil atop each pine box.

"Come, Frances," George whispered as he swept back to her side. "Let's get you in where it's warm . . . the baby."

She nodded, then gazed up at him in the pewter half light of early afternoon. A strange glow surrounded George Grummond's head, reminding her of the halos she had seen atop the heads of angels in those childhood Bible storybooks.

Her knees softened. George caught her as she collapsed.

"I'll carry you down to the fort, dear." He swept her up.

Frances stared, mesmerized at the pale corona surrounding his head.

"The baby, George. Our baby!"

Chapter 28

*I*n his seventeen winters Curly could not remember a
robe season any colder. The wooly smother of snow
on the land did not dampen winter's bite.

The rivers had begun to freeze while the north winds
sculpted every snowdrift into jewel-glittered fans surrounding the gold stubble of prairie bunch-grass. Even
now the bullberry along the bottoms stood naked against
the onslaught. Across the sunny slopes the willow had
surrendered its last red leaves, wind-driven across the
frozen hills like bloody arrowheads left behind come this
season of sleep upon the land.

For days after their fight with the soldiers, many of the
Sioux argued among themselves. Many sided with Yellow
Eagle, who had planned and led the main attack on the
wood train. He said they had done right in trying to pull
the soldiers from their horses rather than shooting them
from cover. A growing number of young warriors, however, followed the words of Curly.

"Never again should we let soldiers live merely because we covet their horses," he had explained around
lodge fires in those days following the fight. "We lost the
horses . . . and the soldiers got away."

"Curly has the heart of a warrior." Man-Afraid had
silenced much of the criticism flung at his young protégé.
"I agree. We must kill soldiers. Forget the horses. We

must keep our eye on one thing only—death to *all* the soldiers at Pine Woods."

Each night in those villages stretched like a buffalo-rawhide lariat for some forty miles along the headwaters of the Tongue River, they debated the lessons to be learned from what had taken place in the opening days of this new moon. Argued, yes—yet everyone among them certain they had found the secret to crushing the soldiers who had come to profane Sioux hunting ground.

From late summer through the frosty days of fall, more and more recruits had ridden into the Sioux camps gathering no more than fifty miles north of the soldier fort. Not only the Sioux confederation, but Cheyenne under Roman Nose and Medicine Man. Arapaho under Little Chief and Sorrel Horse. Yet not until that fight in the valley of the Peno was there universal agreement among the chiefs and principal warriors. To all the villages runners had been sent to gather a great council. Tonight they would decide how to kill many soldiers, driving the rest from Sioux land—for all time.

Curly slid to the snow from his pony's back. The wool greatcoat kept him warm. The soldier who wore yellow bands on his arm no longer needed it. Curly had smashed an axe into the back of the soldier's head, leaving him to die because other white men hurried to the ridge-shadows where Curly killed the soldier leader and Yellow-Bands-on-His-Arms. Too many soldiers had escaped.

"Tonight, we have agreed how to assure that no soldiers escape our next attack." Red Cloud's voice rose over the lodge.

"It is good," Black Shield of the Miniconjous replied. "We are ready to fight together."

"So that we will never have to fight the white man again," Roman Nose agreed. "One big battle."

"With the white man driven from our land," Sorrel Horse echoed hope.

"We saw how we can overpower the soldiers . . . destroy any army sent against us!" Red Cloud roared in a voice that sent fiery chills along Curly's spine. "The first day after the next full moon we will lay a trap of all our warriors."

"Attack their slow wagons!" Man-Afraid cheered. "They always send soldiers out to protect their slow wagons!"

Red Cloud nodded. "Let a few lure the soldiers to their deaths."

"Who will lead the decoy?" Black Shield asked.

"Who among our young men should have this honor?" Red Cloud echoed.

Muttering filled the council lodge. Worry crossed their faces. The bands had agreed to a battle plan and when to spring their trap. Now their harmony appeared threatened. Curly grew anxious that all the good done would fall asunder.

"Brothers!"

Man-Afraid's voice rang out, silencing every man in the crowded lodge.

"There is but one among us who should bear the honor of leading the decoy that will lure the soldiers into the trap where the many will wait to spring."

"Who?" one old Oglalla called out.

Roman Nose stood. "I agree with Man-Afraid. He should lead the decoy!"

The ripple of a cheer began its trickle through the lodge warmed by fire and body heat—until Man-Afraid raised his arms and silenced the chiefs and head men.

"No," he answered, nodding to Roman Nose. "The Cheyenne chief humbles Man-Afraid by this honor. Yet Man-Afraid himself says there is but one to lead the decoy."

"Who is better qualified than you?" Sorrel Horse demanded.

"Yes," Red Cloud agreed. "None is braver than Man-Afraid."

The Oglalla shook his head with a smile. "In days gone by there was none known braver," he said, slapping a hand against his warshirt. "Comes a new day—there is one who no longer stands in my shadow. His courage spurs us all! He shall lead the decoy. He shall lure the soldiers to their death like the sage hen draws the wolf. He who has a heart of iron!"

Man-Afraid flung his arm out, pointing across the fire at his young protégé. Surprising him.

The young man stood slowly, unsure at first. Then squared his shoulders as the chant grew louder, and louder still, ringing off the buffalo-hide walls, thundering in his ears with a mystical power all its own. A call for blood.

"Curly! *Curly!* CURLY!"

He hadn't smelled a woman's perfume in . . . it had been a long time.

The fragrance of her almost made his mouth water as he turned from throwing some wood on the fire in a tiny sheet-iron stove that was her only source of heat in this small cabin. No more than a low-roofed, one-room log hut the army provided for the few families of enlisted men stationed at Fort Phil Kearny. Fortunate for her and the baby, at least, that it did not take much of a fire to knock the December chill off the place.

Seamus turned to find Abigail Noone still nursing her infant daughter, sitting in the only chair in the room. For a moment he questioned again why he had come here tonight after the funeral. Bowers and Bingham and Noone. But looking around the little hut, he again realized he felt sorry for her. That sympathy he rarely showed brought him to her doorstep this night as the wind howled beyond the plank door. Taking pity on her, for Abigail had followed her husband west with the 18th Infantry. Bringing their daughter, now six months old, and all they owned in the world.

One chair. And two battered trunks.

The army had provided a small pine-board and rope bed on which lay a lumpy tick bulging with musty straw.

Atop a crude washstand Abigail had placed her fine china washbowl and pitcher. Suspended from a nail above them hung a mirror, a corner of its mercury-glass broken, like one spindly strand of spider's web.

He pulled up one of the old wooden trunks by the stove and eased himself down. For the longest time he watched her nurse the baby. Fascinated, for it was the first time he had witnessed this passing of life from one body to the next.

When Abigail looked up to find him watching, she turned slightly, more to give the impression of propriety than to hide her engorged breast pendant from the front of the black dress borrowed from Margaret Carrington.

"I . . . I've never owned anything black," she had explained to him when he first came here this evening, not long after the last stragglers scurried back to the fort from the post cemetery. "Mrs. Colonel Carrington let me wear it. I'm . . . good that she's so . . . full-bodied that a nursing mother has room to fit in it."

He remembered her saying it without embarrassment. Talking to him as if he were but one of the women here when he had approached her door.

Sitting there in Kinney's place earlier as the light seeped from the sky like a room gone dark when a lamp snuffs itself out, Seamus had stared for the longest time into his red whiskey. Sensing what, he was not sure. Having himself experienced loss before. Grappling with it like a man might work at skinning the hide off a deer he had shot. Slowly, working his knifeblade through the thin, opaque membranes like a sharpened finger on his hand. Careful not to cut through the spongy hide itself. Steadily working down, down until he had decided he had no choice but to visit her.

To console another with a need at this hour greater than his own.

Finding the Noone cabin easy enough, he had listened at the door to the subdued voices of several women. Donegan withdrew to the shadows and waited out of the

wind. Nearly an hour later he recognized the scrape of
the plank door on its doorjamb. The soft glow of lamplight spilled across the entry as three women stooped out
the door, bid their good-byes and hurried off across the
snowy parade.

Margaret Carrington. Lieutenant Grummond's preg-
nant wife. And a third he could not identify. Likely the
wife of the post surgeon.

Looking back on how he had shown up at her door,
Seamus found it interesting that no look of surprise or
wonder had come into her reddened eyes when she found
him there in that pale lamplight seeping onto the trampled snow. Instead, it was as if she had expected him all
along, motioning him inside without a word. She had
offered him the last of some tea she had warmed for her
guests. They sat for the longest time, talking of the trip
north from Laramie last summer. Both of them carefully
avoiding that awful day spent on the Crazy Woman, until
the baby awoke and began to cry.

"It's not normal for her to wake up," Abigail had apologized, with her eyes mostly. "It's been . . . a trying
day for us all."

"I'll build up the fire." He had risen from the trunk as
she went to the rifle-case Frank Noone had made into a
crib with soft cotton batting and blankets. "Knock some
of the chill off, Mrs. Noone. Most like' the baby's cold."

"Thank you," she had replied, settling to the one chair.
Then slowly, deliberately slipping one button at a time
from their tiny loops at the front of her mourning dress.
Sensing his eyes on her, but resolved to feed her daughter
in front of him. "You must call me . . . Abigail. We are
not strangers, Seamus."

"No, we're not . . . Abigail."

She slipped the rigid nipple between her daughter's
open, grasping lips. "All of us who survived that horrid
day share a bond few others can ever appreciate."

"You and the others . . . you women—come through

something that made many a man tremble and cry out in fear during the war," he explained quietly.

She had nodded silently, stroking her daughter's face. Seamus waited a few moments, then pushed split firewood through the stove door. As he listened to the wet *nng-nng-nggg* sounds made by the hungry, confused infant eager at her mother's breast.

"I suppose that's why I came here this evening. I know everyone else tells you they're sorry for what—for Frank. But me—I want you to know I really am sorry for the way things worked out for *you* here. The baby."

As she sighed, he heard the rattle of a sob in her chest. For the moment she tried to conceal her hurt by cooing at the infant, then turned again to the Irishman.

"We had such dreams, Seamus. Frank and I." She stroked her daughter's hair. "Frank asked for duty assignment. We talked about it before coming West. He knew he could not be a musician the rest of his life . . . to support a family." Abigail held one of the tiny, pink hands wrapped around a single finger. "He asked for duty out here. But now Frank's girls must go on . . . without him."

"Will you head East?"

She nodded once without looking at him. "The next chance there is to leave. Colonel Carrington says it will be at least a week before the next mail escort attempts a trip south. Lieutenant Bisbee took his family south today after the . . . the ceremony. I imagine we'll be able to leave with an armed escort as well."

"You need anything between now and then, Abigail— have someone come for me."

She looked at him full now, her face alive with a soft glow radiating from the single oil-lamp perched atop the table made of rough-hewn planks laid across hard-bread boxes. With those eyes so stark and reddened, the soft light made it appear as if her face itself was aglow. Translucent.

"Do you have any whiskey with you?" she asked.

He started for his coat hung from a peg by the door. "I always——"

"Just that I remember that day by the Crazy Woman——"

". . . carry a small flask with me——"

". . . how good your Irish whiskey tasted——"

". . . tell everyone it's for medicinal purposes only——"

". . . watching you pull that arrow from the lieutenant."

"I'm sorry you had to see that . . . I wasn't thinking——"

"Don't apologize."

"In a fight, I forget me manners." He sighed. "Sorry you ripped up your petticoat for bandages."

"There was nothing better we could use." She eyed the small flask he held in his lap. "May I?"

Wordlessly, Seamus worried the cork free and watched her drink, delicately at first. Taking a sip, and licking her bottom lip with the pink tip of her tongue. He found himself aroused, watching her draw at the neck of his flask. Without breaching the silence in that tiny cabin, the Irishman watched the baby feed at the rounded breast, watched Abigail nurse at the bottle. When finally the infant slipped off the damp nipple, soundly asleep, Abigail made no attempt to cover the breast as she passed the flask to Seamus.

Once the baby lay buried beneath her covers in the rifle-case crib, the young mother turned to find Donegan standing at the stove. She started toward him, her boot-toe stubbing an uneven plank on the rough floor. As Abigail pitched forward, he caught her before she fell to the burlap sacking she had stretched out in her little home as proudly as any rich carpet.

Slowly he rose with her cradled in his arms. Finding her shudder, gently at first. Growing in intensity until Abigail sobbed pitifully, her shoulders shaking violently, like the frantic efforts of a bird to free itself from his hand.

Yet this bird clung to him. Reluctant, refusing to let go. Not wanting him to free her.

It was some time before she calmed herself, huddled there against him. As he stroked her fragrant hair. So, so damned long since he had smelled a woman's perfume. Seamus encircled her within his arms as he watched the solitary lamp slowly burn itself out, the wick become a red glow, the chimney filled with curls of black smoke as the room snuffed into darkness.

Dark, but for the orange glow of firelight creeping round the stove's ill-fitting door.

Abigail pulled herself away from him, gazing up into his eyes. She made no attempt to swipe at her damp cheeks, to clear away the tears smudging her face-powder and rouge. Nor did the young mother hide her breast. As if it were again that hot July day at the Crazy Woman, both brought together here, as they had been in the cool, dim light of the Noone's ambulance.

He felt his heartbeat throb at his temples, gazing at her flesh. The muscles along his jaw tensed like rope gone taut as his eyes fixed on the firm curve of that milky breast. He looked up once. And found her eyes locked into his, as if she wanted him to admire her. As he had that hot summer day on the Crazy Woman.

Tenderly Abigail slipped her tiny, slim fingers round his big, callused hand and raised it to her bare breast.

As his flesh met hers, the woman's head tumbled back, rocking from side to side as she slowly ground her hips against him.

"Abigail——"

Her fingers flew to his lips. Silencing him. "I . . . I need you tonight, Seamus. I'm so . . . never been this alone before."

He shook his head, confused. Feeling such an overpowering lust for this young mother barely three days a widow. Her flesh like soft velvet to his hands grown more accustomed to clutching hickory axe-handles or mule-harness. "I . . . I can't, Abigail."

"You must . . . please—you must," she pleaded. "Surely your need is every bit as great as mine."

She whispered against his chest, unbuttoning his wool shirt quickly. Her breath-words warm and moist against his flesh as she pulled aside his long-handles.

The Irishman shuddered. Knowing at once he tread on dangerous ground. Believing he should flee. Realizing he was already powerless to stop. Admitting he hungered for a woman as badly as she needed him. A part of him feeling like a sham dodger, for Abigail had chosen him among the many. While Seamus Donegan would likely have bedded most any moist and warm female given half an invitation.

The simple elegance of Abigail Noone's graceful body was an added pleasure.

She stood before him now as his hands pulled away the top of her widow's dress, hurriedly ripping open her white bodice to free both engorged breasts, her clothing hung a'swirl from her waist. Like the paws of some fevered animal, Donegan's hands raced over her warm, trembling flesh. While most men would look at Abigail and see a plain woman not attractive enough to warrant a second glance, Seamus instead now gazed upon the striking firmness of her slim body. And found a wanton embodiment of physical desire that had for too long remained hidden by layers of restrictive clothing.

At the edge of the bed where he removed her high boots and long stockings, he at last found beneath all those layers an even warmer flesh tingling over a body that yearned up at his hungrily. Pulling him downward atop her, seeking a fevered, anxious mating.

Instead, the Irishman drew back when she held her arms up to him. Gazing upon her while he ripped his own clothes free. Watching Abigail writhe atop the coarse blankets as her eyes narrowed on his readiness for her. She reached out as he came to her. Took him in both hands, kneading him gently as he sank to the protesting bed beside her.

His nose and mouth found the nape of her neck, pushing her black hair aside to suck deep of the smell of that perfume he had been too long in recognizing. Too many months. So many lonely nights without a woman. And thanking his God that the woman who would break his fast was one as hungry for him as was Abigail Noone.

When his lips wandered down her neck, into the crevice of her rigid flesh, Seamus heard Abigail gasp once, then a second time. Perhaps for how he excited her now. Perhaps as she felt him grow in the midst of her pleading hands.

Grow he did. For with each breath he took in the heated, moist musk of her rising to his nostrils.

And when his tongue found a rigid, milk-damp nipple, Donegan heard the groan rumble from the back of the woman's throat. Like some untamed beast. At once her body grew rigid. He worried that he should not touch that flesh. After all, he sensed immediately, perhaps Abigail believed her breasts belonged to her infant daughter alone. He pulled back, licking his lips damp from the brief taste of her warm, sweet milk.

Surprised was he when she suddenly relaxed, putting her fingers in his curly hair, pulling his head down to her once more. Nuzzling his face in the warm, moist, milk-fragrance of one breast. She wanted him there. Donegan licked the droplets oozing from her motherhood. Gently taking the nipple in his mouth. Sucking hungrily at her breast. Everytime he drew her more insistently between his lips, Abigail pressed him against her with a greater need.

Until she could wait no more and one hand again found his rigid flesh, guiding it within her.

Abigail arched her back, throwing herself against him frantically as he began to rock above her. She clawed at him, crying out in her own way at this flushing of her overpowering grief. Lunging at him, fighting the Irishman moving atop her, within her. Lunging to exorcise the devils of loneliness and despair.

Until they both found together what Abigail had wanted. That release of the poison for three long days building at the core of her being. Finding this private healing that would allow her the strength and dignity to carry on, if only for her child. Rather than collapsing into a hideous, grieving, incomprehensible mass unable to stand the test of this great wilderness.

As Seamus cradled the tiny woman against him like some small, crippled birdlike creature, he realized it was not love she had made with him. But a mutual rending of what had been her love for Frank Noone. Needing tonight a man to possess her. To drive away her loneliness and loss. Her way of cleansing this wilderness from her.

With the stove's red light aglow on her shoulders, Abigail fell quickly asleep. The first she had enjoyed in three long days. Sweeping some black hair from her cheek, Donegan knew that Abigail Noone had needed his body to lash back at the wilderness that loomed outside these log walls. There above them, on the Peno Head and Sullivant Hills. The cold, unforgiving wilderness that waited just beyond the crest of Lodge Trail Ridge.

An empty wildness that had ripped Frank Noone from her.

The same savage, horrendous maw waiting to swallow them all.

Chapter 29

*I*n those first days of the third week in the *Moon of Deer Shedding Horns,* hundreds upon hundreds left their families behind in the villages huddled along the headwaters of the Tongue River. Only warriors would journey in this severe cold-time. From Oglalla, Miniconjou, Hunkpapa and Sans Arc camps they came. Northern Cheyenne, Arapaho and Big Belly. Red Cloud's Bad Faces, ready to stare down the white soldiers in one big fight.

Over the past few days the cold had grown even more intense. In all his winters, Curly had never seen his people so desperate. A second winter of starving. And still the white man wanted to steal the road and the game and eventually the hills themselves. While his people starved. But no more!

Behind him rode the pick of the Oglalla. Hand-chosen to lead the attack on the white wagons. Specially selected by Curly to join him in seducing the soldiers into the trap.

Hunkering beneath buffalo robes with the thick fur turned in or wearing blanket capotes, most of the Oglalla had traded brain-tanned buckskin for the warmer, wool-blanket leggings. Around their feet each man had lashed knee-high buffalo fur moccasins after wrapping scraps of wool round and round like stockings.

When an opportunity arose, small groups drifted off the southbound trail to hunt for elk or deer or a rare chance at a snowbound buffalo. But Curly would eat the pemmican his aunt had packed in a skin bag. Nothing would turn him from this medicine call. Instead, he would eat atop his pony and not allow himself to tarry on this war-trail. Curly pointed his ponies toward the Peno country. And Lodge Trail Ridge.

Each of these first warriors to leave the Tongue River villages plowed south through the frozen drifts, urging the pack animals they rode between every heaving lunge. Behind him each warrior pulled more pack animals struggling beneath burdens of food and lodge. Curly's Oglallas would not ride their favorite war-ponies. Yet. Fleet-footed, barrel-chested mustangs, every one. Saved for the coming fight.

In a sheltered valley behind the Peno Head, the first arrivals under Curly made camp, awaiting the many hundreds who would follow in two suns. No man could say how many would make the ride, wanting to join the big fight. Among the Lakota the biggest number counted was ten-times-ten. Yet many of Curly's young Oglalla grew astonished as the camps filled. By the setting of that second sun, Man-Afraid strolled through the three camp circles: Sioux, Cheyenne, Arapaho. In awe, he counted more than fifteen of the ten-times-ten.

As the allied chiefs held councils and argued battle plans, Oglalla scouts came and went from camp through shrinking daylight hours. Along the ridges and ribs jutting into the valley of the fort, the young warriors flashed their mirrors and waved their blankets in signal. But there would be no more raids until they had decided all the details of the coming fight. For almost two weeks they had ignored the soldiers and woodcutters, leaving the wagons to scurry between the Pine Woods and the fort without a care.

For the first time in their history, the Sioux and Cheyenne had decided on a new tactic. Instead of attacking small parties of whitemen and wagons along the wood-road, the warriors would now lure a large force of soldiers to their deaths. Enticing them with a decoy while the rest waited in ambush along the bottomland at the forks of the Peno. Halfway between the soldier fort and their great warrior encampment.

A trap, ready to spring.

One morning, cold and clear as looking glass, every man young and old alike journeyed to that bottomland, each warrior marking his place of hiding in the brush along both sides of a narrow spur jutting north from the Lodge Trail. On this frozen ground they would rehearse their plan, sending Curly's decoy party up the ridge.

Here lay the stroke of Red Cloud's genius that proved this Oglalla chief's powerful vision alone. The strength of his leadership dictated that he convince his warriors they must no longer fight the white soldiers as they had for years past. This recent, forceful penetration of the soldiers to the very heart of Sioux hunting ground required a new, bold strategy. And if that new strategy were to succeed, Red Cloud knew his warriors would require practice.

Among the Indians of the northern plains, the *berdache* remained a creature of powerful medicine. A person born half man/half woman with a special mission. So it was only natural that to a Miniconjou *berdache* Red Cloud gave the honor of announcing the coming of the soldiers to those warriors laying in wait. Again and again the bands practiced, the young man/woman racing back from the top of the ridge repeatedly, each time announcing an ever-growing number of soldiers approaching—marching into their trap. It was a ride rehearsed until every warrior hidden in the brush understood they were not to spring on the few.

Instead, they were to wait for the many.

Though winter man continued to crush the land beneath his icy, white grip—they realized this would be a time for all Lakota to remember. For time beyond would

the People remember how the Oglalla lured the soldiers
into their trap. Long would the Sioux remember the
young warrior who lured so many to their deaths. In
those winters yet uncounted, across the years yet to
come, the bands would tell the whites how for the first
time they had come together. How for the first time the
bands had rehearsed their roles in this bloody drama. For
the first time. But not the last.

He jerked awake, sweating in the cold, dark lodge.
Nearby lay the crimson coals of a dying fire. His breath
froze before his face. Still, his copper skin was moist to
his touch. He tingled with excitement.

"Uncle," he called out, tapping the warrior who slept
to his right. "You are awake?"

"Yes," Man-Afraid answered. "I listened to you fighting the dream-maker."

"I did not fight the dream-maker, Uncle," the young
Oglalla replied. "Instead, I have seen a new medicine-
helper."

Aiiyeee! Man-Afraid whispered loudly.

"What is it!" Yellow Knife rose to one elbow. "Can't a
man get his——"

"Hush!" Man-Afraid commanded, watching the others
in the war-lodge rise from their robes and blankets. He
threw some pieces of dry wood on the coals. In a moment
tiny flames brightened the frosty lodge. "Silence, all of
you. We must hear of a new medicine-helper."

When Man-Afraid nodded for him to continue, the
young warrior swallowed hard, his heart pounding, his
breath shallow and ragged. The vision no less clear than
it had been in his dream.

"I watched the soldiers follow me . . . like bees after
a boy who steals honey. They followed, until I led them
to the foot of the ridge. They were trapped. As they circled among themselves, scared—like cornered snowshoe
hares—we swept down on them from all sides. Then I
watched a young warrior ride among the soldiers . . .
racing in and out among them, swinging an axe in one

hand, a club in the other. Back and forth he rode while others cried out that he must be foolish . . . that he must be crazy . . . that he courted death riding among the soldiers."

He swiped a hand across his dry lips, sweat beading his upper lip. Sensing the silence in the war-lodge as if it were a tangible gift laid before him, in respect and awe.

"The others called him crazy . . . yet it was his horse I looked at next. Streaked with lightning bolts of white clay . . . spotted with hailstones of oxblood red. The horse carried its master back and forth through the soldiers . . . until there were few left standing. They ran among some rocks to hide. But the young warrior dashed after them. Alone. Into the rocks his wild steed carried him—slashing, hacking at the last of the soldiers. Until no soldier lived."

"This will happen?" Yellow Horse asked, gazing at Man-Afraid.

The chief scowled. "Do you doubt the power of this vision, Yellow Horse?"

Before the war-chief could answer, the young dreamer continued.

"As the warrior atop his horse cut down the last soldier, all warriors swept 'round him—chanting, shouting, singing his praises for his bravery in battle. They danced round and round him—calling out his name: 'Crazy Horse!' 'Crazy Horse!' 'Crazy Horse!' "

Man-Afraid leaped to his feet, pulling the young Oglalla up with him. "This will come to pass! Brothers! No longer do we look upon the young warrior called Curly . . . behold, before you stands the powerful medicine of . . . *Crazy Horse!*"

"Captain Powell!"

"I see it, Colonel!"

Powell waited at the bottom of the crude steps as Carrington half tripped, half slid down from his watchtower.

On Pilot Hill the picket frantically waved his flag in the morning air, signaling an attack on the wood train.

"You'll lead the relief," Carrington thumped, out of breath.

"Sir? Fetterman's the senior——"

"Captain! *You* will lead this relief!"

"Yessir!" His eyes darted over to the stables where soldiers tightened cinches, shoved bits back into horses' mouths and snugged caps down on their heads. He turned to Metzger, who stood nearby blowing Boots and Saddles.

"Bugler! Enough!"

"Captain?" Adolph asked.

"Get to your horse!"

"I can go with—Yes, sir!"

As Powell slipped a foot into the hooded stirrup and swung atop his saddle in one movement, Carrington rushed to his side.

"Heed my orders, Captain." He looked up at Powell, more imploring than ordering. "Remember the costly lessons of the sixth. Do not pursue the Indians across the Lodge Trail."

He nodded, lips pressed in a thin line as he pulled his sorrel round. "Lieutenant Grummond!"

"All present and accounted for, sir!"

"Let's ride!"

Powell and Metzger led out. Immediately behind them, Eli Garrett bellowed commands at C Company, cavalry. "Troop forward at a trot! Guide—center. HO!"

Bringing up the rear, Grummond flung his arm forward, leading his mounted infantry through the gates. "Keep it tight, boys! We're gonna make Red Cloud pay today!"

. . . through a cheering forest of soldiers and civilians thronging to watch the rescue dash down the slope onto the wood road toward the Sullivant Hills . . . through the first bare knuckles where the wind had scoured the snow into an icy rind blanketing a gray land . . . riding face on into a stiff westerly breeze.

Enough to make Powell's cheeks ache like burnished rawhide. Every bit as stiff and hard as the knitting-kit on his belt where the ammunition for his Springfield rattled. He prayed the rifles would work today. As cold as it was. So many badly in need of repair.

Overhead the sun hung like a pale yellow glob of butter atop cream in the churn back home. So cold the air sparkled in those rare glimmers of sunlight, alive and moving. *They're running off!*

"Sergeant!"

"Captain?" Garrett answered.

"You'll stay with me today. Understood?"

"What if the warriors divide when we give chase?"

"You have your orders, Sergeant!"

Powell watched Garrett swallow his curse in the midst of that blond beard.

"You bet I do . . . *sir.*"

Garrett dropped back along the column of twos, just as the Sioux disappeared over the hill. Breaking off their attack on the wagons. Those soldiers and civilians hunkered behind mules and wagons stood cheering, wagging their rifles over their heads. Delivered once more.

Powell swept his horse soldiers past the wagons without losing a step. Over a low brow at the western end of the Sullivant Hills the warriors enticed their pursuers.

Along the pine-covered slope of Peno Head signal mirrors glittered in the pale sky. Immediately the Sioux split, a dozen climbing the Head into the valley of Peno Creek. Another dozen or so tearing off to the right, whooping and hollering, beckoning the soldiers on and on. Up the hard, barren, windswept slope of Lodge Trail Ridge.

Powell watched the mirrors glitter atop the ridge. The signals disappeared as suddenly as the fleeing warriors.

"Captain!"

Powell turned, watching Grummond straining, beating his mount to catch up with the head of the columns.

"Captain! Request permission to break off . . . chase those devils running——"

"Permission denied, Lieutenant!" he flung his words into the wind. "You'll ride with me all the way!"

"But, sir, you don't need all these . . . my mounted infan——"

"Get back with your men, Lieutenant!" Powell barked. "You follow orders today!"

He liked Grummond. Really admired the bright, energetic officer. But Carrington had told Powell how Grummond had galloped off on his own. Only to scamper back minutes later, running for his life.

As soon as his troops reached the western rim of Lodge Trail Ridge, Powell raised his left arm. "Sergeant Garrett! Halt the command!"

Back along the columns soldiers ground to a halt, their horses spraddle-legged from the mad scramble up the slope, ribby sides heaving, heads down and steaming into the frosty air.

Grummond skidded to Powell's side. Garrett not far behind.

"Captain!" Grummond pointed down the slope toward Peno Creek. "You can damn well see them!"

He growled, "I damn well can, mister!"

"Request permission to pursue——"

"No, Lieutenant!"

"What?" Garrett shrieked. "Lemme take twenty cavalry, sir! Show 'em some steel!"

"I said *no,* Sergeant!"

"Begging pardon, Captain." Garrett wore that smirk of his. "But the captain doesn't know a damn about cavalry work. Perhaps I can show 'im——"

"Get back with your men, Garrett!" he barked. "I'll call you when I have need of your . . . your insolent help!"

Below in the valley two dozen warriors shouted and gestured obscenely, taunting the soldiers, begging for the chase.

"Let me take some men, Captain. We can show——"

"No, Lieutenant. I have my orders from Colonel——"

"Carrington be damned!" Grummond screamed. "He's a goddamned coward——won't fight. See! Look down there! War is all those bastards understand. Fighting. Blood! Let me draw some blood, Captain!"

Powell waited a moment while Grummond spent himself like a spring-wound toy running down.

"Lieutenant," Powell sighed, sniffling the cold dribble back from the end of his nose, "any soldier rides down there ain't never coming back."

Chapter 30

*H*e had scarcely stirred through the better part of two days. Huddled here beside Judge Kinney's stove, warming a ladder-backed chair and drinking round after round of whiskey tempered with black coffee.

Yesterday, Donegan had moved twice. Once to relieve his bladder at the slip-trench. A second time to watch Powell's troops march back through the gate. Not a single casualty, he had brooded, sipping at his steamy elixir. *Captain remembered that it takes more than just a brave sojur to win a war . . . takes a smart sojur most of all.*

Amid the groans, jeers, and angry mutterings of his troops, Powell had turned back to the fort. The warriors faded away. Crisis averted. Both Fetterman and Brown, who had not marched with Powell, rebuked Carrington again for his order against pursuit beyond Lodge Trail Ridge. Waiting on the porch in front of his office for Powell's return, the colonel reminded the soldiers that he intended to continue his long-held policy of utmost caution until Cooke's promised reinforcements arrived. In the meantime, he explained, work to complete the fort would continue with the highest priority.

"The Indians accomplish nothing," he had shouted over the hubbub as soldiers and officers complained. "While I'm perfecting all details of the post and preparing for active movements."

"Active movements?" Fetterman echoed. "We're preparing an assault on the hostile camps?"

"Not . . . yet," Carrington had answered.

"When, by god?" Brown demanded. "When will you let us stand like men and fight back?"

Donegan had watched Carrington flinch. "Not long, Captain."

"Pray it isn't, Colonel," Brown growled. "Pray it isn't long at all."

A light snow had fallen that night, flakes as big as wood-ash curls. Enough to fill a man's footprints and dust the sill outside the smoky window where Donegan sat nursing his whiskey. More times than he cared to remember he allowed himself to wallow in the cups. To forget a dark-eyed older woman, perhaps a cat-eyed young temptress, or most of all that husky-voiced colleen left behind. Or simply to ease his mind as it turned something unknown over and over again—the way the children on the parade turned the new snow over and over in their mittens that afternoon, forming perfect snowballs.

Try as he might, Seamus wasn't in any condition to make sense of anything right now. Only the taste of the whiskey washing against the back of his throat. The dull ache of a long-empty heart.

The scrape of the door across pine planks was seconded by a jolt of cold air. Boot-soles scraped to the bar. Happy voices cheered new arrivals.

"Two of your best whiskey, Judge!"

Seamus recognized Brown's voice.

"Water on the side?"

"No." That was Fetterman, Donegan decided. "Barefoot'll do."

Two priggish officers come to drink their fancy whiskey. Enlisted men and poor-mick Irish drink what's left. Giving thanks for the blessed forgetfulness it brings——

"Did just as you suggested, Judge," Brown droned after he had swilled down the first cup and Kinney poured a second.

"How's that?"

"With Carrington," he explained. "Me and Judd just came from there."

"Paid him a visit, you say?" Kinney asked.

Brown felt the room grow quiet, voices falling off and men shuffling close to the bar to hear the latest post gossip. "Judd and I asked him again. Told him we had fifty armed civilians took an oath to ride with us to the Tongue. All we needed was him to give us fifty mounted soldiers. Clean out that nest of vipers once and for all. Then we'd get some peace to see the winter through."

"A hundred men's all it'll take, Judge," Fetterman echoed.

"So, what'd the colonel say to you?" the sutler asked as his ample belly pressed against the bar.

"What the Hades you think the sniveling coward said?" Fetterman snapped.

"I'll tell you!" Brown hollered, gesturing wildly. "That spineless bastard calmly picked up his morning report and flung it at me. Said if he let fifty seasoned men go with Judd and me—he'd have nothing but shavetails left to guard his precious post! Couldn't keep General Cooke's mail moving . . . not enough for picket duty——"

"His well-worn cowardice," Fetterman growled before he sipped thoughtfully at his whiskey.

"Claimed he couldn't spare fifty horses for those seasoned men either!" Brown went on. "Showed me Ten Eyck's report for this morning—forty-two mounts in service. Forty-two!"

"Colonel'd do better making another his post commander," Kinney clucked like a gossipy hen at the back fence. "That Ten Eyck does no soldier good. But enough of what the colonel said. Tell me, gentlemen—how'd you lay into him?"

"Told him I'd be leaving for Laramie soon after Christmas—what with my work done here," Brown grumped. "Wanted a chance to 'raise hair,' as the frontiersmen say!

Just one more good fight, I begged. Something a real soldier could sink his teeth in."

"What'd Captain Fetterman say to Carrington?"

"When I saw that the colonel had no intention of authorizing a punitive expedition to the Tongue River, I got up to leave——"

"Without saying a goddamned thing, Judd!" Brown interrupted.

"Bastard knows damn well how I feel already!" he snapped.

"On the other hand," Brown slapped his chest, rattling the spurs looped through a buttonhole of his greatcoat, "I told him that I'm certain I can kill a dozen myself! Given half the chance——"

Brown stopped right in the middle of his own sentence. The tin cup frozen before him. Every man's eyes followed the captain's as a tomblike silence fell over the cabin.

Through the tumble of fog filling his brain and the glaze of his half-closed eyes, Seamus gazed up at Kinney's plank bar. And found every man in the place staring back at him.

"My . . . my! Just look at that pitiful excuse for a man," Captain Brown sneered before he brought the whiskey to his lips.

"Word has it he was branded a coward during the war," an old infantryman piped up, eager to hop right in.

"Lost his stripes, was it?" Judge Kinney asked of no one in particular, giving the rough planks a swipe with a dirty towel.

"Sergeant Garrett told the story that way," Fetterman said, turning back to the bar.

"And Donegan didn't deny it," Brown added, an elbow propped on the bar, glaring at the loner huddled in the corner by the sheet-iron stove. "Can't deny it 'cause it's true—ain't it, Seamus Donegan?" His voice hammered with the flat, metallic sound of a sixteen-pound sledge on a cold anvil.

For a long moment Seamus returned Brown's glare.

Then his eyes began to water and he turned away. He gazed out the smoky window at the clearing sky, bright pinpoints of light exposed that spelled another subzero night. Bridger himself had said it. That Brown was one to be watched, like a rattler in a sack.

"Look! You all see that? The goddamn story must be true!" Brown harangued the crowd. "I gave that bastard Irishman another chance to deny it—here and now before you men—and what'd he do?"

"Turned away, s'what he done!" one of Brown's civilian lackies chimed in.

"Right!" Brown swilled at his whiskey, then banged the hollow cup on the bar. "Fill 'er for me, Judge. Then I think we oughtta have us some military justice done right here. If the truth of Seamus Donegan's disobedience of a direct order was never settled in the Shenandoah back to 'sixty-four, by all that's holy, we'll hold our own court of inquiry here and now!"

A sudden cheer erupted that filled the sutler's cabin like a foamy head bubbling over a glass of dark Boston ale. Seamus sensed something about to overwhelm him. But he was long past the point of caring.

He watched Brown swagger over like a prairie cock. He dropped his cup on Donegan's table then unbuttoned his coat. Seamus appraised the captain—seeing his leggings lashed tightly round his calves, ready for riding at any alarm. And those two revolvers stuffed in the waistband of his britches.

"Loaded for bear, ain'cha, Cap'n?" Seamus asked as he collected his thoughts.

"I've found me bear enough for now, Seamus Donegan." Hatred lay unconcealed in his dark eyes. Brown beckoned the others. "C'mon, boys. Need a jury to decide this defendant's guilt. Judge Kinney here will make sure its a fair trial, won't you, Judge?"

"You're having fun with him, Captain?" The sutler ambled to the edge of the crowd, squeezing in on Donegan's corner.

"Fun?" Brown echoed, not taking his eyes off Donegan. "I've shot cowards and deserters before, Judge. Always something a professional soldier had to do. But I can't say as I ever looked forward to it . . . till now."

The laughter rocked against Seamus like tangible, mocking fists swung at him. He ground at his eyes with both hands, hoping to clear them.

"I'm sure the court's heard the charges . . . as explained by Eli Garrett. If necessary, the prosecution'll call the sergeant for more——"

"No!" a soldier behind Brown hollered.

"Don't need to! Get on with it!"

"Right," Brown echoed as he stuffed his thumbs in his belt next to the pistols. "Now let's hear from the defense. Mr. Donegan—what have you to say in your behalf?"

His head hurt from punishing the whiskey for the better part of two days. Before that he had spent most of a month in the guardhouse—eating their swill, scratching at lice, freezing beneath two thin blankets grudgingly given him. Until the colonel finally freed him, and forced Brown into giving Donegan his settlement pay. From that day, Seamus had worked at nothing better than drinking his way through sutler Kinney's whiskey barrels, or his civilian pay—whichever came first.

And now—Seamus wanted to be left alone. Nothing more. Just find himself a warm, quiet place where no man would talk to him and he wouldn't have to answer. But most of all, someplace where he didn't have to look at Brown's leering face.

Slowly, unsteadily, Donegan pushed the chair back and rocked to his feet, glaring down at the captain. A full head above any man in the room.

"Cowardice, Cap'n?" he asked, gazing into Brown's laughing face. "Shall we talk about cowardice, you reeky scut? Just so you can get some Injin's bleeming scalp afore you prance back to Laramie and your next cushy assignment—you'll drag every man here to his death!" His finger swept the room. "Begora! You'd even sacrifice the life of your best friend . . . if it'd grant you a scalp and your bleeming promotion! Right, Cap'n Fetterman? Won't Brown forfeit your life just to earn his oak clusters!"

"I don't think he'd———"

"Tell 'im, Brown! Your best friend, and he don't even know you good as I!" Seamus roared, easing his bulk around the crude table. "I've seen what rests in the soul of ambitious men like you—men who'll sacrifice a wife and family. Hell, what's a friend to an ambitious bastard like you?"

Seamus recognized it in the captain's eyes, even before he watched Brown's right hand swing toward the pistol at his belt.

You stare enough men in the eye, toe to toe, and you get to where you can recognize that look—just when they're ready to make their play. All you got to do is be a little quicker.

He had to admit he enjoyed feeling his fist cracking against Brown's jaw, sensing that parting of his knuckles against the bone as his arm straightened behind the volcanic power in his shoulder. Watching the captain flung back into the crowd like a limp rag-doll. Caught by two soldiers, the rest flowing like water around a boulder in a stream. Reaching for him. Grabbing with a hundred hands or more. Tearing for a piece of Seamus Donegan. Yelling about justice and a firing squad. As he grabbed the big infantryman in front of him, Seamus wondered who the coward was they were screaming about.

It seemed easy enough to pick up the big soldier and fling him to the side. Unplanned, but oddly beautiful the way the soldier soared through the crude window onto the narrow porch outside. A blast of cold air rushed in to the tinkle of glass. He suffered the first punch, then caught the next fist he saw headed his way, crushing it, pulling the man into him. He swept the soldier off his feet, tossing him back against the surging crowd.

Seamus needed fighting room. The door stood too far

away, and there were too damned many of them anyway.
But at least he could make himself some fighting room.
He cracked heads and ducked from flying chairs. A mug
smashed against his temple. He enjoyed the homey taste
of warm blood at his lip. The dribble of crimson at his
nose.

Someone smacked a chair-leg across his brow. Startled,
Donegan rocked back, watching bright meteors. He'd
just seen the stars appear behind the clouds through the
window . . . some time back . . . so long ago now.
The soldier with the chair-leg swept his arm back for a
second go at Seamus. At the same time at least five of
them dove at him. All legs and arms, pummeling the
Irishman as they roared curses in his ears. He sensed six
on him now, tearing at his arms. Then seven kicking at
his legs, trying to bring him down.

Finally the clean, solid clunk of metal against his skull.
Seamus Donegan recognized that sound well enough. *So
bleeming many times before they've brought me down with
a crack of a wee pistol.*

Blessed, bleeming darkness.

Chapter 31

*A*fter failing to lure the soldiers into their trap, the tribes argued through the next day and into the night. Huddled round their fires behind saddle-blanket wind-breaks as the snow fell. Then melted, before a cold wind swept out of the arctic itself. *Wasiya,* the Winter Giant glazing the weary land.

"Perhaps another should lead the decoy," Crazy Horse suggested.

"No," Man-Afraid stated firmly.

"Some stronger medicine——"

"There is no stronger medicine than yours, Crazy Horse."

"Man-Afraid speaks the truth," High-Backbone echoed. "I will lead the ambush . . . and I want Crazy Horse to use his medicine to bring the soldiers to my *wickmunke,* our trap."

"If you don't believe, Crazy Horse," Man-Afraid clamped his hand on the young warrior's shoulder, "you'll find no success at the end of your ride. No one can give you any more power than you find within yourself."

Crazy Horse studied the two faces before him. High-Backbone's penetrating eyes seemed to implore him to complete the ambush as planned. While Man-Afraid's fiery glare urged him to believe in himself.

"I will lead many *nisma wica,* the hair-mouth soldiers to High-Backbone," he declared evenly. "We will catch many in the hand!"

Behind him erupted the grunts of approval and the rhythmic, *"H'g'un . . . h'g'un . . . h'g'un!"* The Lakota courage word.

"Woyuonihan!" Man-Afraid shouted above the clamor. "I salute you, Crazy Horse! Your power is your own best *wyakin,* your war charm!"

"Simiakia." The young warrior bowed his head, feeling the praise heaped on him by the warriors of all the tribes. "Again, I have faith in my own medicine."

While the pale rind of a winter moon slipped from the sky, most of the warriors crawled beneath warm robes and blankets to try at sleep. For most, sleep was not an easy thing. Their medicine was strong once more, so announced the shamans who had studied the entrails of a young doe shot for dinner.

With the coming of the new sun, the last day of the third week of the *Moon of Deer Shedding Horns,* the soldiers would be swept away.

"Your young men are ready?" Man-Afraid stepped up beside Crazy Horse the next morning.

He gazed down from atop his war-pony painted with the lightning bolts of white clay, crimson hail-stones dabbed in buffalo blood.

"Those who come with me are the youngest . . . perhaps the most reckless," Crazy Horse answered with a smile that danced at his eyes. "They are the best to ride with me—for they have blood running in them hot as a rutting bull."

"It is good." Man-Afraid stroked the war-pony's withers. "Soldiers will come running after you this time. They will not stop until they are in the jaws of death. High-Backbone is ready to lead his warriors to the white-man's road near the foot of Lodge Trail Ridge. He gave the Arapaho and Cheyenne their choice of hiding places.

They will lay in wait among the brush along the west side of the road. The Lakota will hide on the east. I will hold ten-times-ten on ponies with me behind a low ridge. If needed, we will sweep through the walk-a-heaps, swinging our clubs."

"You do not fear killing all the soldiers?" Crazy Horse asked.

"No, none will escape." He smiled. "We will have no trouble against the soldiers and their *mazawakans,* their rifles."

Crazy Horse straightened a moment, looking over the heads of the young warriors who would lure the soldiers into the trap. Behind them as far as the eye could see, more warriors tied bridles and pad saddles to their warponies. Some smeared clay on the animals' flanks for power and speed. Others tied feathers and hawks' bells in bushy manes. All men bound up the long, brushy tails in strips of red trade-cloth. The color of war.

"Aiyeeee!" the young Oglalla exclaimed. "How many will be waiting for the soldiers I lead into the trap?"

Man-Afraid smiled broadly. "It fills my heart, *Tashunka Witko!* Earlier this morning the chiefs counted twenty ten-times-ten ready to fight!"

"Tunka sila le iyahpe ya yo!" Crazy Horse shouted back to his young decoy warriors. "Father! Receive this humble prayer! We will lead many into *Wanagi,* the Land of Shadows, before the sun rides low in the sky!"

Man-Afraid slapped the neck of the war-pony. "I may not see you until it is over, young friend. I wish you well, *Tashunka Witko.*"

"H'g'un!" the young warrior shouted at Man-Afraid. The louder the better, for this was the courage word of the mighty Lakota warrior.

Man-Afraid touched the fingertips of his right hand against his forehead, *"Woyuonihan!* I salute you, Crazy Horse! May you ride like the wind!"

"Come, my brothers!" the Oglalla yelled to those anx-

ious young warriors prancing behind him. "It is a good
day to die!"

Man-Afraid watched until the last Oglalla war-pony
disappeared from sight, the pounding of their many hoofs
fading from his ears.

"The scouts tell me our spotters are on the ridges with
their mirrors," High-Backbone said quietly as he stepped
alongside the Oglalla war-chief. "All is ready."

Man-Afraid nodded. Then gazed down the trail Crazy
Horse had led his young bull-hearts. "Yes, High-Backbone. It is a good day for many *soldiers* to die!"

Damn cold. His rheumatism bothered him so badly
that he hadn't even crawled out of the blankets to
scrounge some breakfast. Bridger lay still, trying to ignore the dull pain until Lieutenant Wands banged on the
door to his little room among the noncom staff, near the
cavalry yard.

"Colonel wants you come as soon as you can, Mr.
Bridger," he explained.

Wearily, Jim swung his creaky legs to the side of his
rope cot. "What for?"

"We got some Cheyenne at the gate."

"What day is it?"

"Why—it's the twenty-first. December."

"No, day of the week, son."

"Friday." He waited while Bridger dallied in tucking
his woolen undershirt into his breeches. "Two Moons's
the leader."

"He's the one come through here on his way north few
weeks back," Bridger said as he tugged on the first boot.
"Wanted to go hunting up on the Tongue."

"That's what he claimed," Wands answered impa-
tiently.

"Bet ol' Two Moons's hunting something else."

"How's that, sir?"

He leveled his blue eyes at the lieutenant. "I figure
Two Moons is hunting soldiers this morning."

"How could he be hunting——"

"Red Cloud got his ol' friend Two Moons to get inside the fort." Bridger yanked his second boot on then swept his old blue army coat off the bed. "Where's the colonel?"

"He wants you to talk to Two Moons first . . . at the gate," Wands said. "Before he'll let the Cheyennes into the fort."

Bridger smiled. "You pay attention to the colonel, son." He knew well enough that Wands didn't stand on Carrington's side in any of this. "The man's growed pretty smart since he come to the mountains. Heap smarter than the whole lot of his goddanged officer staff." Wands headed for the door. "Paper-collar soldiers fighting rebs down South . . . don't know a goddanged peedoodle 'bout fighting Injuns. Nary a one!"

Overhead the sky hung the color of skimmed milk. The sun flung against it no brighter nor no warmer than a pewter button. As he and Wands walked across the parade to headquarters, Jim saw most of the snow from yesterday had already disappeared, though icy, white collars still clung to the lee side of ridges and down in the coulees. The air felt cold and dry, stinging a man's face if he didn't watch out. Down in the valley, both creeks lay frozen from bank to bank, bubbling and tumbling beneath winter sheets of translucent ice.

"Morning, Jim!" Carrington waved to a chair by the sheet-iron stove where the old scout would be warmer. "Coffee?"

"Don't mind a'tall, Colonel."

"Mr. Wands. Three coffees, please."

"Three?"

"You'll join us, won't you, Lieutenant?"

"Certainly, sir."

"Before I let Two Moons in, want to talk with you first."

"You done the right thing, Colonel."

He smiled briefly. "Had a good teacher in Jim Bridger. Something here doesn't feel right."

"Listen to your innards, Colonel. Two Moons's a cagey one. I'd trust Black Horse with my wife and children. That Two Moons—I'd not trust him with another man's dead skunk in a burlap sack."

"Exactly why I want you with me. For some reason, he and his cronies are back at our gates."

"Begging again, Colonel," Wands offered as he set coffee before the two men.

"Mr. Wands remembers Two Moons's last visit."

"I heard some of your hotbloods almost rubbed out the bunch of 'em."

"Saved us all a lot of trouble if they had!" Wands said.

"Lieutenant, if you please?" Carrington gestured for his adjutant to take a seat. "Tell me what your intuition says, Jim."

Bridger sipped at the scalding potion Wands had served. "That sawed-off runt of a two-timing, back-stabbing sonuvabitch will require some watching. But," and Jim replaced his frown with a grin, "let's give the ol' boy a real show of it."

"Now you're talking!" Carrington agreed and slapped a knee. "A real dog and pony of it!"

"That's the idea, Colonel!" Bridger grinned even wider.

"Dog . . . and pony?" Wands asked.

"Shut your mouth and pay attention, Lieutenant," Carrington said as he rose. "You're liable to learn a thing or two this morning from Mr. Bridger. Now, Mr. Wands —if you'll go to the gate and have the sergeant of the guard escort our Cheyenne guests to my office."

"Sad in a way, Colonel," Bridger admitted later, after he had been palavering with Two Moons for half an hour. "Just as I figured. This big-mouthed runt don't have the stomach to stand up to Red Cloud's bunch like Black Horse. Two Moons's riding a Sioux pony for sure."

"Riding a Sioux pony?"

"Way of speaking, Colonel. Two Moons's no better'n a Lakota now."

Carrington wagged his head, watching the Cheyenne chiefs' eyes studying him and Bridger. "I was afraid of that. All right—let's tell Two Moons what he really wants to know, Jim."

Bridger grinned like a coyote about to pounce on snowshoe. "Be purely pleased." He turned to Two Moons and the chiefs who had spread blankets across the floor near the stove, where they could warm themselves during the council with the pony soldier chief.

"Two Moons," Bridger began, "take word back to Red Cloud and his warriors that they'll never steal into this fort."

Two Moons played his best look of shock. "Big Throat Bridger does not speak straight of Two Moons. I am Cheyenne. Not Sioux!" He ran a finger across his throat to sign the Lakota.

Bridger smiled. "Big Throat knows where you've camped the last two moons. On the headwaters of the Tongue, where you smoked with Red Cloud." He did not wait while Two Moons chattered angrily, but flung his hand in the air, telling the chief to shut his mouth.

"You are as much a fool as the Sioux if you plan to attack this fort. The soldiers' hearts are big. Your warrior friends will lose the fight if you attack the fort—and there'll be much crying in your villages."

Two Moons rocked back. "Big Throat tells a mighty story!" he sneered.

"Colonel, think it's 'bout time to show these red cutthroats."

"Show them our fort?" Wands squeaked, lunging forward at the old scout in disbelief. "You can't show the red bastards our defenses . . . our, our powder magazine——"

"Relax, boy," Bridger replied, wagging a gnarled hand in the air. "If your soldiers out there doing their job, we got no worry of any one of these red niggers sneaking on the post and blowing up your precious powder-magazine."

Simply put, with the state of siege that had now existed for the better part of six months around Fort Phil Kearny, no soldier ever gave a second thought to the question of infiltrators creeping past the stockade walls. Every copper-skinned guest to the post was under constant, vigilant watch. And just such a tour as the one Bridger gave Two Moons had to go far convincing the hostiles they had not a ghost of a chance getting past the outer pickets, much less slipping by the sentries who surrounded the soldiers' powder magazine. Besides, if any snake-skinned warrior had gotten that far into Carrington's post, he would have to contend with the multiple locks securing the huge door of forged iron and rough-hewn timbers.

Carrington cleared his throat. "You want us to show this Cheyenne . . . everything?"

"Right," Jim answered. "Better showing. No use telling a goddamned mule-headed Injun . . . show the bastard what we want him to take back to them Sioux hiding on the ridges off yonder."

Once outside the office to begin their tour, Carrington stared a moment at the sky.

"Mr. Wands—appears good weather will hold for the day. Release the wood train for its first run to the Pinery."

"Very good, sir."

Bridger watched Wands leave. "You want your wagons heading down to the Pine Woods, Colonel?"

Carrington looked startled momentarily. "Why, do you sense trouble?"

"Probably nothing," Bridger grumped, volving a painful shoulder. "Feel something in my bones. Maybe just a storm a'coming."

Carrington smiled. "The way I see it, our wood train's safe for today at least. Why, if the Sioux send Two

Moons to look over our fort, they'll wait until he leaves
before trying anything, won't they, Jim?"

Bridger gazed at the colonel a moment before answering. "I rarely give a Injun the benefit of the doubt, Colonel. Just hope . . . better *pray* you're right."

Chapter 32

Carrington's tour hadn't taken long. He showed the Cheyenne the powder magazine and all the stores laid in by the soldiers. Even showed the chiefs a "gun that shoots twice," one of those dreaded mountain howitzers firing canister shot. To top it off, the colonel had a troop of men perform their close-order drill for the visitors.

The soldiers were ready, Bridger reminded Two Moons's delegation as he escorted them to the main gate. These soldiers were ready for any attack on the fort Red Cloud might plan.

The colonel returned to his office, spending the next hour readying his papers so that his month-end report to General Cooke might nearly be complete by the New Year.

"Indians!"

Carrington jerked up, hearing boots thumping the porch outside his window. From the door he saw that the children on the parade had stopped playing their blindman's bluff and stood stock-still, pointing at Pilot Hill.

He wheeled. *Damn their red souls anyway!*

Atop Pilot Hill waved the picket's flag. Down to the side and up. To the side and up. *Many Indians . . . wood train under attack.*

"Bugler!"

"Here, Colonel!" Metzger came running, his bugle clanging against his knitting kit, itself rattling with ammunition as he buckled the pistol belt round his waist.

"Boots and Saddles, bugler! Blow, by god!"

Carrington boiled with sudden anger. Caught lowering his guard. Believing the Sioux wouldn't attack a wood train the same day the Cheyenne visited. He ripped his watch from a pocket. *Just before eleven.*

"Colonel Carrington!"

He rushed to the bottom of those steps leading to the watchtower, cocking his head up the ladder. "What is it?"

"Two Injuns, sir!" the sentry shouted down, pointing. "They just come down the slope of Lodge Trail, big as life itself . . . crawled off their ponies t'other side of the Big Piney."

"What're they doing, Private?"

"N-Nothing, sir! Just sitting there. Wrapped up in their blankets. Just sitting. And watching."

"Watching what, soldier?"

"Us, sir. Watching us."

"Colonel?"

He wheeled. "Captain Powell! You'll ride to the relief of the wood train as you did two days ago."

"Your orders stand?"

"As they did then—do not take your troops over Lodge Trail Ridge."

Powell smiled weakly. "I found out for myself. You don't have to convince me——"

"Colonel Carrington!"

He turned at the shrill voice. "Fetterman?"

"I demand to lead this relief!" Fetterman stomped to a halt at Carrington's boot-toes.

"On what grounds——"

"I'm senior to Powell here," he snapped. "Besides, my Company A is ready to march as we speak."

Carrington looked over Fetterman's shoulder. Soldiers stood at parade rest in front of their company barracks.

Carrington sighed. "Powell accounted well for himself on the nineteenth——"

"I won't waste time lallygagging with you here, repeating chapter, verse, and section . . . if you catch my drift," Fetterman snapped. "I'm senior field officer of the Eighteenth. By god, I'll not have you snatch this from me!"

Carrington glanced at Powell with an apology in his eyes. He watched Powell sag, a look of relief loosening his features. Powell doesn't want to go anyway, he thought as he turned back to Fetterman.

"Very well, Captain. You'll have command of the entire relief party. Move out at once with your Company A . . . and a detachment of cavalry——"

"Where're they?" Fetterman barked.

"You move out with your infantry and the cavalry at once," Carrington fumed. "I'll see Lieutenant Grummond is dispatched with his mounted infantry. They'll catch up with you, Captain."

"Hopefully before we reach the wood train."

"In plenty of time to drive the warriors off."

"There'll be no cat and mouse today, I'll have you know." Fetterman turned on his heel to shout back. "It's a fine day to get our licks in at last!"

"Halt, Captain Fetterman!" Carrington shouted, jarred by the flamboyant boast, suddenly remembering he hadn't issued specific orders.

Fetterman whirled, fuming. His hands clenching, barely containing his excitement. "What now, goddammit!"

"Captain, you'll support the wood train," the colonel began. "Relieve the wood train and report back to me."

Fetterman's bragging—the way he struts. He wants my chair! Gaining that promotion by beating the Sioux at any cost.

"Do not engage or pursue the hostiles at the expense of the wood train, Captain! Under no circumstances are you to pursue the Indians over the ridge . . . Lodge Trail Ridge."

"Is that all?"

He couldn't believe Fetterman had answered with that question. "Do you understand your orders?"

"That's all there is, Colonel?"

"Yes, Captain. That's all."

Fetterman saluted, turned and dashed across the grassy parade, waving. Sergeants barked orders along the columns as the foot soldiers right-faced, lit out for the south gate.

"Colonel?"

He turned to stare into the red face of young Lieutenant Wands.

"Request permission to join Fetterman, sir."

Carrington glanced at Fetterman marching along officers' quarters, nearing the south gate. He wheeled back on Wands. "Request denied, mister. You'll stay with me——"

"But, sir!"

"I need you with me, Lieutenant! You can damn well see that!" Henry sensed the first fissures fracturing his little world, beginning to widen. I'll hold on, he thought. Everything will quiet soon enough.

"As you wish." Wands turned to go.

"Lieutenant." Carrington put a hand out to stop his adjutant. "Catch Fetterman at the gate. Be certain you repeat my orders."

"Y-Your orders?"

"Make sure he understands he's to relieve the wood train . . . and not pursue the Indians over Lodge Trail Ridge."

Wands wheeled without saluting, tearing across the frozen parade, puffing steamy clouds as he ran. It doesn't matter him not saluting me, Carrington brooded.

He glanced at his watch. *Eleven-fifteen. Get your men moving, Fetterman!*

Carrington whirled at the sounds of shouting, hoping

to find the lieutenant in sight. *Where the devil is Grummond?*

Across the parade the colonel watched Wands stop Fetterman in front of the Grummond house, next door to Carrington's home. The captain leaned off his horse, appeared to be listening to what Wands had to say. Then Fetterman rared back for a moment before he presented his hand to the adjutant. They shook. Wands stepped back. Fetterman waved his foot-soldiers and the twenty-seven cavalry forward at once. Accompanied from the stockade by a spotted dog.

To Henry's left arose the shouts and clatter of the mounted infantry, scrambling from the cavalry yard, Grummond in the lead. He halted his detail before Carrington.

"Lieutenant, you understand your orders?"

"Report to Captain Fetterman. Relieve the wood train. We're not to pursue over the ridge."

"Remember the lessons of the sixth, Lieutenant. Report to Fetterman. Obey his orders, and never leave his side."

Carrington didn't wait for a response but turned on his heel and strode quickly down the line of mounted infantry. Inspecting rifles. Here and there he found a man with a faulty weapon or one who hadn't reported in complete light-marching order. He dropped those few from the ranks.

"Colonel Carrington—request permission to join the relief party, sir!"

He whirled, ready to bite another head off. He sighed instead, recognizing the trusted old veteran, Pvt. Thomas Maddeon before him, fully dressed and armed. "Your weapon in good repair?"

"Positively, Colonel! And itching for some action, sir. For months you've kept me busy so I couldn't get a lick in on them red bastards, sir. Excusing the language."

"It's all right, Maddeon. Permission granted. You'll take your personal mount?"

"Aye, I will."

"Fall in with the rest of H Company. You'll ride with Lieutenant Grummond."

Henry glanced at Pilot Hill. The flag waved to the left again and again. *Big party of Indians on the wood road. Big party——*

"Colonel, I've asked Jimmy if he'd let me ride Calico."

Carrington turned, finding Fred Brown riding up on the spotted pony Brown himself had given the colonel's son better than a year before.

"Why you, Fred?" He already knew.

"Like I told you last night—not that much time left here. Job's done. Paperwork's all in line. They want me at Laramie before the new year. By damn, I'm eager for one more chance at these savages, Colonel! Something tells me today's my day! I'll bring back Red Cloud's scalp myself and throw it on your desk before the falling of the sun!"

Carrington glanced down at the little pinto beneath Brown. "Just . . . remember the pony. The boys love him so——"

"Nothing'll happen to him!" He tapped heels and whirled the pony past the waiting soldiers. "What glory mantles our shoulders when God's work we do!"

"Colonel Carrington," Grummond called out. "Two civilians will be accompanying me."

Carrington glanced at the eager volunteers, recognizing faces but not remembering names.

"You are?"

"Issac Fisher," the first answered, tapping the barrel of his Henry repeater against his hat brim.

"James Wheatley."

"Your wife runs the mess down by the stockade," the colonel answered. "You look suitably well-armed."

"Better'n your poor boys with them muzzle-loading Springfields."

"Your repeaters might come in handy at that. Take them with you, Lieutenant."

Wands trotted back across the frozen parade, skidding beside Grummond's horse. "George," he cried out breathlessly, his eyes flaring with apprehension. "I had no idea you'd go too!"

Grummond chuckled. "Of course, Alex. Why not?"

"Good god—your wife! Your child," he stammered, licking his dry lips, catching his breath. "She's standing at your door, in positive dread and horror at the thought of your going."

"Dear girl——"

"She can't believe you want to go . . . after knocking at death's door but three weeks——"

He clamped a hand on Wands's shoulder. "Tell her not to worry, Alex."

"Please, George," he pleaded. "For your family's sake, be prudent . . . avoid rash movement. And above all, heed the order not to dash over the ridge. Powell obeyed and he wasn't——"

"Alex! I'm surprised at you! To think my wife worked you up into such a lather. Be assured, my friend—I have no intention of laying my life down for some half-dressed savage who worships rocks!"

Grummond righted himself in the saddle, saluted Carrington, and moved out. The company sergeant shouted his orders, bringing the files behind Grummond.

"Column half right . . . march! Left! Front into line!"

The lieutenant turned in his saddle and waved. "Goodbye, Alex! Tell Frances there's nothing to fear!"

The hair along Carrington's neck stood on end as he glanced across the parade, noticing Frances Grummond huddled beneath the eve of her doorway, thick shawl crumpled around her shoulders. His heart ached of a sudden.

With his next breath Carrington dashed across the parade. Up the ladder, two steps at a time, he clambered to the banquette above the south gate in time to call out.

"Lieutenant Grummond! Halt!"

"Colonel? What the——"

"For god's sake, Lieutenant, for everyone's . . . remember: under no circumstances are you to cross Lodge Trail Ridge——"

"I heard you the first time, Colonel."

Grummond turned away, signaling to the sergeant he had drilled repeatedly over the past month.

"Column of twos! Center guide—HO!"

Henry watched until the last soldier trotted out the gate, then tore the pocket watch from his tunic. *Eleven twenty-eight. Half an hour gone . . .*

Jim Bridger had watched Carrington lumber across the graveled walks and frozen grass of the parade, scurrying up the ladder to the banquette. After Carrington glanced at his watch, he gazed north, toward the bony ridge once more.

"Where the blazes is Fetterman going?" the colonel asked of no one at all.

When Bridger turned from the stockade wall, it surprised Carrington. "How long you been standing here, Jim?"

"Long enough to see a lot, Colonel." Jim nodded toward Fetterman's columns. "I figured he'd head down the wood road to relieve the wagons. 'Stead, it looks like Fetterman's marching northwest, gonna cross the Big Piney at the foot of Lodge Trail."

"Why the devil's Fetterman doing that?" Carrington leaped to the wall, tearing the looking glass from a sentry's hands.

"Maybeso, Fetterman lays to cut off the Injuns pouring into the valley from the north . . . come to attack your wood train. Maybeso—he figures to jump them Injuns from behind."

"But I gave no such order——"

"Too late to yank back on his reins now."

". . . Just relieve the train," Carrington whimpered into the freshening breeze that swung out of the north.

Bridger sensed that breeze too. *Temperature dropping*

fast. He looked west, noticing the first low clouds had scudded behind Peno Head already, threatening to lock in the valley before long.

"Yes! That might be it, Jim," the colonel answered quietly. "By jove—he's taking the same route I took on the sixth, when I sought to trap the Sioux myself. He's going to run an ambush on them—take the hostiles in reverse, isn't he?"

"Let's hope, Colonel. Hope that's what he's got in mind."

By the time Fetterman's combined forces reached the icy crossing of the Big Piney, Grummond's mounted infantry had caught up. Upon reaching the north bank, Fetterman wheeled left, marching along the creek up the southern foot of Lodge Trail Ridge.

"He's put skirmishers out, Jim," Carrington announced as he brought the glass from his eye. "Driving a few warriors before him as he climbs the ridge."

"Bound on taking the Sioux from the rear, then," Jim said, more hopeful than ever.

"My lord!" Carrington gasped. "I completely forgot in my haste——"

He wheeled to the edge of the platform, shouting for Wands. "Lieutenant!"

"Sir?" He came running, puffing frost.

"I assigned no surgeon to Fetterman's detail. Find Hines! Grab two hospital stewards and dispatch them on the double to the wood train. If the medical team isn't needed there, have them swing around and join up with Fetterman."

Wands tore off, headed for the unfinished hospital.

"They should be able to catch Fetterman," Carrington murmured under his breath. "He's not reached the top of the ridge yet."

"Not yet anyways," Bridger replied.

The clatter of iron-shoes on gravel and frozen ground lured them both to the edge of the sentry-walk.

"God's speed, Surgeon!" Carrington cried out, saluting.

Hines glanced up, continuing without a word, followed by his two grim-faced stewards. Their hoof-beats faded down the wood road.

"Colonel! The picket—Pilot Hill!" a sentry hollered.

Carrington whirled, bringing up the looking glass, though any man could plainly see the waving flag atop the southern knob. Round and round the picket's head the flag fluttered on the cold wind, then carried back and forth along the brow of the hill.

"They've broken off the attack on the wood train!" a sentry shouted.

The colonel slowly took the glass from his eye, staring at Bridger. "Doesn't make a bit of sense . . . why the hostiles would break off the attack without being driven off——"

"Look at the Lodge Trail, Colonel." Bridger pointed.

"Fetterman's halted on the ridge." He sighed. "Good." He held the pocket watch up. "Eleven forty-five . . . and he's halted—just as I ordered."

"Can you glass them Injuns down on the Piney?" Jim asked, pointing at the movement he had spotted.

Carrington studied the trees at the edge of the creek. Loping into the cottonwoods rode two dozen mounted warriors, aiming for the Montana Road crossing. He glanced at the series of small, white flags he had ordered placed at intervals across the valley.

"Soldier, find the gunnery sergeant," Carrington directed. "Have him drop some canister among those warriors at the crossing."

"Colonel," Bridger called from the stockade wall. "He's gone."

"Gone?" he screeched, whirling.

"Fetterman." Bridger pointed, wagging his head.

As Carrington watched, wide-mouthed, the last of Fetterman's combined forces disappeared. Eighty-one men: three officers, seventy-six enlisted, and two civilians.

Gone from the bare, windswept brow of Lodge Trail Ridge like woodsmoke on a stiff breeze.

"They can't . . . they're not going over——"

"You saw it with your own eyes."

He gazed at Bridger, fear creasing his brow. "May God have mercy——"

The howitzer belched its first canister. Two dozen warriors burst from the trees like a wounded covey of quail. A second canister uprooted thirty more. The fort watched as every last one sped his pony into the gray, frozen badlands north of Lodge Trail Ridge.

"At least those warriors won't circle in on Fetterman's rear now," Carrington whispered. "I think we can relax, Jim." He flashed Bridger a grim smile.

The colonel turned and clambered down the ladder, crossing the graveled street in front of officers' row, disappearing into the rear of his office.

Chapter 33

"What in blazes are you doing back?" Carrington bolted out of his chair, scurrying around his desk as Assistant Surgeon C. M. Hines burst through the office door.

Breathless, Hines stomped halfway across the room then stopped. "By the time we reached the wood train, Colonel, the Sioux had broken off——"

"I know that!" he snapped. "If not needed there, I ordered you to join Fetterman's column. What're you——"

"We tried, goddammit!"

"What the devil you mean, 'you tried'?"

"I requested two additional privates as escorts for my stewards, then hurried west down the wood road. I fully expected to find Fetterman coming 'round the north side of the Sullivants——"

"No!" he barked. "He led his columns up the ridge." Carrington watched the surgeon's face blanch. As pale as the foolscap the colonel had been using to write General Cooke in Omaha. "What is it, Hines? Tell me!"

Hines gulped, his eyes flitting, never landing, like an anxious butterfly. "That . . . explains what I saw——"

"Saw what?"

"When I reached the western end of the Hills, Lodge Trail Ridge came full into sight."

"Go on, dammit!" He was close to grabbing Hines, wringing it out of him in one gush.

"Saw more Sioux than I've ever seen in my life. Hundreds of 'em, swarming like bees . . . like ants. Infesting the north end of the valley. Massing along the north end of the ridge. Feathers . . . blankets . . . lances——"

"Fetterman!" he yelled at Hines. "What about Fetterman?"

Hines shook his head, staring at the plank floor. "Not a sign of him, Colonel."

"Did you ride any closer?"

His eyes flashed into Carrington's. "You've got to be crazy! There were more Indians . . . milling and yelling, between us and the ridge—why, I turned my men around and rode here full gallop."

Carrington turned away. Stomping to the glazed window. By now the sky had thickened like blood soup, gray and ready to drop its load of icy snow. A stiff wind kicked along the parade.

"Perhaps things aren't really as distressing as they appear, Mr. Hines." *Lord, do I want to believe it.* "I think Fetterman's returning by the Montana Road," and he turned, snapping fingers, "coming back by one of those trails just north of the Big Piney."

"Along the foot of Lodge Trail, Colonel?"

"Right! That's got to be it." He flashed a smile and curled behind his desk once more. "I appreciate you making an attempt to join up with Fetterman. I don't have any further need of your services at this time, Surgeon—you're dismissed."

"Good morning, Colonel."

He glanced at his watch, nodding at Hines. "Yes. Almost the dinner hour. A few minutes before twelve." Carrington watched Hines close the door, a swish of chill air rustling the coffee-stained papers across his desk.

Moments later as a bugler blew dinner call, Wands flung the office door open.

"Colonel! Sentries report hearing rifle-fire!"

He bolted out of chair. "You hear it?"

"Nosir! Came as fast as I could."

Without another word, Carrington dashed from his of-fice and leaped up the ladder to the lookout roost atop headquarters. Breathlessly he listened, counting six scat-tering shots echoing from the vicinity of the Peno, fol-lowed by a series of distinct volleys. Try as he might, the colonel couldn't make out a thing with the looking glass.

"Lieutenant." He wheeled on Wands. "Tell Ten Eyck he'll lead a relief——"

Wands gasped. "You don't think, sir——"

Carrington shook his head angrily. "It doesn't matter what I think. Get Ten Eyck moving now."

"Sir, all respect," he stuttered, then swallowed hard, "the captain's in a bad way this morning."

"Hung over?"

Wands nodded. "Besides, Colonel, Ten Eyck's a buf-foon. Everyone knows——"

"Mister! I'll not have you talking about the cap-tain . . ." As he said it, Carrington knew his adjutant was right. He gazed down at the soldiers milling about the stockade. Knowing he could send so few, having to hold in reserve a force to defend the fort. "I can't send a lot, you understand. If this is a ruse to draw our forces out . . . then assault the fort . . . why——"

He whirled as the lieutenant reached the ground be-low. "Wands! Bring Ten Eyck to the guardhouse."

"The guardhouse?"

"Just do it! And hurry . . . like you've never hurried before!"

Carrington dropped down the ladder, stomping toward the guardhouse which sat next to headquarters. "Ser-geant!" he shouted to the first man with stripes to cross the parade reporting for service. "Ride down to the min-ers' camp . . . take my horse if you must. Bring them here to the fort. They'll know of the alarm. Sweep by the quartermaster yard. Bring all the teamsters here too. Now hurry for God's sake, man!"

He gazed up at the lookout along the north wall. "Sentry! Down here on the double! I want you to grab a horse——"

"Sir, the captain took all fit to ride this morn——"

"Take one that'll get you to the Pinery and back!" Carrington growled. "Bring the wood parties home—without delay!"

He whirled, noticing the nervous private pacing before the guardhouse, his rifle at an angle across his chest. The boy's face curdled with fear.

"Private, front and center!" He waited while the young soldier trotted up, his eyes anxious, concerned in leaving his post. "How many prisoners under guard?"

"Seven, sir."

"Release them."

"Release——"

"To me!" he barked. "Tell them I'm waiting outside, to report to me. They'll be on watch—sentry duty."

"Y-Yessir." He turned to go.

"You have a civilian under guard?"

"Yes," he answered, a question brightening his eyes. "Don't know his name——"

"Donegan. Seamus Donegan," Carrington sighed. Funny that as everything was in the process of falling apart, at least some things became a little clearer with that moment. "Release him too. Tell Mr. Donegan he's to report to me."

"Understood, sir."

The private scrambled back to the heavy pine-and-iron door of the guardhouse, where long icicles hung like canine teeth from the eaves of the sloping, snow-covered roof. From a distance Carrington heard more file-firing. Henry glanced at his watch. *Twelve-twelve.* Volley after volley of heavy fire crackled on the cold dry air. *They're holding their own. Holding——*

Carrington shivered, realizing for the first time that he had forgotten to put on his coat. Chilled, as the cold finally bit through his adrenaline.

Minutes later, as the colonel emerged from the guard-house with Donegan and Ten Eyck, back into the pewter light of midday once more, Henry watched a gray-headed civilian ride up, pulling a second and larger animal behind him.

"Cap'n Marr!" Seamus Donegan hollered with a raw throat. "You brought the gray."

"I did, you stupid Irishman!" He smiled, handing over the reins. "Good to see you, Seamus." He tossed a Henry rifle to Donegan.

"Mighty good to see your face, Cap'n. You'll ride along?"

Marr slipped his own repeater from the boot beneath his right leg. "Wouldn't want you to have all the fun."

"Begora, but you're a jealous scut!" and he laughed in that lusty, deep-throated way of his.

"Stay with Ten Eyck," Carrington pleaded. "Like I asked, help him, Seamus Donegan. See that you bring Fetterman back."

"And Cap'n Brown too?" Seamus glared down at Carrington. "I've a score to settle with that'un, Colonel."

Carrington stepped back from the big gray. "I understand." He swallowed. "We'll make it right by you." He watched Ten Eyck saddle up after ordering his foot-soldiers to the gate at the double. He returned Ten Eyck's salute. "Captain. A second civilian will join your relief party." He watched some consternation cross Tenedor's face. "To help. As I remember, Captain Sam Marr's a cavalry veteran. For God's sake, Tenedor, you can use every man, every rifle——"

"Very good, Colonel," Ten Eyck replied, his droopy eyelid twitching nervously as he glanced at Marr. "You'll ride with me."

"We're waiting on you," Marr said, pointing to the gate with his rifle.

Together the three loped through the main gates, catching the small group of foot soldiers as they disappeared over the brow of the hill. Carrington ordered all gates closed, secured, and double pickets placed along the banquettes.

Dear God, he prayed as he hurried back to his office, the stove and his coat, *I pray I've done all that I can. I suppose that's all any of us can do for now—pray. It's in Your hands now.*

Volley after volley echoed from Peno Creek. Spaced further and further apart. Until she heard a few random, scattered shots. Then nothing.

Silence.

An aching nothingness from the northwest. Beyond the ridge nothing but the agonizing echo of silence.

Margaret felt her blood chill as Henry trudged down the steps, one slow step at a time. Never had she seen that look of gray, hopeless dread pinch his face.

By the time he reached the ground his hands shook, his watch held before him like a bird with a broken wing. "Forty minutes," he stammered at her. "Can it be . . . over already?"

The way he looked at her reminded Margaret of something wounded.

"Colonel?"

Both Henry and Margaret turned. Brevet Captain Arnold saluted. "Yes?" Carrington asked weakly.

"You asked for a report, Colonel . . . the number of men left in garrison?"

"Yes."

"One hundred nineteen, sir."

"Including guard?"

"Including *you,* Colonel."

She watched Henry turn away. "Dismissed, Captain."

For moments Margaret didn't speak. Dared not touch him. A grief too private that even she could not share. When he sighed and turned back to face her, she whispered, "Henry . . . Frances Grummond—she knows. Don't ask me how, but she knows."

"You must see to her, Margaret. Their baby . . . *her*

baby." His eyes begged. "If truly George is in God's hands . . . then Frances now rests in yours."

She turned as footsteps crunched on the gravel walk.

"Gunnery Sergeant Hopkins, Colonel." The soldier saluted. "Three mountain howitzers readied, one field piece —twelve-pounder—all in place, charged with canister or grapeshot. Awaiting your orders."

"We all wait, Sergeant," Henry replied. "Keep your crews at ready, for whatever might betide."

"Henry," she whispered when the gunnery sergeant had dashed off. "Frances fears her worst nightmare's come true."

"It is a nightmare." He sighed, letting Margaret slip her gloved hand around his bare fingers. "Were it not for you——"

"Hush!" she whispered. "So many rely on you. I more than any, Henry."

"I . . . I never knew——"

"Both of us had hoped your new post would be a new beginning," she said. "I shared that dream with you."

"So much . . . too late now."

"Go do what must be done, Henry." Margaret kissed his bearded cheek. "So many depend on you."

"Yes," he answered weakly. "My fort won't fall. I can't let it."

With a squeeze to her hand, Henry turned and sped across the parade toward the powder magazine. *I must get back to Frances*, Margaret thought, wrapping the muffler around her face so only her eyes peeked out. *We'll wait together.*

She set out across the parade to fetch Frances. To bring Frances to her home.

I knew Fetterman would ruin things for Henry. She leaned into a gust of wind as strong as any cruel slap could be. *He intended to bring Henry down, one way or the other. To be post commander . . . even district commander. Now, even unto his death—Fetterman's accomplished what he set out to do.*

"Damn him!" she whispered into the muffler. "Captain William Fetterman . . . hero of the Eighteenth. *Damn him!*"

She had seen the reports on Henry's desk. More important, she had watched her husband brood over Fetterman's record. While Henry had been stuck recruiting in Ohio or Indiana throughout the war, Fetterman gained glory and honor. In combat.

As early as the spring of 'sixty-two, Fetterman rode at the head of Company A, 2nd Battalion of the 18th Infantry, making a name for himself at the siege of Corinth. From there he rode to glory at Stone's River, cited for gallantry after more than thirty-six hours of continuous fighting. Fetterman had been the hotspur that saw the 2nd Battalion through Sherman's march to the sea: Peach Tree Creek, Jonesboro, Resaca, Kennesaw Mountain, and Atlanta itself.

Margaret had watched Henry read and reread Fetterman's record in those days and weeks before her husband called the gallant captain up from Fort Sedgwick. She understood how that record destroyed a little more of Henry with every reading:

> "*Captain Fetterman's command marched to my assistance with great promptness . . .*"
>
> "*. . . displayed great gallantry and spirit . . .*"
>
> "*. . . conspicuous for gallantry and bravery . . .*"
>
> "*. . . the conduct of Captain Fetterman in throwing up a salient and maintaining his positions against repeated attempts to dislodge him by the enemy, is worthy of particular notice.*"
>
> "*. . . breveted Lieutenant Colonel for bravery . . .*"

Chapter 34

"Goddamn these bastards!" Fetterman roared. "I've stormed rifle-pits, laid siege, held men under artillery bombardment . . . but I've never seen anything like this!"

Moments ago the captain had halted his entire force at the western lip of Lodge Trail Ridge. As soon as the decoys saw the soldiers stop, they turned and swept back along both brows of the ridge. Taunting, slipping behind their ponies or waving blankets to frighten soldier horses. Trying to draw fire from the skirmishers, Fetterman had deployed on both flanks of his march up the bare rib of ground, climbing into a thickening, gray sky. Back and forth the young Sioux warriors urged their little ponies, yelping like coyotes, luring, seductive.

"Shoot!" he shouted at his infantry skirmishers. "What the devil you waiting on? They get close enough, knock the bastards outta the saddle!"

With each volley of rifle-fire the decoys fell back. As soon as the shooting ended, they surged back toward the foot-soldiers.

The Montana Road itself snaked up from the Big Piney Crossing toward this spur of bare ground that extended northwest from Lodge Trail Ridge. Near the saddle that separated the spur from the east side of the Ridge, the Road angled to the right, curving north along the crest of the spur for little more than a mile. At the northern tip of the spur the Road dropped into the valley of Peno Creek.

Where the warriors circled and taunted, urging the soldiers off the high-ground.

"Captain, request permission to engage the bastards your infantry can't hit."

Fetterman wheeled, seeing Eli Garrett's wolfish grin. "No," he snapped.

"We'll damn well do better at it than your infant——"

"As you were, Sergeant! I'll have no insubordination." "Judd!"

Fetterman found Fred Brown darting up atop the calico pony.

"There go more of the devils!" Brown pointed out a group of more than thirty warriors racing along the brow of the ridge, up from the Big Piney, joining the decoy party beckoning from the Bozeman Road below. As they watched the warriors dance about in their front, some random shots echoed from the rear of the column.

"Sergeant Garrett," Fetterman turned and growled. "Those shots came from the cavalry. Find out what the devil's going on!"

Eli tore back along the infantry to rejoin C Company and Grummond's mounted infantry. He was no more than halfway back when the brow of the hill exposed more than two hundred warriors. They had crept up from the south side of the ridge, hidden for the most part, until they began taking shots at the white horsemen.

"I damn well see for myself!" Fetterman exclaimed as Garrett slid to a stop beside him.

"They're moving down the ridge, Judd!" Brown shouted, straining to control the excited pony. "They'll join the others in no time."

"I can see that, Fred!"

Garrett watched Fetterman brood on it, his eyes squinting into the distance, attempting to catch a glimpse of something that . . . perhaps no man could see.

"We'll hold here," Fetterman announced.

"Hold!" Brown screeched. "Dammit, Judd—you don't strike that bunch in front of us now . . . those other bastards on our tail can join up——"

"Shuddup, Fred!" He swung a fist in the air. "I'll hold here."

"We can cut 'em up quick, you gimme a chance!" Brown demanded.

"Captain's right, sir," Garrett agreed. He liked Brown's bravado. "We charge, they'll run anyway. Have to fight 'em in pieces eventually. Let my twenty-seven men show you how it's——"

"Sit tight, Sergeant!" Fetterman hollered, hearing the shouts and yells of soldiers all along the column exposed atop the ridge.

"Dammit, Judd, you——"

"Don't bully me, Fred!"

"Bully you?" Brown shrieked, pointing at the warriors. "You may not get another chance like this in your life!"

"Chance for what?"

"Your damned promotion, Judd. Mine too!"

"Is that why you're so hot to chase on down there——"

"Yes, goddammit! Aren't you willing to risk a little something to be a soldier again, Judd? Hell, I remember the warrior you were at one time. Now you and Carrington are two old ladies——"

"I've a notion to order you back to the——"

"You won't send me back, Judd. 'Cause I'm one of the few real soldiers you got riding with you. And I know you well enough too . . . know you're itching to lay into 'em, just like me."

"I'm ordered not to cross the ridge."

"Whose orders?"

"You know whose goddamn——"

"That sniveling coward Carrington? You're gonna listen to that doddering old fool?" Brown laughed, throwing his head back in the crude way he had that showed off his tonsils. "He isn't a fighting man like you or me! We're soldiers, Judd. By damned, let's go do what soldiers do best!"

Minutes ago the decoys had watched the soldiers halt, deploying skirmishers on their flanks. Time and again young warriors dashed along the fringes of the column, attempting to seduce the troopers down the ridge. The shivering soldiers didn't budge.

In desperation, one young warrior sitting atop a pony painted with lightning bolts and hailstones flung his blanket coat to the ground. To him had been given the honor of drawing the soldiers into the trap below. Now he embraced this challenge of luring the white men off the ridge. Wheeling, he shouted courage to his companions. In turn they sang out their prayers for him as he galloped headlong for the soldier lines. Unlike the rest, who zigzagged to escape the soldier bullets, intent only on taunting the troopers, this solitary warrior sped on a collision course with the spear-point of the enemy columns. To force the day.

"By damn, that buck's mine!" Eli Garrett shouted, cocking his Spencer repeater.

"No such luck today!" Fred Brown swung, knocking aside the sergeant's rifle. "He's mine, Sergeant!"

The captain raised his Starr carbine, watching the young warrior on the earth-painted pony steer directly for him over the blade at the end of his barrel. Brown squeezed. The warrior skidded to a stop, threw up his hands then screamed at the soldiers. Fifty feet away. And still alive.

"Goddamn, you missed!" Fetterman cursed as the warrior pranced his pony to the side, urging the chase.

"I bloody well won't miss again!" Brown shrieked. "If you're not man enough to fight these bastards, Judd, I sure am! Go ahead, sit here like that desk-soldier Carrington ordered—I'll have that bastard's scalp and he'll scream in hell before this day's out!"

Brown savagely flayed the little pinto's ribs, tearing

after the solitary warrior. Instead of fleeing immediately, the Sioux turned his back on Brown, raised his rump in the air, exposing his bare, brown flesh to the soldiers. Brown's maddened cry hung suspended on the cold breeze as the calico charged downhill.

"Captain Fetterman, you can't let him go alone!" Garrett prodded.

He growled, "Those goddamned orders of——".

"Blood's the only thing those bastards understand!" Garrett fumed. "Give 'em a taste of what they want!"

"By damn, Sergeant," Fetterman growled back, "William Judd Fetterman never was a coward! And he won't start now! Let's give those bastards a taste of steel and blood!"

"Whaaaa-hoooo!" Garrett flung his arm in the air, signaling his cavalry enthusiastically.

"At a walk, dammit!" Fetterman ordered. "Keep my infantry in sight!"

"At a walk, Captain!" Garrett cheered. "Long as we gut some of these devils in the process!"

Garrett watched his soldiers strain at the bit, controlling their nervous mounts. The screaming. Gunfire. Waiting for action.

"Front into line, goddammit! By fours . . . guide center, forward at a walk—HO!" Garrett shouted to his horse soldiers.

The last he saw of Fetterman, the captain was glancing back at Fort Phil Kearny far across the valley. A moment later, as they dropped down off northern rib of Lodge Trail Ridge, both Garrett and Fetterman could no longer see the fort.

For the moment, neither Carrington nor his orders mattered anymore.

By the time Grummond and Garrett caught up with Fred Brown, the captain sat reloading, grumbling at his poor weapon. All three stared after the seductive decoys flitting farther and farther down the ridge, in the next breath cursing the plodding infantry Fetterman prodded down the windswept ridge on the double. Straining to catch the mounted soldiers.

Off the spur raced the decoys. Time and again they stopped, turned, taunted and hollered. Urging the soldiers on. Watching the cavalry surge against itself restlessly. Following the decoys obediently, Brown led the mounted troops onto that snowy rib pointing like a bony, skeletal finger to the northwest, down into the valley of Peno Creek. Down, down into the maw of the valley they plunged, the infantry winded, struggling to keep up. Past a field of huge boulders, chasing the warriors who circled and jeered down near the creek itself.

Once Grummond's horse soldiers plunged off the end of the spur, the Sioux whirled, hollering among themselves. Their ponies broke ice scum to the north bank of the Peno. Fetterman's infantry thumped along at a ground-eating double-time, plodding after the eager cavalry inching farther and farther away.

As the foot-soldiers entered the maw of the valley itself, the decoys across the creek split into two groups. Each band dashed away like scattering quail, suddenly turning, doubling back, crossing the path of the other.

With that signal the valley instantly sprang alive. Two thousand shrieking Sioux, Cheyenne and Arapaho leaped from bushes and tall grass. From hiding places behind rock and tree. Shouting. Shooting guns. Firing arrows. Screaming. Hurtling lances. Wielding axes and clubs.

Garrett yanked back on the reins. His mount stumbled, pitching over. His mouth went as dry as if he'd swallowed trail-dust. He clambered to his feet, reins still in his hands, his ears pounding with demon shrieks. Back up the spur behind Fetterman's foot-soldiers the trap slammed shut. Across the creek ahead the hillside throbbed with warriors leaping from hiding. From both sides of the spur sprang hundreds. Eli realized they were outnumbered better than twenty to one. *Gotta make a stand of it.*

"Holy shit!" he hollered, whirling as a bullet struck the soldier beside him, brain splattering hot blood across Eli's cheek.

Nearby, Brown's pony crumpled, pinning the captain's leg. Amid the crush of warriors and the panic-ridden raw recruits, Garrett pulled Brown free. By the time Eli turned round seconds later, his own horse had dashed across the creek, several arrows bobbing in its withers and flanks.

"Get back to Fetterman!"

Garrett looked up, finding Grummond in the saddle, pistol in hand, pointing, shouting orders. Urging soldiers back up the spur where Fetterman was having a hot time of it. From all sides the warriors swarmed like maddened red ants.

Grummond raced among the soldiers, kicking, shouting, shooting. Covering the retreat as best he could. Closing the file as the cavalry dragged their wounded with them. Most soldiers horrified at the terror of battle. Some going to pieces and screaming. A few throwing useless weapons away.

Into their midst plunged the two civilians. Firing their repeaters coolly, Wheatley and Fisher held fast, blunting the first wave of Black Shield's Miniconjou who were given the honor of making this first assault.

Eli whirled, sweeping an abandoned carbine from the frozen ground, running in a crouch back to the civilians and a handful of soldiers kneeling in a small fortress of boulders and horse carcasses.

"Glad you could join us, Sergeant!" James Wheatley hollered above the clamor.

"No place like home!" Garrett slid behind a horse still jerking in its death throes.

"Don't waste time," Issac Fisher growled. "More'n enough for us all, soldier!"

Garrett swept his sights to the left and fired. Then swung right. Seeing Grummond drive the cavalry up the spur, joining Fetterman's infantry at the foot of the ridge.

As he turned back, one of Eli's young cavalrymen buckled, crumpling into the snow, thrashing on the ground a moment. Until he lay still. White powdering his back.

Private Burke, Eli thought, and pulled his trigger again. *By god, the boy was a soldier after all!*

Lead slammed into the horse carcasses about them, going home with the flat thud like a hand slapping wet putty. None of the carcasses moved anymore. Arrows hissed through the grass. Bullets hummed overhead. Behind it all rose the constant drone of eagle-wingbone whistles keening for white blood. Soldier blood.

Out of the swirl of Sioux flitted blurred forms. One moment atop their ponies, the next gone. Arrows whispering through the cold air: *whit. Whit. Whit-tukk! Swiss-thung!*

Garrett watched the last soldier in the little horse-fort sink over a carcass, a shaft buried deep in his throat. A moment later he could no longer hear that wet gurgle in the trooper's throat. Fisher, Wheatley, and Eli Garrett remained. In the span of five minutes the Sioux had killed Burke and four seasoned veterans around him.

His gun jammed. Garrett ducked, dragging another Spencer from beneath a cavalryman's body. Once, twice, three times he aimed and fired. Watching a warrior fall for each bullet. Those last three marksmen exacted a terrible toll on the Sioux that day beneath a milk-pale sun hidden behind the thickening, snow-swollen clouds.

"My gun . . . God . . . dammit!"

Garrett whirled, watching Wheatley catch Fisher. A long shaft quivered from the base of Fisher's neck, the bloody iron point dripping from the other side.

"I'll pull it——"

"No!" Fisher shouted. "Give the soldier . . . my gun. Give 'im my . . ."

Wheatley looked up, imploring Garrett. "Take his rifle, goddammit!" he growled, tears clouding his eyes. "He don't need it no longer."

Eli pulled the weapon into his shoulder and fired. Until

it clicked empty. His hands dug through Fisher's pockets, finding the loose .44/40 shells. Four. Five. Six he jammed into the rifle. Then sprang upright to fire.

Looked down at his chest. Seeing the iron tip poking like a stickpin from a gentleman's tie. Dripping with his own fluid.

"You reloaded yet, soldier?" Wheatley hollered, his back turned, pumping and firing. Knocking a warrior from the saddle with every round. Deadly with his Henry. "C'mon, goddammit—you ain't got all day to reload the sonuvabitch!"

Eli turned slowly, jaws pumping, trying to speak. Say anything. He put his cold, bloody hand on Wheatley's shoulder. Then sank in silence. The eagle-wingbone whistles ringing in his ears.

As his eyes locked on the dirty sky overhead.

Chapter 35

*L*ittle Adolph Metzger, eleven-year veteran, filled one hand with his tin bugle, his revolver clamped in the other. Time and again he galloped back to fight at Grummond's side.

The young infantry lieutenant rawhided the cavalry like cattle, driving them back toward Fetterman up the ridge. Warriors swarmed over him. Falling away as quickly.

His saber slashed through the cold air with a whistling hiss. Grummond lopped off the head of an attacker. Fired his pistol into the breast of another, so close the warrior's blanket coat smoldered.

The Sioux rolled over him again. Grummond swung the saber. It bedded itself deep in the shoulder of a warrior who galloped away, already dead. Grummond ran out of luck. His saber gone. Pistol empty.

The lieutenant sank slowly from his saddle. A stain like dark gravy moist across his chest. Sinking slow and thick from his horse, as if he were tired. His legs buckled as he hit the ground. Sitting in the muddy snow beside his horse, reins still clutched in his glove.

Metzger raced up, easing Grummond back onto the trampled snow. He stared up at Adolph's face coming into focus over his.

"Tell Frances——"

Metzger had heard that gurgle too many times before. "You're a brave soldier, Lieutenant. Your wife will know you hung back to cover the retreat. I make that promise to you," Adolph whispered. His fingers pulled the pasty eyelids down.

Metzger fired his pistol. One, then a second warrior tumbled out of the saddle before Adolph realized he was alone. Not a single horse left. He had a choice. Race down to the little rock fortress where Garrett and two civilians worked their devastation on the Sioux with every shot. In a scattered ring surrounding the fortress lay the bodies of better than fifty dead or dying Sioux. Some trying to crawl away. Most still as stone while other horsemen surged toward the fortress.

Or he could run the gauntlet to rejoin Fetterman. Chances better with the more soldiers, he thought, bursting off on a dead run, hunched over like a crab as he scrambled through grass and brush.

Metzger suddenly sensed his heart leaping in his chest like a slippery fish breaking water in the mountain streams of his boyhood. *Germany . . . my beautiful Germany. So much like these mountains.*

"Gottamn dem!" Adolph cursed under his breath, watching the mounted troops clatter uphill, abandoning Fetterman's infantry.

Leaderless and confused, they plunged through the infantry, headed up the ridge, where they were stopped a hundred yards beyond a group of huge boulders. Milling about like some headless, crazed beast while the warriors swept around them, among them. Over them. Knocking the green recruits from their saddles with shrieks of bloody glee.

A blood-chilling scream rose down the slope. Adolph wheeled, fired. Dropping one warrior close enough to touch him with a lance. Metzger watched Wheatley stand. Alone now in his little fortress. Swinging his rifle

like a club. Knocking warriors aside like sheaves of wheat
until they swarmed over him. A second later Wheatley
stood alone again. Bloody from a hundred wounds. A
warrior swung a cruel, nail-studded war-club, taking the
top of the civilian's head with it. Metzger's stomach
pushed up against his tonsils. He turned away. Racing.
Gulping cold air.

He neared the boulders as the cavalry farthest up the
ridge dismounted like ragged tin soldiers. Leading their
horses onto the crest of the ridge. He glanced to the
south. Figuring the horsemen hoped to cross the top and
retreat back to the fort. Adolph watched them draw up
on the glazed, icy snow, short of the top.

The south slope of Lodge Trail Ridge erupted hundreds more mounted, screaming warriors.

Any hope of escape cut off like a last whimper of wind.

Pvt. Ephraim Rover whirled and fired again. Downhill
from where he stood, a solitary cavalry soldier scrambled
on foot. Rover aimed and dropped another warrior. He
would cover the soldier, the way he had covered the retreat of his infantry bunkies. Swinging and firing the carbine he had picked up along the slope, Rover recognized
the irony in his joining the army to escape a family and
trouble in Chicago—hungering for excitement. At the
moment he had more than a lifetime's staring him cold in
the face.

As the little soldier neared Rover, a warrior on horseback swung alongside. Ephraim fired, dropping the Sioux
on top of the trooper. The fallen man dragged himself
from beneath the Indian's body and scrambled alongside
Rover.

"Sank you," he growled with a thick accent.

"Let's go!" Ephraim shouted, watching the old soldier
scamper up the slope toward the boulders and the rest of
the waiting infantry. He leaped to his feet, running back-

ward, stumbling over brush and snowdrifts, firing as the Sioux surged up the hillside. His throat hurt.

Ephraim realized he was yelling at the top of his lungs.

Miniconjou warrior White Bull snugged the war-shield along his wrist, swinging the feathered lance through the air, urging his pony up the snowy slope. Bursting through puffs of gray gunpowder that stung his nostrils. The reek of death and voided bowels profaned the cold air. Three more joined him. While they carried bows, White Bull preferred his lance.

Though he was closest to the solitary soldier, an arrow from one of those who rode at his side struck the trooper first, bringing him to his knees. Slowly the soldier crumpled backward. White Bull charged in, the first to count coup. As he galloped over the soldier, the Miniconjou warrior slapped his lance point across the enemy's head, knocking off the blue hat.

Crazy Horse reined up beside White Bull, bullets hissing about them like mad hornets. The young Oglalla whirled as warriors nearby shouted. Word came that more soldiers were marching from the fort. Already they were crossing the first creek on the valley side of the ridge.

"We must finish these quickly—now!" Crazy Horse commanded. "Fight! Sweep these soldiers from the face of our mother!"

"Aiiyeee!" White Bull shouted, following the young Oglalla's courageous charge up the hill toward the boulders.

Spurred by Crazy Horse's exhortation, his brothers in war charged from all directions. Down from the ridge. Up from both sides of the road along the narrow spur. And closing the circle rode those joining Crazy Horse in a wild assault charging up the hill. Throwing themselves against volley after volley of soldier fire, the Sioux pressed closer. Yard by bloody yard, closer still, caring not for the bullets singing overhead or hissing into the frozen ground at their feet.

On the outer fringe of the low boulders soldiers stood to meet the Sioux charge. Flailing away with their rifles while warriors swung clubs, jabbed with lances, slashed with scalping knives, hacked with axes.

Crazy Horse trampled over warriors riddled with arrows. On all sides of the boulders lay the scattered bodies of his brothers sacrificed in the cross-fire of a savage attack. Already this place stank of death. Blood turning black on the trampled snow. Hair clotting the nails of his war-club, he swung again and again. Screeching his wild cry of death.

His moccasins slipped and he nearly fell. Across the ground wriggled coils of greasy blue gut streaming from a soldier's belly. Steaming. Stinking. He stared down into the wide eyes full of fear and pain. Then slammed his war-club into the face.

Pict. Pict. The bullets rang off the rocks around him. He swung again. The side of another soldier's face disappeared in a halo of red spattering Crazy Horse like hot grease. He wheeled, looking for another, his blood lust feverish. Watching brave soldier spirits rising to the heavens like breathsmoke from a dying man's mouth in winter.

Many of his brothers died around him, paying for this victory before the other soldiers could arrive. Sioux, Cheyenne, and Arapaho died bravely. Their deathsongs in their mouths.

Many dead, for they fought not with guns. But close, staring their enemy in the eye.

Yard by yard Adolph Metzger fell back, reaching the center of the tiny ring of boulders. He realized it was only a matter of minutes, perhaps only seconds now.

"Fred!"

Behind him he recognized Fetterman's voice. Brown

lumbered past the German bugler. Only a handful remained now, surrounded. Adolph wheeled, watching a warrior fly off the rocks overhead, landing on a soldier, swinging a club. Back against the rock he stumbled.

Just beyond, Fetterman and Brown pressed their pistols against each other's temple.

"One . . ." Fetterman rasped.

"Two . . ." Brown quickly echoed.

"NO!" Metzger shouted, leaping.

"THREE——"

He flinched as both heads flung backward, spraying red coronas as bullets slammed through bone and brain. Brown and Fetterman gone.

Cowards lead other men to their deaths, he thought. Then realized he was thinking in German.

Click.

The hammer fell. Again he pulled the trigger. *Click.* His .44-caliber revolver empty. Metzger hurtled it at a warrior crouching on the boulder overhead, about to leap.

He backed up, searching for a weapon. Scooping up Fetterman's pistol, he pulled the trigger. *Click.* Empty.

Saved the last bullet for himself.

Adolph stumbled over bodies, searching. His back slammed against the rocks. The bugle jabbing his ribs. He yanked the braided cord over his head, gripping the bugle like a short club. Swinging. Swinging. Listening to that whistle of the dry breeze in the horn's bell. Hearing startled grunts from warriors he hit as they swarmed over him. His tin bugle a shapeless thing in his hands.

Dear Gott—I'm the last!

Left to right, then back again, little Adolph swung, battering his enemies with that dented horn. It sang in his hand, as beautiful as any call to Boots and Saddles. Thinking now only of twilight . . . and taps.

No suicide, he thought in German. *I have always been a soldier. I will die a soldier.* Recalling the mountains of his boyhood home. Hearing the sweet, sweet notes of a distant bugle call.

Bringing the soldiers home at last.

Crazy Horse heard the others hollering from the top of the spur, shouting that soldiers had reached the crest of the ridge.

Like fevered ants the warriors set about their grisly work. Shouting. Laughing. Cutting and hacking. Stripping bodies. Cutting off hands and feet. Gashing legs. Disemboweling. Scalping forehead to nape, including ears. Firing one arrow after another into the naked soldiers. Every corpse stiffening in the cold. Each body looking helpless, like the pale, white-belly of fish snagged from a summer stream.

Crazy Horse jerked, hearing the iron-hoofs clatter up the frozen slope. Only a soldier horse, chased by two young Miniconjou. A big, white soldier horse. Reins dragging from its jaw. Saddle swaying beneath its belly. Arrow shafts quivering from its withers and rear flanks. It clattered over the hill, the boys in joyous pursuit.

The warrior next to him screeched his victory song, holding aloft a soldier's manhood parts in his bloody hand. The Oglalla danced a moment with his trophy, then stuffed them into the soldier's gaping mouth. Next he pried apart the white man's belly, hauling the entrails across into the dirt and trampled snow. Blood turned the ground black and slick. Quickly freezing.

Crazy Horse watched the first soldiers appear along a brow north of Lodge Trail Ridge. Unmoving. They dared not ride into the valley.

"Brothers!" Crazy Horse exhorted his friends, "Invite these soldiers to come and join these!"

Many laughed, jeering the soldiers—urging, taunting these new troops. Each warrior feeling they could defeat anything the soldiers might throw at them this day. Unafraid. Daring. Mighty.

The dog darted past him. Crazy Horse leaped back,

hand clamped to his mouth. Blindly scurrying in and out of the warriors, the animal scampered for the top of the ridge.

"Kill the soldier dog!" one warrior shouted. "I saw it march into the trap with the soldiers!"

"No," shouted White Bull. "Let it go. We have our dead. Let the dog carry his news to the soldier fort."

"No!" Crazy Horse screamed, surprising himself. From the wolfskin quiver at his back he ripped his bow and a single arrow. His arrow struck the dog midstride. It toppled over, legs a'quiver. Then lay still.

"Nothing!" Crazy Horse glared at White Bull. "Nothing shall live this day. No one is to allow even a dog to escape our great victory!"

With no more whitemen to butcher, the warriors retrieved every arrow that had not been broken, blunted or bristled from a soldier's body. Although he had no way to accurately count, Crazy Horse marveled that so many arrows had been fired in so short a time. More than two thousand warriors, each having more than twenty arrows in his quiver . . . all that in the space of time it takes the sun to move two lodgepoles. A very short battle.

Below him, near the creek, others dragged their dead and wounded aboard ponies or travois. Marching back across the icy creek. Over the hills to their battle-camp. Leaving nothing but their dead ponies behind.

Dark smears upon the cold ground to mark the fall of each warrior.

While it had been a great victory, Crazy Horse realized theirs had been a costly fight. He nosed his pony toward the creek, assured he was the last to abandon the battlefield. Steam from soldier wounds tissued like filmy gauze into the cold air. A trooper's horse struggled in death, legs flailing. His nostrils stank with death.

As he gazed over his shoulder at the soldiers waiting atop the bare spur of ground, the young Oglalla warrior sensed that his people had won but the first battle of a long, long and ugly war.

Chapter 36

$\mathcal{A}$t the Big Piney, Ten Eyck's soldiers removed their shoes and wool stockings. After crossing the ice-swollen water, they put the warm, dry socks and shoes on once more. Forming into columns. Seventy-six in all. Captain Ten Eyck and Lt. Winfield Scott Matson, along with surgeons C. M. Hines and Jeremiah Ould. Seventy-six, that is, plus one Irishman.

To Seamus it had seemed like a dreadfully long time, but Ten Eyck had moved his troops out in less than a quarter hour, the foot soldiers jogging double-time down the road to the icy crossing.

As they left the creek behind, Donegan listened to the distant rifle-fire echoing beyond the ridge. Shots growing more scattered. No longer any volleys. Sporadic. And fading.

He looked at Ten Eyck.

"I hear it, Donegan. Sounds like Fetterman's beat off the attack . . . run the savages off."

Donegan wagged his head. "That, or it's all over, Cap'n."

Ten Eyck steered clear of Fetterman's route along the base of the Ridge. Nor did he stay on the Bozeman Road. Instead, the cautious Dutchman led his rescue detail to the right.

"Captain, why're you taking us way off over here?" Lieutenant Matson demanded, galloping up.

"The high ground ahead's better for a defensive stand. I'll take the men——"

"Defensive stand?" the lieutenant snorted. "Better to show these red bastards we're ready to attack . . . or we'll need rescuing ourselves!"

"I want something from you, I'll ask for it!" Ten Eyck snapped.

"The colonel said you were——"

"Carrington isn't here, is he, Lieutenant?" Ten Eyck snapped. "I'm taking the advice of Donegan here—leading the men to the safety of that high point ahead. From there we can see what lies before us . . . and defend ourselves if need be."

The young lieutenant glared icy daggers before he wheeled away.

The last gunshots echoed from the heavy sky as Ten Eyck's soldiers reached the crest. He signaled a halt. Like black, maddened ants scurrying over the snow, the valley of the Peno below swarmed with warriors.

"Dear God! There's not one of Fetterman's men in sight!" Surgeon Hines gasped, bringing his horse to a halt beside Ten Eyck.

Up the slope raced some young warriors, slapping and thumbing their buttocks. Yelling obscenities. Taunting. Urging these new soldiers down into the valley.

"Fetterman's men're down there." Donegan sighed. Both Ten Eyck and Hines glanced at him, disbelieving. "We just don't see what's left of 'em yet."

"Orderly!" Ten Eyck cried out.

"Captain?" Pvt. Archibald Sample raced to Ten Eyck's side.

As he dragged a small tablet from his tunic pocket and licked the end of his pencil, Ten Eyck ordered, "I want you to take this message to the colonel. Fast as that horse will carry you."

Sample blinked, seeing only the officers and surgeons

on horseback, realizing he was handed the dangerous assignment because he had left the fort mounted. Archibald swallowed.

"Mark the time, orderly," Ten Eyck demanded.

"Twelve forty-five, sir."

"Very good," and he saluted Sample. "God's speed, son."

Sample bolted away, across the spur to the crest of the ridge, heading for the Big Piney Crossing and Fort Phil Kearny.

"Cap'n," Donegan announced, "looks like the Injins done with your boys down there."

Ten Eyck followed the Irishman's arm. Like a wave ebbing from the shore, the Sioux fell back from the slope. Still taunting. A stunned gasp swept over Ten Eyck's foot-soldiers as they witnessed the first of the carnage. Long distance.

Naked bodies—starkly white in the hazy, winter light. Mottled with dark, black patches. Bits and pieces of once-warm humanity freezing beneath a sky that spat loose an icy flake now and again.

Seamus Donegan had seen his fill of death. Yet nothing like this.

Gettysburg had been about the worst of it. The rains coming like a blessing from heaven at the end of that final, third day—settling the dust that choked every man's nostrils . . . washing the blood and brains from the rocks and leaves. Settling the stench of young lives snuffed by the gods of war. He had seen his fill of death.

Yet even Seamus Donegan was unprepared for what he found at the bottom of Lodge Trail Ridge.

Just past the Big Piney Crossing, orderly Sample watched twenty-eight soldiers jogging down the road from the fort. He reined up as the soldiers ground to a halt.

"Where you coming from?" a young private demanded of Sample.

"And who's asking?"

"Private Seth Aikens, C Company, Second Cavalry—that's who."

"What the hell's cavalry doing out here?" Sample inquired. "And where's your horses?"

"Ain't got any," he answered. " 'Bout every last horse rode out with Fetterman. So, the colonel dispatched us to help Captain Ten Eyck."

"That's where I just come from."

"Where's he?"

"Up the ridge." He pointed. "Yonder a ways."

"We'll push on," Aikens said, turning to fling an arm toward the twenty-seven behind him.

"Don't look like there's none of your cavalry left what rode with Fetterman!" Sample hollered after the dismounted, double-timing horse soldiers.

When no one answered him, the orderly nudged heels against his fatigued mount, kicking the animal into a hand-gallop once more.

His mind raced as the cold wind scarred its way across his cheeks. *Maybe the colonel seen something from the fort we didn't see. We was behind the ridge for a long time. Maybe the fellas in the fort watched Fetterman whip them Indians.*

Halfway up from the crossing a rumble of iron-tired wheels clattered over the brow of a hill. Close enough to cause Sample's mount to shy to the edge of the road. He watched as three drivers sang out to their teams, yanking back on reins, leaning into brakes. Behind two wagons and an army ambulance rode some forty armed men.

"Ho, son!" the lead driver hollered out. Dressed in civilian clothes.

"You with Fetterman?"

"Un-unh," and he shook his head. "Colonel's orderly, Private Sample."

"Name's Sam Marr, son."

"You coming from Pine Island?"

"Nope. Me and the rest come outta the fort. Civilians.

Your colonel had us load three thousand rounds of
Springfield and two cases of Spencer for Fetterman's
men. Where's the fight?"

"Ain't no fight, Mr. Marr. Likely all dead."

"Don't say!" he gasped, glancing round at some of the
civilian teamsters and woodcutters who edged close.
"Ten Eyck whipping the Injuns now?"

He shook his head. "If the captain tries, like as not
he'll get his ass whupped something fierce too."

Marr looked around again. "Thank you, son. We best
skedaddle now. Likely someone'll need our help up yonder."

Except for the pounding of his horse's iron shoes on
the frozen road, the silence shrank in around Private
Sample once more. Up the gentle rise, across some trampled snow, and through the main gates on the north wall,
all without slowing his lathered mount. Amid shouting
sentries and the excited, hopeful screams of dashing children, Sample skidded up in a shower of icy crystals at
headquarters steps. Just as Carrington leaped off the
porch.

"Ten Eyck sent me!" he shouted, sliding from the saddle, flinging his reins to another soldier.

"Tell me!" Carrington ordered.

"Here, sir." He slapped the crumpled paper into the
colonel's hand.

Carrington poured over the scrawl, trying to make
sense of it. "I can't read some of this, Sample! What's
going on up there!"

"Captain says he can't see nothing . . . can't hear
nothing of Fett . . . Captain Fetterman!" Sample
gushed.

"Where in God's name!"

"The Injuns are on the road below him . . . shouting
for him to come down."

Carrington shook his head, glancing at the window of
his home. Seeing two worried, women's faces staring
back at him. "How many Indians are there?"

"I don't rightly know, sir. Just . . . the valleys for miles 'round filled with the screaming bastards. Don't see how Fetterman live through it . . . if he gone down in that valley."

"I've sent reinforcements. You meet them on the road?"

"Yessir. Captain Ten Eyck wanted one of them mountain guns of yours."

"A howitzer?"

"Yessir."

He brooded a moment longer. "I want you to take a message back to Ten Eyck."

"My horse is used up, Colonel."

"We'll get another," and he waved at a soldier to bring a mount from the stables. Quickly he scrawled his message across the back of a sheet of foolscap.

> *CAPTAIN: Forty well-armed men, with 3,000 rounds, ambulance, etc., left before your courier came in.*
>
> *You must unite with Fetterman, fire slowly, and keep men in hand; you could have saved two miles toward the scene of action if you had taken Lodge Trail Ridge.*
>
> *I ordered the wood train in, which will give 50 more men to spare.*
>
> H.B. Carrington
> Colonel Commanding

Sample leaned over the message, whispering in the colonel's ear. "Captain's afraid Fetterman's party is all gone up, sir."

Carrington straightened, gazing into the orderly's face. "I can't send the howitzer. Explain that to Captain Ten Eyck."

"I run across some cavalry too, sir."

"They should've joined Ten Eyck by now." His voice rang hopeful. "I'm down to forty-nine men in the post . . . counting myself."

A soldier jogged up, holding the bridle of a large, gray stallion.

"Orderly, you'll ride my horse," Carrington announced, handing the rein to Sample. "Off with you, quick! My Gray Eagle will take you back as fast as the wind."

"Yessir." He saluted.

"Our prayers are with you all," Carrington called out as Sample turned sharply, putting the stallion into a gallop. Then he whispered when none could hear. "Our prayers . . . for those God can still help."

He had to work to keep his breakfast from shoving up around his tonsils. Seamus had seen his fill of death, but nothing so ghastly. Grapeshot and artillery, minié ball and saber . . . he had seen what weapons did to a human body. Never before had he set eyes on the enraged handiwork of man.

The naked, half-frozen bodies had that translucent color of old honeycomb beneath a winter-pale sun. As he saw it, the battle had been fought by three groups. Farthest up the hill, Donegan and the others ran across most of the cavalry and mounted infantry, bodies bunched, stripped of uniforms, mutilated and scalped. Many rolled over on their faces after butchering.

Halfway down the slope around a group of boulders lay even more of the dead men, piled like cordwood, jumbled in a confusion of army horses and Sioux ponies. Inside the rocks they found a couple dozen more.

"That's him. That's Fetterman, all right."

Donegan turned. He watched a soldier pull the buffalo bag from the officer's head. It took a moment, but he recognized the dark, mustached face of Capt. William Judd Fetterman. A hole in what remained of his left temple. After the Sioux finished beating the heads to jelly.

Tangled in Fetterman's legs lay another body. Seamus knelt, pulling the buffalo-skin bag from the head. What he had for hair had been left untouched. His dark penis and scrotum hung from his mouth, draped over his bearded chin. A broken lance had been rammed up his rectum, the bloody point dripping with frozen gore like an obscene erection from his belly.

Seamus felt his own insides draw up as if they'd been salted with alum. *No trophy torn from that bastard's bald head.*

"Looks you won't settle that matter with Brown now, will you?"

Donegan turned, seeing Ten Eyck's droopy eyelid twitching. "No. Look at 'em," Seamus said. "Two of a kind, aren't they? Reeky scuts! Shot themselves afore the Sioux get their hands on 'em."

"Didn't want the Indians capture . . . torture 'em," Ten Eyck advised.

"Wrong, me friend. Look 'round you. These Injins wasn't about to take a single prisoner. There was bloodletting and bloodletting only on the wind this day." He rose and sighed. "The Sioux put them bags over their heads 'cause the two were cowards."

"Balderdash!" an old soldier roared, shouldering Donegan against a rock. "Fetterman's no coward!"

"Shot themselves," Donegan replied. "See yourself. Injins put them bags over their heads—they aren't brave men, fit to see in the next life."

"Butchered by them dirty savages, that's what!" The old veteran glared at Donegan.

"Whatever you wanna believe, sojur. Whatever you *have* to believe."

Seamus turned, for the first time noticing a boot protruding from a buffalo robe near ring of boulders. Pulling the hide back, the Irishman recognized an old friend from the 2nd Cavalry. Company bugler. Veteran soldier.

"Krauts and micks," he said like a prayer. *Weren't for Krauts and micks, there'd be no American army.*

"Sojur!" Donegan shouted, wheeling on the old infantryman. "I'll show you a brave man—braver than any ten of your Fettermans or that bastard Brown. Cast your eyes on a real sojur!"

In utter disbelief the infantryman stared down at the body of Adolph Metzger. "Why, sweet god, he ain't touched!"

"That's right, you stupid scut! Didn't touch him 'cause he was brave. Look at that damned horn of his. Last weapon he held. Them red h'athens showed their respect . . . putting his face to the sky . . . covering him this way without stripping or butchering him . . . or scalping."

"I . . . I can't——"

Donegan grabbed the soldier's arm and jerked him back. "Hold on, friend. Don't want you to forget the face of a real sojur!"

He ducked as the infantryman swung. But wasn't prepared for the other two who charged him. Seamus knocked the first aside as Ten Eyck's voice cracked the air.

"STOP!"

Grudgingly, the soldiers released Donegan's mackinaw.

"I'll take the next one of you who swings back to the fort as my prisoner!" Ten Eyck's eyelid quivered.

"Come a time, Irishman." The soldier shoved his friends away. "Come a time, you and me talk about real soldiers, eh?"

Donegan nodded. "Count on it, Private."

"You best stay close to me," Ten Eyck whispered.

"I'm not afraid of any——"

"Fetterman had him many friends here," the captain interrupted. "Even Brown was well-liked."

"Never been one to have a lot of friends, Cap'n. Only good ones."

Donegan stomped past the boulders. Downhill he found the last of the soldier dead. From what he could tell of the brief skirmish, Fetterman's forces had splintered into three groups, none in view or hopes of support

from the other. Farthest up the slope lay the cavalry and
mounted infantry. Among the boulders, most of Fetterman's infantry. And in the tiny ring of horse and pony
carcasses below lay seven stripped, butchered bodies.

Fisher, his mind whispered as he recognized what was
left of the face. *Wheatley too.* Seamus stepped over the
frozen carcass of a pony, its legs stiff in death, remembering the way sunlight had brought her skin alive there in
the water of the Little Piney. Her long, auburn hair.
Those perfect breasts . . .

*Dear, sweet Jennifer. Abby was first alone, left alone
and abandoned in death . . . gone East now. Gawddamn! This cold, unforgiving wilderness is no place for a
woman. Now another . . . another woman, made alone
once more . . .*

He stopped suddenly by a body. "Damn," he whispered.

You were a sojur at the last, weren't you, Eli Garrett?

Donegan sank to his knees, gazing down into the gray-
blue eyes that stared into the darkening sky. He felt an
aching emptiness, an incompleteness now that Garrett
was gone. A friendship gone awry. With all hope gone
now of ever mending the riven circle of their lives.

Ah, Eli . . . Eli . . . He looked about for the dead
man's clothing. Nearby, Donegan found the torn and
bloody shirt. With a folding knife he took from his
pocket, Seamus set to work on the faded, crimson-stained
chevrons sewn to what was left to the sleeves of Garrett's
blouse.

*War changed us both, didn't it, Eli? All that killing just
made some of us predators. The rest of us left behind to
wonder why. I suppose it was there at Front Royal that we
tore ourselves apart . . . you like the wolf—just liking the
blood of it all. And me, not understanding why a few men
tell the thousands they must march off and die.*

He licked at the salty moistness dripping into his mustache.

From Front Royal we both changed, didn't we? There I

first began to question the hunting of men . . . like sport it was to soldiers like you and Custer . . . like sport.

Finished, Seamus blinked his smarting eyes, glancing over the scene encircling the ring of boulders. More than seventy dark patches marred the trampled snow surrounding the little fortress.

Took a lot of the bastirds with you, didn't you, boys?

Civilians and seasoned veterans alike had been horribly mutilated. Muscles of calves and thighs slashed. Stomachs, breasts and arms hacked. Ribs gashed and exposed; eyes poked out, pendant on cheeks.

"A damn bloody way to go."

Seamus jerked up, surprised. Finding Ten Eyck. "I'tis." He got to his feet.

"I've something for you to do, Donegan," Ten Eyck began quietly. "No hurry. When you're done here."

"I'm finished." Seamus glanced up the hill, seeing the wagons and ambulance arrive.

"We'll take back as many as we can," he explained. "Packing 'em in like butchered hogs. The rest . . . well——"

"What you need with me, Cap'n?"

Without another word, Ten Eyck led him up the slope past the boulders, near the field where the cavalry had fallen. A gray horse lay struggling to rise, its legs flailing. Around it stood a dozen young cavalrymen.

"What'm I to do with this?" Seamus asked.

"It's a cavalry mount, Donegan," he explained. "Second Cavalry. The rest of these men . . . they're just shavetails. You, Sergeant Donegan, served the Second for many years."

"What's that got to do——"

"These boys decided you're the one to take care of the horse."

"Take care of the——"

"Sergeant . . ." One of the young men stepped forward. "Mr. Donegan, this here's a special horse—name o' Dapple Dave. Rode by Sergeant Garrett. We . . . us

—figured you'd put the animal outta its misery. Only fitting."

Seamus watched his hand accept a pistol from the young private. He knelt by the animal's head, stroking between the ears as he eased the muzzle against the cold hide. The horse struggled, trying to rise. Closing his eyes, Donegan pulled the trigger.

Rising, he slapped the pistol into the private's belly, then pushed his way free of the crowd until he found that big, gray stallion he had killed a rebel officer for. The animal that would carry him back to Fort Phil Kearny.

Chapter 37

"*I* can tell you nothing more," Henry Carrington explained to the officers' wives gathered in the Wands's cabin. "Only to repeat my assurances that you should entertain no apprehension for the safety of the fort itself. I beg you to wait patiently, to be ready for the return of all our troops."

Frances Grummond watched him go, duty and his own anxiety calling. What seemed like hours ago, the teamsters and woodcutters from the Pinery had arrived, taking their places along the banquette with what few soldiers remained in the fort. The incessant banging of hammers throbbed in her tortured mind. Across every window and over most doors men nailed boards in the event of the attack every man, woman and child feared. Her mind conjured wild imaginings now that her worst nightmares had sprung to life.

Frances stared glassy-eyed from the window, watching the final preparations at the corner of the parade ground. Around the large hole the fort used as its powder magazine, soldiers and civilians worked feverishly pulling wagon bodies off running gears. Wagon-boxes tipped on their sides round the magazine in three ever-wider circles.

"Frances, you mustn't concern yourself with soldier duties."

She gazed up into Margaret Carrington's grave face.
"Have you no words that bite any deeper?" Then she
stared out the frosted window once more while the light
drained from the sky. "I remember seeing so much war
. . . in that land so far away from us now. So much
suffering. So much blood. I remember soldiers throwing
up barricades before an attack. Margaret—those men are
preparing for the Indians."

She took Frances's hand in hers. "You fear too——"

"Please," she begged in a whisper. "Tell me the truth."

Margaret's eyes misted over. "Yes," she whispered.
"When the Indians attack, our men will hold out as long
as possible. Then, the order will be given to fall back to
the wagons-boxes. It's there our final defense will be
made . . . and when our cause is lost . . . Henry will
order the magazine blown."

Her eyes darted back to Margaret's. "Taking us with
it."

"You mustn't say a word to the others . . . or the
children——" She stopped, watching Frances gaze down
at her swollen belly.

"Yes," Frances replied, caressing the swollen mound,
"we mustn't tell the children."

Shouting arose outside. Frances started, fearing the
savages had chosen twilight to breech the fort itself. Yet
as she and the others crowded to doorways and windows
to watch and listen, it became clear from the sentry
voices that no Indians had been sighted.

Instead, the pickets announced seeing Ten Eyck's forward scouts at the Big Piney Crossing.

With the first shout, bandsman Frank Fessenden hurried over the iron-hard old snow to the gate, hopeful of
finding good news to cheer the soldiers who had remained behind in the stockade.

Darkness curdled over the fort. Beyond the walls he
recognized the familiar rattle and squeak of wheels and
frozen axles. The first mounted soldiers crept wearily

through the yawning portal. Next rumbled the ambulance, followed by the two wagons. No man in the fort uttered a word. Each one suffered in private his own horror, witnessing the ghastly cargo of naked bodies, severed arms and legs frozen in death, bouncing along like butchered hogs come to market. With every bounce of the wagons, bloody arrows trembled from cold flesh. Unashamed, Fessenden began to cry with many who watched old friends coming home.

"Schmitty had ten days to serve!" one veteran shrieked. "Ten . . . God . . . damn . . . days!"

"Goin' home in ten days," another whimpered, spotting a bunkie.

"They're not all here," whimpered one of the footsoldiers plodding through the gate. He sighed and stopped, trying to explain it to those who had waited—those who hadn't witnessed the horror at the base of Lodge Trail Ridge.

Fessenden watched the old infantryman blanch with his vivid memory. "Ten Eyck counted only forty-nine when the sun fell outta the sky. Ordered us back before dark."

"You left the rest out there?" A little man stepped forward. "With them bloody savages? Think what they'll do to 'em out there——"

"Nothing!" the infantryman shouted to shut the little man up. "Nothing they ain't done to 'em already." He shook his head. "Ain't a horror they can do to them boys they ain't already done."

He'd thought it couldn't possibly grow colder than it had been near sundown. But now, after dark, Carrington found his little stove struggling to keep his inkwell and pen nib from freezing as he scribbled maddened, meandering dispatches he would send to Fort Laramie, bound for Omaha and Washington City. With no real sense of what he wanted to say, Carrington scattered his words across the pages in an unintelligible scrawl for sentences at a time. With no pattern. Pressed to express his desperate fear for their situation at Fort Phil Kearny. Outside, a light snow had begun to fall.

General Cooke: Do send me reinforcements forthwith. Expedition now with my force is impossible. I risk everything but the post and its stores. I venture as much as any one can, but I have had today a fight unexampled in Indian warfare.

Returned with forty-nine dead. Must recover more than thirty remaining on the field, weather and conditions permitting on the morrow. Fetterman, Brown, and Grummond, all taken from me. Grummond not located before dark.

No such mutilation as that today is on record. Depend upon it that the post will be held so long as a round or a man is left. Promptness is the vital thing. Give me officers and men. Only the new Spencer arms should be sent; the Indians are desperate; I spare none, and they spare none.

When he had finished his plea to Cooke and warmed his frozen fingers over the stove, the colonel copied the dispatch so that it would accompany his letter to General Grant.

I sent copy of dispatch to General Cooke simply as a case when in uncertain communication, I think you should know the facts at once. I want all my officers. I want men. Depend upon it, as I wrote in July, no treaty but hard fighting is to assure this line. I have had no reason to think otherwise. I will operate all winter, whatever the season, if supported; but to redeem my pledge to open and guarantee this line, I must have reenforcements and the best of arms.

"May God Himself hold my couriers in the palm of His hand," Henry whispered, shivering with the growing cold. "God Himself."

* * *

John Phillips hunched his shoulders beneath a heavy
blanket coat, scurrying across the snowy parade as flakes
lanced out of the blood-thick sky. Here and there fragments of lantern-light scoured dirty-yellow patches
across the darkness. He wondered what could be colder
than death itself, if it weren't for this damned night.

Funny, to think of death, when I just cheated it, he
brooded. Wondering if he deserved to cheat the reaper
this time around.

*Wheatley and Fisher gone. Partners. Nothing left for me
now. This—the last thing I can do for these soldiers. For
that poor woman.*

Nicknamed Portugee long ago, Phillips wondered why
he had been spared in the great drama of things. Assigned by Quartermaster Brown to fill the post's water
barrels at the Little Piney that morning when the first
alarm rang out. Hauling water while Wheatley and
Fisher volunteered to ride with Fetterman.

Volunteered their lives in the bargain. He stopped on
the porch, knocking packed snow from his hog-leg boots.
The last thing I can do for this poor woman.

He rapped at the raw-boarded door.

Margaret Carrington answered. "Yes?"

"I come to see the officer's wife," the swarthy caller
explained.

"Mrs. Grummond?"

"That's her," the man in his early thirties answered.
"Please."

"What in God's name for——"

It appeared the colonel's wife suddenly understood the
look in his eyes.

"Come in . . . out of the cold." She opened the door
wide enough for him to slide into the lantern-lit parlor.
"You wait here. I'll bring Mrs. Grummond."

He stared at the slivers of yellow light through the
crazed frost patterns on the thick windowpanes until he
heard the soft scuffling of feet behind him in the narrow

hall. Phillips turned, feeling his heart surge against his throat. Her eyes had been a long-time red from crying, her cheeks rouged with the bitter cold that found its way through every chink in Carrington's raw-boarded cabin.

"Do . . . do I know you?" she asked, clutching the wool coat about her shoulders.

"No, ma'am, you don't," he stammered, then remembered the buffalo cap on his head. With it crumpled in his hands, Portugee continued in his soft accent. "I give my service to the colonel. To ride to Laramie with his letters. I'll bring help—men and guns. Don't you worry . . . please."

"You'll ride to Fort Laramie with Henry's dispatches?" Margaret asked, seeing a glimmer of mist cross the stranger's eyes.

He nodded. Then he gazed at Frances once more. "Going to Laramie for help. I'll go if it costs me my life. Only wanted to tell you . . . I'm going for your sake."

"My . . . My sake?" Frances gasped.

"Yes'm." Portugee reached out, touching the back of her hand. "The baby, ma'am. You and your baby."

He glanced down at the furry black and gray bundle he clutched beneath his left arm, handing it to Frances. "Here, ma'am. My wolf robe. Take it, please. A gift from me to you . . . your baby. I bring it for you to keep. For you to remember me by if you never see me again. You and the baby to remember that . . . I tried."

Frances accepted the soft, lush wolfskin, clutching it to her belly. Suddenly aware of the sting at her eyes. She caught her lower lip between her teeth, suppressing the sob about to overwhelm her.

Portugee saw the tears well in her eyes as she leaned forward to kiss his bearded cheek. "God's speed, good man," she whispered.

He touched her hand once again, then swept out the door into the cold, jamming the buffalo cap on his head as he remained a moment on the porch.

"Who was he, Frances?" he heard Mrs. Carrington say.

"I don't even know his name," she answered. "Told me . . . said he was going for us all . . . for my baby—and I don't even know his name."

"Dear God," Margaret Carrington whispered. "With this brutal storm that man is riding hopelessly into, it's as if Nature herself has conspired with the Indians to swallow us all."

Portugee crossed to the corner of the parade, satisfied that he had talked with her. Loose ends tied up as neatly as he could.

Tiny wisps of sleety snow swirled around him like bothersome gnats swarming around his sweating face last summer. Cutting through the cavalry stables, hurrying across the wood yard, past the teamsters' mess and mechanics' shops.

"Mr. Phillips?" a voice called out from the dark.

He stopped. "Yes?" he answered softly.

A shadow took form. Carrington's face beneath a buffalo cap. "You'll need these, for your ride."

Portugee quickly slipped the long buffalo coat over his shoulders after he pulled the buffalo-fur leggings up to his thighs. "A horse? Said you'd get me a good horse?"

"My own," Carrington sighed, leading Portugee to the railing at the blacksmith's shop. "Gray Eagle. A Kentucky thoroughbred, Mr. Phillips. He'll carry you all the way."

He stroked the big white charger. "A good animal, Colonel."

"You have provisions?"

Phillips held up the saddlebags. "Hardtack."

"Nothing else?"

"Won't have time to eat nothing else."

"And the horse?"

Portugee shook a leather satchel. "A nosebag and twenty pounds of your oats, sir."

"Good," he answered. "You're ready?"

"Yes."

Carrington led Phillips toward the water-gates at the southeast corner of the quartermaster yard.

"Halt!" a voice cried out from the darkness. "Who goes?"

"Your commanding officer!"

"Colonel?"

Portugee watched the young soldier loom out of the night. "S-Sorry, sir . . . Private John Brough, Second Cavalry, Colonel."

"Never mind," Carrington replied. "Open the gate for me."

"Open the——"

"A rider's leaving, Private. See to the padlock quickly."

With the narrow gate pulled open, Brough stepped back, watching the two men beside the nervous horse.

"You're my first, Mr. Phillips. I'm sending William Bailey, another miner, after you. In an hour. I must copy more dispatches first."

Portugee nodded. "In case I don't make it, Colonel?"

"I'm hoping one of you will."

Phillips gazed longingly at the snowy yard, his home since August. "May not see you . . . this fort again."

"A deadly undertaking, volunteering to make this ride . . . 235 miles of wilderness."

"Man does what a man has to, Colonel."

Carrington yanked Portugee's hand into his, shaking it tenderly. "I trust we'll meet another day, Mr. Phillips."

Portugee swung into the saddle, adjusted the bulky coat around his furry leggings, then snugged the heavy cap on his head. Hands encased in mittens, he saluted, urging the anxious charger through the narrow opening. Darkness instantly swallowed the horseman like coal cotton.

"May God help you, Mr. Phillips!" Carrington whispered into the night. "May God help us all!"

For no more than a minute the colonel could hear the

muffled hoof-beats. He stood by the narrow opening, head cocked, listening breathlessly. When he could hear his Kentucky-bred charger no longer, Carrington straightened.

"Good," he sighed. "He's taken the softer ground at the side of the road."

Stepping back from the gate, Carrington finally sensed just how cold the night was. *Mercury motionless . . . well below zero.*

"Close and lock the gate, son," he directed Private Brough. "Stay warm on your watch."

"A damn bloody cold night, Colonel, excusing my——"

"No offense taken, Private." Carrington turned into the swirling buckshot snow, heading back to headquarters.

"May God help us all."

Chapter 38

*W*inter finally swept down upon the land with an unrelenting vengeance.

Throughout that bitter night, Carrington scurried about the post. Seeing that sentries were relieved every half hour so that no man froze to his death along the windswept banquettes. In the maddening swirl of icy snow, every soldier remained mesmerized by those Sioux signal fires blinking from the ridges and hills surrounding Fort Phil Kearny.

A glacial cold greeted the gloomy gray of the new day, finding Carrington red-eyed. Fearing a dawn attack like every other man. Huddled in Henry's office sat Bridger and Donegan, scouts Jack Stead and Henry Williams, captains Powell and Ten Eyck, Chaplain White, surgeons Horton, Hines and Ould, in addition to lieutenants Wands, Bradley, Skinner and Matson, along with civilians Leviticus Carter and Judge Kinney. Seventeen sleepless, grumpy men. Some anxious. Others plainly scared.

Orderlies and sergeants came and went, giving their whispered reports at the door. Carrington dragged himself out of his chair, cleared his throat, and opened officers' council.

"Company rolls show thirty-one enlisted still missing," Wands announced.

"And Grummond," Ten Eyck added.

Carrington nodded. "As none came in overnight, we'll assume the thirty-two are lost." His eyes slewed around the room, studying the haggard faces. "Our first concern becomes the recovery of the bodies."

"They will attack you, sir," Ten Eyck said.

Carrington glared at him a moment. "Captain, they did not attack you yesterday."

Ten Eyck nodded, embarrassed. "Surely had a bellyful of the killing, Colonel. A bellyful of the . . ."

"No matter," Carrington sighed, looking at the floor. "I must go—if I do it alone."

Powell stood, uneasy. "Respectfully, Colonel—I don't advise a rescue. Ten Eyck came out lucky yesterday. By now, the hostiles've regrouped and'll be loaded for bear again."

"Damned Injuns out there in the hills," Bridger growled, "even them savages manage to recover their dead warriors."

Matson stood. "I support Captain Powell. It'd be hazardous to return to the battlefield while the Sioux are celebrating their victory over Fetterman. We should sit tight for now."

"Colonel, I'm an old man," Bridger grumbled, wagging his head. "I've no time for these paper-collared fools of yours. Your own damn soldiers laid out there in them hills all night. It's time we fetched them boys back. Like decent folk would."

"Anyone else?" Carrington asked.

"Ahh-hem." Kinney cleared his throat, rising, pink fingers interlacing in his galluses. "I second what prudence Captain Powell advises, Colonel. If a party to rescue the dead leaves our gates, the lives of those left behind will be in peril."

"Not necessarily, Judge——"

"Most emphatically, Colonel! I want you to understand I've not found much to like in your handling of matters—and should you decide to send out a rescue col-

umn, I stand against you again, and most wholeheart-
edly."

"I'm well aware that you've sided against me on most
issues, Judge. It's quite well-known you're a proslave
man. Unable to reconcile why Lincoln removed you from
your Utah judgeship . . . you despise my antislave
stand. But, be that as it may, I frankly don't give a damn
for your shortsighted and selfish opinions."

For a moment Kinney stood silenced. He finally stammered, "Think hard on this, Carrington. I've friends in
power . . . why, my life savings are invested in that
post——"

"To hell with your sutler's goods, Kinney," Carrington
interrupted quietly. He flung an arm to the west. "I'm
thinking of those good men—butchered, left to the
weather . . . and God knows what else."

"You pompous sonofabitch!" Kinney shrieked. "If you
send a rescue party out, all of us will fall prey to those red
bastards."

"I agree, Colonel!" Powell leaped up again. "We don't
have enough men to do both safely. Take some to go after
what's left of Fetterman's men—we can't leave enough to
defend the fort. But if enough men remain behind to defend the fort while the rescue party is out—the Sioux can
easily overwhelm those who've gone to bring the bodies
back. We can't win!"

"Gentlemen." Carrington motioned the men to their
seats. "I want you each to listen carefully to me. Through
the long hours of the night I've tried as never before to
think like an Indian."

"Cockleheaded fool!" Kinney spouted.

"I have the floor, Judge. If you choose to interrupt, I'll
see you're excused from this council." He waited for silence. "I could not but feel that if I'd been a red man, I
would've fought as bitterly—if not as cruelly—for my
rights and my home as the red man fought since last July.
Especially as he fought yesterday."

"What does that have to do with rescuing the dead?" Wands inquired.

"Coming to that, Lieutenant. Knowing a little more now than I ever have about the Indian mind, I won't let the Indians entertain the conviction that our dead cannot and will not be rescued."

He circled the desk then leaned against it. "If we cannot rescue our dead, as the Indians always do at any risk, how can we send details out for any purpose? Realize, by not going to rescue our dead, that single fact will give the Sioux an idea of weakness here, Judge. And, Captain Powell—that idea just might stimulate them to risk an assault on the fort at any hour. On any day."

He lumbered around the desk, gazed at his coffee-stained maps, then declared, "Therefore, gentlemen, the matter is decided. I'll lead the rescue myself—taking eighty men, soldiers and civilians. I alone will decide who'll go with me. Ten Eyck, you'll lead me to the battle-field. Surgeon Ould, you and Lieutenant Matson will accompany me. Captain Powell will be in charge of the fort in our absence. We leave in an hour, gentlemen. Dismissed."

"Colonel?"

"Yes, Mr. Donegan."

"I'd like to ride along with you."

"So'd I, Colonel." Bridger rose on creaky knees.

"You're in no shape for it, Jim." He shook his head. "But I need you along. See that Jack Stead hangs close to Powell. The captain might have . . . need of Jack's horse sense while we're out." He patted the old scout on the shoulder, then turned to the tall Irishman.

"But as for you, Mr. Donegan," Carrington smiled weakly, "seems the army's a lot to repay you . . . after locking you up the better part of a month. Brown's dead. There's no need you risking your life going with——"

"My ass's been hung over many a fire before, Colonel," Donegan replied. "Figure I better go 'long on one more wee ride up the Lodge Trail with you this morning."

Bridger watched Carrington's eyes moisten. "You're more than welcome to ride at my side, any time, Seamus Donegan."

In the Carrington parlor adjoining Henry's office, Margaret and Frances Grummond overheard every word spoken during the council. His meeting over, the colonel turned from the Irishman, crossed the floor and knocked on the pine door before entering.

"Henry!" his wife gasped, surprised. She rose from the window where she had been watching the frantic activities on the parade as men carried boxes and barrels to the powder magazine.

Frances had been reclining on a settee nearby. Both scrambled to their feet as Carrington closed the door behind him.

"Sorry to startle you, ladies. I knocked as a courtesy——"

"Of course, Henry," Margaret replied, crossing the room and taking one of his hands in hers.

"Hush for once, Margaret. And listen to me. I've decided to lead the rescue myself."

She nodded, her eyes misting. "I . . . heard, Henry. I'm so . . . so very proud of you."

Margaret watched him swallow a knot in his throat before he turned to Frances. "Mrs. Grummond, I shall go in person. On my word as an officer and a gentleman, I promise to return the remains of your husband to you."

"Colonel——"

"Say nothing," Carrington silenced her.

In the next breath his cheeks flushed as Frances stood on her toes to kiss his cheek.

He turned to his wife. "To know I've done right is reward enough, Margaret."

"God bless and keep you." She embraced him, feeling for Henry more than she had felt for such a long, long time. "Come back, Henry. Come back to me."

Without another word, Carrington turned, closed the

door, and stepped into the arctic cold pounding life from the Big Horn country like a icy hammer on a frozen anvil.

Donegan watched Carrington climb atop a broken-down sorrel with a bad case of wind-galls. Not much left in the way of good horseflesh at Fort Phil Kearny, he brooded.

Yet it comforted a battle-scarred veteran like Seamus to know that every last man at the post had volunteered to march with Carrington, to rescue the bodies of comrades and friends. The colonel chose eighty of those most fit to march.

"Captain Powell?" Carrington called out. Powell stepped up. "You understand your orders?"

"I'm to fire the sunset gun as usual, running up a white lamp to the mast head on the flagstaff. If the Indians appear near the fort, I'm to fire three shots from the twelve-pounder, at minute intervals. Then hang a red lantern from the flagstaff instead of the white."

"Very good, Captain. You remember as well the orders you are to keep secret from the rest of the men . . . women and children?"

Powell barely whispered this time. "If the hostiles attack in overwhelming numbers, I'm to put the women and children in the magazine with food and water. When all is lost, strike a match to the powder. Let no man, woman, or child be captured alive."

Carrington nodded. Saluted. "God's speed, Captain."

Powell swallowed. "Good luck, Colonel."

The colonel waited until the last man in his rescue party had cleared the gate, then listened while sentries inside drove the bolt home.

Donegan rode with Carrington to the head of the columns. At both sides of the road marched a cordon of mounted cavalry. Most of the remaining infantrymen bounced along the frozen road in mule-drawn wagons. Bridger saw to it that pickets were stationed on the high ground along the ridges. A pair of soldiers left at every station, within sight of two other stations, so that a continuous line of communication would link the rescue column to the fort.

A day wine-clear and as still as a buzzard's shadow hung over high-meat. Growing colder by the hour. Silently, Carrington's column climbed the long, frozen ridge, now laying bare, silent. Everlasting.

Past sage and yucca. Through bunch-grass and wildrose. Down into thickets of allthorn, following the crooked trail like some dark, bloodied scar beneath the brooding sky. To the very end of the naked ridge itself.

Ten Eyck and Donegan pointed to the boulder field below, then began their descent into hell once more. On their way down the snowy, trampled slope, they crossed that narrow rib of ground where most of the cavalry had died. Horses strewn over the bare ground in a space barely forty feet wide. The head of every one pointed toward the fort.

Donegan pointed to the boulders. There, he explained, they would find most of Fetterman's dead. Arrows sprung like sunflower stalks from the frozen ground, pointing every which way. Soldiers completely surrounded.

The dreary, stomach-churning work began. A man had to hold the head of every mule frightened at the smell of so much frozen blood as others stacked the remains and body parts into the wagons like cordwood. When the first freight wagon had been half loaded, the mules kicked and lunged, throwing their handlers aside, strewing the bodies across the frozen ground and darting off. Only six of all the bodies showed bullet wounds. The rest had been killed by arrow, with lance, club, knife, or axe.

"Close and dirty work. Hard way for any sojur to die." Donegan stopped beside Carrington. "There're more, Colonel."

"We've loaded every man here." Carrington turned and climbed into the saddle. "The Eighteenth endured snow and ice before Shiloh. It marched through a brutal plains winter to its new post in Nebraska just last year. These men lived on parched corn before Kennesaw Mountain, and moldy pork here at the foot of the Big Horns." He swiped a hand beneath his nose, knowing he should brood on it no longer. "Ten Eyck, I'll follow Mr. Donegan. Bring the wagons down the road."

Over the next mile they located four more bodies. Then came across Lieutenant Grummond and Sgt. Augustus Lang. Carrington stared at Grummond's body for the longest time before he slid from his horse to kneel over the remains. The lieutenant's head had been nearly severed from the neck, and his naked body bristled with arrows. Placing something in the pocket of his greatcoat, Carrington rose and returned to his horse.

Near the bank of Peno Creek they found Jimmy Carrington's little calico pony, its head butchered.

"Injins ever scalp a pony, Jim?" Seamus inquired.

"Wouldn't put it past the sonsabitches, Irishman," Bridger growled. "Way of showing how they hated the man what rode the animal."

"Brown," Carrington replied. "Fred Brown."

"Injuns!"

Seamus jerked around with the first shout. More soldiers took up the alarm, pointing up the ridges.

"The bastards come to get us!"

"Run for it!"

Soldiers and civilians alike lunged for their horses and wagons. Forgetting the bodies. Ignoring the dead.

"The Sioux come back to finish us!"

Donegan gazed up the ridge where the soldiers pointed.

"Colonel!" Seamus grabbed Carrington. "Your soldiers think the pickets Jim left on the hills are Injins!"

Bridger nodded. "Best you get your boys under control now. Gonna have a full-scale ruckus here."

Carrington dove into the center of the pandemonium, quieting the men enough to speak. He pointed out that they had seen their fellow soldiers. "Like being scared of your own shadow, men." Then he wagged his mittened hand. "Any man among you too afraid to stay long enough to finish this work, let him leave now!"

He listened to angry grumbling before continuing. "Go on back to the fort best you can if you're afraid. But understand, those of you who go will leave your guns and ammunition behind. I'll not allow one armed man to leave until the last body's rescued."

With the disturbance quelled, a hundred yards away Donegan brought Carrington to the desperate stand of Wheatley, Fisher, Garrett and the cavalry veterans.

"From the looks of it, they put up one devil of a defense here," Carrington offered as he viewed the dead carcasses of horses and ponies alike.

"Look at them black patches on the ground," Bridger pointed out. "A warrior knocked outta his saddle for every one. These boys made a fine account for themselves while they lasted. Injuns hated 'em something fierce. More'n a hundred arrows in every man's body here. Sioux didn't take kindly to the toll these fellas took."

"Even young Private Burke," Seamus added. "Company C."

Carrington inched closer to another body, pointing. "Isn't that . . . the cavalry sergeant——"

"Eli Garrett, Colonel."

"Appears he acquitted himself honorably," Carrington said.

"Eli always was a good soldier," Donegan answered. "Sometimes, he just forgot what being a good soldier means."

By the time the wagons were loaded along the frozen Peno Creek, the low rumble of the sunset gun echoed over the ridge. A cold, desolate feeling like nothing he had felt before seeped to Donegan's marrow while the columns climbed the bare, scarred finger onto Lodge Trail Ridge.

"Praise God," Carrington sighed, gazing south as twilight settled over the fort, "from whom all blessings flow."

"Your white lantern hangs high on the flagpole, Colonel," Bridger added.

"Yes," Carrington sniffled. "Like a welcome star of blessing. A homing beacon, calling the wanderers home. Praise God—our people are safe."

Chapter 39

"**Y**our husband lays in the guardhouse, Mrs. Grummond. With his comrades," Carrington explained, squeezing her hand. It was just past ten o'clock when his rescue party crawled back through the fort gates.

Beside her sat Margaret, clutching her other pale hand. "Can I——" Frances choked on the sob.

"No," he whispered. "I think it best that——"

"I . . . understand, Colonel Carrington," she whimpered, dabbing at the end of her nose with a damp kerchief.

"I'm deeply sorry," he continued, stuffing a hand into his pocket. "I only wish I could express the sorrow I feel at this moment. For you . . . for your child, Mrs. Grummond."

He held before her a small, sealed envelope. "I . . . brought something from your husband's last field of battle. I knew you'd want to have it—as a memento of George."

"George?" she squeaked.

"Yes," he answered. "God knows you've suffered the worst loss imaginable. No one can ever say you'll get over it, Mrs. Grummond. I'm not saying you should ever get over it. Just that, the best thing is to make a place for that hurt, that loss in your life . . . and walk on. Make a place for that pain, and let it give meaning to your life."

As Frances took the envelope into her trembling fingers, Henry turned to Margaret. "Come, dear—we must excuse ourselves. Give Mrs. Grummond time to herself."

She watched the Carringtons close the door, then all was silence once more. With quaking fingers she tore at the sealed envelope, finding inside a lock of George's hair. Frances held it to her breast, tears welling from eyes she had believed all cried out.

"George. Dear, dear George," she whispered with a sob. Then remembered.

The locket I gave you our first Christmas together—only a year ago. The miniature portrait I had done of me so you'd have your Frances to look upon . . . wherever the army took you.

The tears came easily, sobs welling up from deep in the marrow of her.

Who carries that portrait now, George? Dear God, what dark-skinned savage wears my locket now?

As if held in abeyance by some divine hand, the blizzard that had threatened the land waited until Carrington returned with his grisly cargo. Temperatures plummeted to thirty below as brutal winds drove icy snow across the land. That night the colonel ordered pickets rotated every half hour.

By morning of the twenty-third the snow had drifted so high along the west stockade wall that a soldier could march out of his company barracks, up the icy drift and over the stockade timbers. Starting at first light, soldiers struggled in relays to dig a ten-foot-wide trench outside the wall to make it harder for the hostiles to breech the stockade. As hard as the work became, they made little progress through the day. The keening winds never died, sweeping still more snow into the trench as Carrington's troopers labored on through the endless hours.

Throughout that day and into Christmas Eve, the men prepared the bodies of their comrades for burial in the guardhouse and Horton's hospital. Grim work, assembling mutilated fragments. Identifying the butchered remains. Wrenching what arrows they could from the frozen corpses, cutting off the rest. Cleaning the waxlike flesh, then draping each body in a dress uniform donated by a friend or bunkie.

Half of the headquarters building had been turned over to the carpenters, who sawed and hammered pine planks into coffins. All too quickly they ran out of sheet-tin to line the simple boxes, working day and night. Not until after dark on Christmas Eve did those coopers finish nailing the lid over the last of the Fetterman coffins.

By mid-morning the day after Christmas, two pits it had taken the men three solid days to dig yawned like ugly black scars in the middle of the graveled street along officers' row. One small grave for the three officers killed, each placed in a separate coffin. Along the gaping maw of a nearby fifty-foot hole dug seven feet deep out of the frozen soil, the enlisted dead lay boxed, paired in thirty-nine coffins carefully numbered for future identification.

The sun hung low in the east like smudged, gray ash as Donegan watched solemn troopers lay the pale boxes beside the ugly trenches dug from soil hard as iron plate. His eyes smarted with a biting wind, his face hidden behind the muffler wrapped round his face. Staring at the soldiers, women, children and civilians who trundled up in tiny knots to the edge of the gaping holes.

". . . the severity of the weather," Carrington droned over the mourners, many of his words swept away as quickly as they were spoken in the swift-footed wind, ". . . brief ceremony . . . saddened, without benefit of military honors."

The colonel nodded to Reverend White, who shuffled forward, a gray wool muffler tied beneath his chin, protecting both old ears and white head.

"Here me, O children of the chosen land! Our Republic lives because there have always been men who loved Her more than life itself. Trust in Him who has forced into the nostrils of the living the very breath of life! Trust! For the mighty God of our fathers' fathers will not desert thee! The Lord who led his people from Pharaoh's bondage will not abandon those who march into battle beneath his banner. The God of Hosts will not forget those who have shed their blood in His name's sake."

White coughed, his dry throat straining to last his prayer through. "Our Grand and Fair Republic likewise will not forget those who are committed to the bosom of this land today. Dust to dust . . . ash to ash—the flame of freedom burns on! The blood of these now mingle with blood shed by patriots ninety years gone. In this, our cause, no less shining than those who stood at Concord Bridge . . . waited atop Bunker Hill, or froze in the snows of Valley Forge. My solemn oath to these brave patriots we commit to the soil this day—they'll not be forgotten!"

The reverend opened his eyes, lifting his speckled chin. White gazed a heartbeat longer at the Irishman, then finished, "A-men!"

"Amen," echoed a hundred other voices, drowning out the embittered sniffle of man or the quiet whimper of woman.

Carrington edged beside White, waving the burial crews to the edge of the pits, where they began lowering the first coffins.

Alone or in small, black knots, the mourners dispersed across the snow like humpbacked beetles scurrying for warmth to one raw-boarded building or another.

"Seamus?"

Donegan turned, finding Sam Marr before him, a woman and two small boys huddled against him. "Cap'n," and he nodded to the woman. His eyes flicked over the two youngsters who clung like burrs to their mother's dark greatcoat. Seamus recognized it as a man's —oversized, swallowing the woman's small frame as it slurred the ground with every insistent gust of cruel wind.

"Mrs. Wheatley," Marr began, instantly snagging the

Irishman's full attention. "I introduce Seamus Donegan. A Union soldier, like your late husband."

He yanked his floppy hat from his head and took a step closer, for the first time straining to get a good look at the face hidden in shadow beneath the hooded cowl.

"We . . . we've met before, Sam," Seamus said quietly into the cruel wind that flung itself against them all. *Another young widow . . .*

As she tilted her head back to look up at the tall man before her, Jennifer's red-rimmed eyes met his for the first time since that midsummer day on the banks of the Little Piney. Though ravaged by countless tears, those green eyes still held an unspeakable magic for him. This close, almost feeling the heat she gave off. Those full lips, rouged by the wind. Somehow, he imagined her imploring him in some unspoken way.

Seamus cleared his throat self-consciously. "I knew James, ma'am. Mightily sorry . . ." He gazed down at the youngsters. "Sorry he's took from you and the boys. My . . . deepest condolence."

Only then did the cowl fall back, taking the face from shadow, allowing Seamus to fully study the dark, liquid, almond-shaped eyes so red and swollen.

Her pale, ivory cheeks rouged with bitter cold quivered a moment longer as her teeth rattled in the wind. Those full, trembling lips stammered, "T-Thank you, Mr. Donegan."

Glory, but she's even more a beauty up close.

"There's anything I can do," Seamus found himself saying, "to help you—the cap'n. You call me."

She extracted a mittened hand from one of the boys, presenting it to the tall Irishman. "I won't forget your kindness, Mr. Donegan."

He looked down at the mitten, remembering how she had clasped both hands over herself to hide those perfect, freckled breasts that summer day as the sunlight and water teased him every bit as much as she had from afar.

In that moment he touched her hand through the

coarse wool now, Seamus sensed a warmth . . . a warmth the likes of which he hadn't felt in a long, long time.

"Mrs. Wheatley," he nodded, bowing slightly, seeing her yank at the hooded cowl, once more hiding her face from view.

Marr lead the young widow away.

For several minutes Seamus found himself gazing after her, until they disappeared into the quartermaster's yard. A gust of wind nudged at him insistently, reminding him of the gaping, open wound along officers' row. Seamus Donegan stuffed his hat atop his dark curls, tugged his collar round his neck, then grabbed a shovel to lend his shoulders to the task at hand.

Frozen clods of spoil clattered atop the pine boxes like a hollow thump of an insistent hammer. Seamus dug into the pile of dark earth, again and again and again. Remembering the warmth her touch had bestowed upon him.

"You're a fool to push onto Laramie!" John Friend declared, rising from his warm telegraph key at Horseshoe Station. He had just finished condensing and transmitting the dispatches of Col. Henry B. Carrington to Fort Laramie some forty-five miles to the south.

"Fool or no, I promised," the swarthy rider replied. "Both of us." Portugee Phillips flung his thumb at miner William Bailey, who busied himself wrapping burlap sacks round his legs before climbing back into the buffalo-fur leggings.

"We promised the colonel we'd hand his letters to the Laramie commander," Bailey added. "Personal."

Bundled back into their buffalo coats, Phillips and Bailey crawled onto their cold saddles, pointing their weary animals south once more.

"It's Christmas Eve, by god!" Friend shouted into the howling wind. "Stay . . . enjoy the warmth of what cheer I can offer."

Phillips waved, never hearing a word Friend flung into the cold. He had promised, after all. Portugee swore a private vow he could stay in the saddle the rest of this day. Until he reached Laramie.

A few miles north of Horseshoe Station, Bailey had come up on Phillips. For a few minutes there, Portugee had convinced himself a Sioux warrior had been trailing him. From hiding he watched the plodding horseman hove into view, hunched over his saddle horn, frozen to the marrow.

"Ho!" Phillips had hauled the big Kentucky thoroughbred from the thicket beside the road.

Bailey jerked up, startled. Yanking back on the reins and nearly tumbling from the saddle. "Who the Sam Hill are you!"

"Phillips," he answered. "Who're you?"

"Portugee? That you?"

"Yes. How you know my name?" he asked, searching for something familiar in the shadowed face hidden behind a muffler.

"I'm Bailey. Bill Bailey, by god! Can't believe it's you!"

"Colonel said you'd be coming down."

"Sent me out an hour after you galloped off. Wanted to make sure."

"Sure one of us got here," Portugee echoed as he drew alongside Bailey, slapping the rider's arm crusted with icy sleet. "C'mon, Bill. We'll both make Laramie now."

"Horseshoe ain't but a couple miles, Portugee."

"They got a key there?"

"About all there is at Horseshoe. That, and a stove."

"Blessed Virgin Mary!" Portugee exclaimed, crossing himself. "Let's drag our cold bones to Horseshoe!"

Within the warmth of Friend's telegraph shack the couriers had talked. Finding they both had ridden south along the Montana Road, yet never venturing onto the road itself. More important, both had survived by traveling only the long nighttime hours, hiding out the day.

Come winter on the high plains, a man can eat up a lot of ground riding at night. Keeping a promise.

Undeterred by Friend's appeal, both riders pulled away from the telegraph station near Bridger's Ferry at the North Platte Crossing. With one thought in mind. The same thought that had compelled them across 190 miles of Sioux-infested, blizzard-buried wasteland. To complete the job they had started.

Portugee welcomed the fish-belly gray of twilight. By now it felt like liquid sand rolled beneath his eyelids. The day's bright sun glaring off the wall-to-wall prairie white had tortured his eyes. They rolled in a thick, liquid fire.

Sowbelly snow clouds scudded low out of the west just as darkness swallowed the land. A bright winter moon crawled into the southern horizon below the leaden clouds, beginning to cut its nightly trail across the sky just as snow began its white scurry across the trackless hills. The bottom went out of the thermometer, cold cutting a man to his marrow.

"Can't go no more," Bailey moaned.

"You must," Phillips replied. "Wait! Look there! A light, yonder!"

Bailey squinted against the swirl of buckshot snow. Afraid his eyes deceived him, or that this was some trick of Portugee's, until he too saw the faint light flickering through the icy mist.

"Who goes there!"

Phillips sat straighter in the saddle. He had aimed the thoroughbred's nose at that faint star of light for the last half hour. And now a dark form emerged from the snowy gloom. Portugee tried to speak. His lips mumbling, teeth chattering. His hands fumbling to say something.

"Great ghosts, man!" The soldier flung his rifle aside, catching Bailey as he slid from the saddle. "Lieutenant! Goddammit, I need your help out here!"

"What you screaming about——"

Lt. Herman Haas leaped from the door to help drag

William Bailey into their guard-post. "Get the other'n, Myers. This'un's 'bout done for."

Back out in the blizzard, Myers tried pulling the second rider from his saddle. But Phillips yanked his arm away as best he could, mumbling into the wind. "C-C-Comm . . . mander."

"Lieutenant!"

"I heard." Haas stood at the door. "You come watch this one. He's in a bad way. I'll take that one up to see Palmer."

Without a protest from Phillips, Lieutenant Haas grabbed the thoroughbred's frozen bridle, leading the horseman toward the lamp-lit buildings of Fort Laramie.

"Look like you been through hell, friend," Haas chattered back at the frozen statue on the saddle. "What's your name? You hear me?"

"Phillips."

"Damnation, Phillips. You're a sight! Icicles hanging off your eyelashes and beard, by god! It'll take a week of Sundays to thaw that snow from your coat!"

"Commander."

"I heard you. Just keep your pants on, fella. That's where I'm taking you right now. Old Bedlam. Having a Christmas Ball tonight. That is, everybody but Lieutenant Haas."

As the officer brought Phillips round the corner of the barracks, Portugee heard the first strains of gay music, saw the first bright smudges of yellow light pouring from the windows along the two-story company quarters. Ahead lay the gaily-decorated bachelor officers' quarters —Old Bedlam.

Haas tied the wheezing horse at the rail, gazing up at the rider. "Phillips, you said. Well, Phillips—you got any idea what time it is? Didn't think so."

He struggled, pulling Phillips from the saddle where he had sat frozen for some eighteen hours. "It's after eleven. Christmas night, by god. The rest of the boys better not've finished off the rum punch. I think there's two of us gonna need some . . . for medicinal purposes, you understand! I figure you earned the first drink too."

Haas dragged Phillips up the steps, across the porch, then shoved open the door. Portugee immediately sensed the warmth, his frozen, half-lidded eyes blinking at the bright light. Tiny candles were pinned along the green boughs, festive red garlands draped around the room.

"Haas!" an officer shouted. "I'll have you on report for interrupting a full-dress garrison ball!"

"Major," Haas answered, struggling to keep Phillips on his feet. "We need to see the general."

"General Palmer?"

"In the worst way, sir."

The major studied Phillips's waxy, frostbitten face. "What the devil's going on here?"

"He won't say. Only he's got to see the commander."

"So?"

"And one other thing, Major."

"Yes?"

"He keeps repeating the word, *'Kearny.'* "

The major nodded, turned and disappeared into the main parlor. Minutes later he had Haas lead the horseman into a small sitting room.

After a warm drink, Phillips began to tell the story of his ride to Laramie's commander. Then stuffed his hand beneath his three shirts. There, next to his skin, he had carried the narrow, leather envelope. From it, Gen. Innis N. Palmer pulled Carrington's dispatches.

After reading them beneath the light of an oil lamp, Palmer gazed at the other officers in the room. "By the saints! That garbled message we got from Horseshoe this morning is true. A massacre of over eighty men at Kearny!"

"Any casualties among the Second, General?" inquired David Gordon, lieutenant in the 2nd Cavalry.

"Afraid so," Palmer answered. He looked back at the dark-skinned horseman huddled by the stove. The general knelt and stared into Phillips's glassy eyes. "Even though I didn't believe it at the time, I want you to know I forwarded the message you sent from Horseshoe, Mr. Phillips. Sent it on to Omaha myself."

"We all thought it nothing but a wild rumor," Gordon added.

"Teach us to listen more carefully to our Indian friends staying the winter near our fort, gentlemen." Palmer sighed and rose. "For the past two days they've tried telling us of a big fight at the new post on the Bozeman Road. We'll know better next time, won't we?"

A loud rap rattled the door a heartbeat before a young officer burst in. "Pardon, General." He swept past Palmer, stopping before Portugee. "That your horse out there, mister?"

Phillips looked up, blinking. "Yes . . . no." He wagged his head. "Carrington's——"

"Doesn't belong to no one now." The officer gazed at the others in the room. "Dead in the snow, blood gushing from its nostrils."

Portugee's face pinched, tears streaming from his eyes. He hid his face for a moment, sobbing. "Sir?" Phillips asked weakly, turning to Palmer. "Could you find me a bed? Haven't had a decent night's sleep in close to a week."

"By the saints, Mr. Phillips! We'll do better than a mere bed! Lieutenant Haas, see that our guest is given a private suite at the post hospital, on the double!"

Chapter 40

Cold weather squeezed the land.

The mid-morning sun edging over the badlands to the east cast an orange glow to the banks of the Tongue River where the wind had swept the snow before it. A brilliant glow of white made his pale eyes tear as he watched the villages scattering. The first of the processions snaked its way to the east, headed for the Powder River country. Black Shield's Miniconjou. In other camp circles nearby, brown buffalo hides fell from the conical lodgepoles as women packed travois, loading both children and old ones for their journey from this place.

Directly below him, in the lee of the ridge where he sat in the sun and wind on this last day of the *Moon of Deer Shedding Horns,* Crazy Horse watched his Oglalla band prepare for their move. First the pony herd would be brought into camp while meat cooked for the day's journey. With property packed, the lodges would come down. When all was ready for departure, Man-Afraid and Red Cloud would send a runner to fetch the young war-chief who had succeeded in luring the soldiers to their deaths. A great battle, worthy of many songs. A battle to stay on the lips of the old and young alike for winters to come. Painted on tribal robes of winter count. A great victory, this "Battle of the Hundred in the Hand."

A hundred, Crazy Horse recalled. *Red Cloud says our*

*fight will drive the white man and his soldiers from our
hunting grounds for all time. I cannot agree. Instead of
scaring the white man away, the "Battle of the Hundred in
the Hand" is but the beginning of a long, long war.*

*Lo, Wakan Tanka! Behold your son, Crazy Horse! My
body is young and strong. My blood runs hot. My people's
fight will be my fight. A long, and ugly war, wind spirits!*

*Behold! I do not cower nor hide. Crazy Horse is ready
for that fight. May you give me the strength to send many
white spirits on the wind before our fight is over. May I
wear many white scalps and see fear on many faces.*

*May it be said many winters from now—Crazy Horse
was the protector of his people!*

Carrington worked feverishly through that next
month. Straining at first to hold on to the dream that ran
through his fingers like sand, then struggling to stand
against Cooke and army brass back East.

With a cold, cramping hand, Henry wrote in his private journal:

> With the arrival of Captain Fetterman, I had sensed this
> change in command on the winds. But with the massacre,
> I clung fervently to the belief that Cooke would allow me
> to stay in charge at my beloved Fort Phil Kearny—the
> dream I designed and watched rise from the bowels of
> this unforgiving land.
>
> While I welcomed Captain Dandy and his reinforce-
> ments, I want the record to show I nonetheless required
> ten times their pitiful number following the massacre.
> Not to mention ten times the replacement arms and am-
> munition if I was to raise a powerful hand against the
> Sioux such as they dealt us on 21 December last.
>
> From that night of the disaster, our men slept in their
> clothes, in reach of their arms, in complete readiness for
> attack on our post. Although, by the advent of the New
> Year, Mr. Bridger informed me we no longer had to fear
> surprise from the Sioux. Every trail, valley, and gully lay

smothered with snow. My chief of scouts claimed even the most hostile of Red Cloud's Bad Faces would be slow to take to the warpath in such weather.

By the fourth of January the weather had tempered so that I could dispatch a mail escort to Laramie. In that long letter to General Cooke in which I agreed to transfer, I firmly stated that the disaster vindicated every report from my pen . . . vindicated my administration of this Mountain District . . . vindicated my begging for reinforcements and resupply . . . proving correct my repeated warning of 1500 lodges of hostiles gathered on the Tongue River.

Since establishing ourselves on this site, my command has suffered the loss of five capable officers, ninety-one enlisted men, and fifty-eight civilian casualties. I cannot count the wounded.

My poor soldiers spent joyless holidays and an uncertain new year, knowing not what destiny held for them. Brave soldiers all—dressed in their buffalo coats and leggings, vests of skin to keep them warm beneath winter's onslaught . . . at their labors standing guard, hauling water or cutting wood without so much as a word of complaint. The whole garrison shared a common gloom. None of us finding much cause to celebrate January 1— the date our beloved 2nd Battalion of the Eighteenth Infantry became the new 27th Infantry.

What final, sweet bleeding of my heart came on the sixteenth when the sentries atop Pilot Hill signaled the arrival of soldiers on the south road. Relief! raised our bugle call. Relief! thundered snare drums on parade.

"Open wide the gates!" shouted some.

"Admit our deliverers!" shouted others.

"At last we are saved!"

"Phillips was saved, saved for us!"

Though I've suffered many indignities, still I found myself at the lookout post, watching that long column led by Lieutenant Colonel Wessels winding its way toward my fort. Replacing me as commander of my be-

loved Phil Kearny. I now had one short week to prepare
for my departure from these walls. One week to close so
dramatic yet bitter a chapter in my life.

The sun creeps over the horizon to the east as I write
this sentence.

23 January, 1867.

> Col. Henry B. Carrington
> formerly commanding
> Mountain District
> Department of the Platte

Relieved of command. And going home.

Epilogue

Seamus Donegan stood on the banquette, high along the south wall of the stockade. There were times he could not help looking down at the crowd clustered in tiny, cold knots near the gate below. Each time, his eyes never failed to find the small form bundled in a long, heavy man's coat. On either side of her huddled the boys, one under each arm.

While he had never suffered the death of a lover, the Irishman had endured loss. As a growing, gangly youngster, Seamus recalled the emptiness of his mother's house following the burial of his father. How he had struggled to be what she needed him to be, his pa gone. What had pulled even more at the sad chords within him was that leaving of Ireland . . . his mother and family and everything he had ever known left behind.

No man ever more lonely than when he had reached Town Boston to find his uncles gone. For years now something more sensed than certain had been telling Seamus that those brothers O'Roarke had come west. Perhaps to the gold streams in California. Could be he might find them among the silver camps dotting the high country of Colorado Territory. Maybe even to run across one or the both along that digging of Alder Gulch a man could find at the end of this Montana Road.

With one man alone had he shared this quest—Sam

Marr. Back in Kansas after they had paired up for their trip west, Seamus told the cap'n he was going to the goldfields near Bannack and Virginia City to find his fortune. What he hadn't shared with Sam until weeks later was that Seamus Donegan marched up the Bozeman Trail to find his uncles. Not until a steamy twilight had settled upon the hills above the Crazy Woman Fork did the Irishman tell the horse-trader that he was, in fact, come here on a manhunt.

Saying he was bound to find the O'Roarkes wherever a man found gold and willing women and lots of strong whiskey. True enough, his uncles loved adventure almost as much as they did the perfumed whores and red rye. That twilight in the rifle pits, Sam Marr had whispered it did not matter why the Irishman had come along for their trip up the Bozeman.

What mattered only was that Seamus Donegan had come. That, and if the two would live to watch the sun rise come daybreak over that Crazy Woman Fork.

Theirs had been a secret Sam Marr vowed never to tell from that dawn they marched away with the Crazy Woman at their backs.

Should I trust another of me secrets to the cap'n?

Seamus brooded as his gray eyes once again found her in the crowd below, the big coat slurring the ground at the insistence of the cruel wind sweeping off the Big Horns.

Trust him now . . . tell him about her . . . what I feel?

Hopes had brought Seamus up the Bozeman, brought him here to this place a'purpose, to his way of thinking. Dreams might hold him here a bit longer.

'Tis a cruel hand grips many a life, he thought as he looked down to that crossing at the Little Piney where the long procession of soldiers, wagons and ambulances had broken the ice and was working its way into the rolling hills leading south to Fort Reno. *Some, like Carrington, never meant to find what they look for. Meant*

*only to seek. Wasting their life searching for that holy grail
of their dreams.*

"By the saints," Seamus whispered to himself, feeling
the press of friends gathered round, "pray, may I soon
find the O'Roarkes."

*And release this death grip the hand of destiny holds on
me.*

"Suppose I can give this to you now, Seamus."

Donegan turned to find Jack Stead pulling a folded
parchment from his coat.

"The colonel gave me two. One he said was for me and
Jim." Stead nodded at the old scout by his arm, "and
this'un for the big Irishman."

Donegan felt Sam Marr press at his elbow.

"Open it, you stupid Hibernian," the old man growled,
smiling in the wind that whipped his long, gray hair and
the ends of his long mustache.

With thick fingers Seamus tore at the seal, first studying the unfamiliar scrawl of ink across parchment before
he began to read aloud:

> My dear Mr. Donegan: Would that I address this to
> Sergeant Seamus Donegan. But I'm certain that remains
> a story for another time. And another place.
>
> I hope by your remaining the winter at my beloved
> Phil Kearny that you might tarry even longer. By no
> means is the army a home for all men, Seamus Donegan.
> But for some the army remains a lodestone, drawing
> those strongest and possessed of a certain will, drawing
> them like flecks of iron to army blue. I trust I'm not
> wrong in appraising your character.
>
> There were times I attempted to tell Seamus Donegan
> what he came to mean to Henry Carrington. Yet now it
> remains for this pale missive to speak my final words to
> you. Rendering ultimately my heartfelt thanks for what
> you meant to the women and children of Fort Phil
> Kearny, but most importantly, what Seamus Donegan

meant to the officers and enlisted of the 2nd Battalion, Eighteenth Infantry.

Moreso, I pray the men of your own C Company, 2nd Cavalry, will long remember the contribution you played in the history of this post.

You've chosen a rough and difficult road, once more, Sergeant Donegan. Yet I'm sure you smile now as you read this—for you're no stranger to hard roads. My most-Catholic prayers go out to you . . . hoping our God and redeemer will hold you in the palm of His hand, while you raise your mighty arm to protect and defend.

I leave without bitterness, but with despair that the corridors of army command are not filled with real soldiers. Instead, I've come to agree with Mr. Bridger— too many paper-collars choking too many fat, well-fed necks!

Instead of putting an end to the Indian problem in the West, the army's high command has instead put a match to the tinderbox, I'm afraid. Where I had entered this land bright with hope of bringing peace to the northern plains, I now see instead that the army is but beginning its war on the Indian. Where that long and bitter war will lead thousands upon thousands of young soldiers, no one but God can answer at this crucial moment in history.

When that bloody war will end, no one but God knows. The only safe bet is that far too many of those young soldiers and far too many Indian warriors will spill their blood among the grass and sage, along the creeks and rivers of these far western lands before it is decided. And only God knows when it will be over.

Von Clausewitz set down his inspired military treatise many years ago, yet his words remain no less true for us today as we begin this struggle.

"The commander of a besieged fortress sees that his own moral courage grows within him as the situation without becomes more difficult. Every man of leadership has like courage and sustenance to pit against the day. The true hero? Nay, how rare it is to find the same courage and steadfastness in the face of reverses! Only those with the true mantle of courage will exhibit the qualities of steadfast leadership. Only then may their number be counted on Olympus."

I believe few are ultimately counted among the truly brave, Sergeant.

Seamus Donegan occupies a lonely, lonely perch. I salute you, Sergeant. As I would salute all true soldiers. God's speed, dear Irishman.

Henry Carrington

Seamus glanced up at the gleaming eyes of the three friends gathered round him. Not one among the civilians ventured a word as the tall Irishman swiped at his nose, blinked his smoky-gray eyes and stepped to the stockade wall.

Far below him Carrington's columns disappeared like a black centipede inching its way across the white table-land, retreating from this dark and bloody ground.

Stuffing the crumpled parchment in a pocket, Seamus Donegan brought his right arm up, a powerful right hand pressed to his brow. The final salute given Henry Carrington by a born soldier.

For the space of two heartbeats, with his hand still held against his brow, the Irishman glanced down at that small, lonely figure huddled against both the wind and immensity of this land, turning now from the gate with her young boys.

One woman got away from you, Seamus. Best you not let this one go.

Seamus Donegan vowed he would stay.

HERE'S AN EXCITING PREVIEW OF *RED CLOUD'S REVENGE*, BOOK 2 IN *THE PLAINSMEN* SERIES:

Prologue

G od, how he hated these primitive savages.

All their hocus-pocus and hoo-doo witchcraft, he brooded to himself.

What he needed most now was a good dose of fumaric in those bloody holes in his belly . . . and a jolt of whiskey down his gullet.

"Captain" Robert North adjusted himself on the bed of elk robes, easing a wool blanket from his shoulder to study his wound one more time. More to assure himself again that the soldier's bullet had passed on through his belly, out the small of his back. Sighing, he sank back on the buffalo robes, quietly whispering the words to the old Confederate song.

> *"I'd rather be in some dark holler,*
> *Where the sun refuse to shine,*
> *Than to see you another man's darling*
> *And know you'll never be mine."*

His nose filled with the smell of this winter-place. The lodge reeked of smoked hides, sweet-grass and pungent roots a'boil.

That old harpy better not spit into my bullet hole no more, he thought, yanking the blanket over his bare skin and singing more.

> *"I don't want your green-back dollars,*
> *I don't want your diamond ring,*
> *All I want is your love, darling,*
> *Won't you take me back again?"*

All that remained of his left hand were stumps of fingers an exploding pistol had left behind many years ago. With them North scratched at a week's worth of whiskers. Wondering how long it had taken his Arapahos to drag him back to this winter camp on the upper Tongue River. Their village sat upstream from Red Cloud's Oglalla Bad Face band. Opposite Black Eagle's Miniconjous. Within hailing distance of Sitting Bull's Hunkpapas.

Where the hell's that stick?

His fingers felt through his war-bag at the side of his bed by the fire. Finally finding the peeled willow stick. He counted the notches he carved in it every sundown. The only calendar a white man like North had to keep track of the days and weeks and months with these savages. Down from the twelfth ring carved clear round the stick he counted twenty-nine notches.

December . . . gawddamn . . . thirtieth today.

He struggled, fire through his belly and pain in his head, trying to remember how long ago he had been shot.

Seventh . . . no—the sixth, gawddammit.

He and his Arapahos had joined Red Leaf's Miniconjous, Crazy Horse's Oglallas and the rest when they ambushed the soldiers on the sixth of December, 1866. If his count was right, he'd been lying here more than three weeks, mending. His belly full of puggle and his wounds oozing poison. Worst of it was he'd even missed the big fight. The Sioux and Cheyenne called it their "Battle of the Hundred in the Hand." With their leader wounded and unable to move, North's Arapahos had followed Red Leaf and got in a few licks, too.

For three days after that big fight, the bands had danced over soldier scalps and feasted.

"Just as sure as the dew falls
Upon the green corn,
Last night she was with me,
Tonight she is gone."

He closed his eyes. They burned the gritty lodge-smoke, tearing like he'd bitten into a raw prairie onion.

Yesterday he heard talk of the tribes breaking up for the rest of the winter. Going their separate ways. They were due, North figured.

By gawd, they killed every last one of those sonsabitches!

Ambushed. Trapped at the foot of Lodge Trail Ridge. And butchered to the last man. Every last army horse killed. Not one thing left living on that bare-bone, snow-crusted ridge.

Shit! How I wished I'd been there to see that!

He twisted to the side, his arm cradling his gut. The fire had come back, in a bad way. He fumed, wondering when that handful of Arapahos would get back from Fort Peck with his whiskey. Two hundred miles. Almost due north—cross the Yellowstone, then ride for the Missouri. He'd sent them there with some hides to trade for the white man's whiskey.

Bob North had always needed whiskey more than anything else. With it, he'd kill the pain in his belly. And then he wouldn't care that those two holes in his gut still oozed. Then he wouldn't care how their festering stank up this winter-lodge. Whiskey . . . and a woman now and then. Bob North could be happy with the simple things.

His thirst for whiskey had led to his capture by Union forces back in 'sixty-three. A tall, muscular Confederate cavalry officer—knocked from his horse by the concussion of artillery exploding around him . . . knocked senseless and captured. Ending up in irons and shipped to one hellhole after another. Time and again they shoved a paper under his nose . . . telling him to sign it . . . swear allegiance to the Union and they'd make him a soldier . . . wearing Union blue this time . . . and stationed on the frontier to fight Injuns.

The iron locked on his wrists and ankles grew heavier, and one day Bob North signed—just so he could get something to eat. And maybe a little whiskey if he was good.

Gawddamn 'em!

"Galvanized Yankees" is what they called those former Confederates, officers and soldiers both, who had sworn allegiance to the Union, sent west to fight Indians instead of wasting away in a Federal prison. At least until this last sixth of December, things had been working out a whole hell of a lot better for Bob North.

He'd deserted, escaping from his detachment up on the Powder River. Country the Union officers were calling hostile territory at that time. But to Bob North, freedom itself beckoned, and he didn't much give a damn about where he tried to run. Lady Luck was at his side two days later when he ran into a small hunting party of Arapaho. Had they been Sioux . . . well, Bob North tried not to dwell on that.

A few days later in the Arapaho camp he was taken to, North began carving on his willow sticks, making his calendars. And riding out with the Arapaho on raids into Absaroka to bring back Crow ponies. Scalp raids against the Crow and Ute and Snake and Flathead. With each new success, Bob North grew more daring. Until he started leading his own war-parties out. If he couldn't find an enemy village, Bob North always knew where the soldier forts were. The Arapahos liked that in their renegade leader.

They said he had big bull's eggs.

Damn right. I've got balls! Who the hell else is gonna let himself get seen time and again by them white sonsabitches?

But after three summers of daring and killing and living with the Arapaho, the army moved their posts farther north . . . right to the foot of the Big Horns . . . into

· the heart of Sioux and Cheyenne and Arapaho hunting grounds. To protect their Bozeman Road that took settlers and miners to Bozeman, farther still to Virginia City —Alder Gulch and gold.

From July of this year, 'sixty-six, through the twenty-first of December when the tribes had wiped out eighty-one soldiers in a spare forty minutes, Red Cloud's confederation had harassed the forts, killing civilians along the trail and those working in the hayfields or timber. Last summer Bob North made sure Red Cloud and the other chiefs understood what the word "*siege*" meant. Bob North made sure the tribes never let up their pressure on those forts hunkered defensively along the white man's Montana Road.

And then he took that bullet in the belly. Bob North had missed the finest day of fighting any of the tribes had ever seen. Forced that day to lie here on these robes, drinking the last of his whiskey . . . waiting for someone to return to camp with news of the success of the ambush and battle.

Damn, did he hate white men.

Bob North chuckled. "You're getting half crazy, ol' coon," he whispered to himself. "You got white skin yourself, gawddammit."

He recalled that during the last full moon he had led this small band of his adopted Arapahos to the upper Tongue. To join in struggle against other white men. But those white men weren't his kind. Where Bob North wanted to be left alone, those soldiers down at the new fort wanted to stir shit up. Where soldiers went, he knew, the shit always got stirred.

Bob North had learned that much by following Stephen Watts Kearny in and out of Mexico back in '46.

Suspiciously he eyed the old woman who hobbled through the door flap and scooted 'round the fire in his direction. She bent over the kettle simmering at the edge of the fire and nodded, smiling toothlessly at him.

Gawd-damn! My belly hurts. This bitch goes sticking

roots and other shit in them holes . . . could do with more whiskey . . . these brutes ever come drag this old harpy away . . . they ever show up with more whiskey like I told 'em. How many days ago now . . . I got knocked outta the saddle?

Back on that murky dawn in the first week of a white man's December, renegade Bob North had led his Arapahos to join the Sioux attacking the soldiers stationed in that new fort on the plateau. Dawn—and time for North to prove himself to Red Cloud's boys.

The sky had never really snowed. It just oozed icy, lancing flakes once the gray of pre-dawn streamed along the hills to the east. Everything made slick and wet. Their short bows not worth much in such damp weather, the Arapaho would have to rely on their numbers. Their speed. And the incompetence of the fort's officers.

North could always count on that. Incompetence. Few officers like Captain Robert L. North in either army anymore—those not raving lunatics by now had become roaring drunks.

Wish they'd get here with that whiskey of mine! he fumed, watching the old woman guardedly and grinding his hip down into the elk-robes. *Could use me some drink.* He remembered the good red whiskey aged in those Tennessee kegs. Not at all like this amber-colored, tobacco-laced grain the traders sold to the Indians along the Upper Missouri.

Just 'nother drink . . . help me sleep.

As directed, his warriors had raced down on some soldiers, then turned and darted away while the soldiers followed obediently behind them. After a ten-mile chase took North's Arapahos into the badlands northeast of the fort, North had suddenly turned his warriors as the Sioux closed the trap behind their hapless pursuers.

Rather than shooting at the white men, the Arapahos and Sioux had tried to pull the soldiers from their horses. Two soldiers died along that trail. But the rest escaped.

Soldiers retreating, their withdrawal covered by a lone civilian.

Bob North would never forget that solitary civilian standing behind his big horse while the soldiers scampered past him, dashing over the hill to safety.

Now his side hurt more than ever thinking about that son of a bitch. *Gawddamn brazen file-closer . . . what he was. Covering the rest of them . . . coolly covering their retreat.*

Again and again North had exhorted his warriors into charging the civilian. Each time he watched a warrior fall. Each time he swore in English. The big civilian had carried a brass-mounted repeater that day north of the Lodge Trail Ridge, using it to hold North's warriors at bay until the soldiers were on their way.

Until Bob North himself grew furious with defeat, growling ugly curses about cowardly Injuns, and charging the civilian on his own.

He remembered getting hit, with the slap of a painful claw around his belly. Tumbling to the ground like a sack of wet oats. Seconds later he remembered being yanked across the wet sage between two flying Arapaho ponies. Rescued. Dragged from the field.

The angry warriors had watched the big white man leap atop his horse and disappear. Then took Bob North to this camp on the upper Tongue to lick his wounds.

And remember that big, gray horse.

He would not easily forget the soldiers and civilians he had fought that snowy dawn. He would not forget the feel of white man's lead burning an icy track through his belly. And Bob North vowed never to forget the tall, bearded one who stood beside his big gray horse, firing that brass-mounted repeating Henry rifle of his . . . again and again and—

Until Bob North suffered the sting of that big man's bullet.

The renegade had stayed with the Arapaho to be left

alone. To lay with the women now and again when it moved him.

But now them Yankee soldiers come to protect their gawddamned road. Bringing these civilian sonsabitches in their shadow . . . like camp-dogs.

His head hurt. Hangover, he figured. He was due for a whopper of a hangover, all right.

It's gonna be fine, he told himself. *You're not a white man any longer, Captain North. You play by Injun rules now. You get hurt . . . you hurt back.*

North closed his eyes, hungering for his whiskey, gritting his teeth as the old woman ground the root fibers into his mean, oozy wounds.

He grit his teeth . . . and brooded on the tall, bearded man sheltered beside his gray horse. Dreaming how good it would be to wear that tall bastard's scalp one day soon.

"*I'd rather be in some dark holler,*" he growled out the song's words against the pain in his gut, a pain he was beginning to think would never be washed away with all the whiskey at Fort Peck. Or with all the time in the world.

"*Where the sun refuse to shine,*" and he coughed again.

"*Than to see you another man's darling,
And you know you'll never be mine.*"

He shoved the old woman's hand away as she tried to feed him some slick, scummy meat.

Lordy, I wanna wear that tall bastard's scalp one day real soon!

One day real soon, he promised himself.

Chapter 1

The old scout gazed over his steaming cup of coffee at the big Irishman sitting across the table. Jim Bridger had to chuckle a bit inside with it. After better than forty-four winters in these Shining Mountains, Old Gabe had seen a few he-dogs come west. And this big strapping youngster had to be one of the few himself, Bridger figured.

But it seemed Seamus Donegan had himself a natural-born talent for attracting trouble.

No matter the package, Jim Bridger figured. Whether it was one of Red Cloud's warriors, or an army captain, or a pretty young widow-gal—Seamus Donegan attracted trouble like bees drawn to honey.

"You're punishing that whiskey, Seamus," young Jack Stead advised. He was Bridger's young partner, a former English seaman who had become a competent scout in his own right, marrying a Cheyenne woman and settling into a life of working for the army as it sought to pacify the Far West this second year following the end of the Civil War. Stead himself admired the big, taciturn Irishman. Something about his twinkling eyes attracted friends.

Perhaps Seamus Donegan had been born that rare breed of soul who is blessed with as many good friends as he was cursed with mighty enemies.

"I haven't a right to drink my whiskey, you're saying?" Donegan growled over the lip of his tin cup. "Winter's got this land locked down tighter'n a nun's kneecaps . . . and not a nit-prick of us venturing out the stockade if he don't have at least a company of sojurs behind him for fear of getting butchered like Fetterman's boys—bless their souls. Jack, me boy—seems drinking the sutler's red whiskey is all that's left a man to do."

"Then drink yourself silly again today, damn you!" Jack roared in laughter. "Can't think of a reason why we shouldn't get sacked together."

Bridger watched them clang their cups together, sloshing some of the strong liquid onto one of the rough-hewn tables in the sutler's cabin. He grinned behind his beard, despite the ache in his bones and the icy pain the rheumatiz stabbed at his every joint. And he remembered another cold day barely one month past.

A day Fetterman and Brown and Grummond rode out at the head of seventy-eight men to chase themselves some Sioux scalps, Jim brooded darkly to himself with the memory. *Twenty-one December last, 1866—when Fetterman's entire force disappeared over that goddamned Lodge Trail Ridge, not a man among the lot of them seen alive again.*

Sighing, the old trapper become army-scout gazed at the hard cut of Donegan's face. The finely chiseled nose set beneath the gray-green eyes. Those full, expressive lips buried within the dark beard. And Bridger recalled the look carved on the Irishman's face that sub-zero night when Donegan returned with the somber rescue party—with word that not a soul among Fetterman's command had survived. Bridger had never asked any more about it, for the look in Donegan's eyes had told any half-smart man not to venture such a question.

Still, the old scout knew the young Irishman had seen far too much of the killing in his few years, what with four of those years spent fighting atop a horse down south against Confederate cavalry, not to mention all that Donegan had seen since he had arrived in Red Cloud's Sioux country some seven months ago.

Seven months to some. A lifetime to most.

No way Jim Bridger would ever forget the look in the Irishman's eyes that winter night. A haunted look that somehow, even with all the time that had since passed, remained a look every bit as haunted still.

"Sun's going down behind the peaks," Stead remarked absently, nodding toward the window where he watched the milk-pale orb settle on the Big Horns mantled in white.

"Matters little," Donegan replied, never looking up from his whiskey cup. "Night or day—still cold enough to freeze the bullocks off a Boston snowman."

"You spent time in Boston, did you?" Stead asked, eager to make conversation to ease some of the constant electric tension forever present around the Irishman like a frightening aura.

Seamus nodded. "It's where I landed . . . come here from the land of me birth. An English ship, filled with dirt-poor Irish farmers . . . come to these foreign shores hoping for better. Too oft handed worse. And me but a young lad shipped off by me mither to this new land with her hopes and her tears."

"She hoped you'd fare better here?"

"Aye," he nodded again. "To look up her two brothers, I was. A lad of fifteen, carrying all I owned in her wee carpet satchel. Most everything I had then a hand-me-down at that."

"Those uncles of yours help you find work there in Boston by the sea?"

Donegan shook his head, staring into the red of his whiskey. "Not a trace of 'em, either one."

"You came to Boston on a cold trail?"

"Nawww," and Seamus lifted the cup to his lips. "Last letter my sainted mither got from her brothers came posted from Boston . . . saying they'd both landed work as city constables." He snorted without any humor.

"That's a bit of a laugh. Them two brothers of hers—constables! And in Irish Boston to boot!"

"What became of 'em?" Stead inquired.

Donegan froze the young scout with those gray-green eyes of his; he finally gazed out the frosted window while the last light slid from the sky. His brow knitted. "No telling, Jack."

"You checked with the constable's office?"

"Never worked as constables," he answered with a wolf-slash of a grin. "But, the constables did know the both of 'em. One was quite the brawler, it seems. My dear mither oft shook her head and said I took after his blood. And me other uncle . . . well, now—the constables said he had a smooth way about him, talking folks out of their money."

"Sounds a bit like sutler Kinney there," Stead whispered, nodding toward the counter.

Jefferson T. Kinney leaned one pudgy elbow on the rough-hewn pine-plank bar, wiping a dirty towel across some spilled whiskey and laughing with two civilian workers who had bellied their way through the crowd to nurse their drinks. A former U.S. Judge out of Utah and an ardent pro-slaver, Kinney had lost his bench when President Lincoln had entered the White House. Kinney had been one of the many who had rejoiced when the Great Emancipator was cut down in Ford's Theater not two years ago come April.

Bridger's eyes joined the Irishman's in glaring at the sutler. Kinney must have felt the heat, for he looked up from the bar, gazing across the noisy, smoky room with those black beads he had for eyes. They locked on Donegan.

"No love lost on that one," Bridger whispered around the stub of the pipe that kept a constant wreath round his gray head.

"Aye," Donegan agreed as he nodded, and went back to staring at his red whiskey. "That's one bastard wishes

Seamus Donegan's body had been hauled back from the Ridge with Fetterman's dead."

"What makes a man like him hate a man like you, Seamus?" Stead asked, gazing at the sutler's plump fingers pouring drinks for civilian workers pressing the bar.

"Man like Seamus Donegan here," Bridger began, snagging the attention of the other two, "always brings out the fear in little men like the Judge over there. And in such men, fear is the worst thing you want. No telling what a fella like him might do you get him scared enough."

"What's a man like Kinney got to be afeared of from me?"

"Seamus Donegan, down inside where that fat little bastard lives, Kinney knows he don't belong out here in these mountains like you do," Bridger explained. "Somewhere in his gut he knows he's bought his way out here— but he can't ever earn what it is you already have for free."

"What's that, Jim?" Stead asked.

"The respect of other men. Strong men. Honest men. The kind of man it will take to tame this land. The kind of man Judge Kinney will never be, but will always try to buy, and failing that . . . will try to squash like a sowbug."

"Pour me more whiskey, Jack," Seamus said as he slammed down his empty cup, "and I'll drink a toast to the sowbug squashers in the world. Appears me uncles have much in common with our friend Judge Kinney over there."

Stead poured from a thick glass bottle packed in straw all the way from Omaha. "What keeps Seamus Donegan from being a sowbug squasher himself?"

The Irishman stared at the red whiskey a moment before answering. "I suppose I'm not the kind content to die peacefully in bed with me eyes closed. Because some time back on a hot, bloody battlefield they called Gettysburg, Seamus Donegan realized he would never die an old man's death. Now some cold and bony finger's always tapping me shoulder, telling me every day's borrowed time."

"The reaper has us all, sometime," Bridger added.

"To the reaper then!" Donegan cheered, lifting his cup. "To the reaper—the last friend a dying man will ever know!"

"To the reaper," Stead joined in, sloshing his cup into the air.

"To the old bastard himself," Donegan added after swilling down some of the burning whiskey. "This god-blessed, hell-forsaken country gonna keep the reaper plenty busy before this war with Red Cloud's over."

Seamus stood shuddering with the cold blast knifing his groin. Quickly as he could, he finished wetting the snowy ground at the corner of the latrine slip-trench behind Kinney's cabin, and he was buttoning the fly on his faded cavalry britches when the voice startled him.

"Should have known, Seamus Donegan. If I don't find you drinking whiskey in the bar, you'd be outside in cold pissing good whiskey away!"

Donegan smiled at his old friend Samuel Marr, as he pulled on a buffalo-hide mitten and swiped at his drippy nose. "Hate the smell of these places. Remind me of sojurs, a latrine like this does."

Marr chuckled. "Where the hell you think you are, boy? You spit in any direction . . . you'll hit a soldier."

"Curses be to 'em!" Seamus growled. Then he grinned and slapped the gray-headed Marr on the back. "Man tries to forget ever being a sojur and fighting that war—there's always mitherless sons like you want to remind him of the bleeming army! C'mon in to Kinney's place—I'll buy you a drink if the bastard will take my treasury note."

Marr stopped, pulling from the tall Irishman's arm. "You can't, Seamus."

"And why can't I?" he asked, both hands balled on his

hips and a wide grin cutting his face. His teeth glimmered beneath the thumbnail moon lingering in the west.

"The girl," Marr replied. "She wants to see you."

"The Wheatley woman?" He felt his pulse quicken.

Marr nodded without a word.

Donegan's eyes narrowed suspiciously, not wanting to hope. "What would the widow be wanting with me?"

"You told her to call when she needed anything."

"Aye," and he nodded, staring at the crusty snow beneath his tall, muddy boots. "The day we buried her husband. Brave man, that one."

"A few who marched with Fetterman were every bit as brave as they had to be on that hellish day," Marr whispered, taking a step closer to the tall man.

"She say what it was?"

Sam shook his head. "Not a word. Just asked me to fetch you to her place . . . small cabin outside the east wall of the quartermaster's stockade."

"I know where it is."

"Oh?"

"I've kept me eye on her since."

"I see."

"It's not what you're thinking, Cap'n," Donegan growled.

"Didn't say it was. Just, I've got a fatherly feeling for the girl. Not yet out of her teens . . . and with two young boys to raise . . . her husband butchered with Fetterman's command but a month ago this day. She's alone in the world now."

"No she's not, Cap'n." Then Donegan slapped a big paw on the older man's shoulder. "She's got you . . . and me both watching out for her and the boys."

Marr winked in the pale light. "Best you get now. I told her I'd send you straight-away."

"You'll be at Kinney's for the evening?"

Marr nodded. "Nowhere else to be, is there, Seamus. You'll find me here." He turned and scuffed off across the old snow, his boots squeaking over the icy crust as he stomped toward Kinney's door.

Donegan watched after him while the old man's form faded from the pale snow. He loved that old man, he did. Captain Samuel Marr, Missouri Union Volunteers.

When Seamus had mustered himself out in those months following Appomattox, he had wandered west with the big gray stallion, his yellow-striped cavalry britches now patched and worn, and the .44-caliber Navy pistol that had carved out a comfortable place for itself at his hip. Wandering into Missouri he had run into Sam Marr, busy buying horses for the newly-organized frontier army. After the canny horse-trader Marr discovered he couldn't buy Donegan's gray stallion, they had learned together of the wealth to be made in the Montana diggings along Alder Gulch. And from that moment had begun forming a fierce friendship frequently tested as they fought their way up the Bozeman Road through Sioux hunting ground.

Seamus Donegan would not do a thing to hurt Sam Marr. Nor would he ever do anything to harm the Widow Wheatley.

Purposefully he slid to the door as quietly as a winter-gaunt wolf and listened. Inside he made out the muffled voices of the two young boys. The oldest, Isaac, named for his father's best friend. Isaac Fisher who had stood and stared cold-eyed into Red Cloud's Sioux ambush at Wheatley's side. Then Donegan made out the smaller boy's voice. Little Peter. Taking after his mother. A beauty she was, that woman. With so much to bear at her young age. He heard her scolding the two, then listened as she laughed.

Never was one to get hard with those boys of hers, Seamus thought, bringing his big fist up to the rough-hewn door.

Two pairs of little feet hammered to the other side of the door, accompanied by excited voices. He listened as her feet scuffled up, her whisper shushing the boys as she drew back the huge iron bolt and cracked the door an inch.

Seamus gazed down at the single eye peering through the crack at him under the pale moonlight. He cleared his throat.

"Mrs. Wheatley. It's Seamus. Seamus Donegan."

Then he suddenly remembered his hat. Quickly he raked the big, stiff, quarter-crowned brown-felt hat from his long, curly hair and nodded.

"Pardon me, m'am. A man out in this country doesn't get much of a chance to be a gentleman."

By this time the door had opened and the shy, liquid eyes were blinking their welcome as she waved him inside. "Please . . . Mr. Donegan. Come in."

He stooped through the door-frame and stopped two steps inside as the woman urged the heavy door back into its jamb and slid home the iron bolt. She came 'round him, shyly reaching for his hat.

"I'll take that, Mr. Donegan," she offered, taking the hat from his mittened hands. "Your coat. Please. Make yourself to home."

Beyond her the two boys stood huddled as one, staring at the tall man who had to hunch his shoulders beneath the exposed, peeled beams of the low-roofed cabin. Their eyes wide with wonder, Isaac finally whispered to his young brother.

"We see'd him afore, Peter. Day we put Papa to rest."

"It was cold, Isaac," the little one whispered. "I don't remember him."

"I do," Isaac replied protectively of his mother, never taking his eyes off Donegan. "I remember *that* one."

Jennifer Wheatley slid an old cane-backed chair across the plank floor toward the Irishman. Donegan slipped the heavy mackinaw coat from his shoulders and shook it free of frost before handing it to the woman. He settled carefully on the chair many-times repaired with nails and wire.

Things had to last folks out in this country, he brooded

as he watched her pull up the only other chair in the one-room cabin.

He saw a wooden box turned on its end that served as a third chair at the tiny table where the family took its meals.

"You'd like coffee, Mr. Donegan?" she asked, pointing to the fireplace of creek-bottom stone and mortar.

"If it's no trouble, ma'am."

"Have some made. But you must stop calling me 'ma'am,' Mr. Donegan," she said as she knelt by the iron trivet where the blackened and battered coffee pot sat warming over the coals.

"You're a married woman, ma'am," he started, then ground his hands over his knees, growing angry with himself for his careless words. Words that caused her to stop pouring the coffee. "You've got two fine boys here," Seamus tried again, hoping it would ease the pain of his thoughtlessness.

Jennifer rose slowly, two cups in hand. She passed one to Donegan. "My name's Jennifer. Family and friends back in Ohio called me Jennie. I . . . I want you to be my friend." For a moment she glanced at the two boys. "We . . . we all need a friend. So, please—call me Jennie."

He sipped at the hot liquid. The coffee tasted as if it had been setting in the kettle, re-heating for most of the afternoon. Seamus nodded. "Make you a deal . . . m'am. I'll call you Jennie—if you and the boys here call me Seamus."

Jennie looked over her shoulder at the boys huddled by the fireplace with wooden horses in hand. They had stopped play to stare once more at the big man sprawled over the tiny chair.

"Boys, I want you come over here now," the woman directed. "Want you meet a kind man who knew your papa."

Isaac nudged Peter across the floor until both stood at

their mother's side. "You knowed my papa?" Isaac demanded gruffly.

Donegan nodded and smiled. "As fine a man as any I've met, Mr. Wheatley was." He stuck out his hand to the boy. "My name's Seamus Donegan. Who do I have the pleasure of meeting?"

Isaac wiped his hand across his patched denims and stuffed it into the Irishman's paw. "Isaac Wheatley, sir. Pleased to meet a friend of my papa's."

Seamus gazed at the youngest when Isaac stepped back. Peter glanced up at his mother. She nodded before he inched forward.

"Peter, sir. I'm pleased."

"Not as pleased as me, Peter." Seamus felt the small hand sweating in his grip. "Your papa would be proud to know how his boys help their mother."

Seamus tried to blink away the stinging tears, glancing 'round the little cabin split in half by wool blankets suspended from a rope lanyard. In the back was barely enough room for the one small bed he supposed the boys shared. Here in the front half of the cabin, another small prairie bed joined the table and chairs, along with a battered old hutch where Jennie kept what dishes had not been broken in her travels west.

When he looked back, he found her staring at her hands in her lap, wringing them silently as she bit her lower lip between her teeth.

"Jennie?" his deep-throated whisper filled the tiny room. "You have nothing to fear now, ma'am. You and the boys got a friend."

DON'T MISS *RED CLOUD'S REVENGE*—
BOOK 2 OF *THE PLAINSMEN*, THE BOLD
NEW WESTERN SERIES FROM ST.
MARTIN'S PAPERBACKS—ON SALE IN
AUGUST

IN THE SHADOW OF THE BIG HORNS,
TWO PROUD NATIONS CLASHED — AND
IGNITED THE LONGEST, MOST DRAMATIC WAR
IN AMERICAN HISTORY.

THE PLAINSMEN

The rugged new Western series by the award-winning
author of *Carry the Wind*

TERRY C. JOHNSTON

Terry C. Johnston was nominated twice for the Golden
Spur Award and won the Medicine Pipe Bearer's Award
for *Carry the Wind*.

SIOUX DAWN (Book 1)
92100-4 _____ $4.50 U.S. _____ $5.50 CAN.
RED CLOUD'S REVENGE (Book 2—coming in August
1990)
92281-7 _____ $4.50 U.S. _____ $5.50 CAN.

Coming in December 1990: THE STALKERS—Book 3

LANDMARK BESTSELLERS
FROM ST. MARTIN'S PAPERBACKS

HOT FLASHES
Barbara Raskin
_____ 91051-7 $4.95 U.S.   _____ 91052-5 $5.95 Can.

MAN OF THE HOUSE
"Tip" O'Neill with William Novak
_____ 91191-2 $4.95 U.S.   _____ 91192-0 $5.95 Can.

FOR THE RECORD
Donald T. Regan
_____ 91518-7 $4.95 U.S.   _____ 91519-5 $5.95 Can.

THE RED WHITE AND BLUE
John Gregory Dunne
_____ 90965-9 $4.95 U.S.   _____ 90966-7 $5.95 Can.

LINDA GOODMAN'S STAR SIGNS
Linda Goodman
_____ 91263-3 $4.95 U.S.   _____ 91264-1 $5.95 Can.

ROCKETS' RED GLARE
Greg Dinallo
_____ 91288-9 $4.50 U.S.   _____ 91289-7 $5.50 Can.

THE FITZGERALDS AND THE KENNEDYS
Doris Kearns Goodwin
_____ 90933-0 $5.95 U.S.   _____ 90934-9 $6.95 Can.

Publishers Book and Audio Mailing Service
P.O. Box 120159, Staten Island, NY 10312-0004

Please send me the book(s) I have checked above. I am enclosing
$ _____ (please add $1.25 for the first book, and $.25 for each
additional book to cover postage and handling. Send check or
money order only—no CODs.)

Name _____

Address _____

City _____ State/Zip _____

Please allow six weeks for delivery. Prices subject to change
without notice.

BEST 1/89